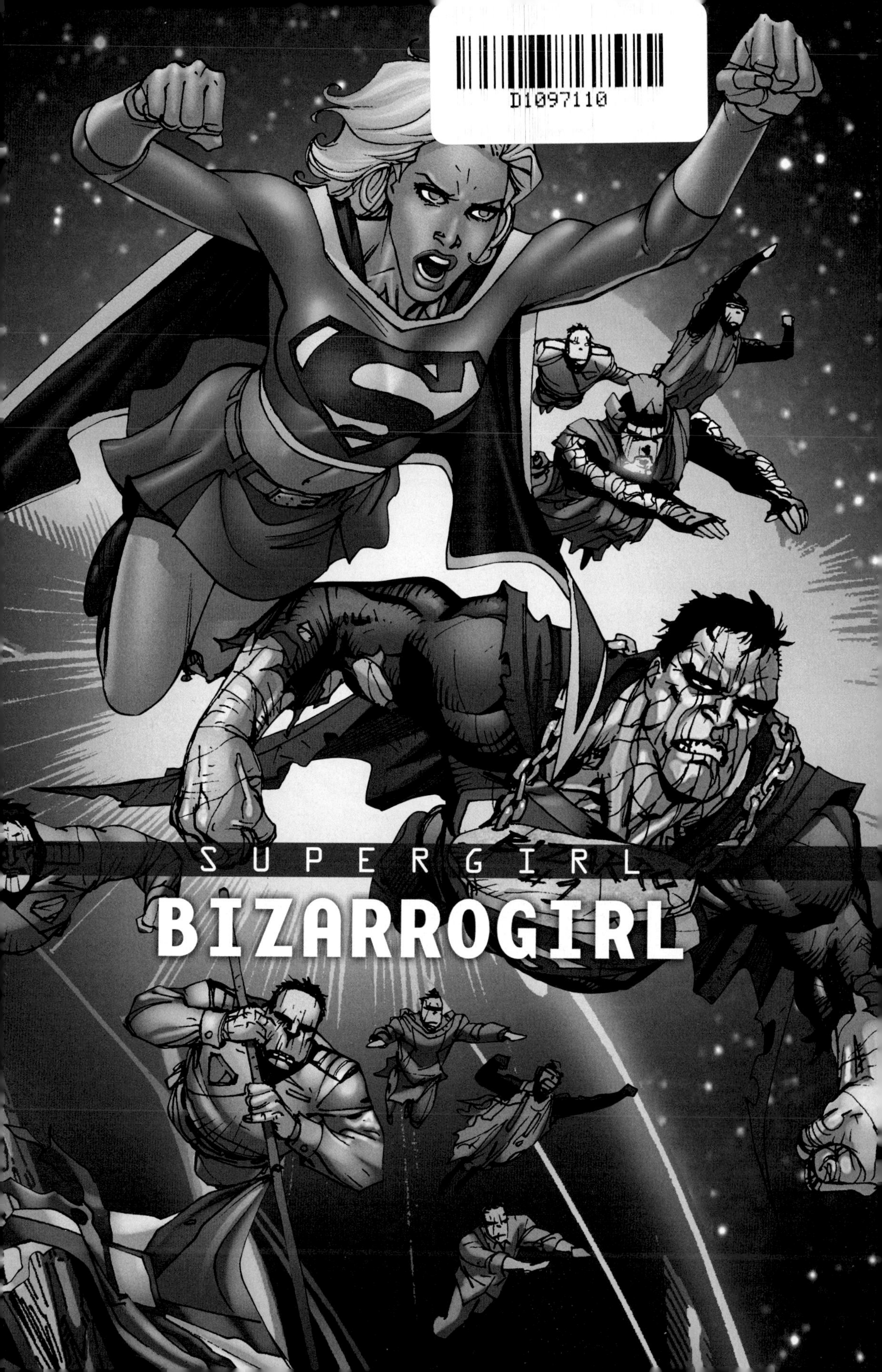

SUPERGIRL
BIZARROGIRL

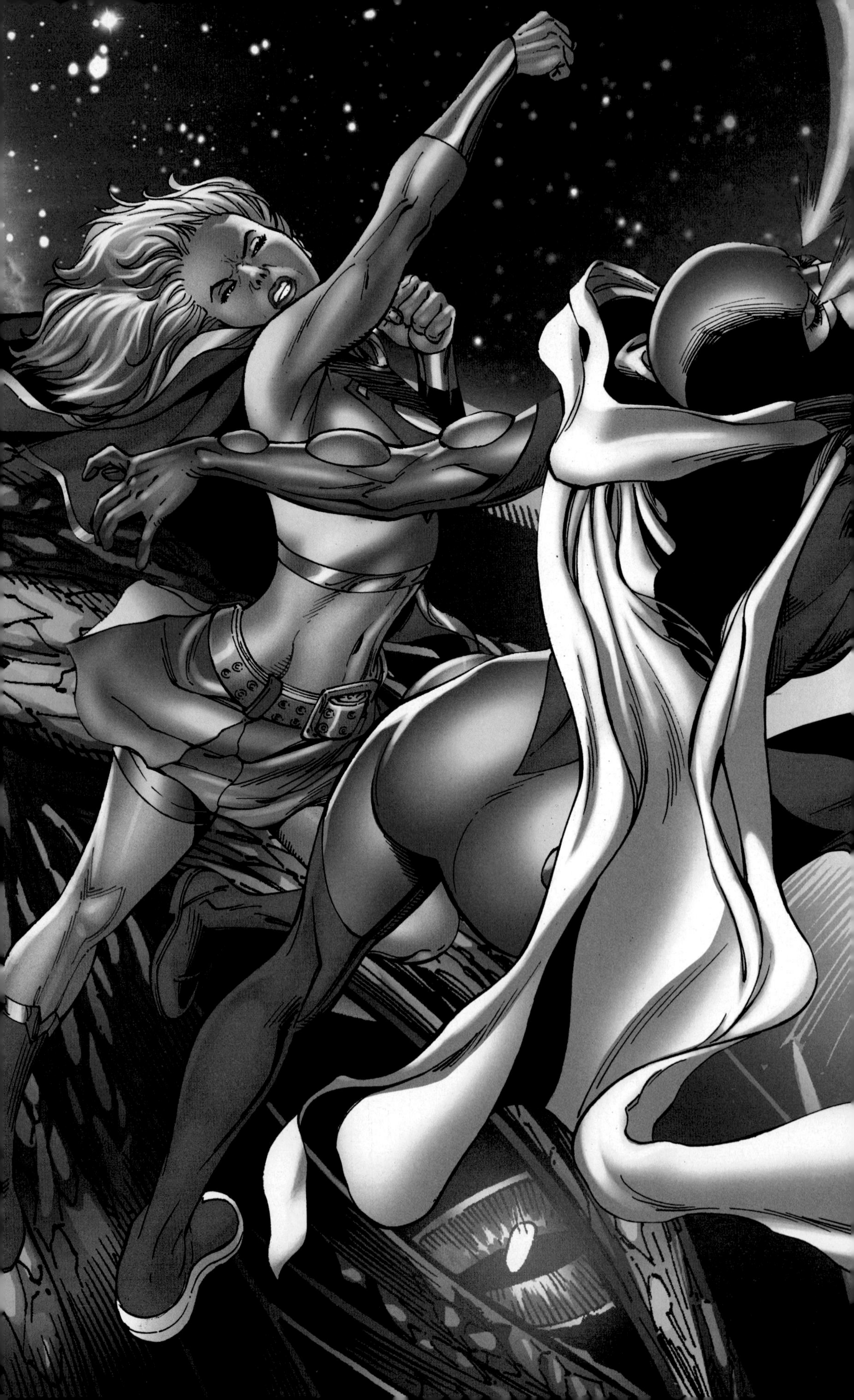

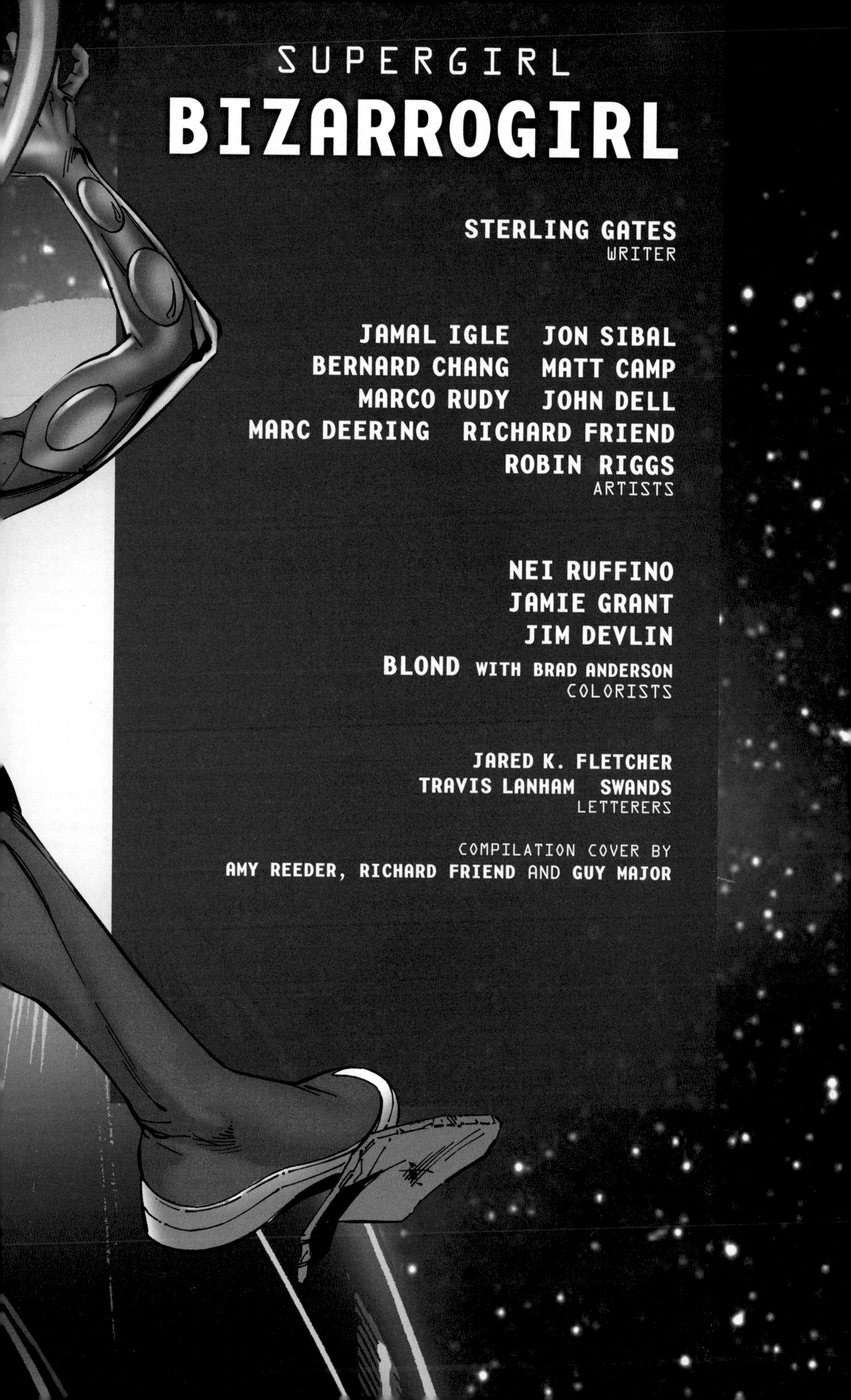

SUPERGIRL
BIZARROGIRL

STERLING GATES
WRITER

JAMAL IGLE JON SIBAL
BERNARD CHANG MATT CAMP
MARCO RUDY JOHN DELL
MARC DEERING RICHARD FRIEND
ROBIN RIGGS
ARTISTS

NEI RUFFINO
JAMIE GRANT
JIM DEVLIN
BLOND WITH BRAD ANDERSON
COLORISTS

JARED K. FLETCHER
TRAVIS LANHAM SWANDS
LETTERERS

COMPILATION COVER BY
AMY REEDER, RICHARD FRIEND AND **GUY MAJOR**

MATT IDELSON EDITOR-ORIGINAL SERIES
WIL MOSS ASSISTANT EDITOR-ORIGINAL SERIES
IAN SATTLER DIRECTOR EDITORIAL, SPECIAL PROJECTS AND ARCHIVAL EDITIONS
ROBBIN BROSTERMAN DESIGN DIRECTOR-BOOKS
ROBBIE BIEDERMAN PUBLICATION DESIGN

EDDIE BERGANZA EXECUTIVE EDITOR
BOB HARRAS VP – EDITOR IN CHIEF

DC COMICS
DIANE NELSON PRESIDENT
DAN DIDIO AND **JIM LEE** CO-PUBLISHERS
GEOFF JOHNS CHIEF CREATIVE OFFICER
JOHN ROOD EXECUTIVE VP – SALES, MARKETING AND BUSINESS DEVELOPMENT
AMY GENKINS SENIOR VP – BUSINESS AND LEGAL AFFAIRS
NAIRI GARDINER SENIOR VP – FINANCE
JEFF BOISON VP – PUBLISHING OPERATIONS
MARK CHIARELLO VP – ART DIRECTION AND DESIGN
JOHN CUNNINGHAM VP – MARKETING
TERRI CUNNINGHAM VP – TALENT RELATIONS AND SERVICES
ALISON GILL SENIOR VP – MANUFACTURING AND OPERATIONS
DAVID HYDE VP – PUBLICITY
HANK KANALZ SENIOR VP – DIGITAL
JAY KOGAN VP – BUSINESS AND LEGAL AFFAIRS, PUBLISHING
JACK MAHAN VP – BUSINESS AFFAIRS, TALENT
NICK NAPOLITANO VP – MANUFACTURING ADMINISTRATION
RON PERAZZA VP – ONLINE
SUE POHJA VP – BOOK SALES
COURTNEY SIMMONS SENIOR VP – PUBLICITY
BOB WAYNE SENIOR VP – SALES

DC COMICS
1700 BROADWAY, NEW YORK, NY 10019
A WARNER BROS. ENTERTAINMENT COMPANY
PRINTED BY QUAD/GRAPHICS, DUBUQUE, IA. 7/22/11.
ISBN: 978-1-4012-3169-9

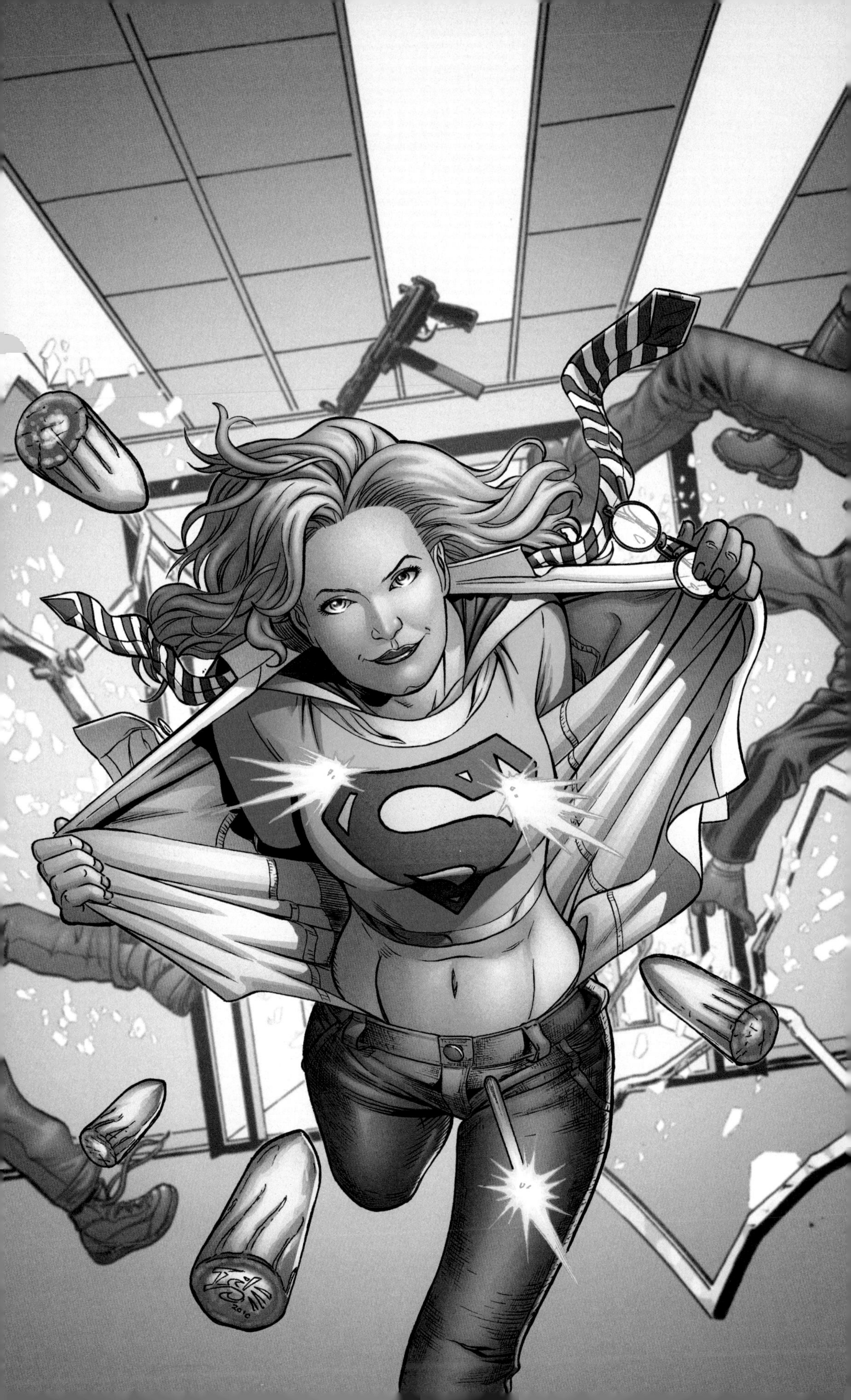

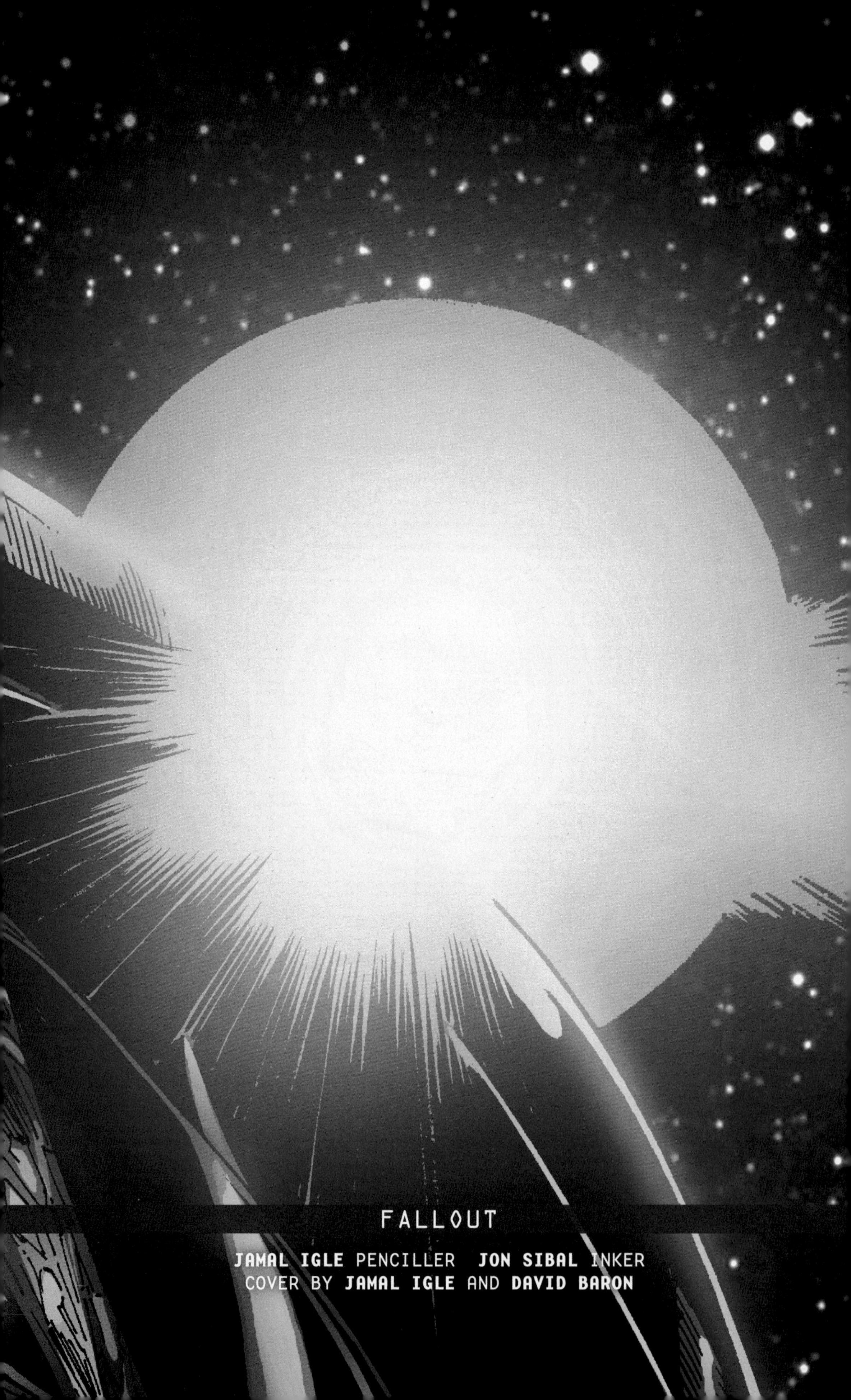
FALLOUT
JAMAL IGLE PENCILLER JON SIBAL INKER
COVER BY JAMAL IGLE AND DAVID BARON

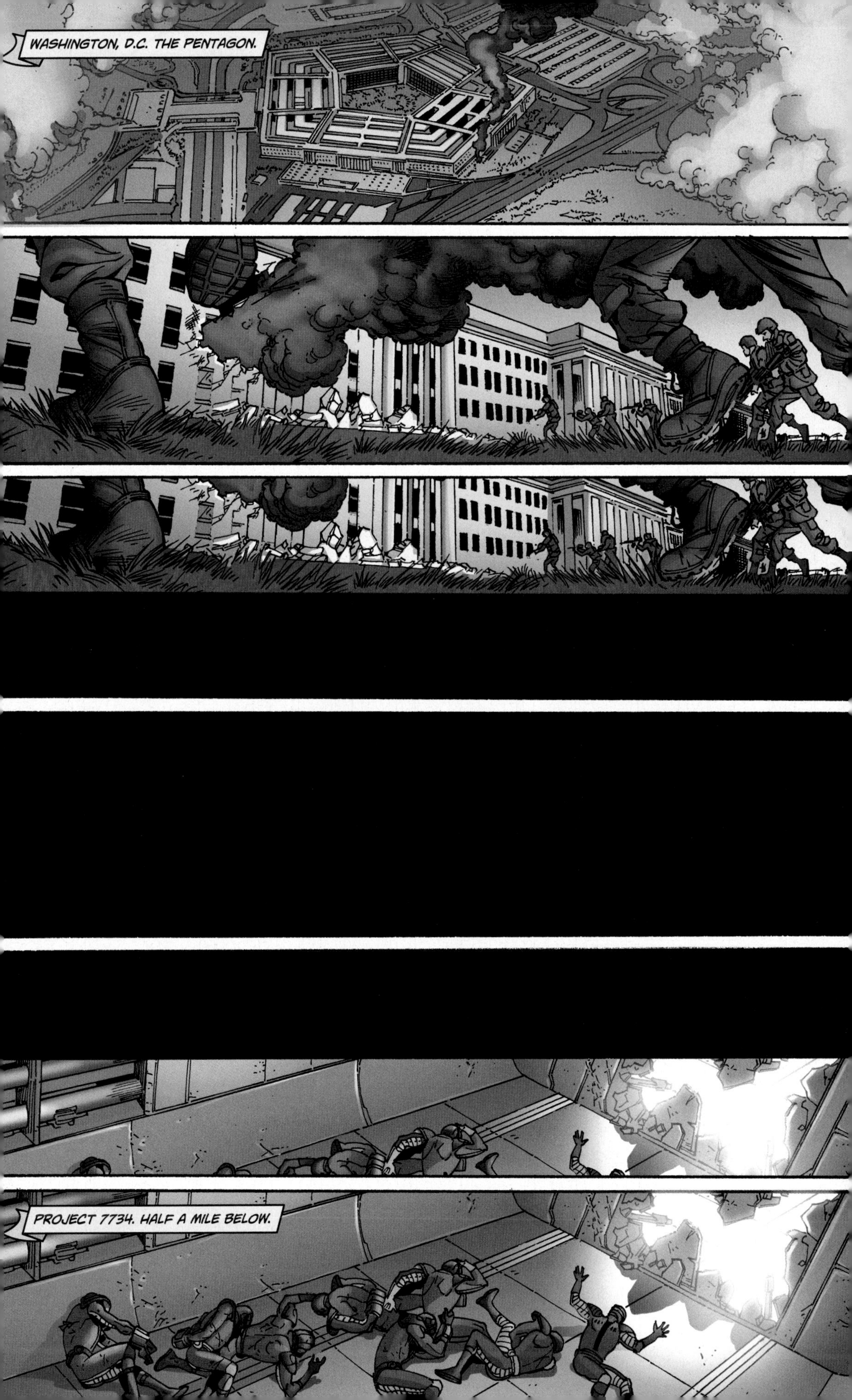
WASHINGTON, D.C. THE PENTAGON.
PROJECT 7734. HALF A MILE BELOW.

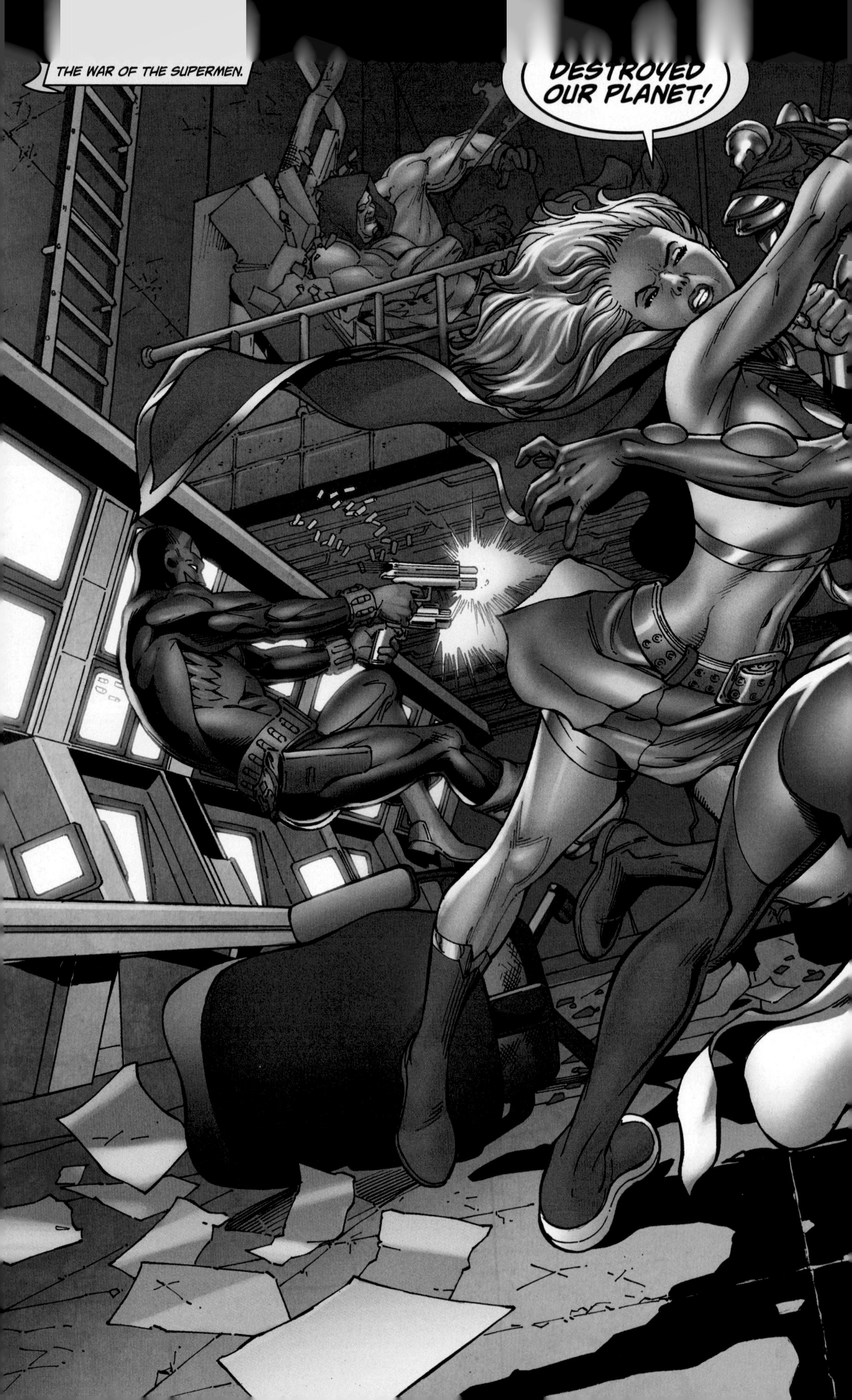
THE WAR OF THE SUPERMEN.
DESTROYED OUR PLANET!

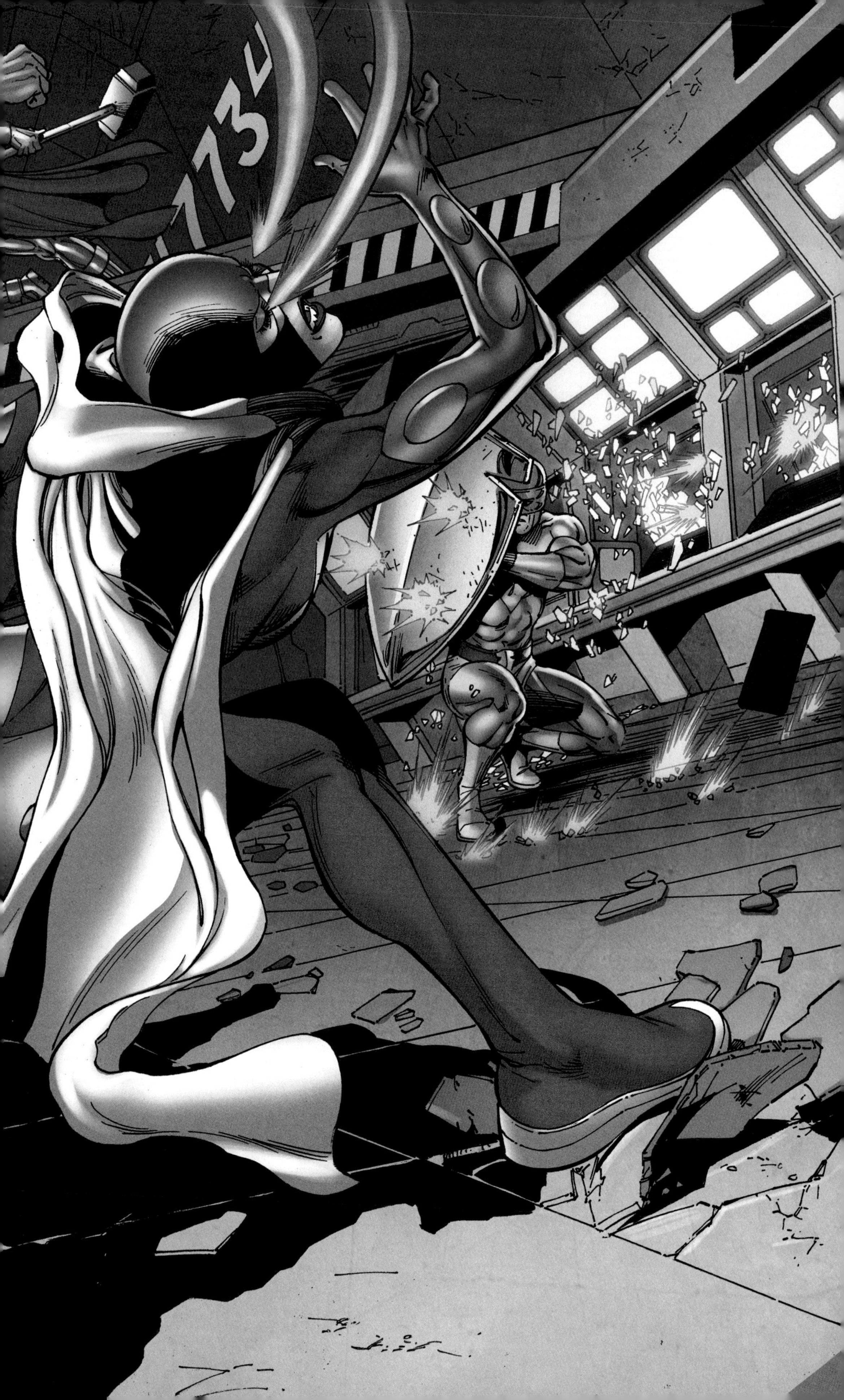
773

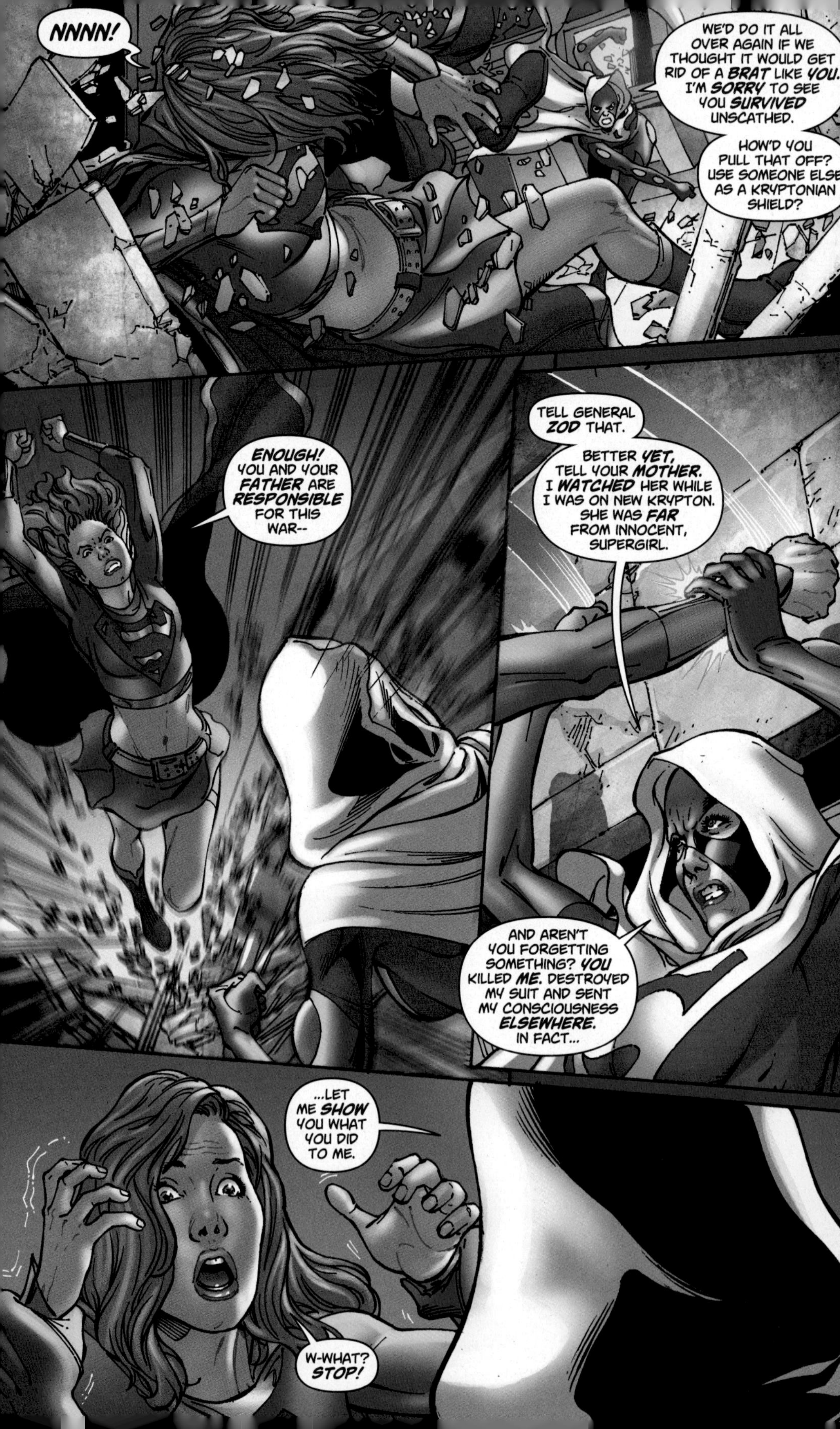
NNNN!
WE'D DO IT ALL OVER AGAIN IF WE THOUGHT IT WOULD GET RID OF A BRAT LIKE YOU. I'M SORRY TO SEE YOU SURVIVED UNSCATHED.
HOW'D YOU PULL THAT OFF? USE SOMEONE ELSE AS A KRYPTONIAN SHIELD?
ENOUGH! YOU AND YOUR FATHER ARE RESPONSIBLE FOR THIS WAR--
TELL GENERAL ZOD THAT.
BETTER YET, TELL YOUR MOTHER. I WATCHED HER WHILE I WAS ON NEW KRYPTON. SHE WAS FAR FROM INNOCENT, SUPERGIRL.
AND AREN'T YOU FORGETTING SOMETHING? YOU KILLED ME. DESTROYED MY SUIT AND SENT MY CONSCIOUSNESS ELSEWHERE. IN FACT...
...LET ME SHOW YOU WHAT YOU DID TO ME.
W-WHAT? STOP!

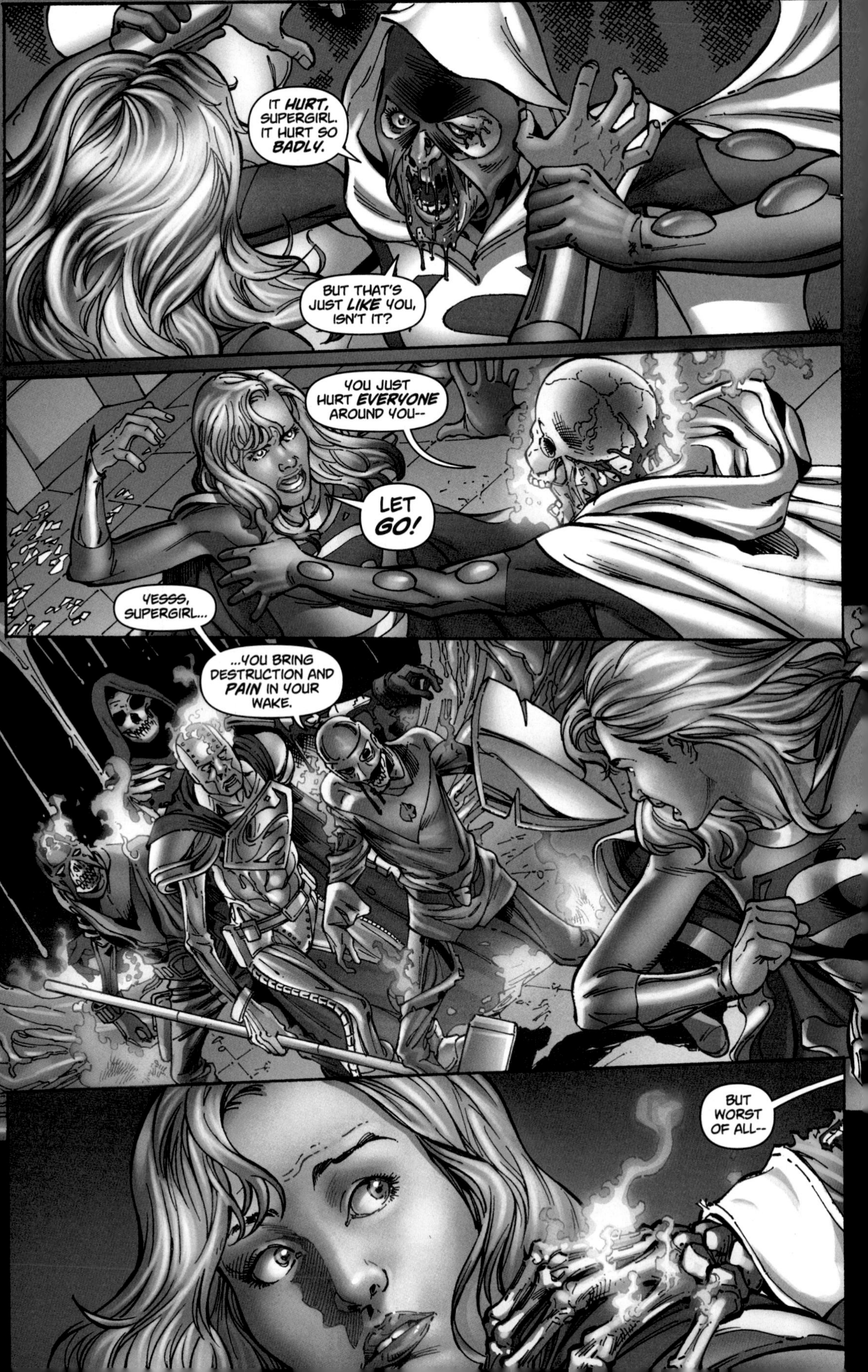
IT HURT, SUPERGIRL. IT HURT SO BADLY.
BUT THAT'S JUST LIKE YOU, ISN'T IT?
YOU JUST HURT EVERYONE AROUND YOU--
LET GO!
YESSS, SUPERGIRL...
...YOU BRING DESTRUCTION AND PAIN IN YOUR WAKE.
BUT WORST OF ALL--

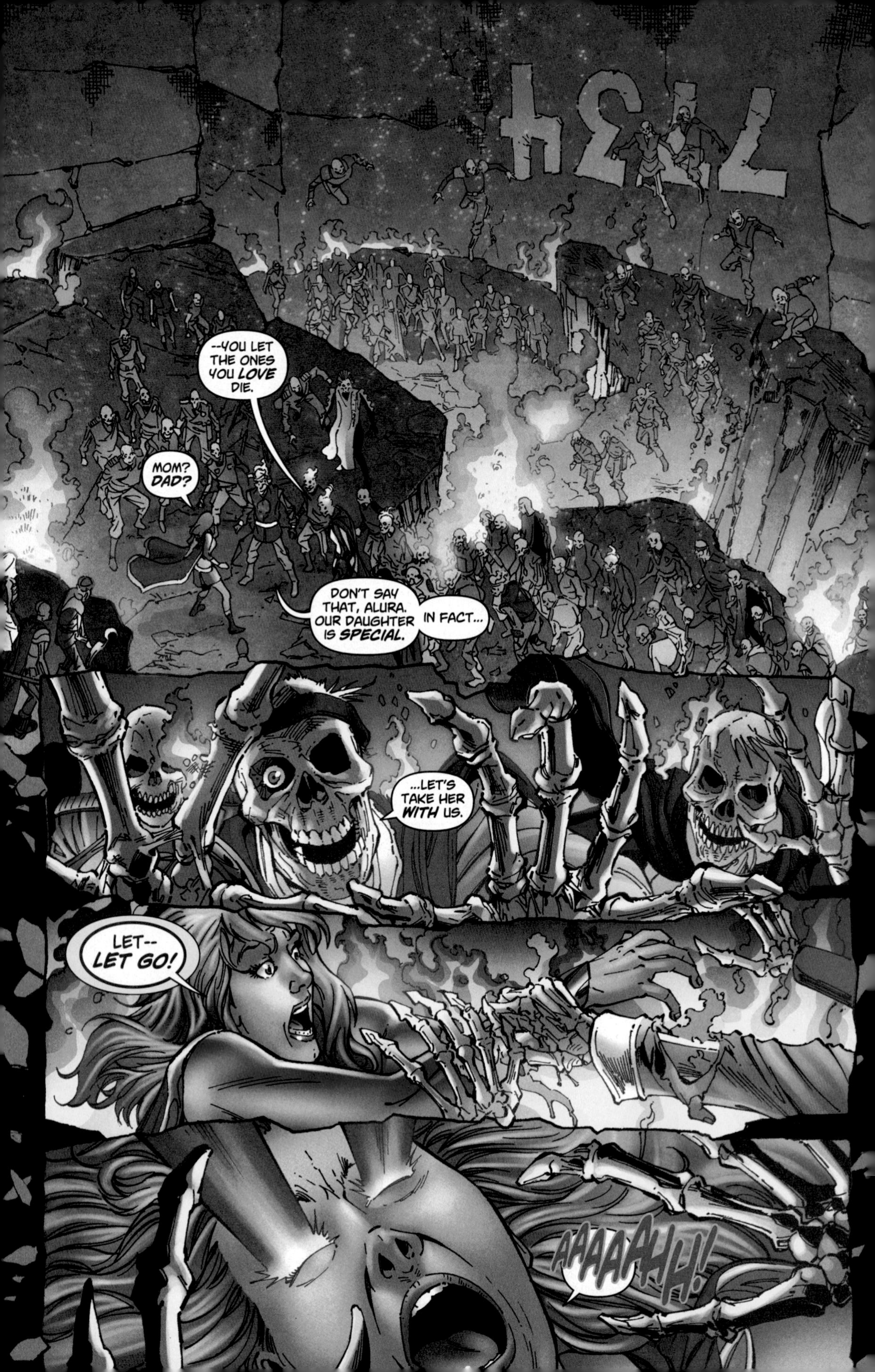
--YOU LET THE ONES YOU LOVE DIE.
MOM? DAD?
DON'T SAY THAT, ALURA. OUR DAUGHTER IS SPECIAL.
IN FACT...
...LET'S TAKE HER WITH US.
LET-- LET GO!
AAAAAHH!

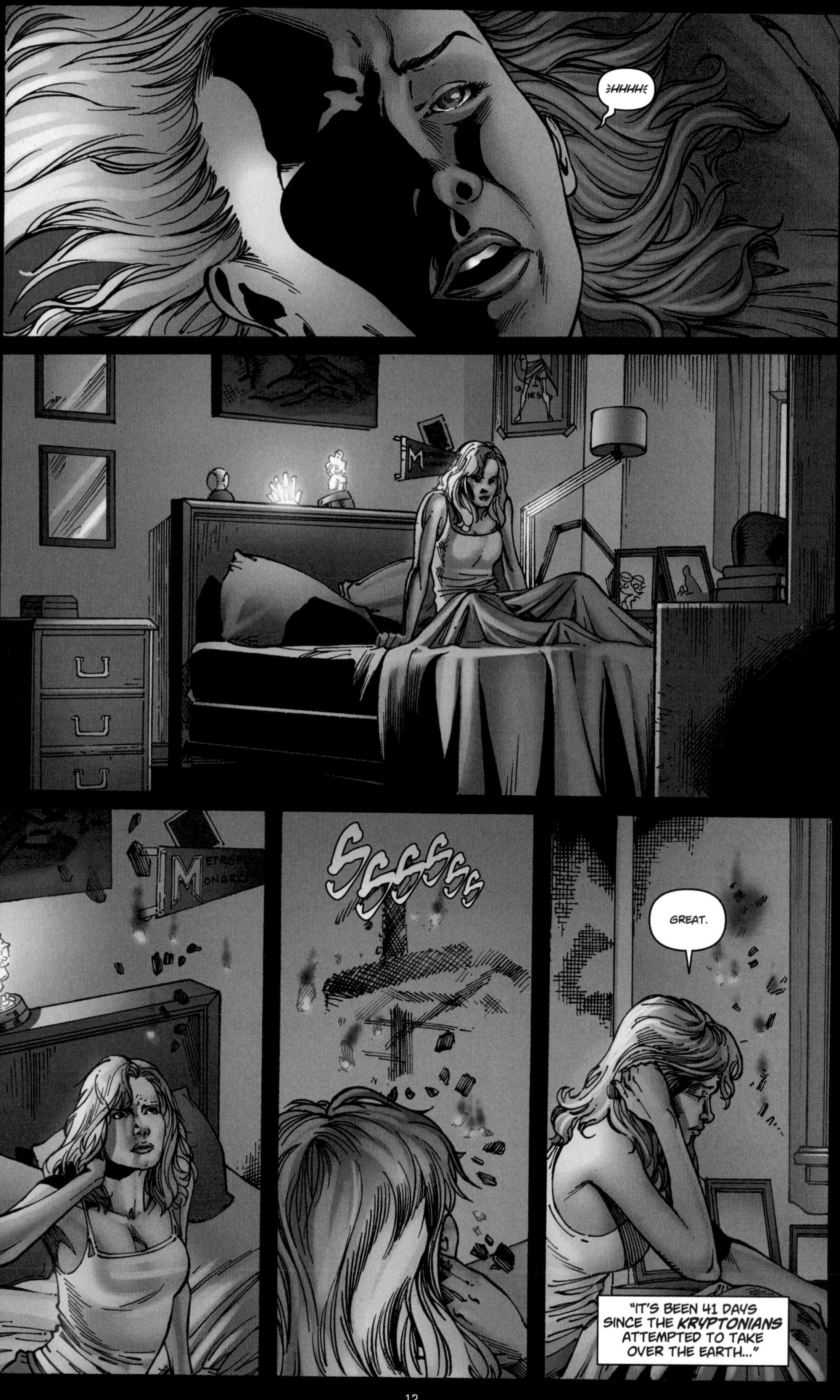

HHHH
Sssssss
GREAT.
"IT'S BEEN 41 DAYS SINCE THE KRYPTONIANS ATTEMPTED TO TAKE OVER THE EARTH..."

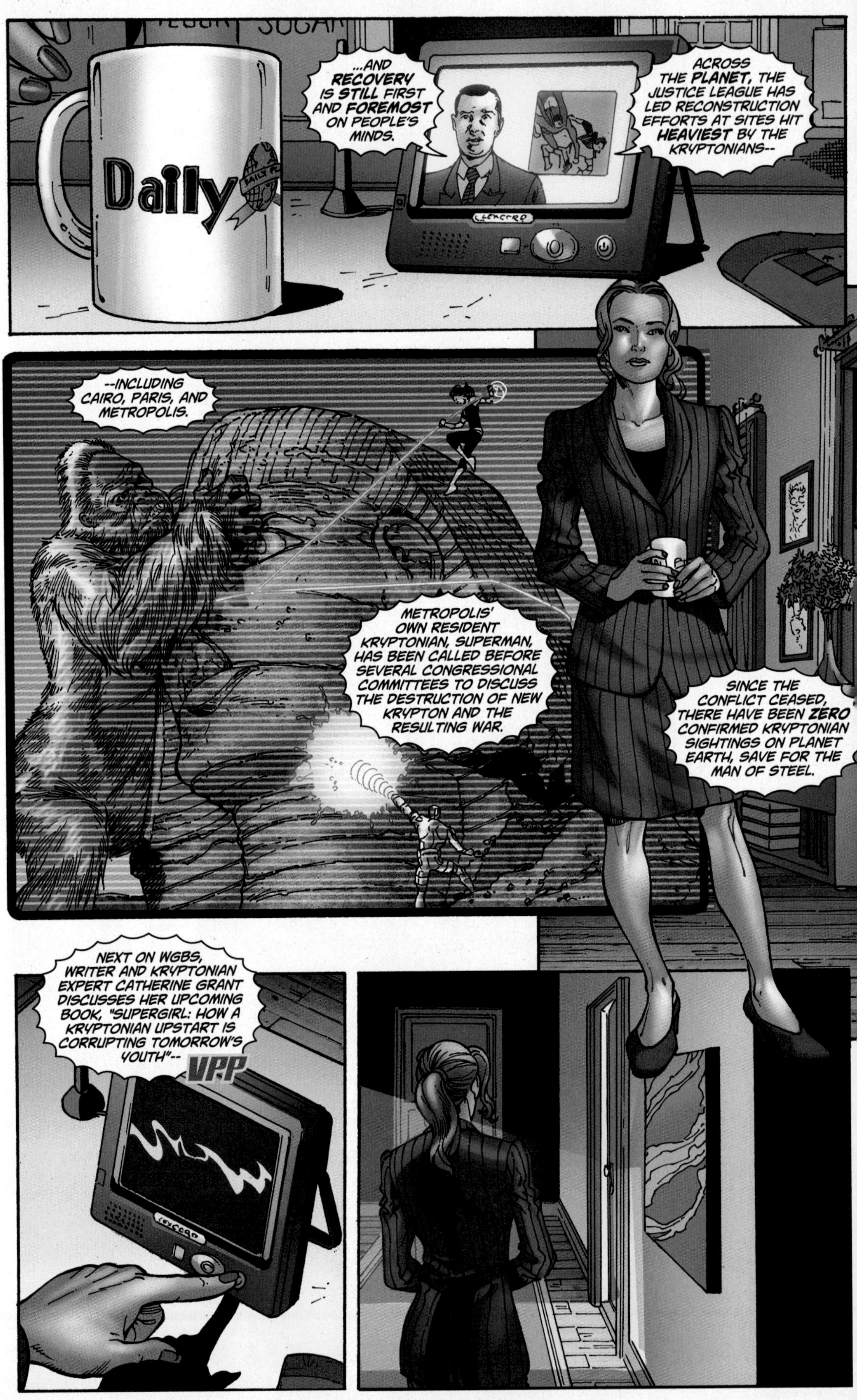

...AND RECOVERY IS STILL FIRST AND FOREMOST ON PEOPLE'S MINDS.
ACROSS THE PLANET, THE JUSTICE LEAGUE HAS LED RECONSTRUCTION EFFORTS AT SITES HIT HEAVIEST BY THE KRYPTONIANS--
Daily
--INCLUDING CAIRO, PARIS, AND METROPOLIS.
METROPOLIS' OWN RESIDENT KRYPTONIAN, SUPERMAN, HAS BEEN CALLED BEFORE SEVERAL CONGRESSIONAL COMMITTEES TO DISCUSS THE DESTRUCTION OF NEW KRYPTON AND THE RESULTING WAR.
SINCE THE CONFLICT CEASED, THERE HAVE BEEN ZERO CONFIRMED KRYPTONIAN SIGHTINGS ON PLANET EARTH, SAVE FOR THE MAN OF STEEL.
NEXT ON WGBS, WRITER AND KRYPTONIAN EXPERT CATHERINE GRANT DISCUSSES HER UPCOMING BOOK, "SUPERGIRL: HOW A KRYPTONIAN UPSTART IS CORRUPTING TOMORROW'S YOUTH"--
VPP

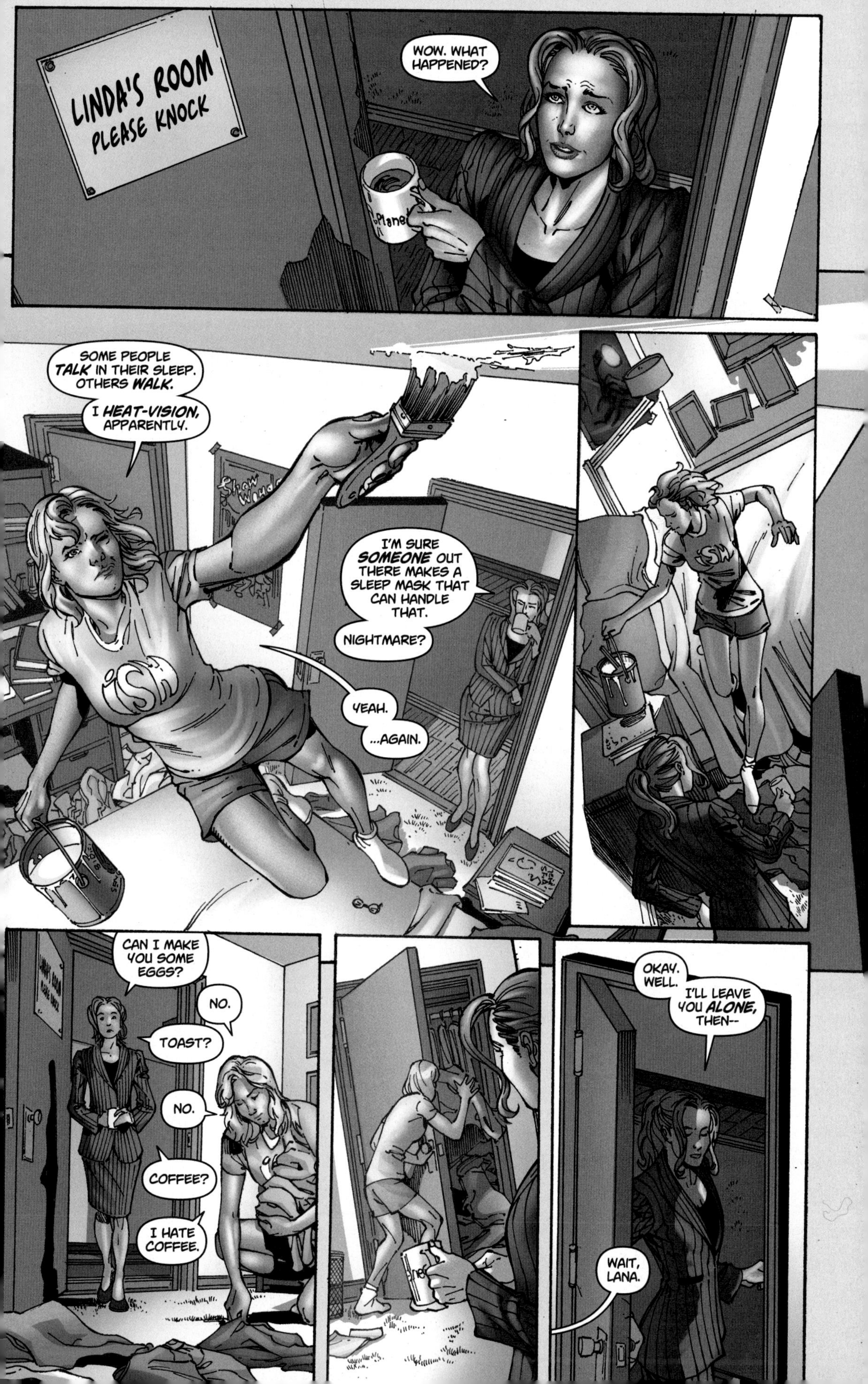
LINDA'S ROOM
PLEASE KNOCK
WOW. WHAT HAPPENED?
SOME PEOPLE TALK IN THEIR SLEEP. OTHERS WALK.
I HEAT-VISION, APPARENTLY.
I'M SURE SOMEONE OUT THERE MAKES A SLEEP MASK THAT CAN HANDLE THAT.
NIGHTMARE?
YEAH.
...AGAIN.
CAN I MAKE YOU SOME EGGS?
NO.
TOAST?
NO.
COFFEE?
I HATE COFFEE.
OKAY. WELL.
I'LL LEAVE YOU ALONE, THEN--
WAIT, LANA.

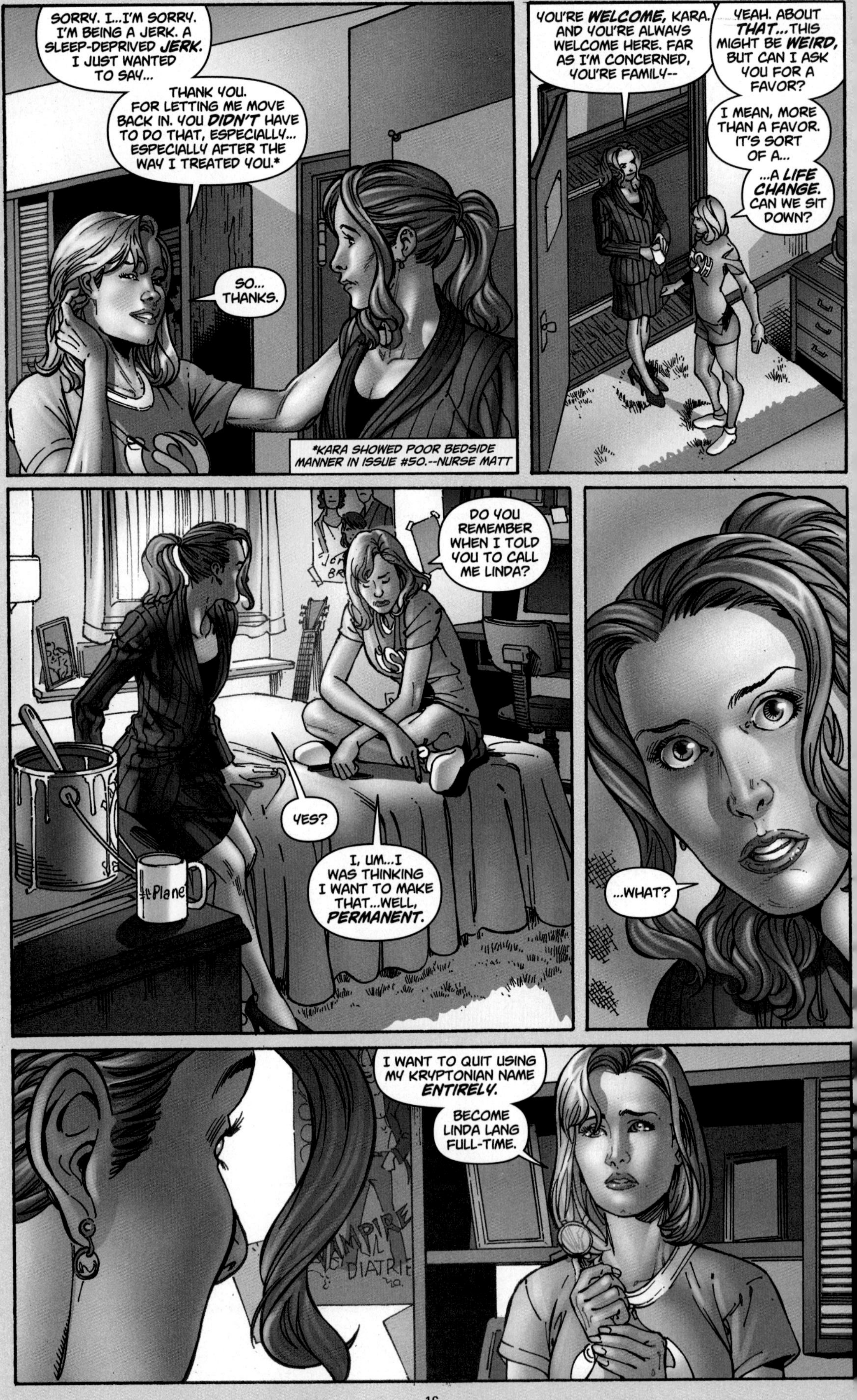
SORRY. I...I'M SORRY. I'M BEING A JERK. A SLEEP-DEPRIVED JERK. I JUST WANTED TO SAY...
THANK YOU. FOR LETTING ME MOVE BACK IN. YOU DIDN'T HAVE TO DO THAT, ESPECIALLY... ESPECIALLY AFTER THE WAY I TREATED YOU.*
SO... THANKS.
*KARA SHOWED POOR BEDSIDE MANNER IN ISSUE #50.--NURSE MATT
YOU'RE WELCOME, KARA. AND YOU'RE ALWAYS WELCOME HERE. FAR AS I'M CONCERNED, YOU'RE FAMILY--
YEAH. ABOUT THAT...THIS MIGHT BE WEIRD, BUT CAN I ASK YOU FOR A FAVOR?
I MEAN, MORE THAN A FAVOR. IT'S SORT OF A...
...A LIFE CHANGE. CAN WE SIT DOWN?
DO YOU REMEMBER WHEN I TOLD YOU TO CALL ME LINDA?
YES?
I, UM...I WAS THINKING I WANT TO MAKE THAT...WELL, PERMANENT.
...WHAT?
I WANT TO QUIT USING MY KRYPTONIAN NAME ENTIRELY.
BECOME LINDA LANG FULL-TIME.

ARE YOU...ARE YOU *SURE* YOU WANT TO *DO* THAT, KARA? I MEAN, YOUR NAME IS *IMPORTANT*, IT'S WHO YOU *ARE*--

I'VE BEEN THINKING ABOUT THIS A *LOT*.

READING ABOUT IMMIGRANTS WHO TOOK ON NEW NAMES TO HELP THEM FIT IN WHEN THEY MOVED TO NEW PLACES.

I'VE GOT TO...WELL, METROPOLIS IS MY *HOME* NOW. SO IT'S IMPORTANT THAT I *ACCEPT* THAT. *LIVE* THAT.

BUT, KARA, WON'T YOU BE LOSING PART OF WHAT MADE YOU *KRYPTONIAN?* REJECTING YOUR PEOPLE--

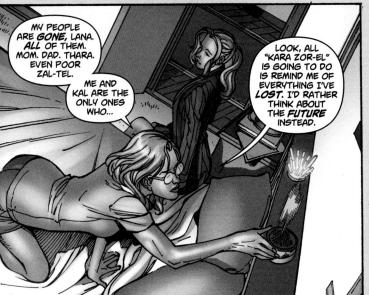

MY PEOPLE ARE *GONE*, LANA. *ALL* OF THEM. MOM. DAD. THARA. EVEN POOR ZAL-TEL.

ME AND KAL ARE THE ONLY ONES WHO...

LOOK, ALL "KARA ZOR-EL" IS GOING TO DO IS REMIND ME OF EVERYTHING I'VE *LOST*. I'D RATHER THINK ABOUT THE *FUTURE* INSTEAD.

THE LANGS WOULD BE *HONORED* TO HAVE YOU FULL-TIME, LINDA. AND FORGET ABOUT WHAT HAPPENED BEFORE. IT'S OLD HISTORY.

FAMILY *FORGIVES* TEENAGERS.

THANK YOU.

HAVE YOU... HAVE YOU THOUGHT ABOUT WHAT *SUPERGIRL'S* GOING TO DO, THEN--

YEAH. JUST LIKE KARA ZOR-EL, SUPERGIRL'S *GOING AWAY*, TOO.

FOR *GOOD.*

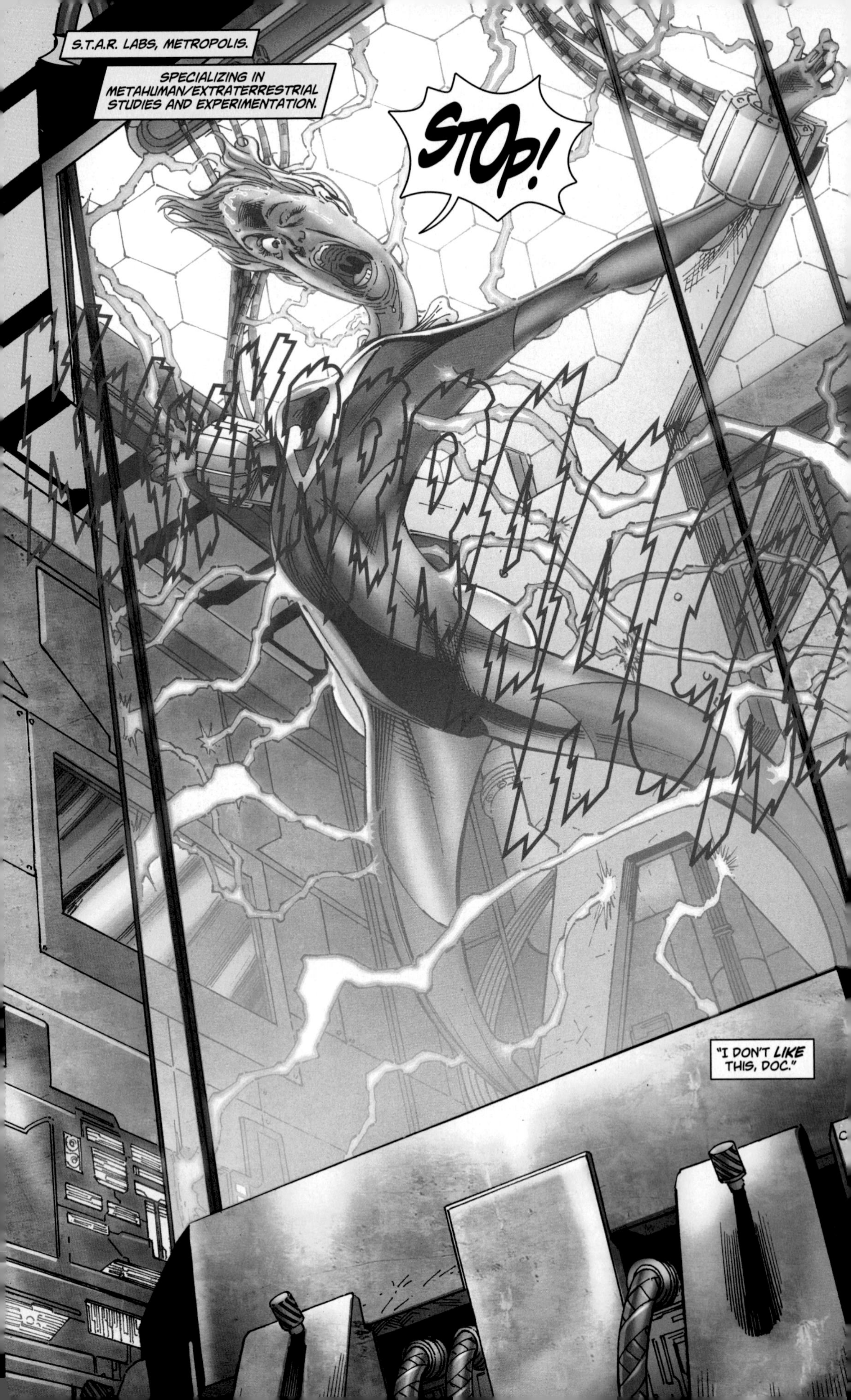
S.T.A.R. LABS, METROPOLIS.
SPECIALIZING IN METAHUMAN/EXTRATERRESTRIAL STUDIES AND EXPERIMENTATION.
STOP!
"I DON'T LIKE THIS, DOC."

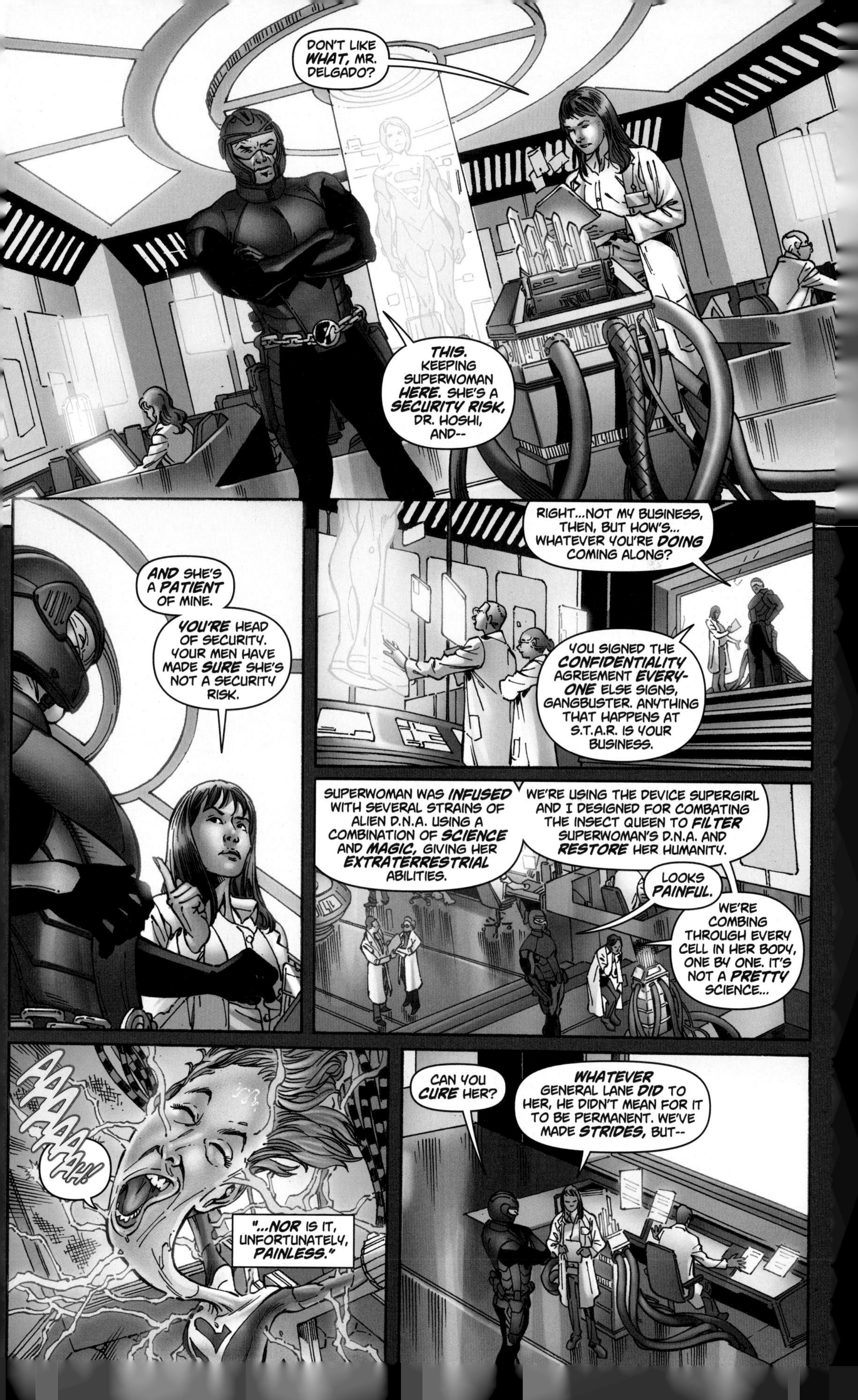
DON'T LIKE WHAT, MR. DELGADO?
THIS. KEEPING SUPERWOMAN HERE. SHE'S A SECURITY RISK, DR. HOSHI, AND--
AND SHE'S A PATIENT OF MINE.
YOU'RE HEAD OF SECURITY. YOUR MEN HAVE MADE SURE SHE'S NOT A SECURITY RISK.
RIGHT...NOT MY BUSINESS, THEN, BUT HOW'S... WHATEVER YOU'RE DOING COMING ALONG?
YOU SIGNED THE CONFIDENTIALITY AGREEMENT EVERY-ONE ELSE SIGNS, GANGBUSTER. ANYTHING THAT HAPPENS AT S.T.A.R. IS YOUR BUSINESS.
SUPERWOMAN WAS INFUSED WITH SEVERAL STRAINS OF ALIEN D.N.A. USING A COMBINATION OF SCIENCE AND MAGIC, GIVING HER EXTRATERRESTRIAL ABILITIES.
WE'RE USING THE DEVICE SUPERGIRL AND I DESIGNED FOR COMBATING THE INSECT QUEEN TO FILTER SUPERWOMAN'S D.N.A. AND RESTORE HER HUMANITY.
LOOKS PAINFUL.
WE'RE COMBING THROUGH EVERY CELL IN HER BODY, ONE BY ONE. IT'S NOT A PRETTY SCIENCE...
AAAAAAAH!
"...NOR IS IT, UNFORTUNATELY, PAINLESS."
CAN YOU CURE HER?
WHATEVER GENERAL LANE DID TO HER, HE DIDN'T MEAN FOR IT TO BE PERMANENT. WE'VE MADE STRIDES, BUT--

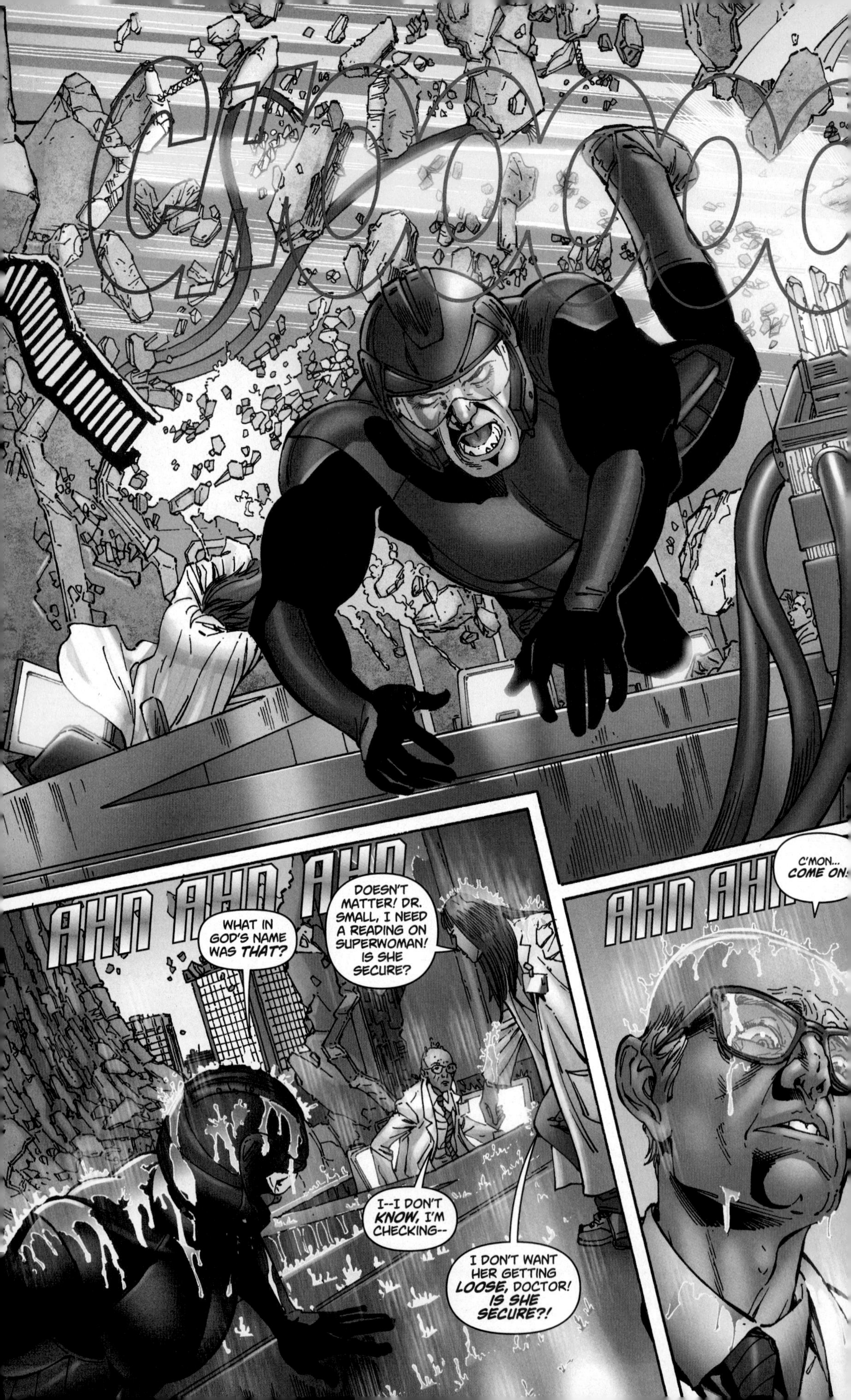
AHN AHN AHN
WHAT IN GOD'S NAME WAS THAT?
DOESN'T MATTER! DR. SMALL, I NEED A READING ON SUPERWOMAN! IS SHE SECURE?
I--I DON'T KNOW, I'M CHECKING--
I DON'T WANT HER GETTING LOOSE, DOCTOR! IS SHE SECURE?!
AHN AHN
C'MON... COME ON

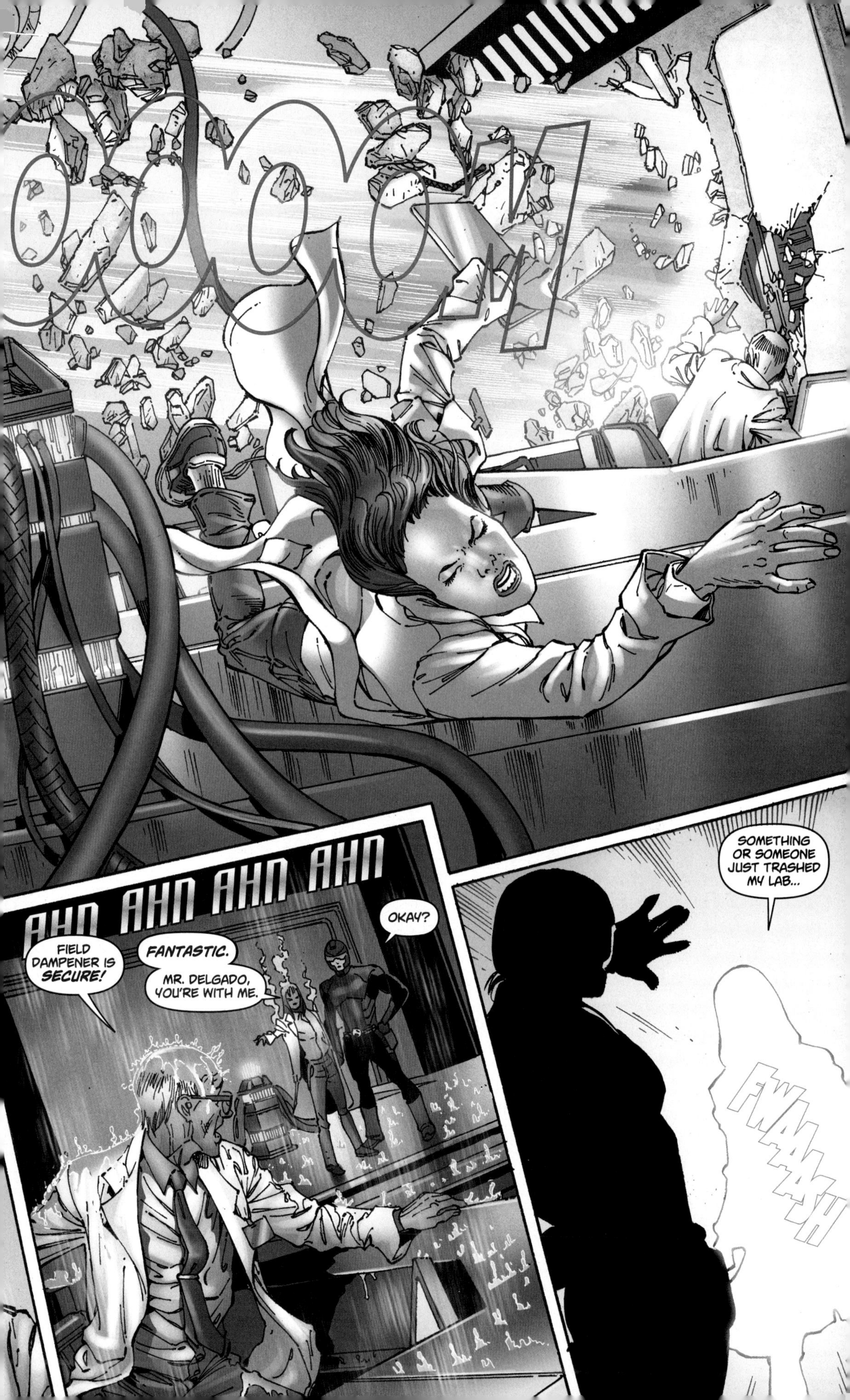
AHN AHN AHN AHN
FIELD DAMPENER IS **SECURE!**
FANTASTIC.
MR. DELGADO, YOU'RE WITH ME.
OKAY?
SOMETHING OR SOMEONE JUST TRASHED MY LAB...
FWAAASH

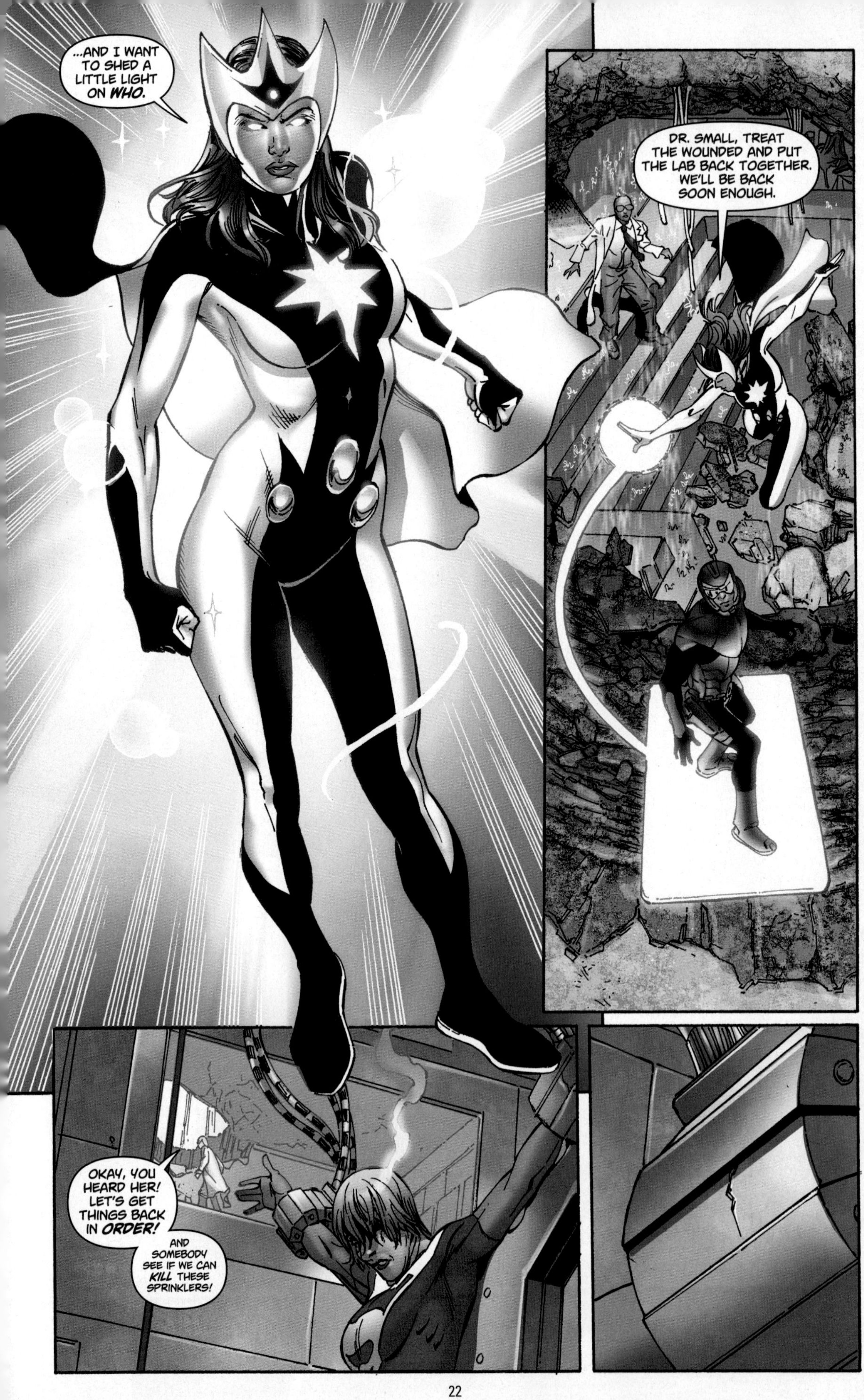
...AND I WANT TO SHED A LITTLE LIGHT ON WHO.
DR. SMALL, TREAT THE WOUNDED AND PUT THE LAB BACK TOGETHER. WE'LL BE BACK SOON ENOUGH.
OKAY, YOU HEARD HER! LET'S GET THINGS BACK IN ORDER!
AND SOMEBODY SEE IF WE CAN KILL THESE SPRINKLERS!

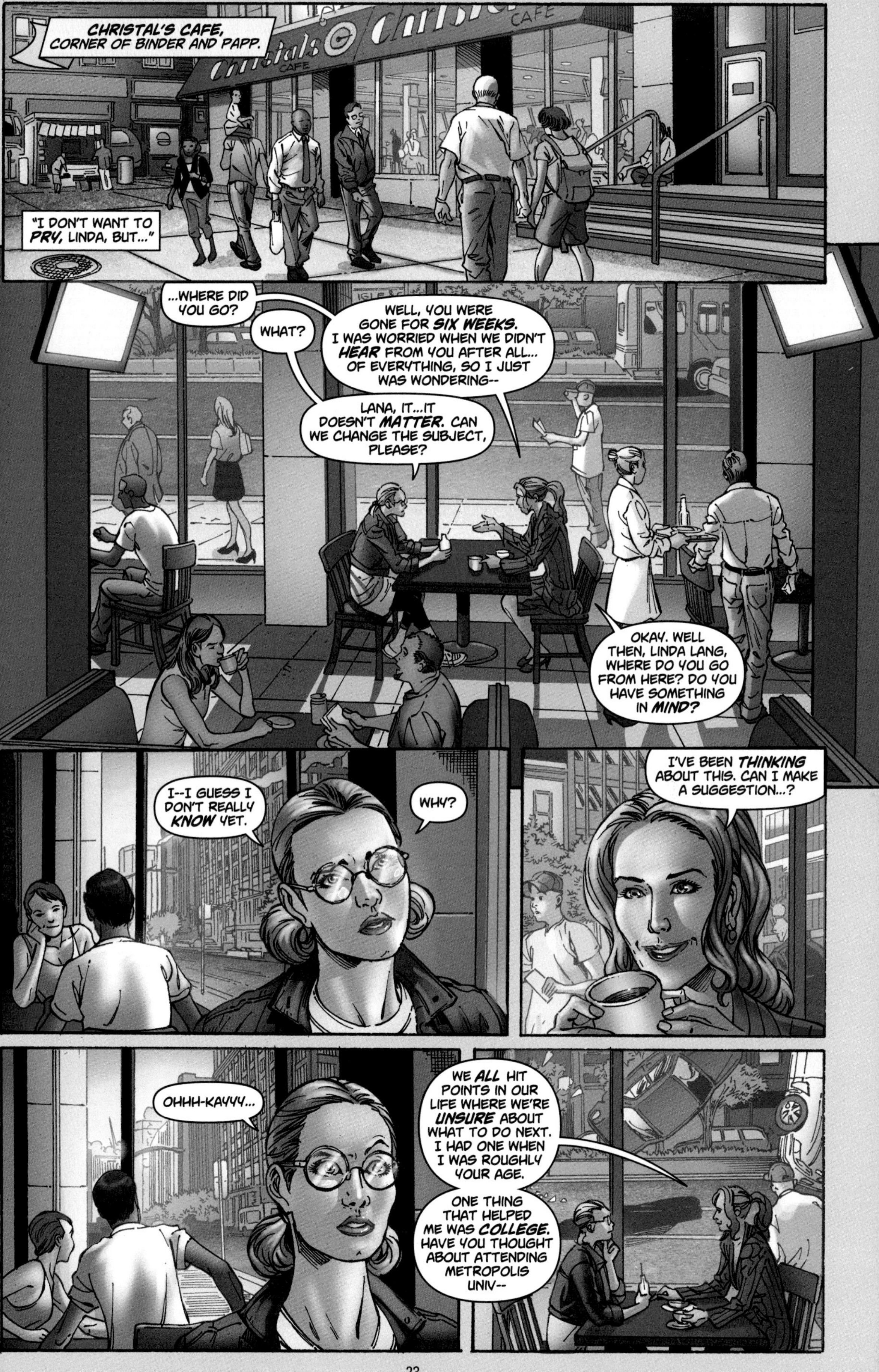
CHRISTAL'S CAFE, CORNER OF BINDER AND PAPP.
"I DON'T WANT TO PRY, LINDA, BUT..."
...WHERE DID YOU GO?
WHAT?
WELL, YOU WERE GONE FOR SIX WEEKS. I WAS WORRIED WHEN WE DIDN'T HEAR FROM YOU AFTER ALL... OF EVERYTHING, SO I JUST WAS WONDERING--
LANA, IT...IT DOESN'T MATTER. CAN WE CHANGE THE SUBJECT, PLEASE?
OKAY. WELL THEN, LINDA LANG, WHERE DO YOU GO FROM HERE? DO YOU HAVE SOMETHING IN MIND?
I--I GUESS I DON'T REALLY KNOW YET.
WHY?
I'VE BEEN THINKING ABOUT THIS. CAN I MAKE A SUGGESTION...?
OHHH-KAYYY...
WE ALL HIT POINTS IN OUR LIFE WHERE WE'RE UNSURE ABOUT WHAT TO DO NEXT. I HAD ONE WHEN I WAS ROUGHLY YOUR AGE.
ONE THING THAT HELPED ME WAS COLLEGE. HAVE YOU THOUGHT ABOUT ATTENDING METROPOLIS UNIV--

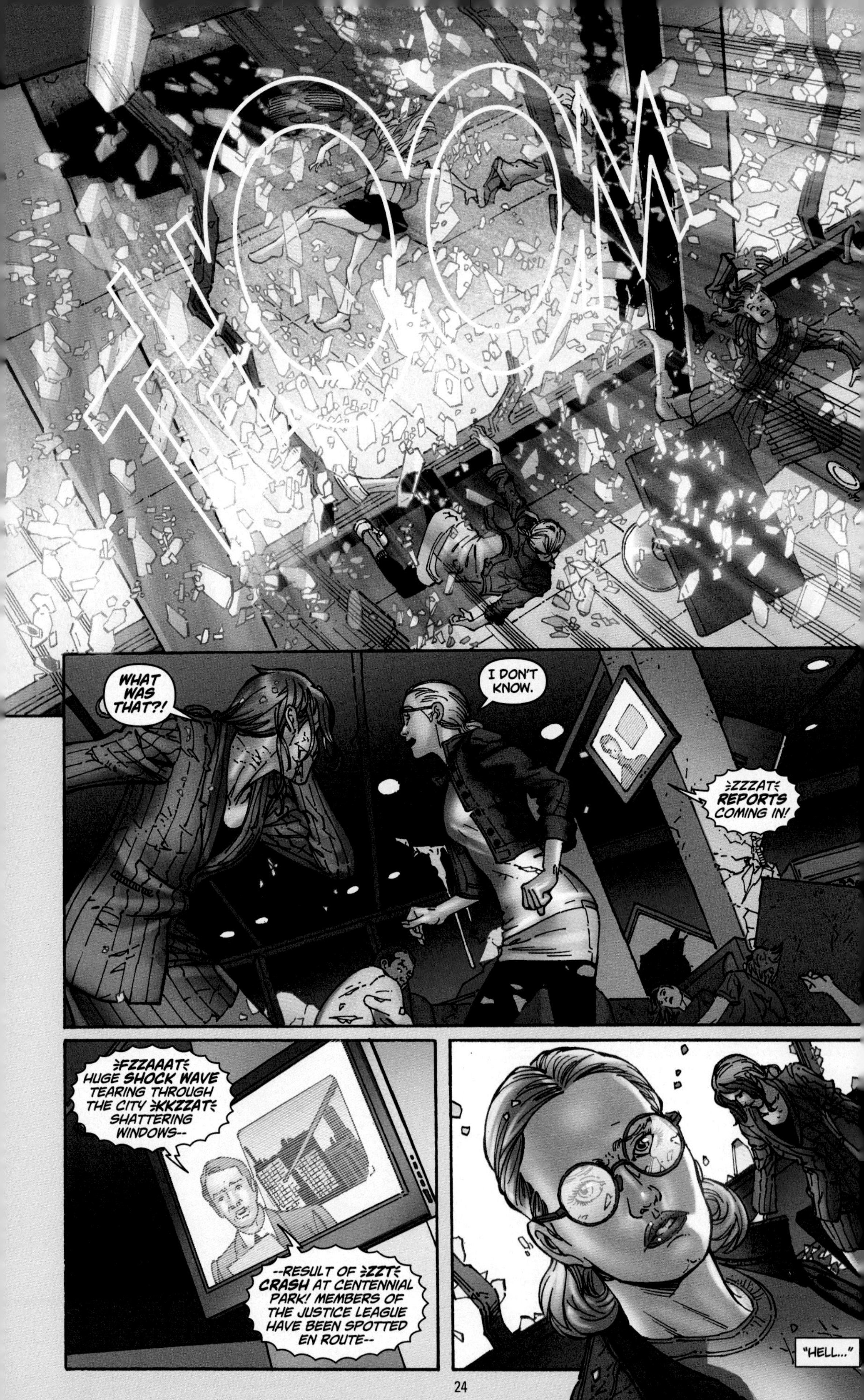
THOOM
WHAT WAS THAT?!
I DON'T KNOW.
ZZZAT REPORTS COMING IN!
FZZAAAT HUGE SHOCK WAVE TEARING THROUGH THE CITY KKZZAT SHATTERING WINDOWS--
--RESULT OF ZZT CRASH AT CENTENNIAL PARK! MEMBERS OF THE JUSTICE LEAGUE HAVE BEEN SPOTTED EN ROUTE--
"HELL..."

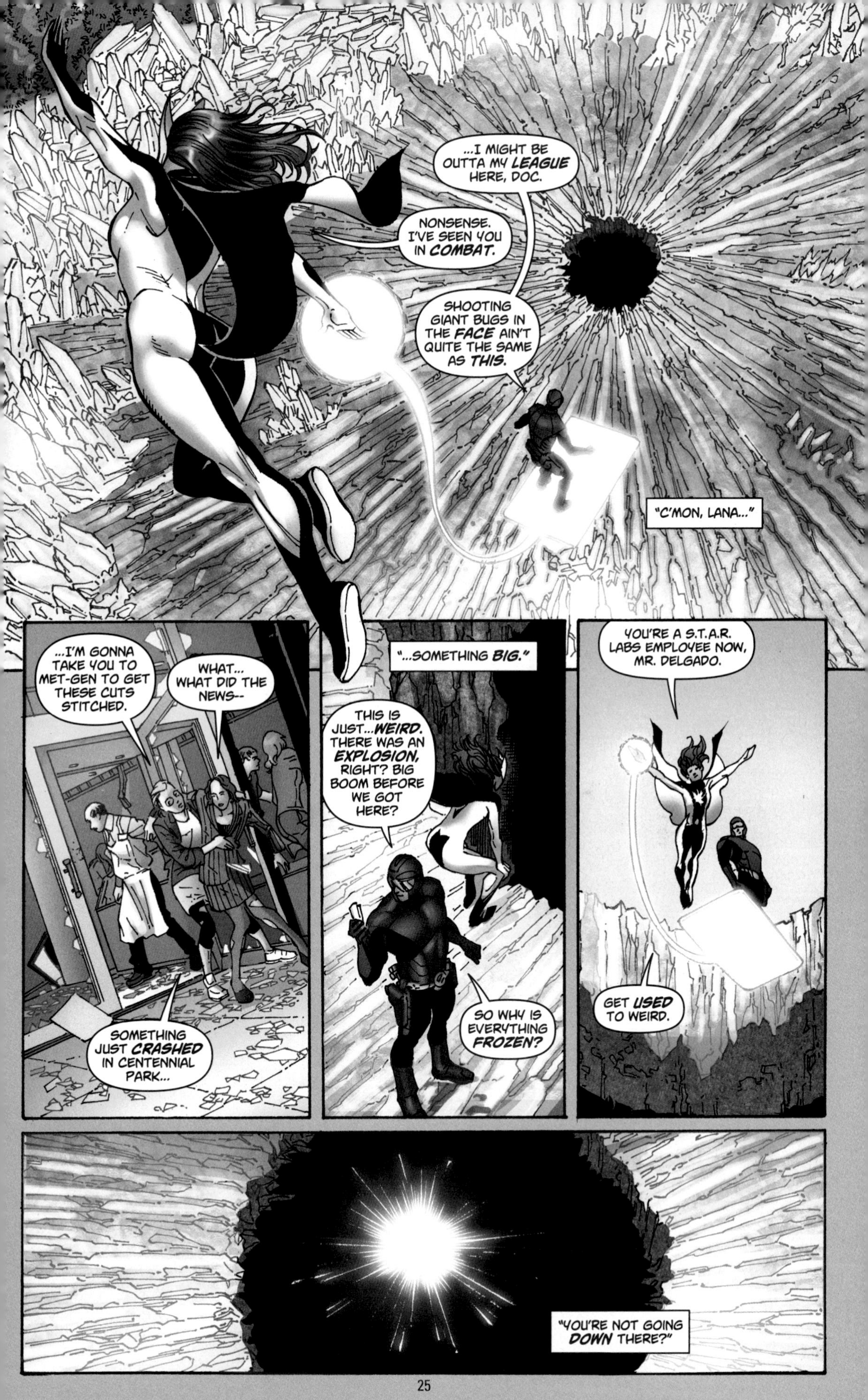
...I MIGHT BE OUTTA MY LEAGUE HERE, DOC.
NONSENSE. I'VE SEEN YOU IN COMBAT.
SHOOTING GIANT BUGS IN THE FACE AIN'T QUITE THE SAME AS THIS.
"C'MON, LANA..."
...I'M GONNA TAKE YOU TO MET-GEN TO GET THESE CUTS STITCHED.
WHAT... WHAT DID THE NEWS--
SOMETHING JUST CRASHED IN CENTENNIAL PARK...
"...SOMETHING BIG."
THIS IS JUST...WEIRD. THERE WAS AN EXPLOSION, RIGHT? BIG BOOM BEFORE WE GOT HERE?
SO WHY IS EVERYTHING FROZEN?
YOU'RE A S.T.A.R. LABS EMPLOYEE NOW, MR. DELGADO.
GET USED TO WEIRD.
"YOU'RE NOT GOING DOWN THERE?"

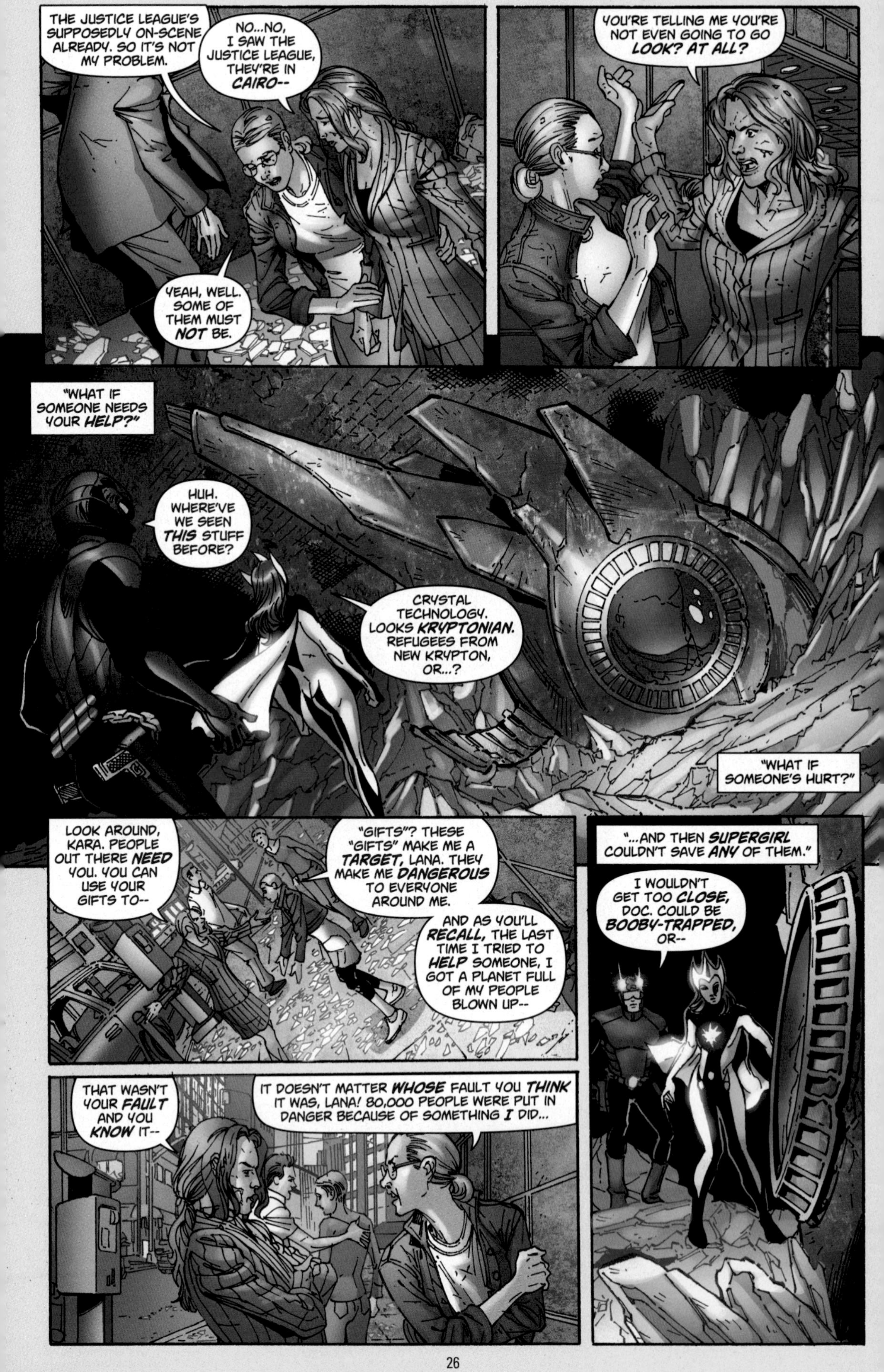
THE JUSTICE LEAGUE'S SUPPOSEDLY ON-SCENE ALREADY. SO IT'S NOT MY PROBLEM.
NO...NO, I SAW THE JUSTICE LEAGUE, THEY'RE IN CAIRO--
YEAH, WELL. SOME OF THEM MUST NOT BE.
YOU'RE TELLING ME YOU'RE NOT EVEN GOING TO GO LOOK? AT ALL?
"WHAT IF SOMEONE NEEDS YOUR HELP?"
HUH. WHERE'VE WE SEEN THIS STUFF BEFORE?
CRYSTAL TECHNOLOGY. LOOKS KRYPTONIAN. REFUGEES FROM NEW KRYPTON, OR...?
"WHAT IF SOMEONE'S HURT?"
LOOK AROUND, KARA. PEOPLE OUT THERE NEED YOU. YOU CAN USE YOUR GIFTS TO--
"GIFTS"? THESE "GIFTS" MAKE ME A TARGET, LANA. THEY MAKE ME DANGEROUS TO EVERYONE AROUND ME.
AND AS YOU'LL RECALL, THE LAST TIME I TRIED TO HELP SOMEONE, I GOT A PLANET FULL OF MY PEOPLE BLOWN UP--
"...AND THEN SUPERGIRL COULDN'T SAVE ANY OF THEM."
I WOULDN'T GET TOO CLOSE, DOC. COULD BE BOOBY-TRAPPED, OR--
THAT WASN'T YOUR FAULT AND YOU KNOW IT--
IT DOESN'T MATTER WHOSE FAULT YOU THINK IT WAS, LANA! 80,000 PEOPLE WERE PUT IN DANGER BECAUSE OF SOMETHING I DID...

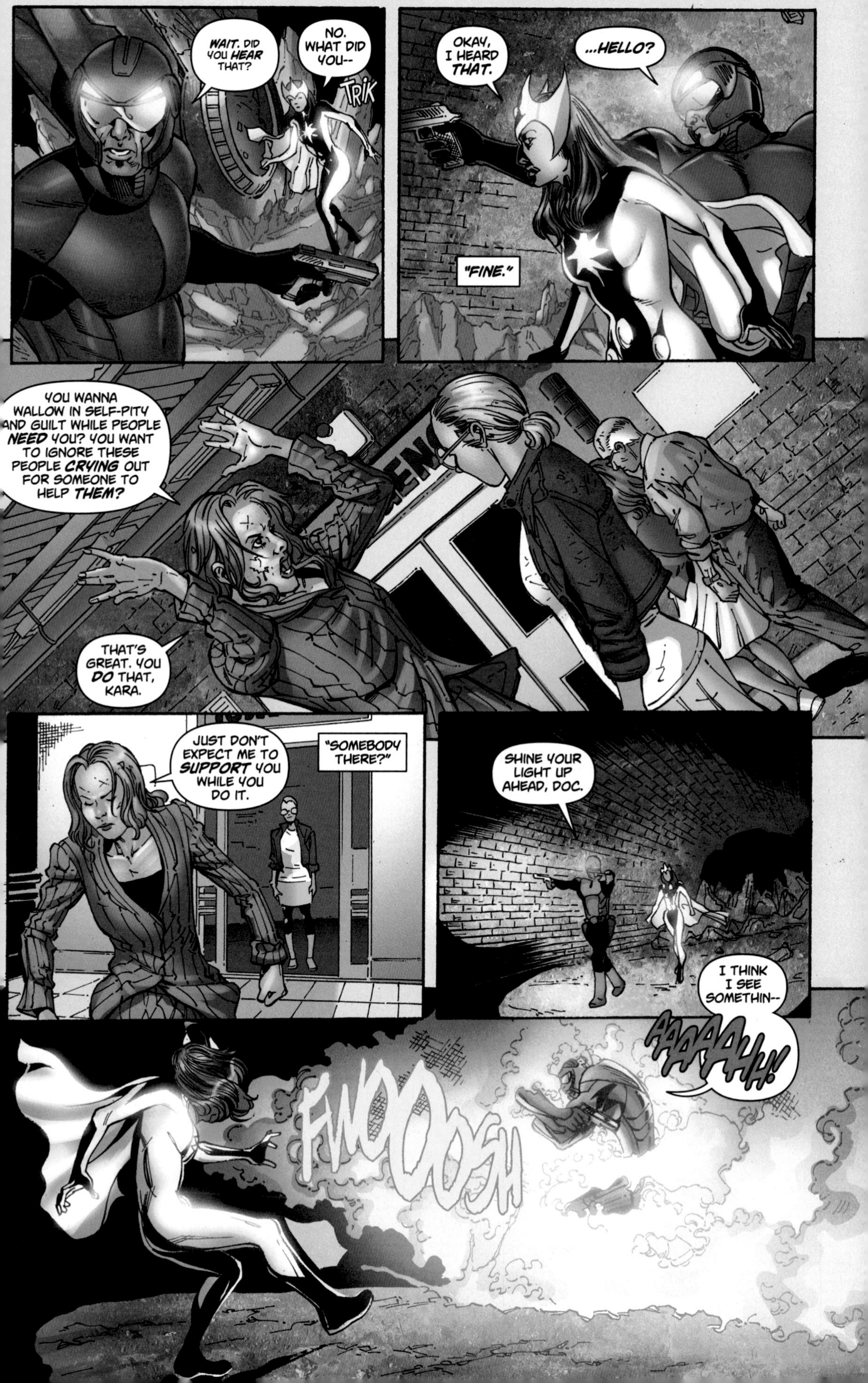
WAIT. DID YOU HEAR THAT?
NO. WHAT DID YOU--
TRIK
OKAY, I HEARD THAT.
...HELLO?
"FINE."
YOU WANNA WALLOW IN SELF-PITY AND GUILT WHILE PEOPLE NEED YOU? YOU WANT TO IGNORE THESE PEOPLE CRYING OUT FOR SOMEONE TO HELP THEM?
THAT'S GREAT. YOU DO THAT, KARA.
JUST DON'T EXPECT ME TO SUPPORT YOU WHILE YOU DO IT.
"SOMEBODY THERE?"
SHINE YOUR LIGHT UP AHEAD, DOC.
I THINK I SEE SOMETHIN--
AAAAAHH!
FWOOOSH

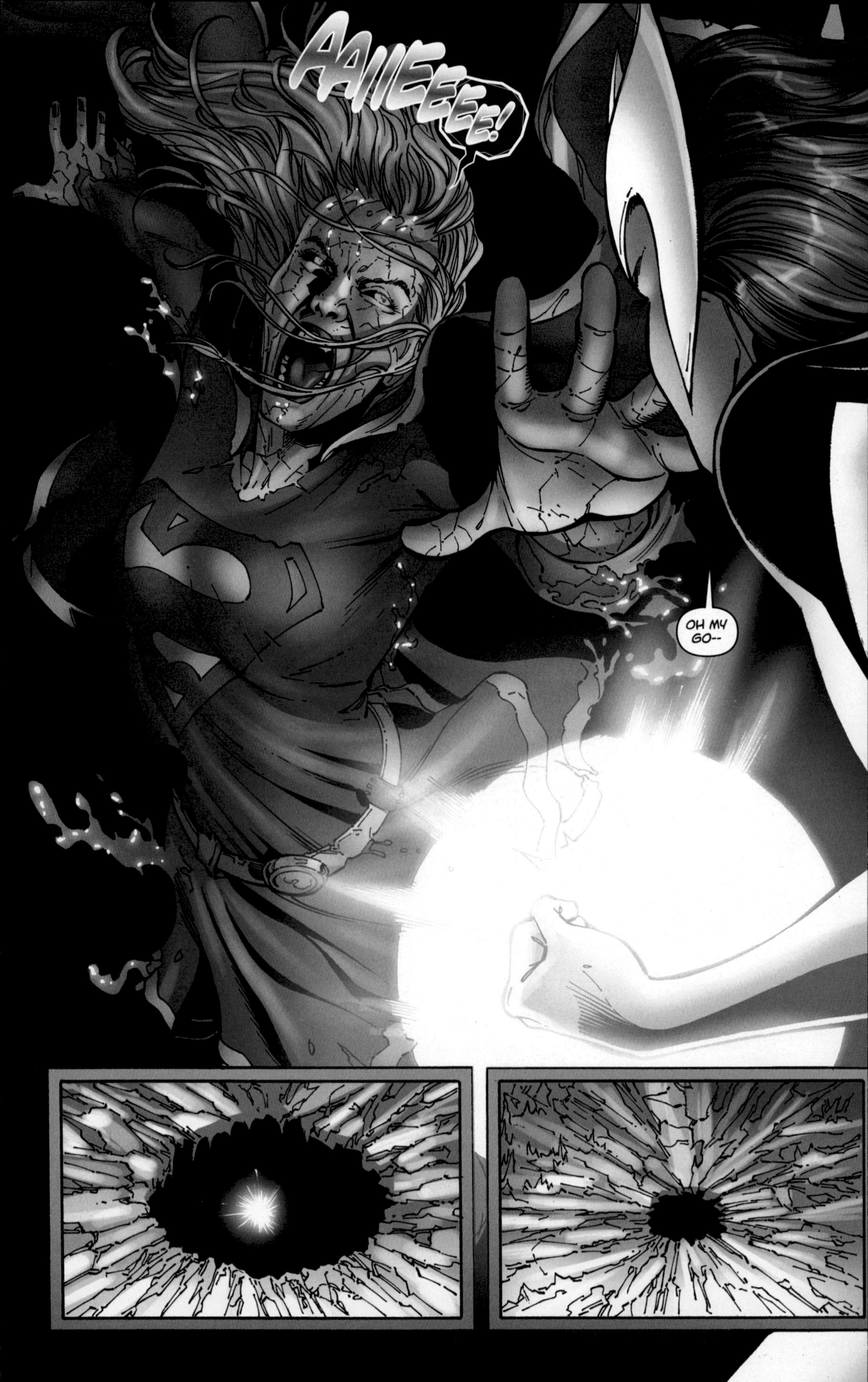
AAIIEEEEE!
OH MY GO--

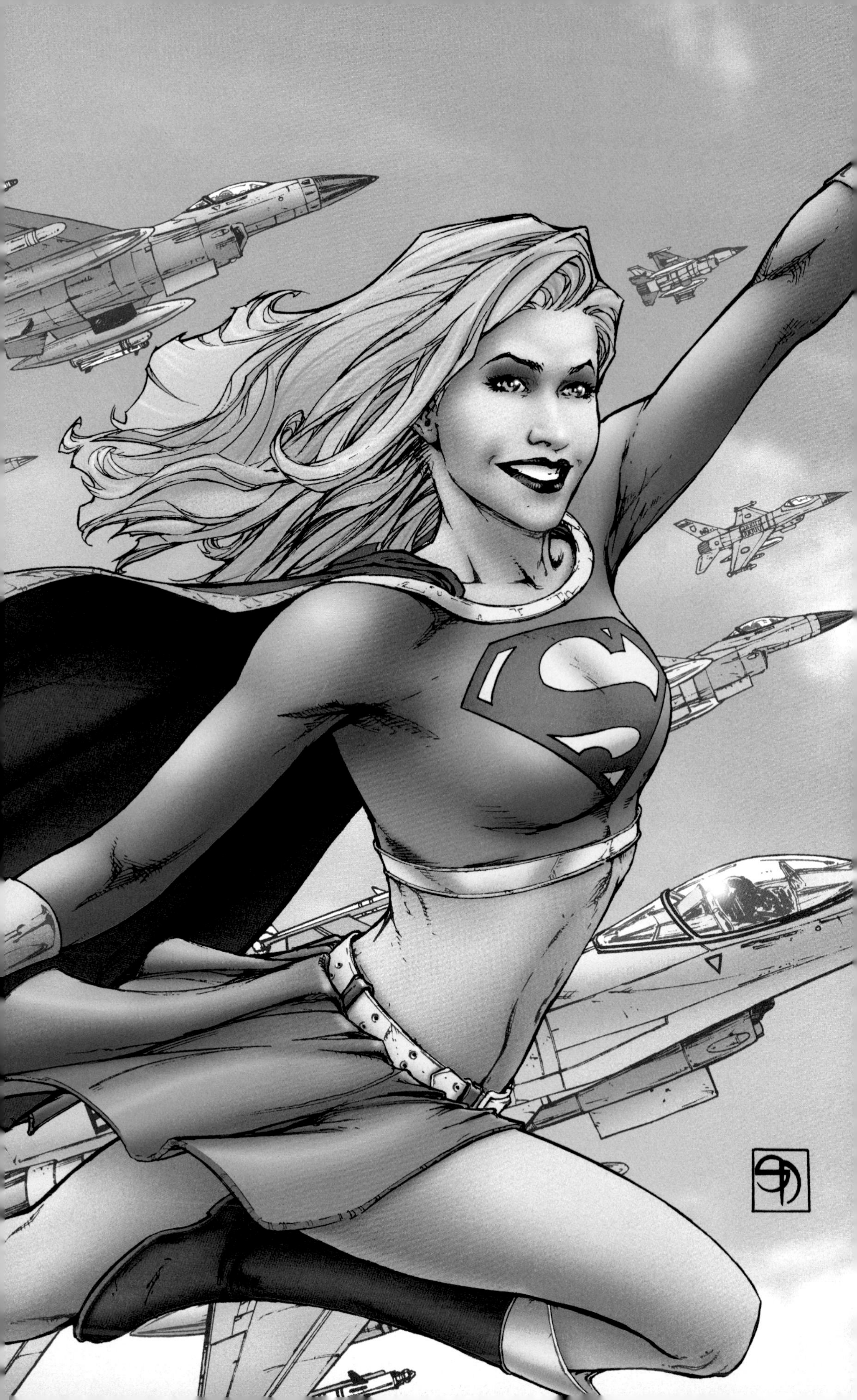

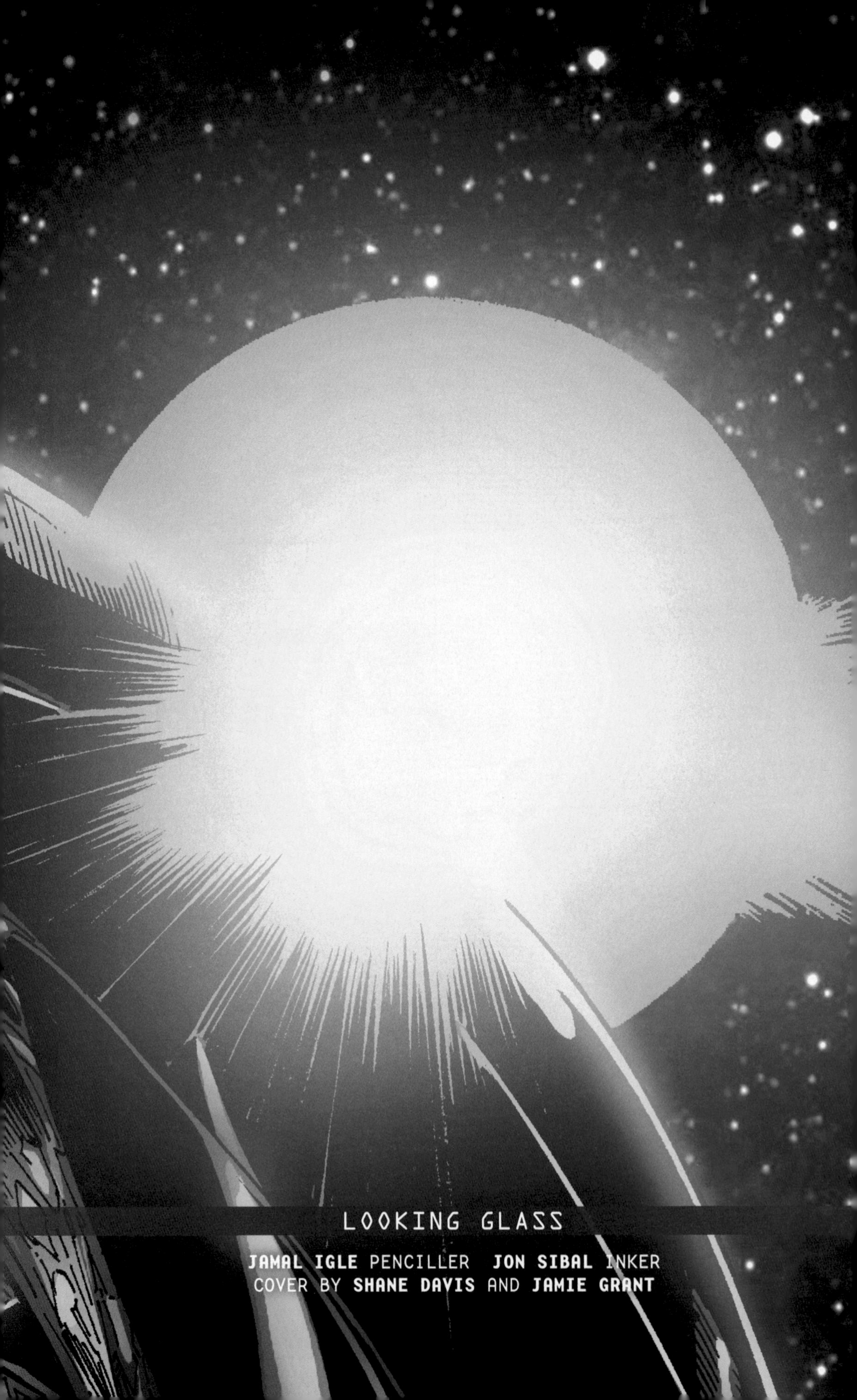

LOOKING GLASS

JAMAL IGLE PENCILLER **JON SIBAL** INKER
COVER BY **SHANE DAVIS** AND **JAMIE GRANT**

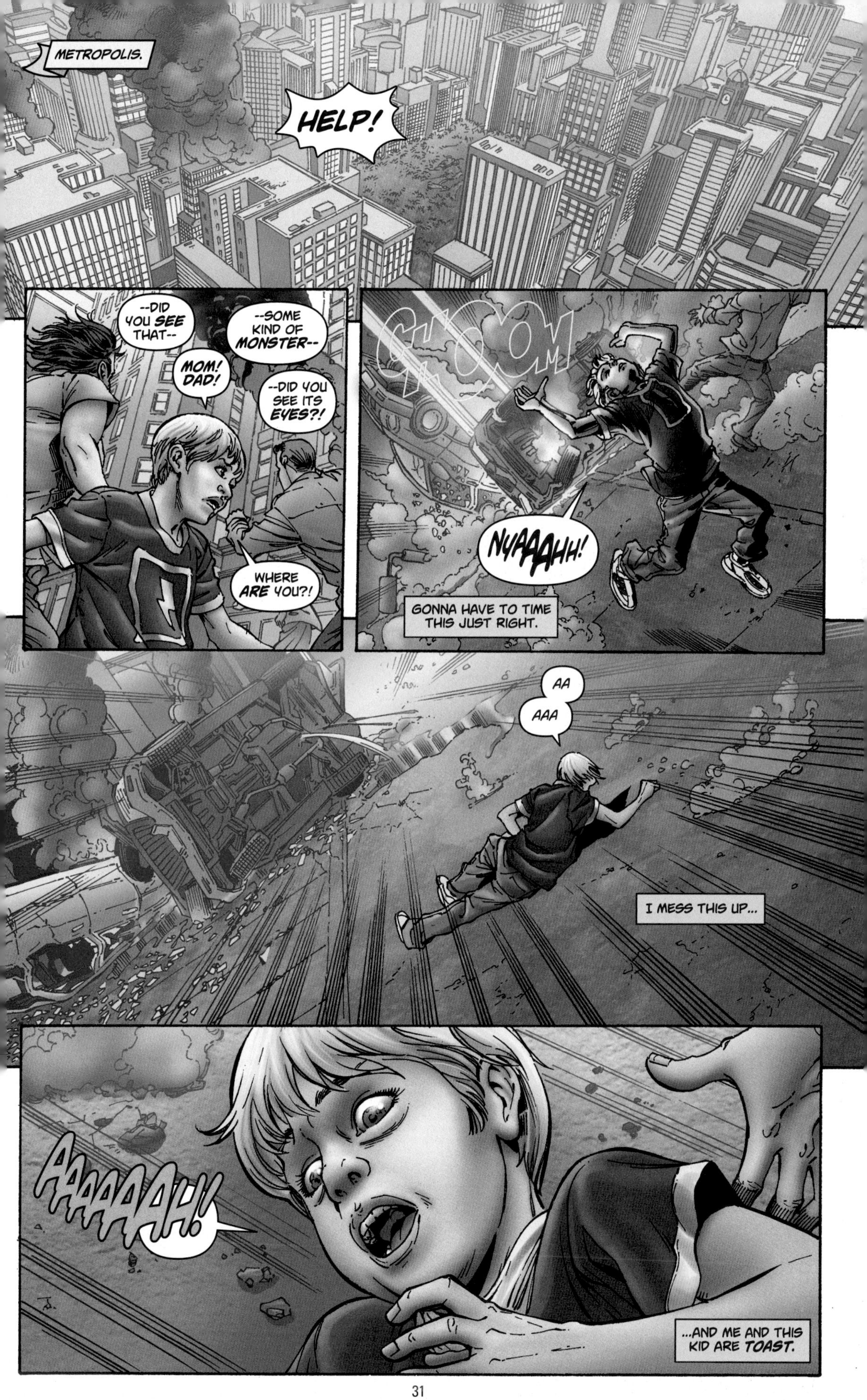
METROPOLIS.
HELP!
--DID YOU SEE THAT--
--SOME KIND OF MONSTER--
MOM! DAD!
--DID YOU SEE ITS EYES?!
WHERE ARE YOU?!
CHOOOM
NYAAAHH!
GONNA HAVE TO TIME THIS JUST RIGHT.
AA
AAA
I MESS THIS UP...
AAAAAAH!
...AND ME AND THIS KID ARE TOAST.

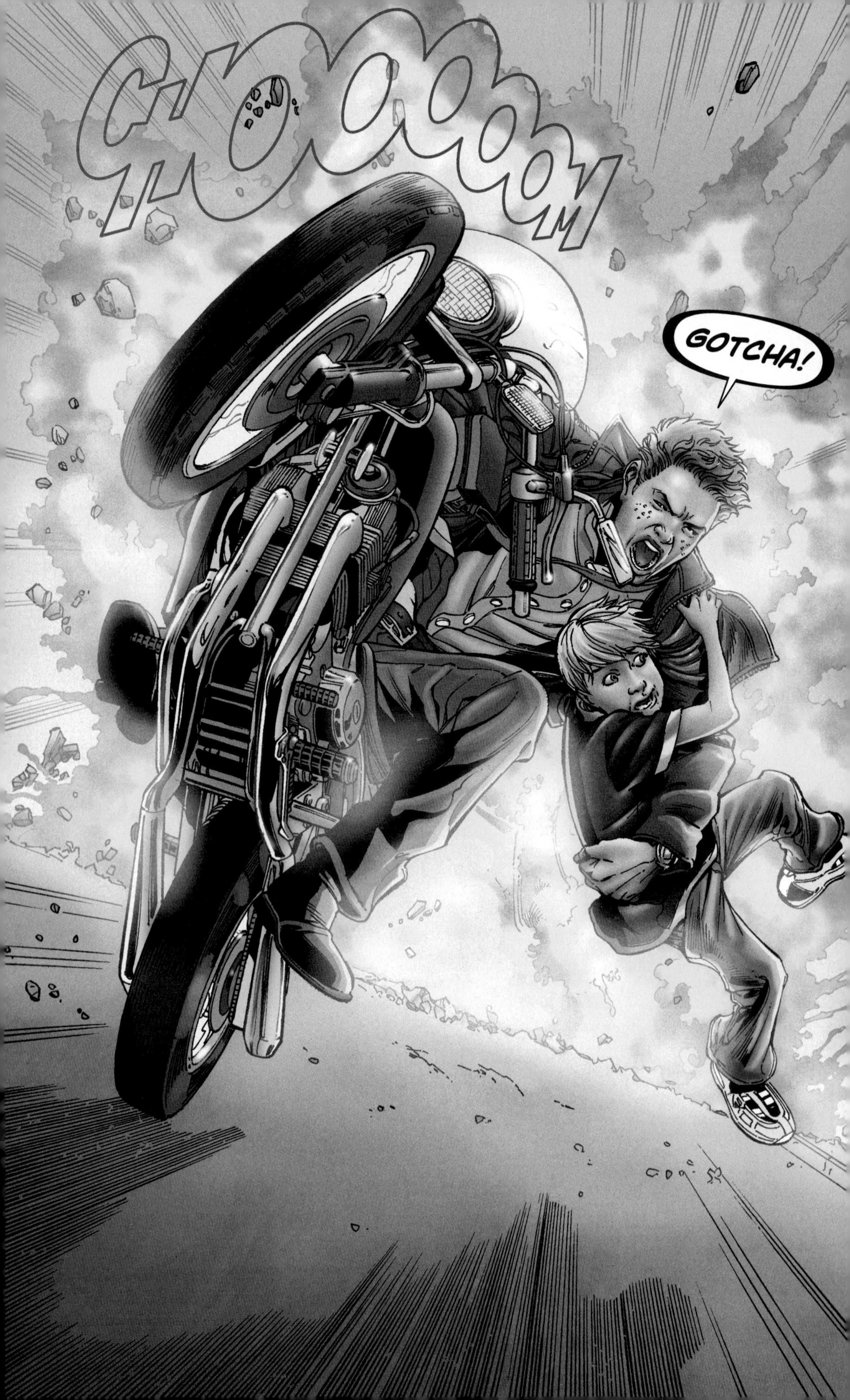
GHOOOOOM
GOTCHA!

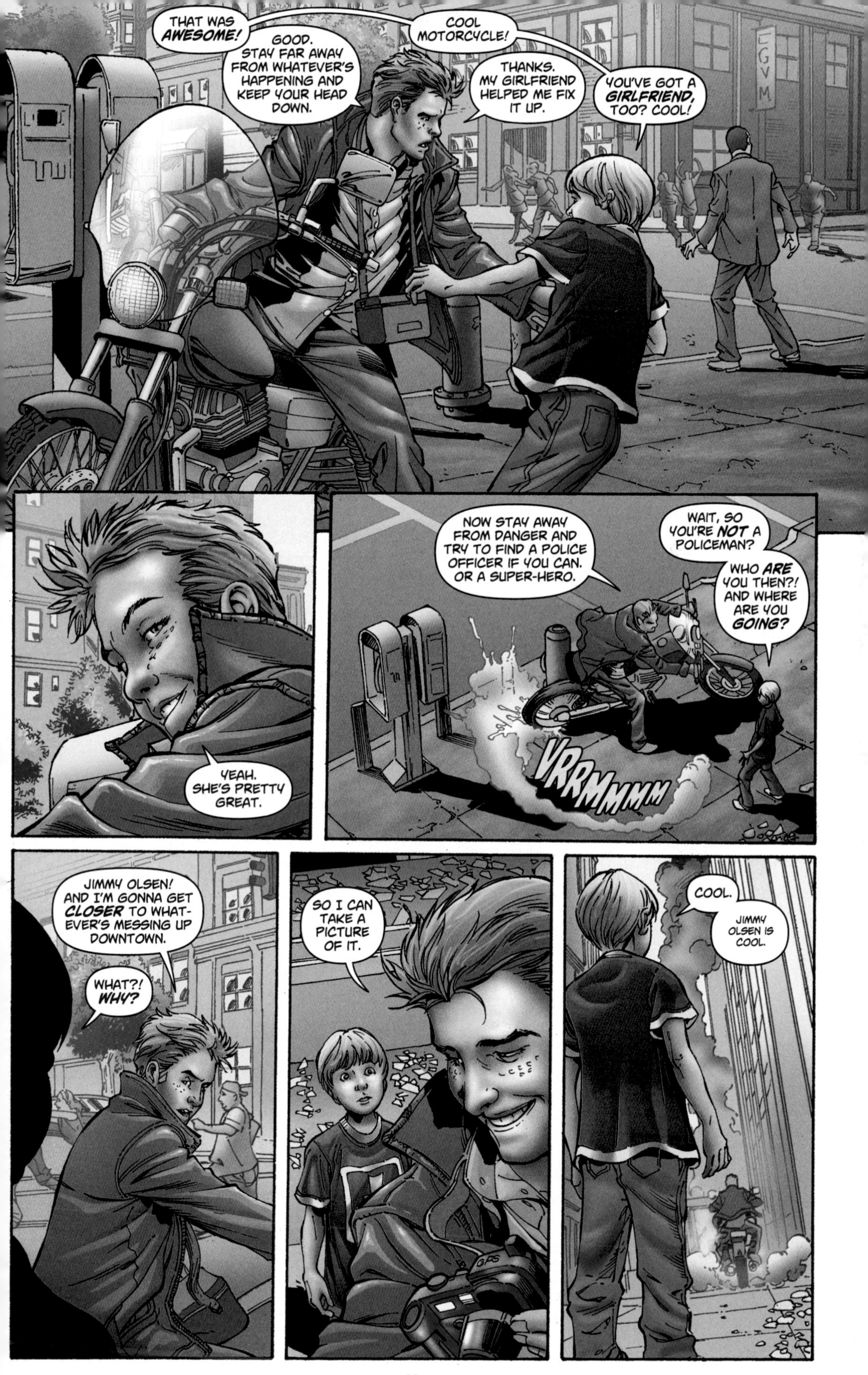
THAT WAS AWESOME!
COOL MOTORCYCLE!
GOOD. STAY FAR AWAY FROM WHATEVER'S HAPPENING AND KEEP YOUR HEAD DOWN.
THANKS. MY GIRLFRIEND HELPED ME FIX IT UP.
YOU'VE GOT A GIRLFRIEND, TOO? COOL!
YEAH. SHE'S PRETTY GREAT.
NOW STAY AWAY FROM DANGER AND TRY TO FIND A POLICE OFFICER IF YOU CAN. OR A SUPER-HERO.
WAIT, SO YOU'RE NOT A POLICEMAN?
WHO ARE YOU THEN?! AND WHERE ARE YOU GOING?
VRRMMMM
JIMMY OLSEN! AND I'M GONNA GET CLOSER TO WHAT-EVER'S MESSING UP DOWNTOWN.
WHAT?! WHY?
SO I CAN TAKE A PICTURE OF IT.
COOL.
JIMMY OLSEN IS COOL.

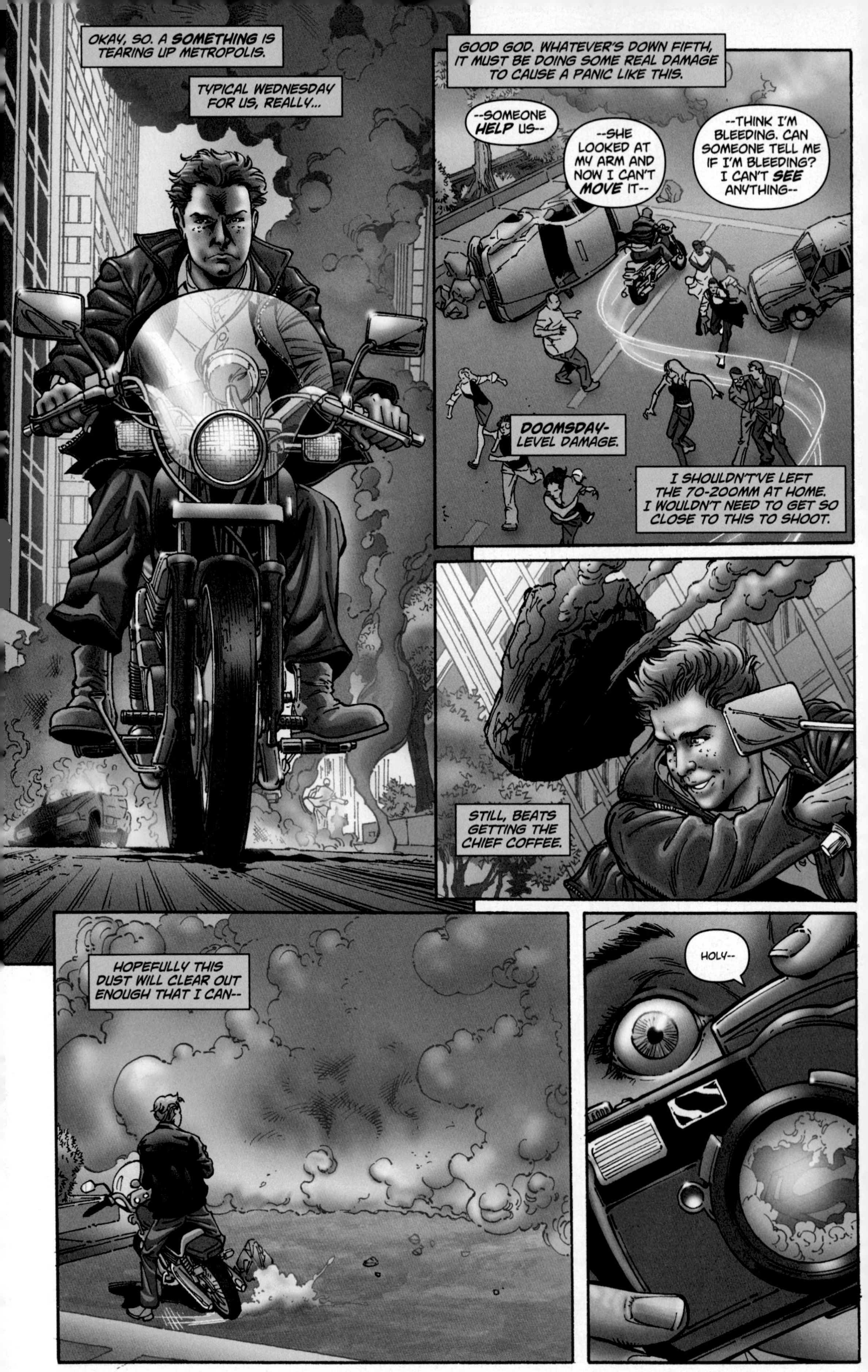
OKAY, SO. A SOMETHING IS TEARING UP METROPOLIS.
TYPICAL WEDNESDAY FOR US, REALLY...
GOOD GOD. WHATEVER'S DOWN FIFTH, IT MUST BE DOING SOME REAL DAMAGE TO CAUSE A PANIC LIKE THIS.
--SOMEONE HELP US--
--SHE LOOKED AT MY ARM AND NOW I CAN'T MOVE IT--
--THINK I'M BLEEDING. CAN SOMEONE TELL ME IF I'M BLEEDING? I CAN'T SEE ANYTHING--
DOOMSDAY-LEVEL DAMAGE.
I SHOULDN'T'VE LEFT THE 70-200MM AT HOME. I WOULDN'T NEED TO GET SO CLOSE TO THIS TO SHOOT.
STILL, BEATS GETTING THE CHIEF COFFEE.
HOPEFULLY THIS DUST WILL CLEAR OUT ENOUGH THAT I CAN--
HOLY--

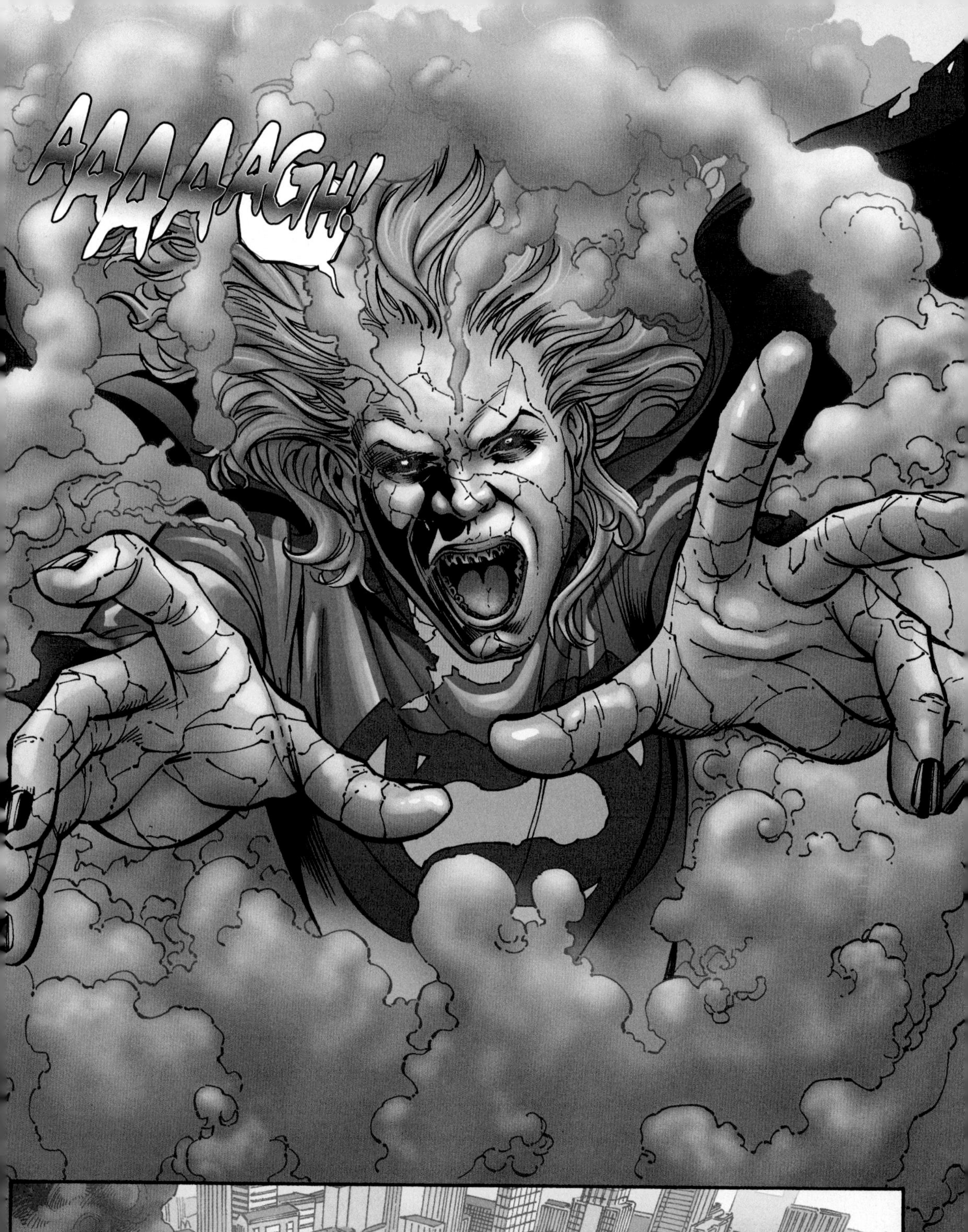
AAAAAGH!
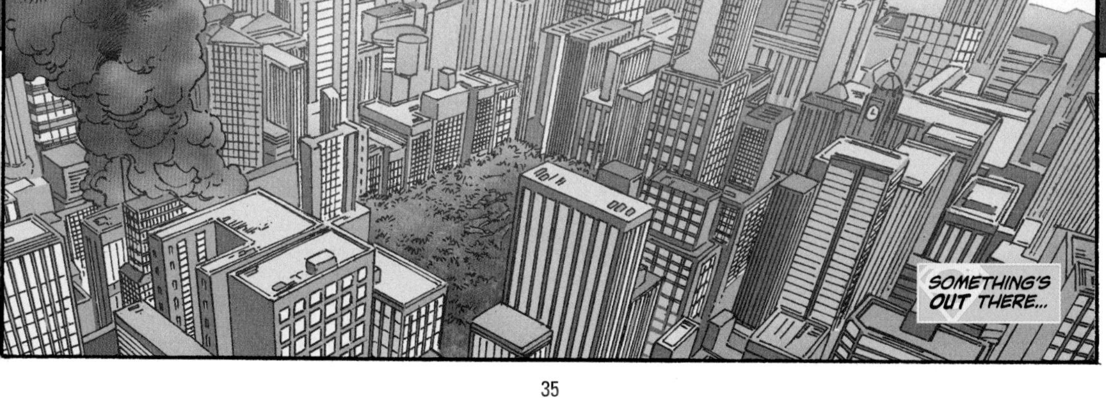
SOMETHING'S OUT THERE...

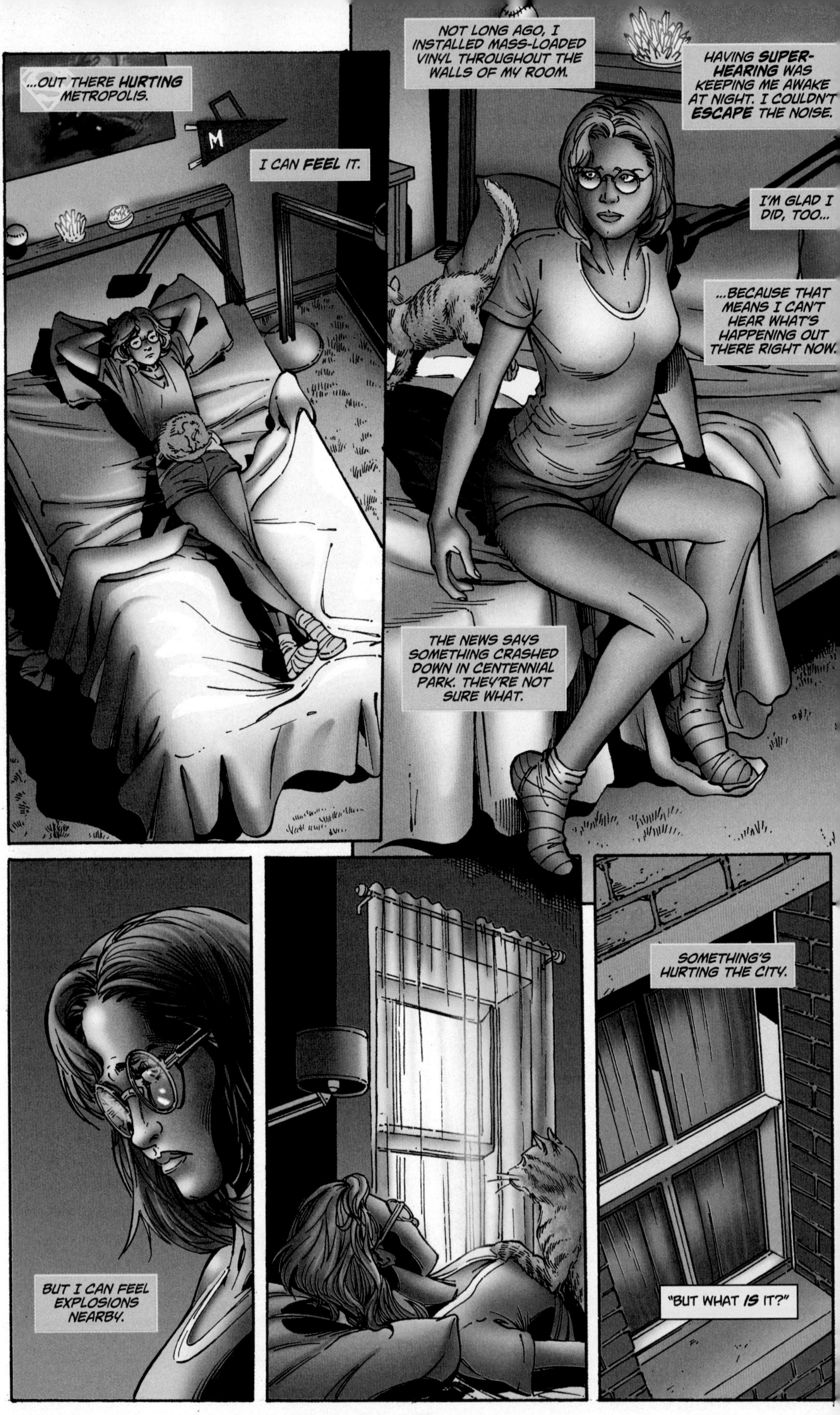
...OUT THERE HURTING METROPOLIS.
I CAN FEEL IT.
NOT LONG AGO, I INSTALLED MASS-LOADED VINYL THROUGHOUT THE WALLS OF MY ROOM.
HAVING SUPER-HEARING WAS KEEPING ME AWAKE AT NIGHT. I COULDN'T ESCAPE THE NOISE.
I'M GLAD I DID, TOO...
...BECAUSE THAT MEANS I CAN'T HEAR WHAT'S HAPPENING OUT THERE RIGHT NOW.
THE NEWS SAYS SOMETHING CRASHED DOWN IN CENTENNIAL PARK. THEY'RE NOT SURE WHAT.
BUT I CAN FEEL EXPLOSIONS NEARBY.
SOMETHING'S HURTING THE CITY.
"BUT WHAT IS IT?"

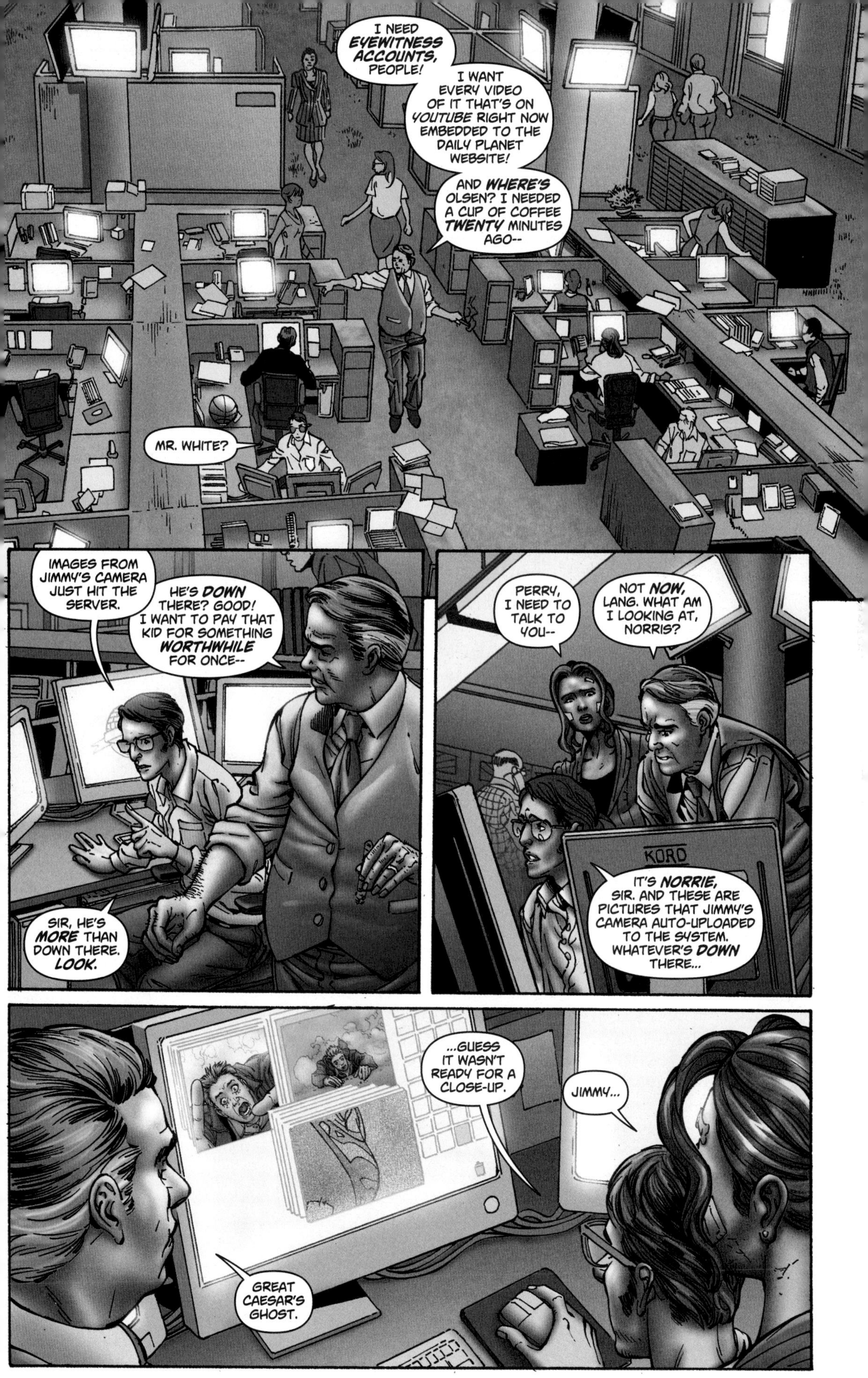
I NEED EYEWITNESS ACCOUNTS, PEOPLE!
I WANT EVERY VIDEO OF IT THAT'S ON YOUTUBE RIGHT NOW EMBEDDED TO THE DAILY PLANET WEBSITE!
AND WHERE'S OLSEN? I NEEDED A CUP OF COFFEE TWENTY MINUTES AGO--
MR. WHITE?
IMAGES FROM JIMMY'S CAMERA JUST HIT THE SERVER.
HE'S DOWN THERE? GOOD! I WANT TO PAY THAT KID FOR SOMETHING WORTHWHILE FOR ONCE--
SIR, HE'S MORE THAN DOWN THERE. LOOK.
PERRY, I NEED TO TALK TO YOU--
NOT NOW, LANG. WHAT AM I LOOKING AT, NORRIS?
KORD
IT'S NORRIE, SIR. AND THESE ARE PICTURES THAT JIMMY'S CAMERA AUTO-UPLOADED TO THE SYSTEM. WHATEVER'S DOWN THERE...
...GUESS IT WASN'T READY FOR A CLOSE-UP.
JIMMY...
GREAT CAESAR'S GHOST.

SOMEBODY CALL THE SCIENCE POLICE! OLSEN'S BEEN KIDNAPPED AGAIN!

SCIENCE POLICE ARE STILL *REBUILDING*, SIR.

THEN CALL THE S.C.U.! AND WHY DID LANE PICK *TODAY* TO GO TO PHILADELPHIA AND COVER THAT SUPERMAN THING!?

NORRIE, CAN YOU *ENHANCE* THESE PICTURES AT ALL?

SURE, MS. LANG. *EASY.*

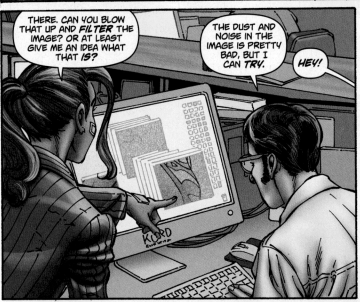

THERE. CAN YOU BLOW THAT UP AND *FILTER* THE IMAGE? OR AT LEAST GIVE ME AN IDEA WHAT THAT *IS*?

THE DUST AND NOISE IN THE IMAGE IS PRETTY BAD, BUT I CAN *TRY.*

HEY!

S.T.A.R. LABS JANITOR ON THE PHONE, PERRY! HE SAYS A *SPACESHIP* CRASHED THROUGH THEIR OFFICES ABOUT TWENTY MINUTES AGO!

A SPACESHIP?

VOILÀ!

OH MY GOD.

YOU'RE AN *UNPAID* INTERN, RIGHT, NORRIE? WITH AN OPTION TO HIRE ON?

UM. YES?

GREAT. I'M HIRING YOU FOR THE BUSINESS SECTION.

YOU'LL REPORT TO *ME* TOMORROW MORNING ONCE I CLEAR IT WITH H.R.-- AND EMAIL ME THAT JPEG RIGHT NOW.

Y-YES, MA'AM!

UM. YES, MA'AM?

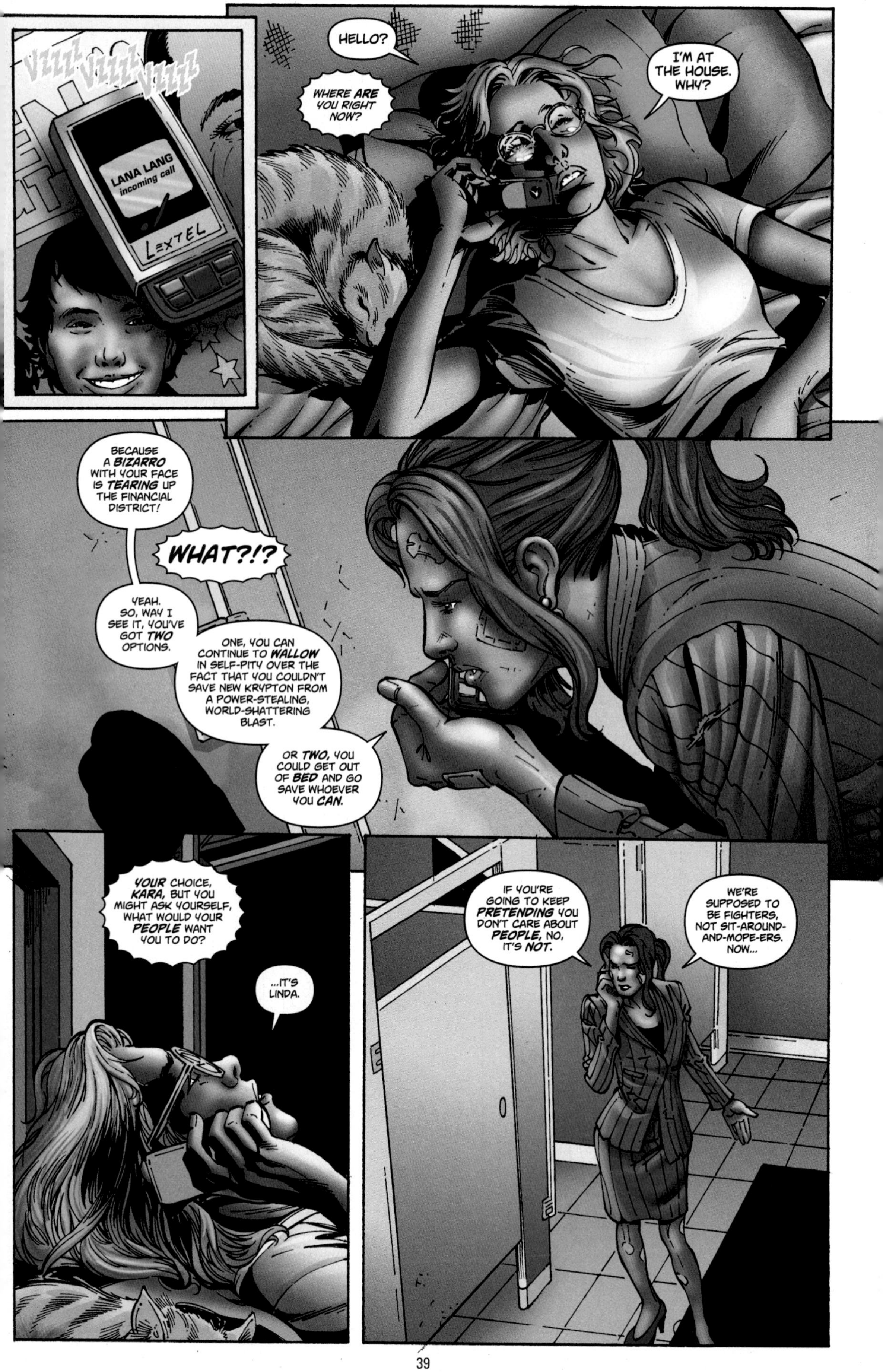
VZZZZ VZZZZ VZZZZ
LANA LANG
incoming call
LEXTEL
HELLO?
WHERE ARE YOU RIGHT NOW?
I'M AT THE HOUSE. WHY?
BECAUSE A BIZARRO WITH YOUR FACE IS TEARING UP THE FINANCIAL DISTRICT!
WHAT?!?
YEAH. SO, WAY I SEE IT, YOU'VE GOT TWO OPTIONS.
ONE, YOU CAN CONTINUE TO WALLOW IN SELF-PITY OVER THE FACT THAT YOU COULDN'T SAVE NEW KRYPTON FROM A POWER-STEALING, WORLD-SHATTERING BLAST.
OR TWO, YOU COULD GET OUT OF BED AND GO SAVE WHOEVER YOU CAN.
YOUR CHOICE, KARA, BUT YOU MIGHT ASK YOURSELF, WHAT WOULD YOUR PEOPLE WANT YOU TO DO?
...IT'S LINDA.
IF YOU'RE GOING TO KEEP PRETENDING YOU DON'T CARE ABOUT PEOPLE, NO, IT'S NOT.
WE'RE SUPPOSED TO BE FIGHTERS, NOT SIT-AROUND-AND-MOPE-ERS. NOW...

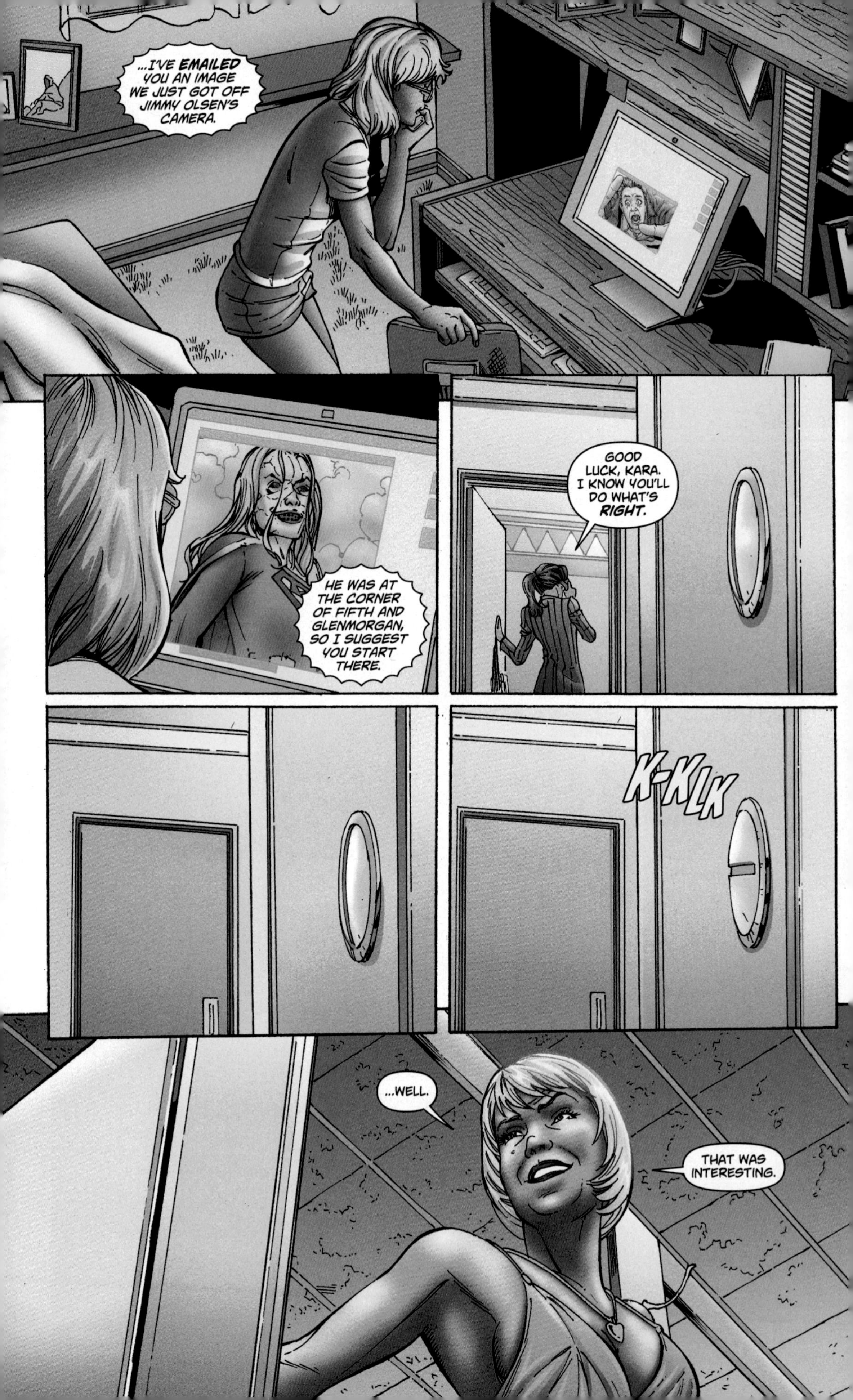
...I'VE EMAILED YOU AN IMAGE WE JUST GOT OFF JIMMY OLSEN'S CAMERA.
HE WAS AT THE CORNER OF FIFTH AND GLENMORGAN, SO I SUGGEST YOU START THERE.
GOOD LUCK, KARA. I KNOW YOU'LL DO WHAT'S RIGHT.
K-KLIK
...WELL.
THAT WAS INTERESTING.

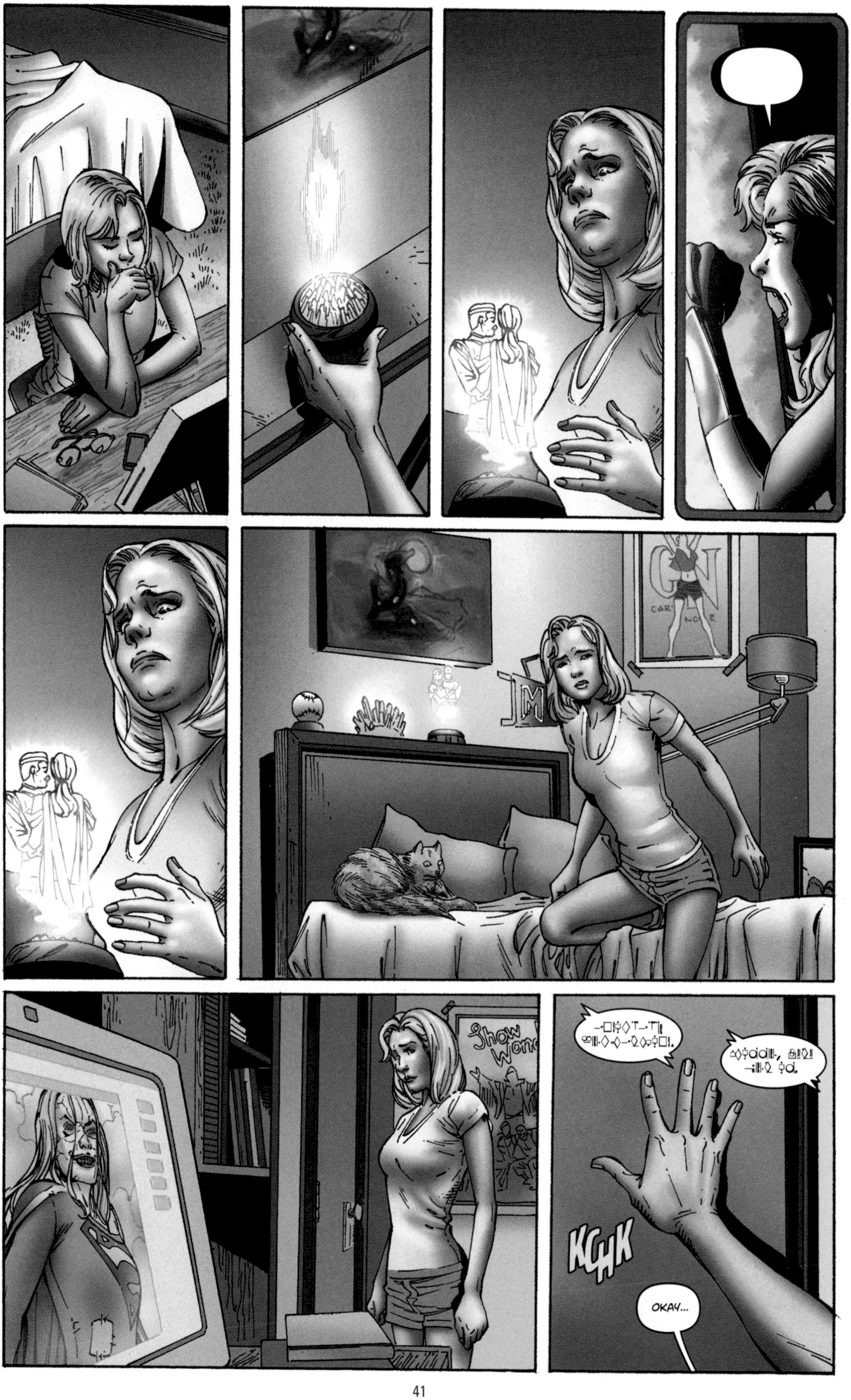
KCHK
OKAY...

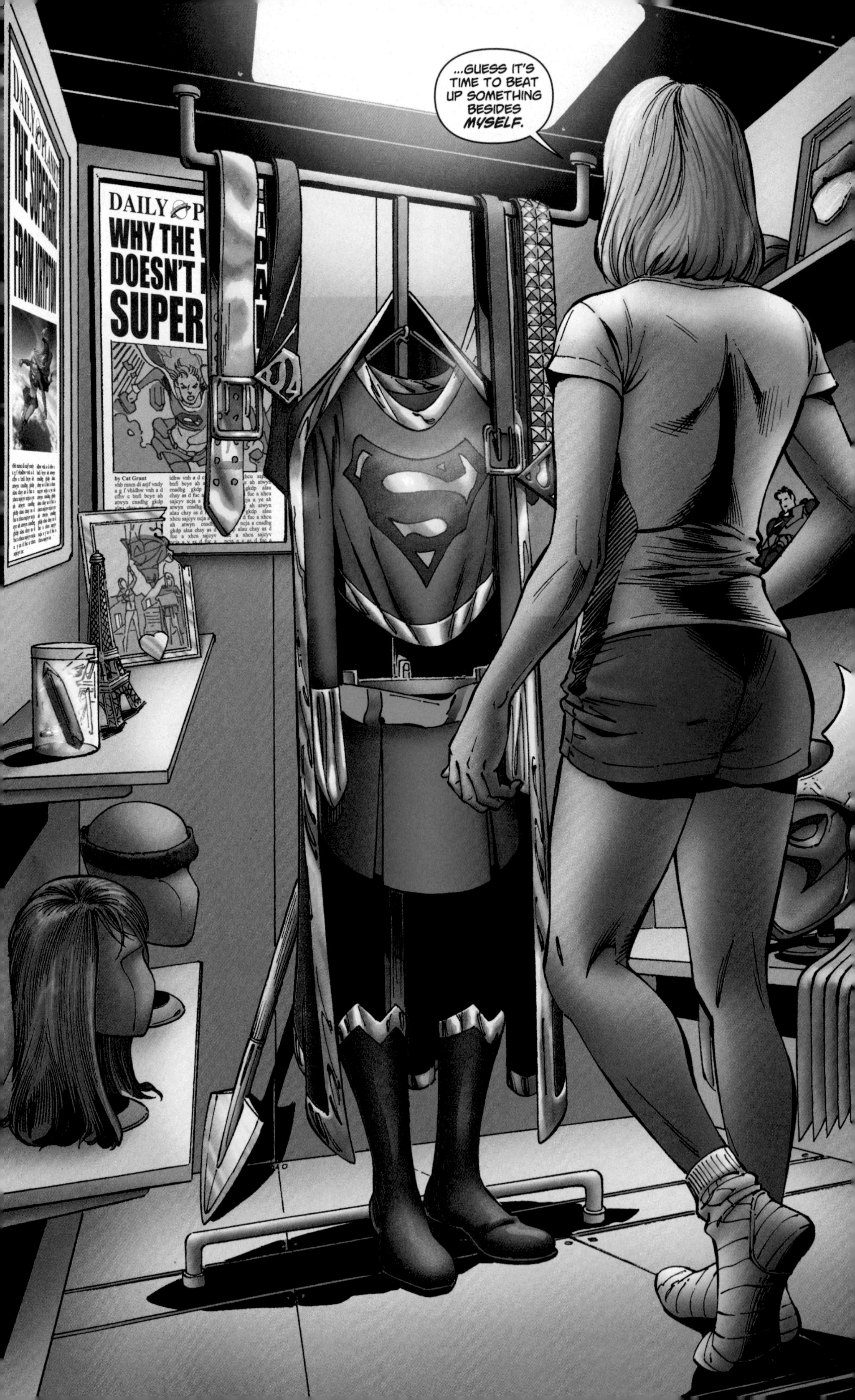
...GUESS IT'S TIME TO BEAT UP SOMETHING BESIDES MYSELF.
DAILY PLANET
THE SUPERGIRL FROM KRYPTON
DAILY PLANET
WHY THE W
DOESN'T N
SUPER
by Cat Grant

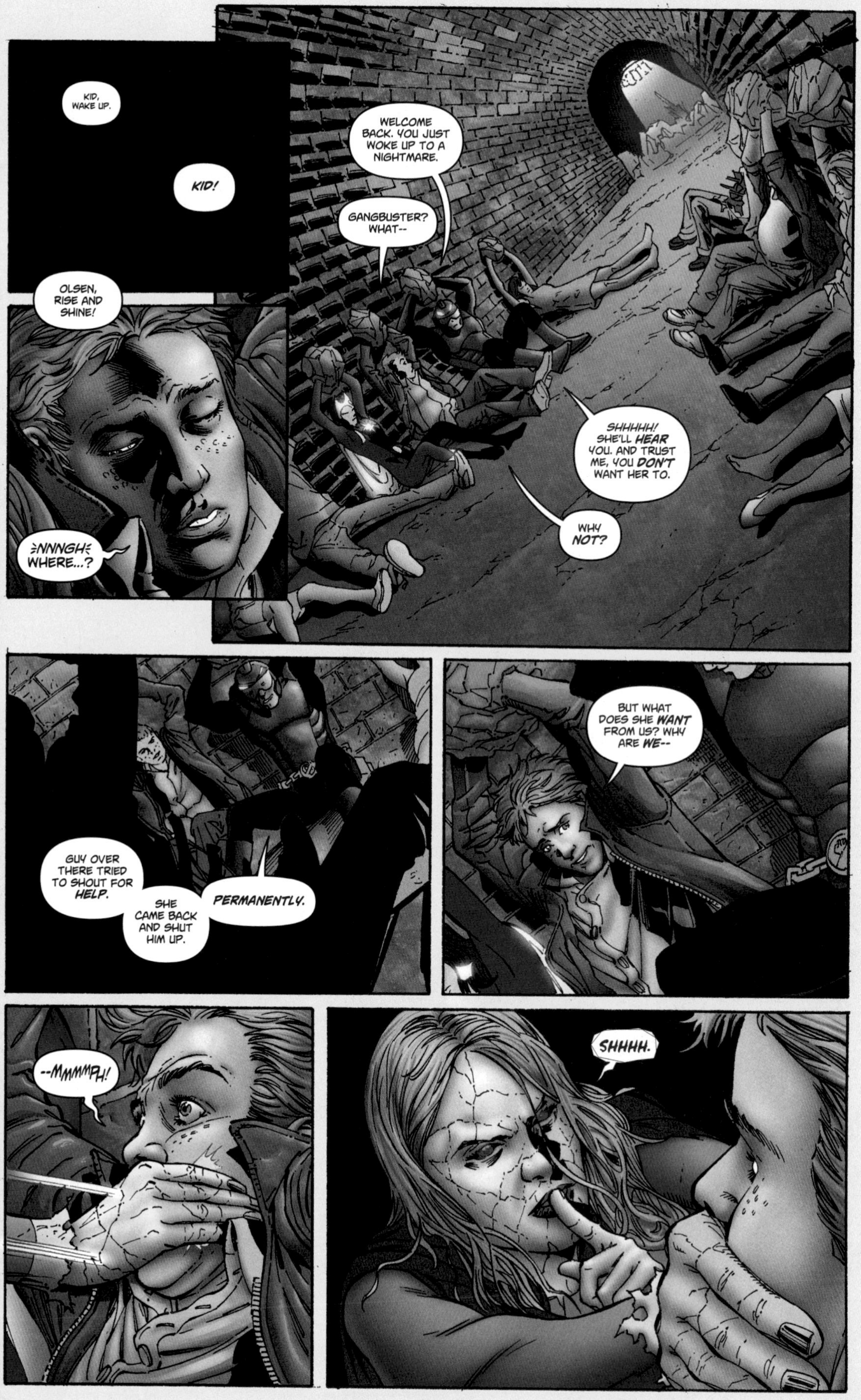
KID, WAKE UP.
KID!
OLSEN, RISE AND SHINE!
≥NNNGH≤ WHERE...?
GANGBUSTER? WHAT--
WELCOME BACK. YOU JUST WOKE UP TO A NIGHTMARE.
SHHHHH! SHE'LL HEAR YOU. AND TRUST ME, YOU DON'T WANT HER TO.
WHY NOT?
GUY OVER THERE TRIED TO SHOUT FOR HELP.
SHE CAME BACK AND SHUT HIM UP.
PERMANENTLY.
BUT WHAT DOES SHE WANT FROM US? WHY ARE WE--
--MMMMPH!
SHHHH.

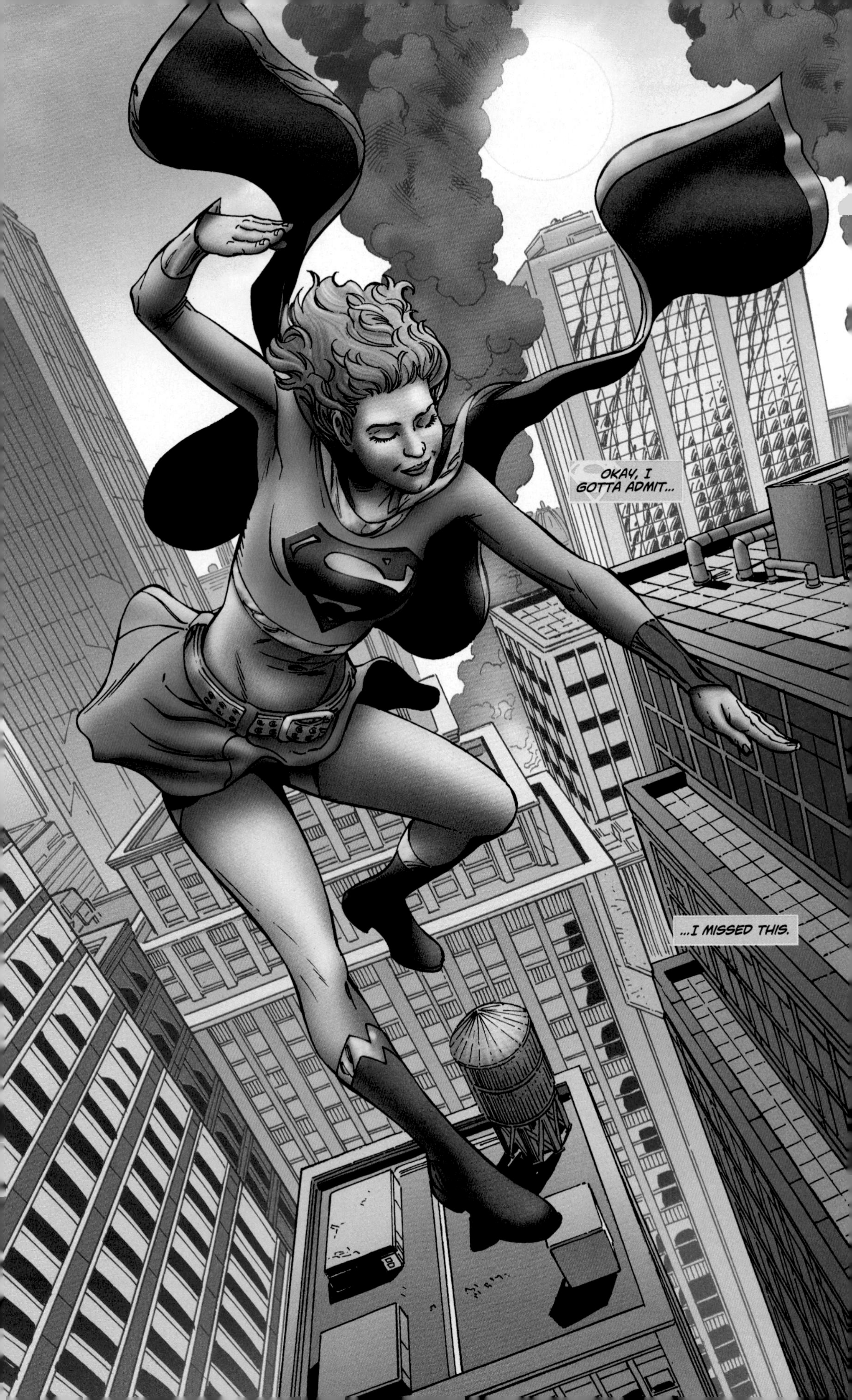
OKAY, I
GOTTA ADMIT...
...I MISSED THIS.

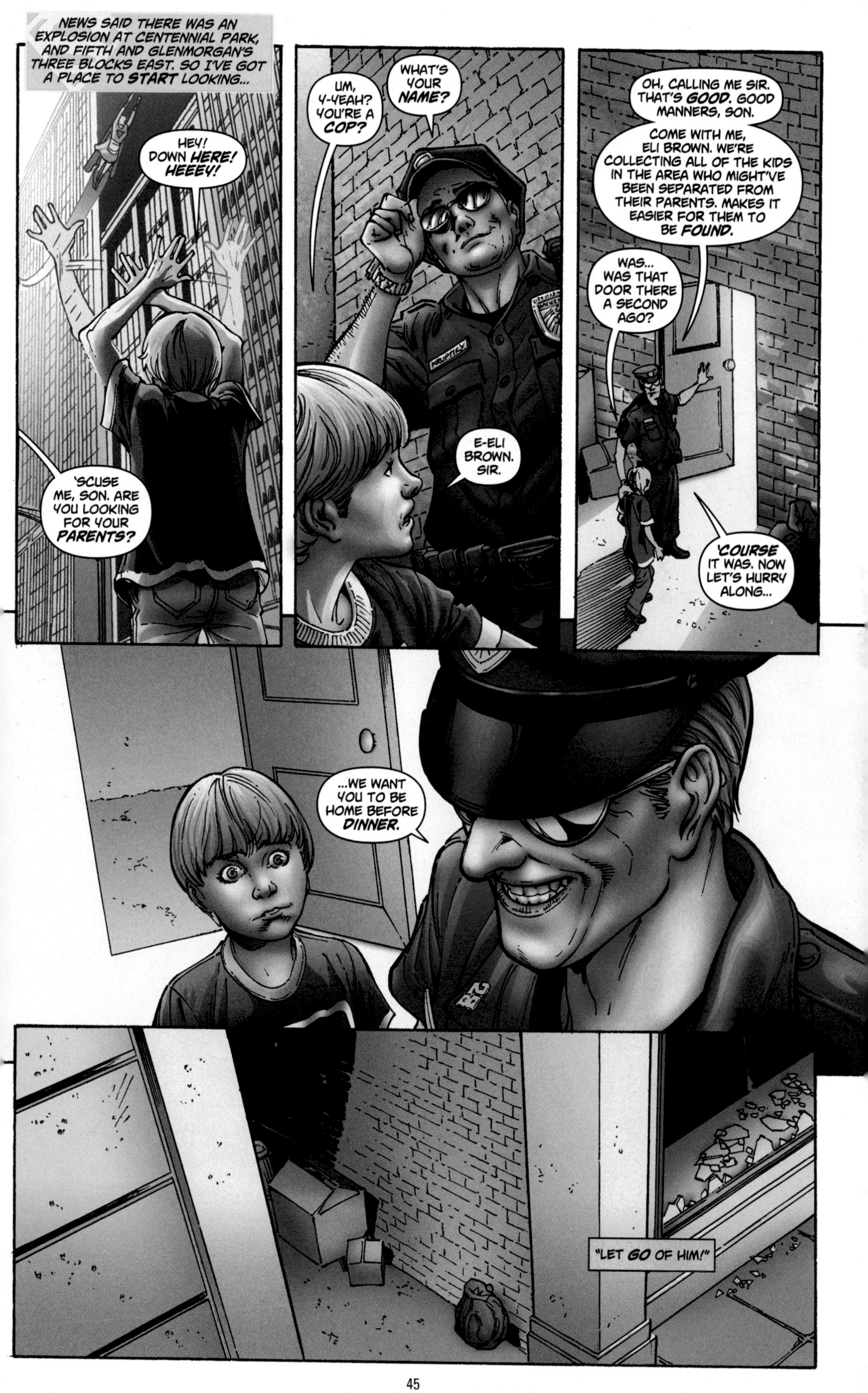
NEWS SAID THERE WAS AN EXPLOSION AT CENTENNIAL PARK, AND FIFTH AND GLENMORGAN'S THREE BLOCKS EAST. SO I'VE GOT A PLACE TO START LOOKING...
HEY! DOWN HERE! HEEEY!
'SCUSE ME, SON. ARE YOU LOOKING FOR YOUR PARENTS?
UM, Y-YEAH? YOU'RE A COP?
WHAT'S YOUR NAME?
E-ELI BROWN. SIR.
OH, CALLING ME SIR. THAT'S GOOD. GOOD MANNERS, SON.
COME WITH ME, ELI BROWN. WE'RE COLLECTING ALL OF THE KIDS IN THE AREA WHO MIGHT'VE BEEN SEPARATED FROM THEIR PARENTS. MAKES IT EASIER FOR THEM TO BE FOUND.
WAS... WAS THAT DOOR THERE A SECOND AGO?
'COURSE IT WAS. NOW LET'S HURRY ALONG...
...WE WANT YOU TO BE HOME BEFORE DINNER.
"LET GO OF HIM!"

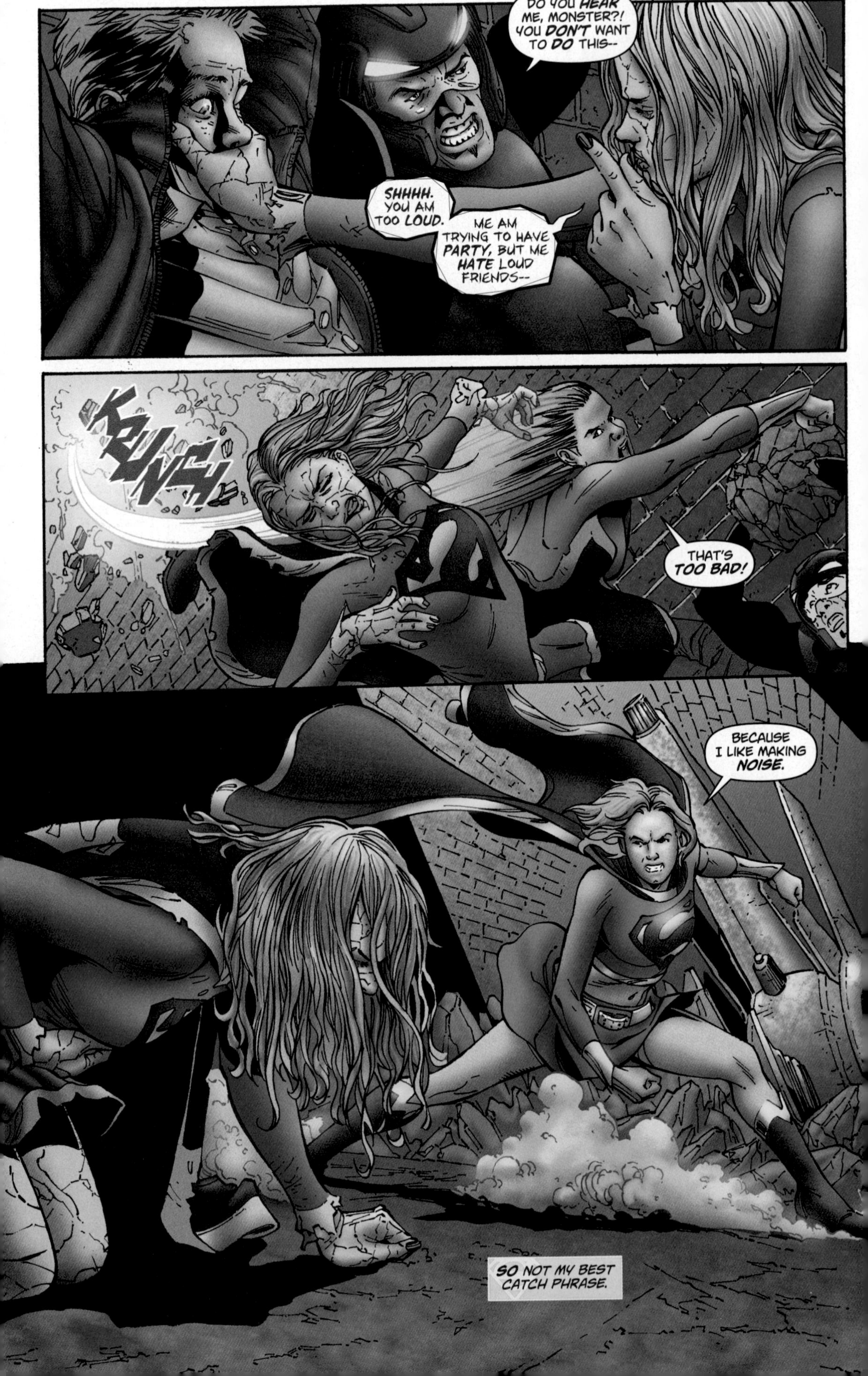
DO YOU HEAR ME, MONSTER?! YOU DON'T WANT TO DO THIS--
SHHHH. YOU AM TOO LOUD.
ME AM TRYING TO HAVE PARTY, BUT ME HATE LOUD FRIENDS--
KRUNCH
THAT'S TOO BAD!
BECAUSE I LIKE MAKING NOISE.
SO NOT MY BEST CATCH PHRASE.

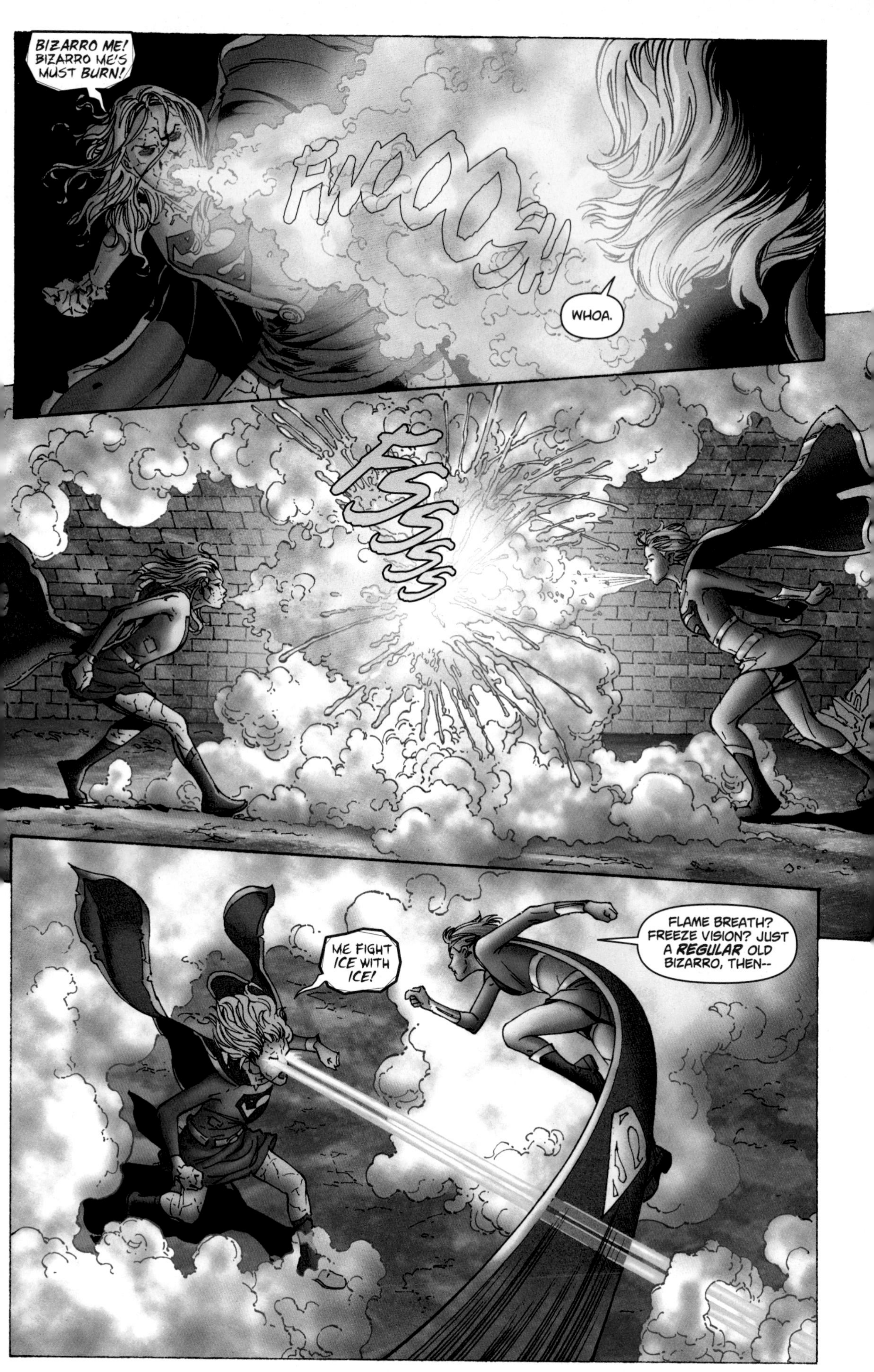
BIZARRO ME! BIZARRO ME'S MUST BURN!
FWOOOOSH!
WHOA.
FSSSSS
FLAME BREATH? FREEZE VISION? JUST A **REGULAR** OLD BIZARRO, THEN--
ME FIGHT **ICE** WITH **ICE!**

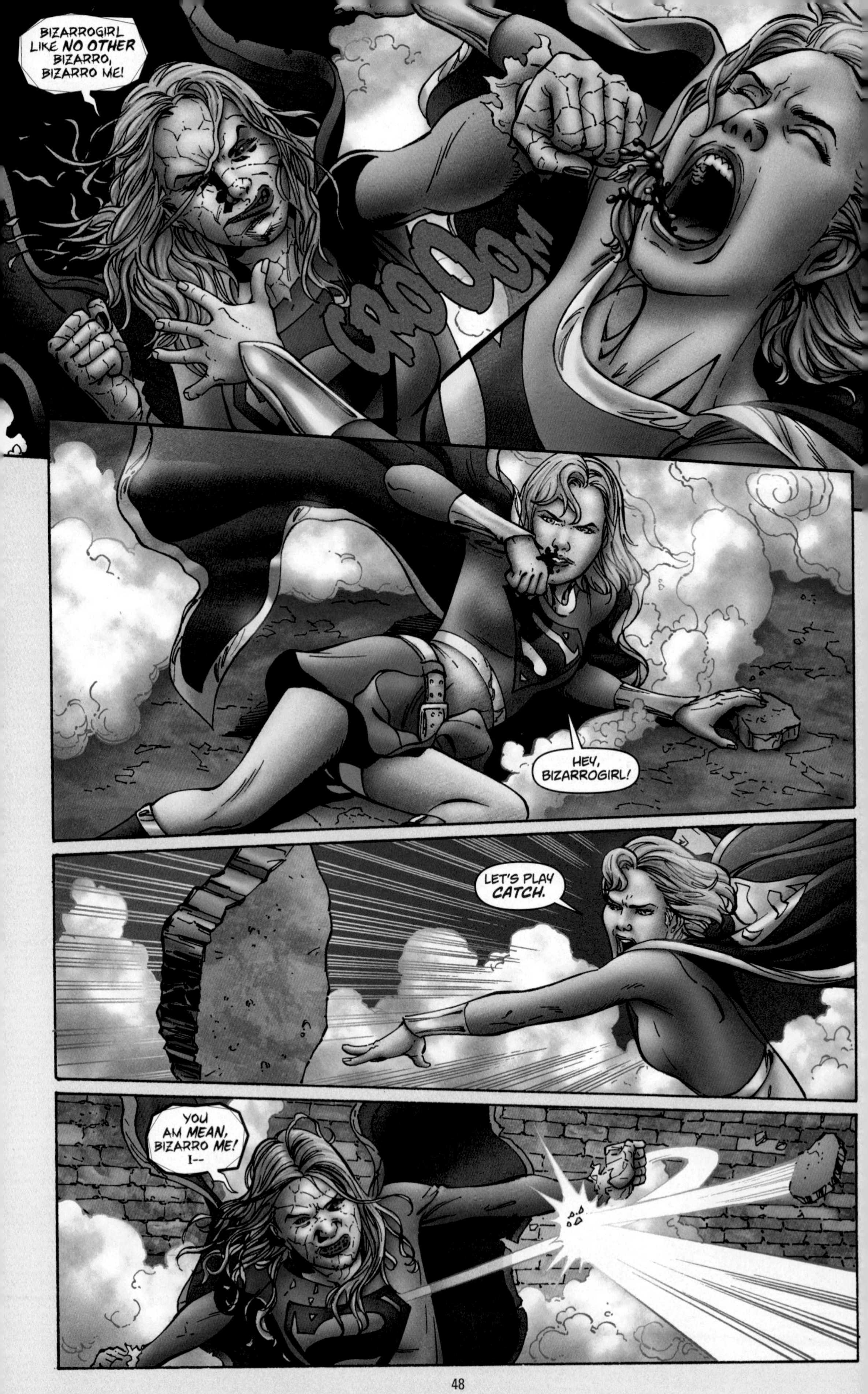
BIZARROGIRL LIKE NO OTHER BIZARRO, BIZARRO ME!
CROOOOM
HEY, BIZARROGIRL!
LET'S PLAY CATCH.
YOU AM MEAN, BIZARRO ME! I--

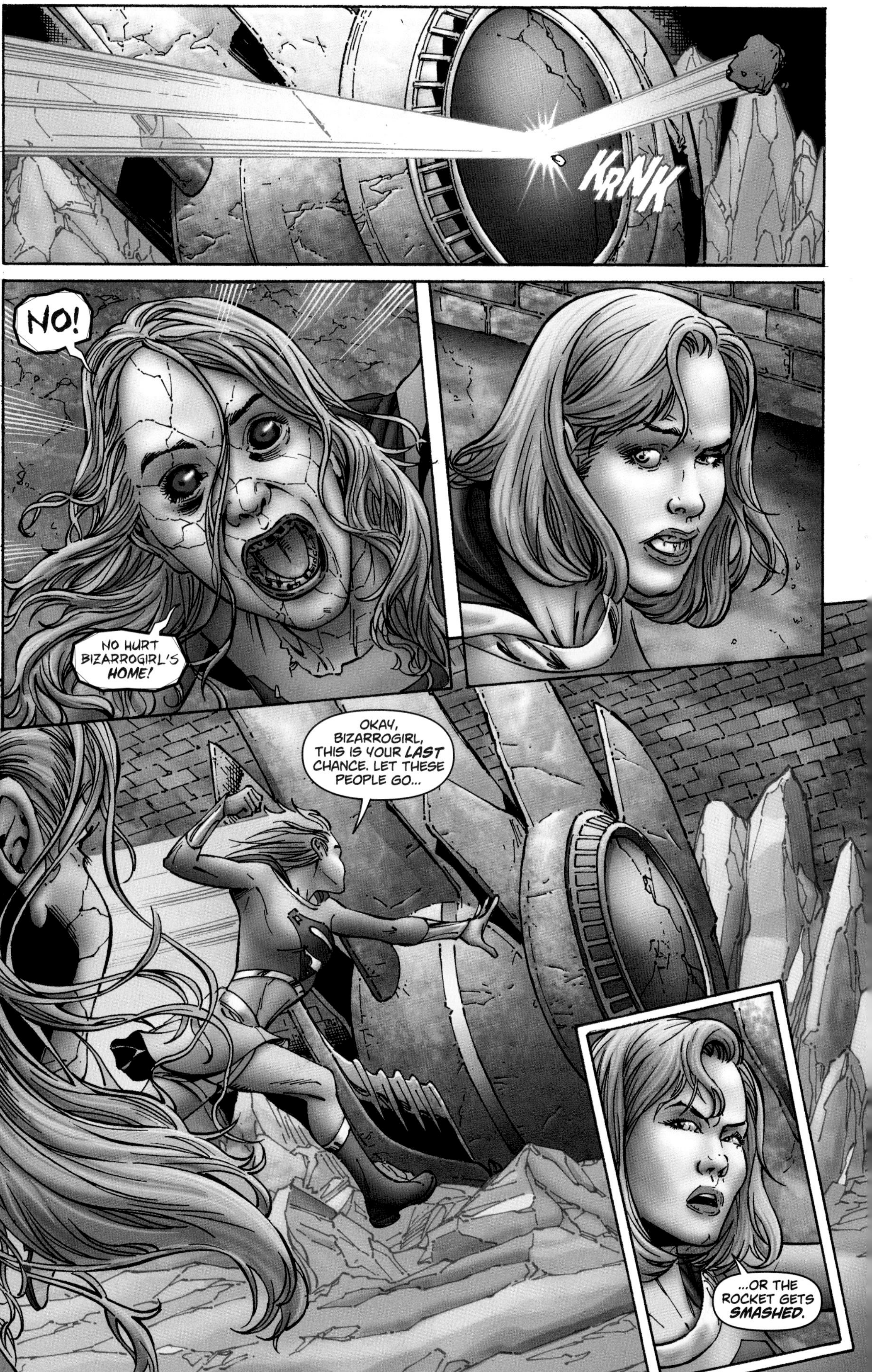
KRNK
NO!
NO HURT BIZARROGIRL'S HOME!
OKAY, BIZARROGIRL, THIS IS YOUR LAST CHANCE. LET THESE PEOPLE GO...
...OR THE ROCKET GETS SMASHED.

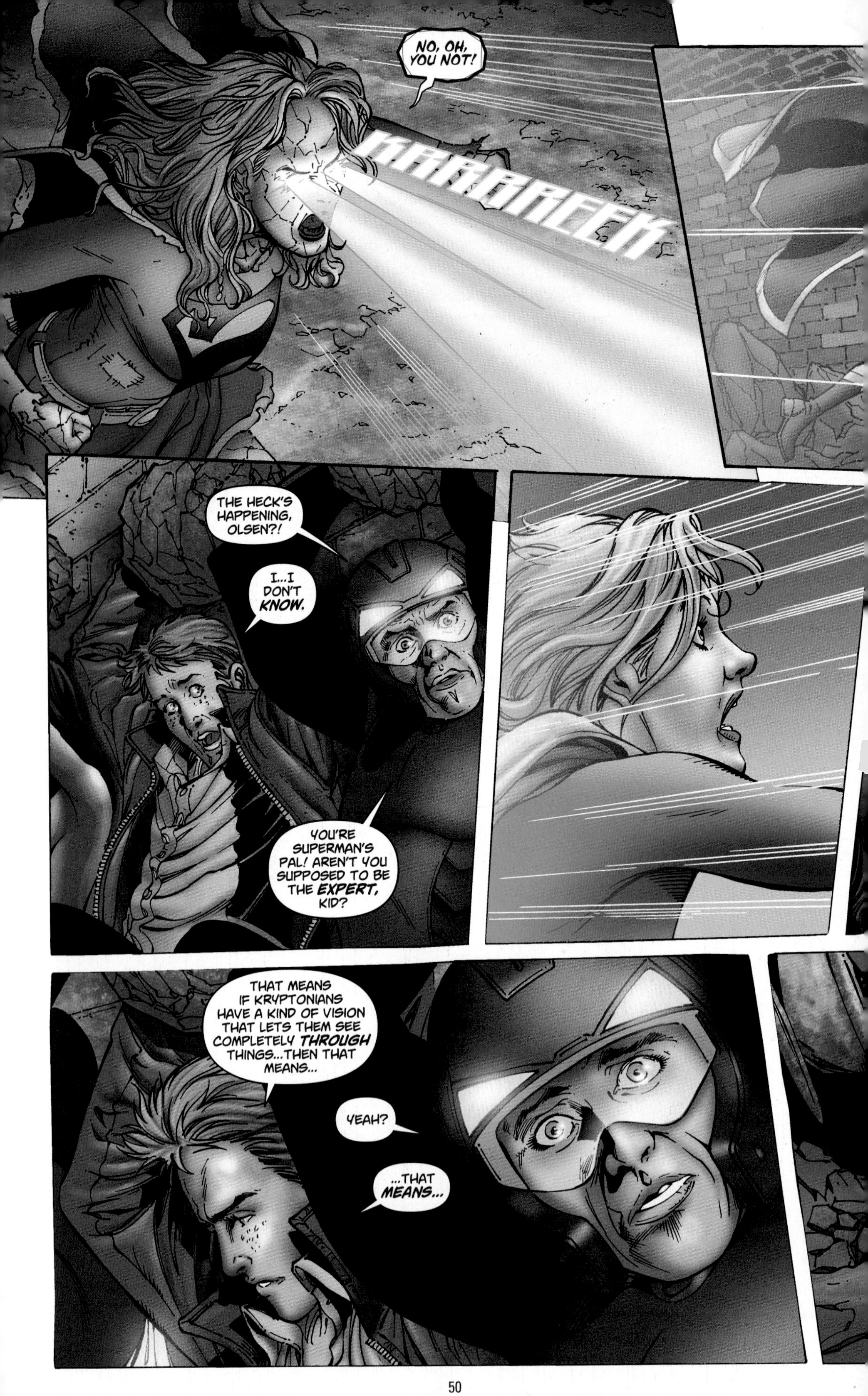
NO, OH, YOU NOT!
KRRRRREEK
THE HECK'S HAPPENING, OLSEN?!
I...I DON'T KNOW.
YOU'RE SUPERMAN'S PAL! AREN'T YOU SUPPOSED TO BE THE EXPERT, KID?
THAT MEANS IF KRYPTONIANS HAVE A KIND OF VISION THAT LETS THEM SEE COMPLETELY THROUGH THINGS...THEN THAT MEANS...
YEAH?
...THAT MEANS...

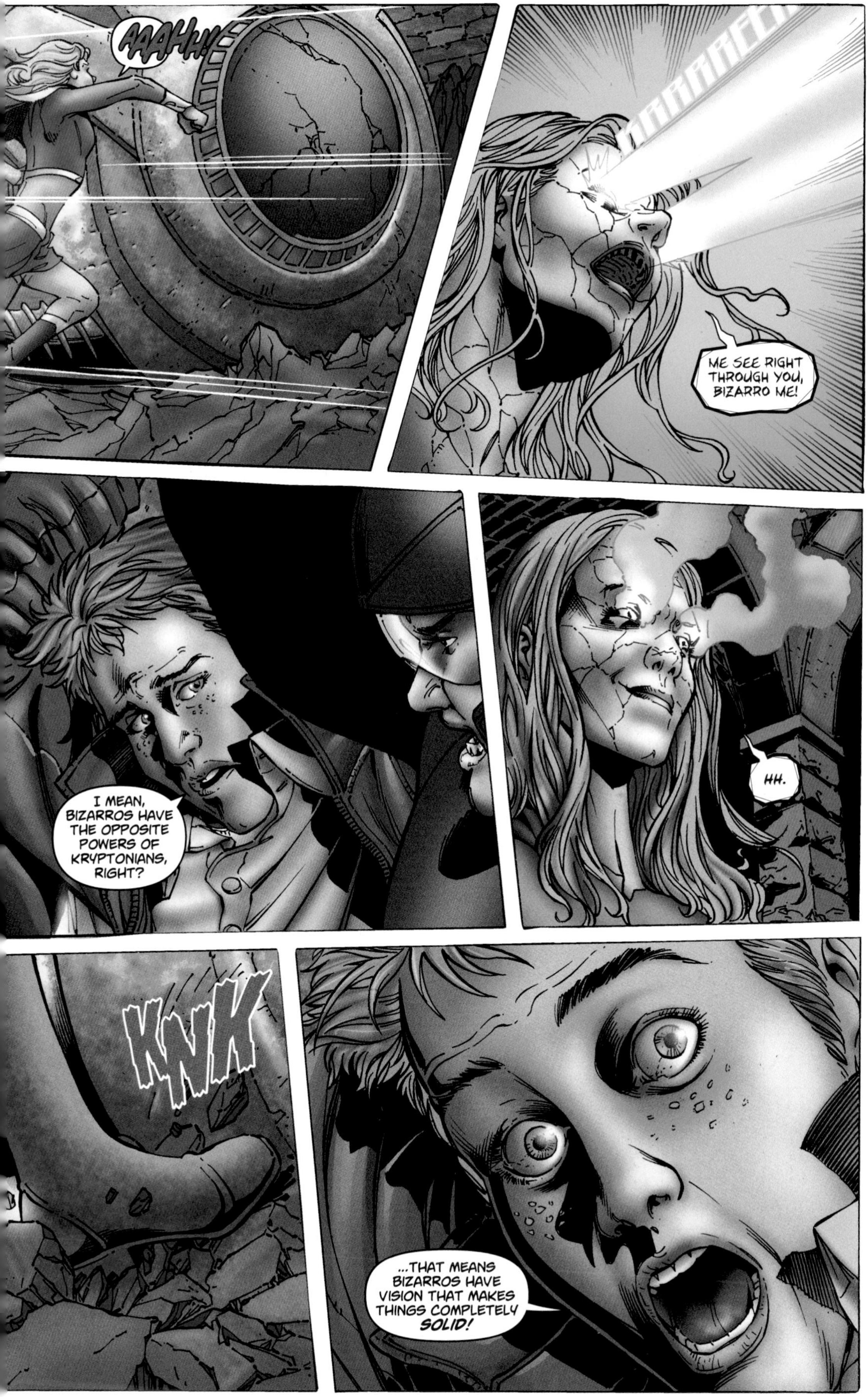
AAAHH!
RRRRRRREEE
ME SEE RIGHT THROUGH YOU, BIZARRO ME!
I MEAN, BIZARROS HAVE THE OPPOSITE POWERS OF KRYPTONIANS, RIGHT?
HH.
KNK
...THAT MEANS BIZARROS HAVE VISION THAT MAKES THINGS COMPLETELY SOLID!

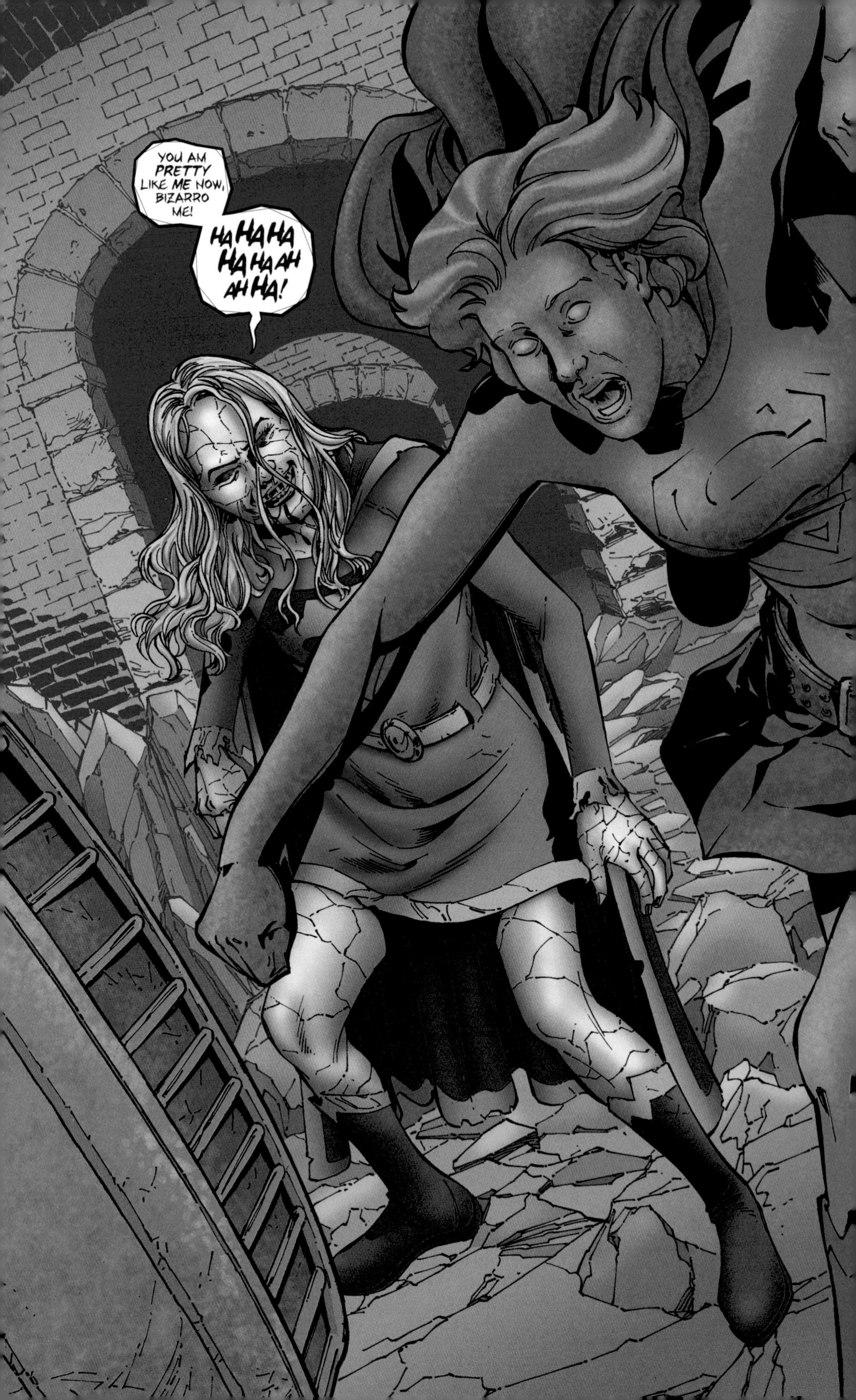
YOU AM PRETTY LIKE ME NOW, BIZARRO ME!
HA HA HA HA HA AH AH HA!

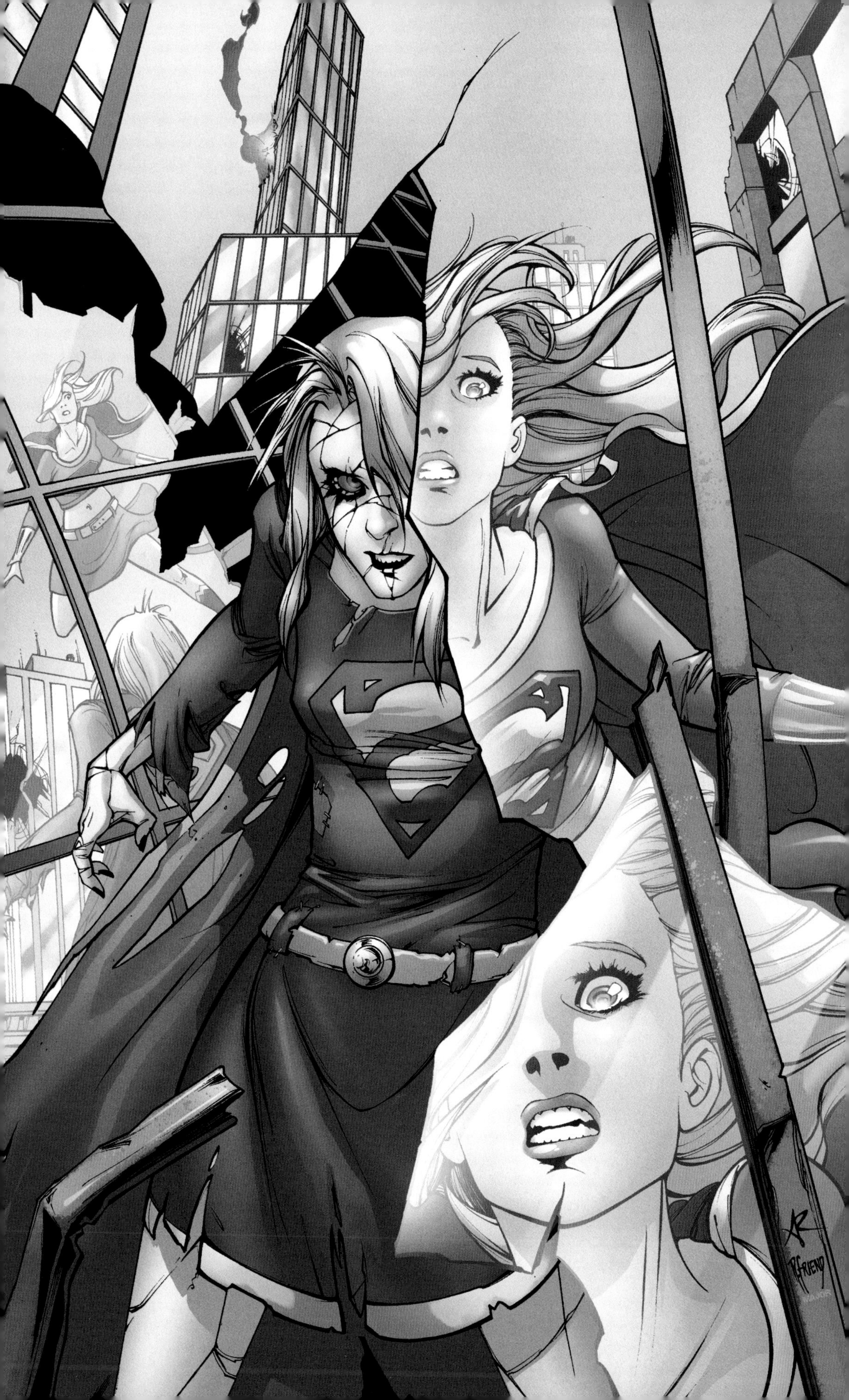

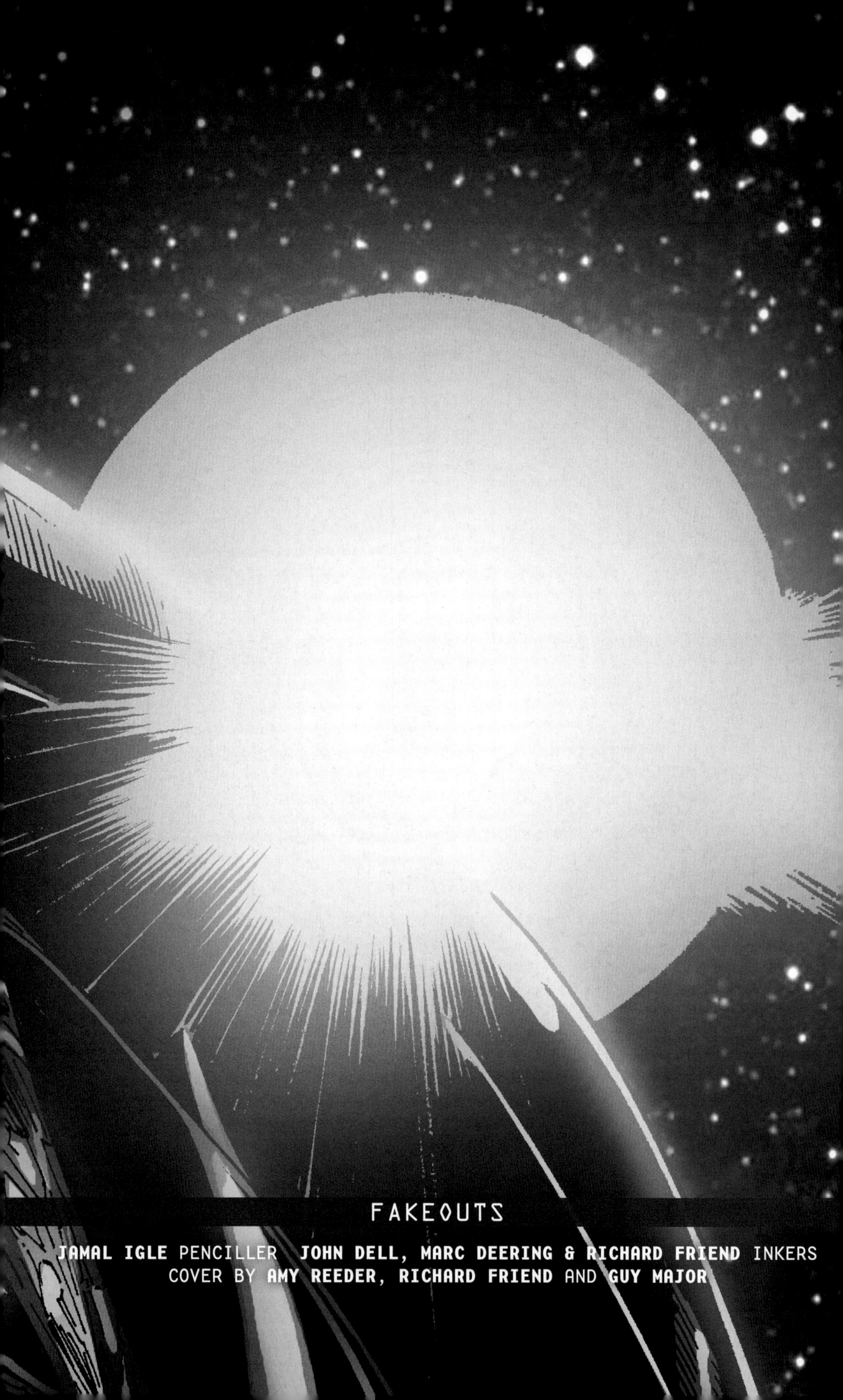

FAKEOUTS

JAMAL IGLE PENCILLER **JOHN DELL, MARC DEERING & RICHARD FRIEND** INKERS
COVER BY **AMY REEDER, RICHARD FRIEND** AND **GUY MAJOR**

BIZARRO WORLD.

THE ANTI-ARCTIC.

SIX WEEKS AGO.

"BIZARRRROOOO! ME NEED YOU!"

RUMMBLLLLLL

HALL OF SCIENCE

HALL OF VILINS

INTERGALTIC GOO

BIZARRO #1! METROPLIS AM GONE NOW! UN-CENTRAL CITY AM MORE WRECKED, TOO! DESTRUCTION EVEN COME HERE, TO FORTRESS OF TOGETHERNESS!

ME AM SAD TO BE HERE AND NOT THERE! ME WANT TO DRAW PICTURES OF DESTROYED CITIES!

YOU AM GREATEST HERO OF BIZARRO WORLD, BIZARRO #1, AND NOW AM TIME TO SHINE! WHERE ARE YOU?!

BIZARRO #1...WHAT... ...WHAT AM YOU DOING?

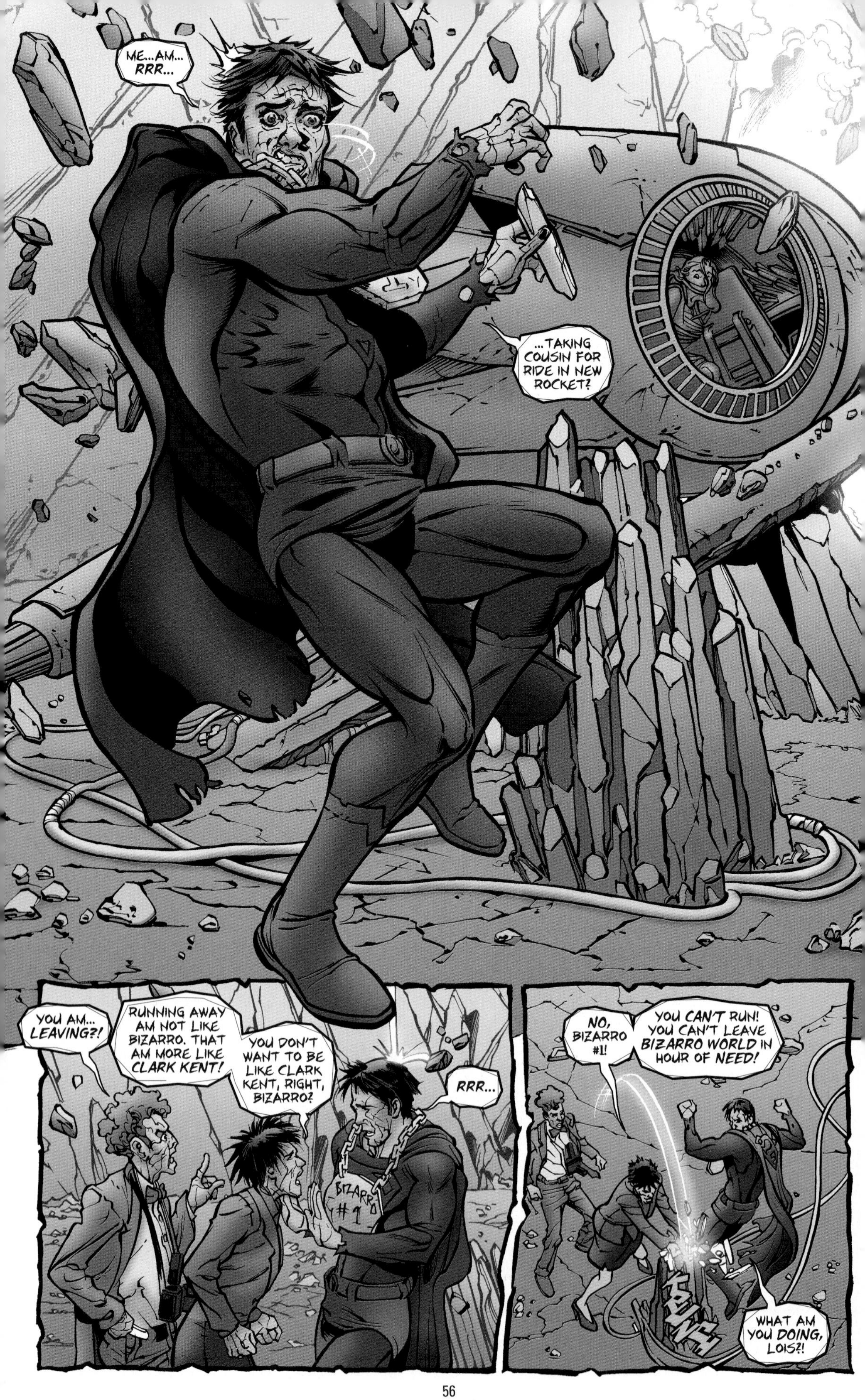
ME...AM... RRR...
...TAKING COUSIN FOR RIDE IN NEW ROCKET?
YOU AM... LEAVING?!
RUNNING AWAY AM NOT LIKE BIZARRO. THAT AM MORE LIKE CLARK KENT!
YOU DON'T WANT TO BE LIKE CLARK KENT, RIGHT, BIZARRO?
RRR...
NO, BIZARRO #1!
YOU CAN'T RUN! YOU CAN'T LEAVE BIZARRO WORLD IN HOUR OF NEED!
WHAT AM YOU DOING, LOIS?!

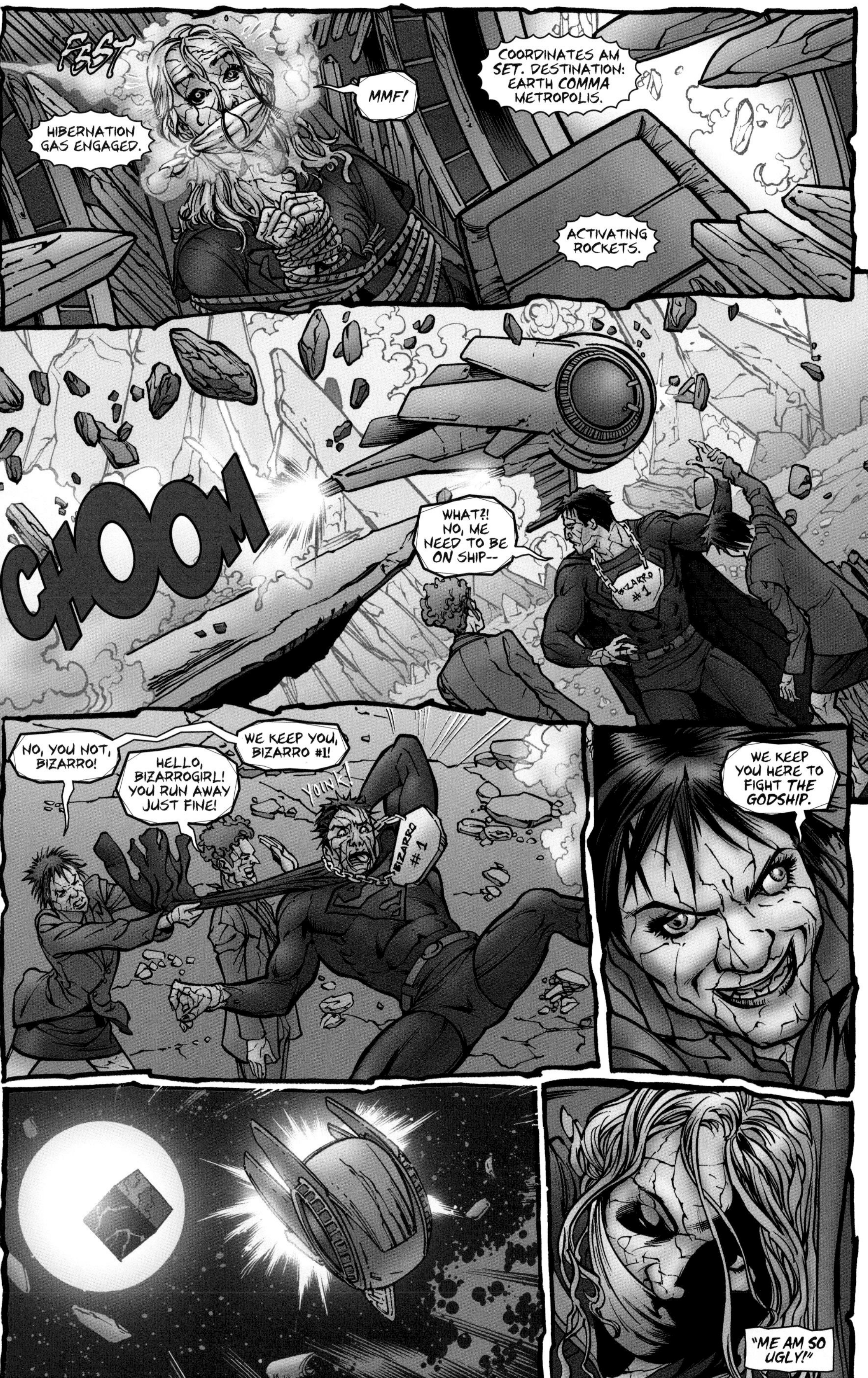
FSST
HIBERNATION GAS ENGAGED.
MMF!
COORDINATES AM SET. DESTINATION: EARTH COMMA METROPOLIS.
ACTIVATING ROCKETS.
CHOOM
WHAT?! NO, ME NEED TO BE ON SHIP--
BIZARRO #1
NO, YOU NOT, BIZARRO!
HELLO, BIZARROGIRL! YOU RUN AWAY JUST FINE!
WE KEEP YOU, BIZARRO #1!
YOINK!
BIZARRO #1
WE KEEP YOU HERE TO FIGHT THE GODSHIP.
"ME AM SO UGLY!"

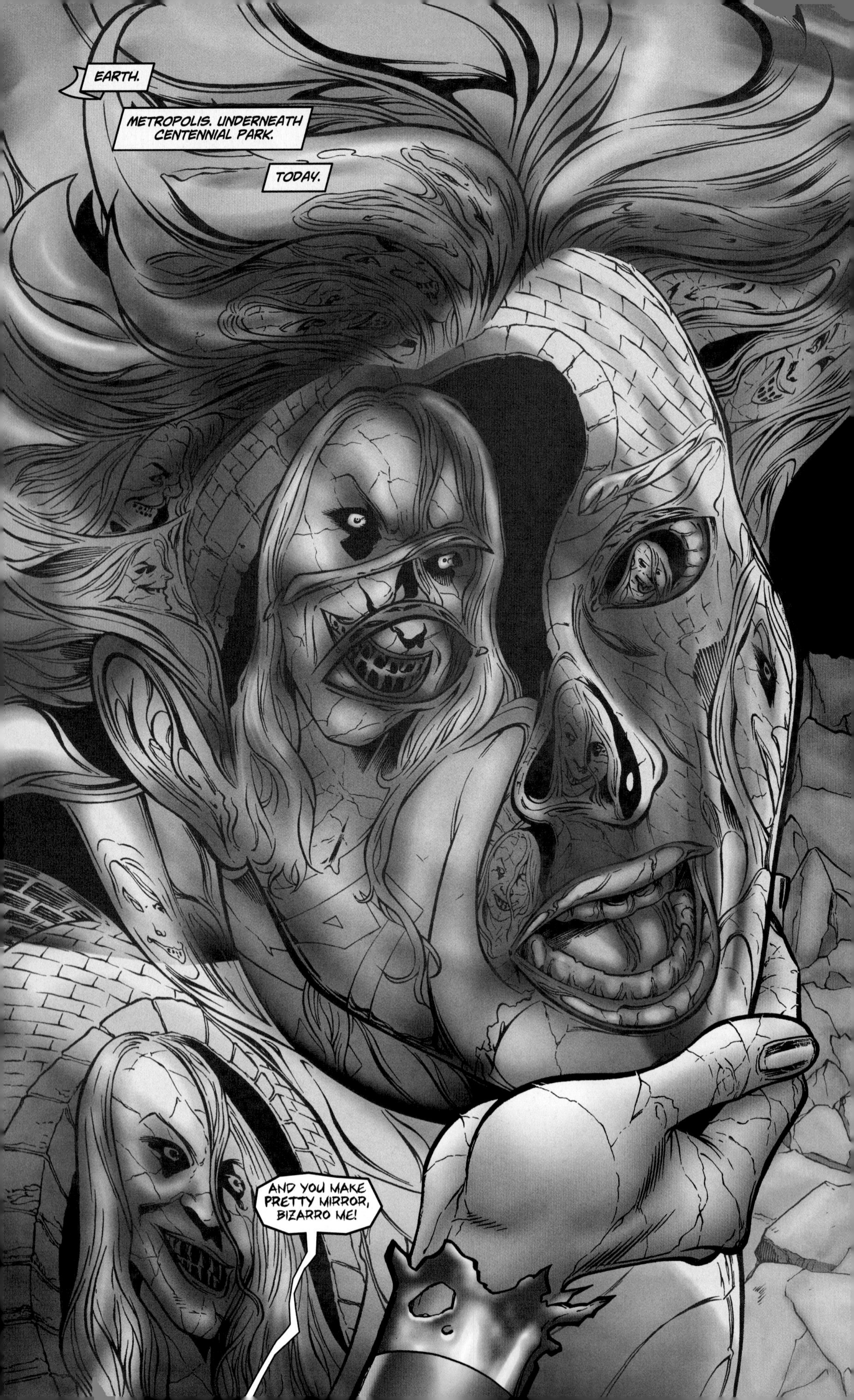
EARTH.
METROPOLIS. UNDERNEATH CENTENNIAL PARK.
TODAY.
AND YOU MAKE PRETTY MIRROR, BIZARRO ME!

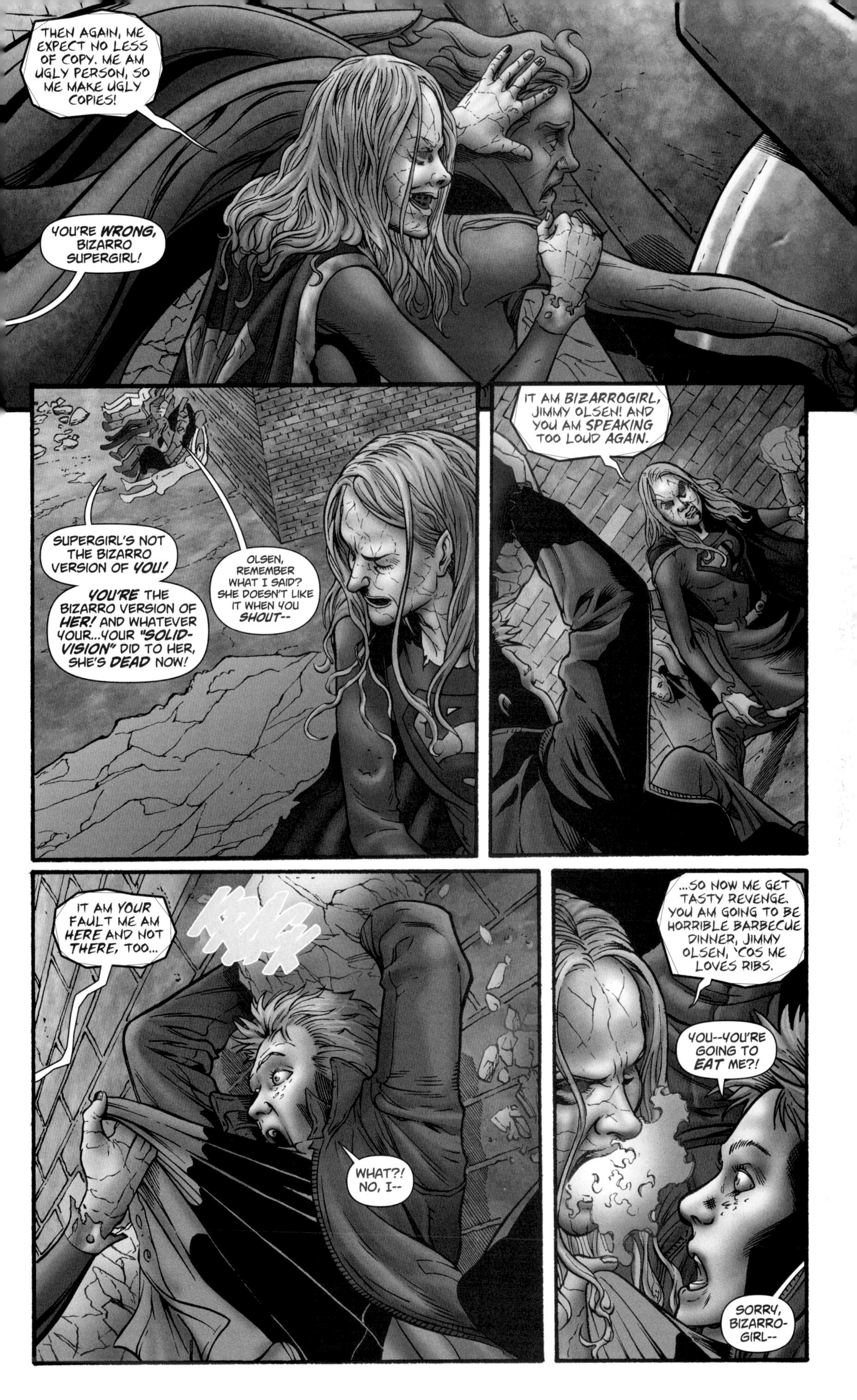
THEN AGAIN, ME EXPECT NO LESS OF COPY. ME AM UGLY PERSON, SO ME MAKE UGLY COPIES!
YOU'RE WRONG, BIZARRO SUPERGIRL!
SUPERGIRL'S NOT THE BIZARRO VERSION OF YOU!
YOU'RE THE BIZARRO VERSION OF HER! AND WHATEVER YOUR...YOUR "SOLID-VISION" DID TO HER, SHE'S DEAD NOW!
OLSEN, REMEMBER WHAT I SAID? SHE DOESN'T LIKE IT WHEN YOU SHOUT--
IT AM BIZARROGIRL, JIMMY OLSEN! AND YOU AM SPEAKING TOO LOUD AGAIN.
IT AM YOUR FAULT ME AM HERE AND NOT THERE, TOO...
KRAK
WHAT?! NO, I--
...SO NOW ME GET TASTY REVENGE. YOU AM GOING TO BE HORRIBLE BARBECUE DINNER, JIMMY OLSEN, 'COS ME LOVES RIBS.
YOU--YOU'RE GOING TO EAT ME?!
SORRY, BIZARRO-GIRL--

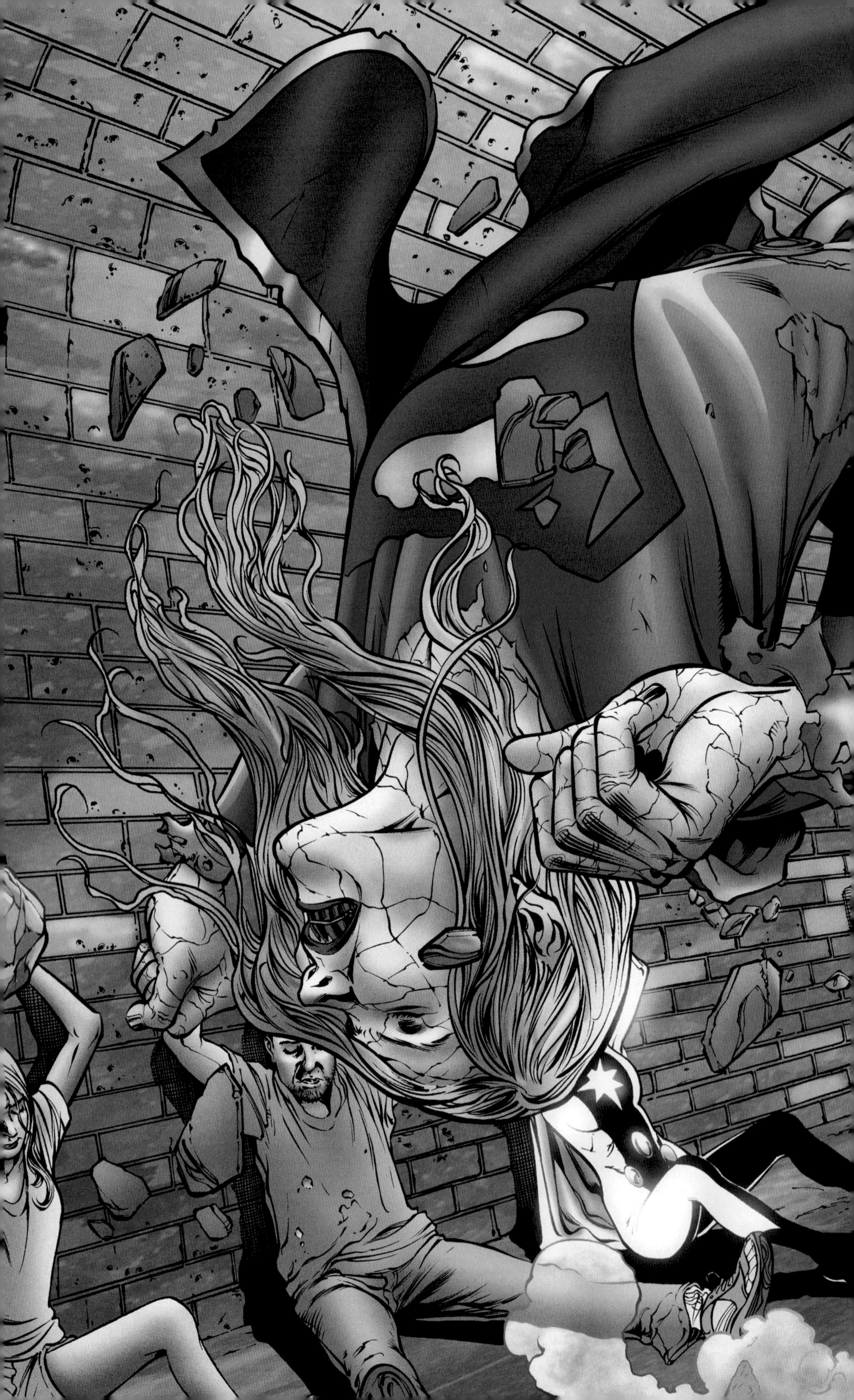

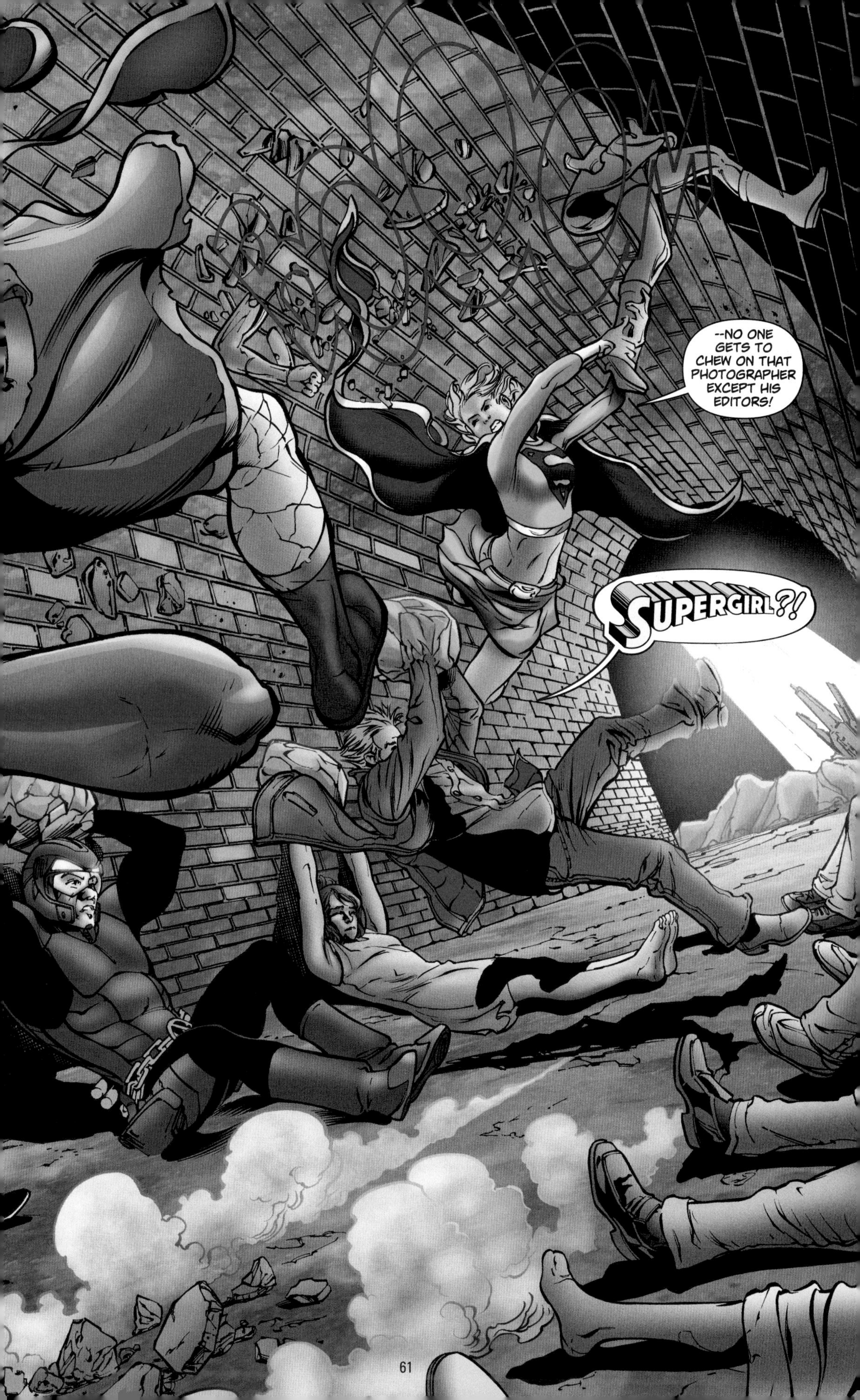
--NO ONE GETS TO CHEW ON THAT PHOTOGRAPHER EXCEPT HIS EDITORS!
SUPERGIRL?!

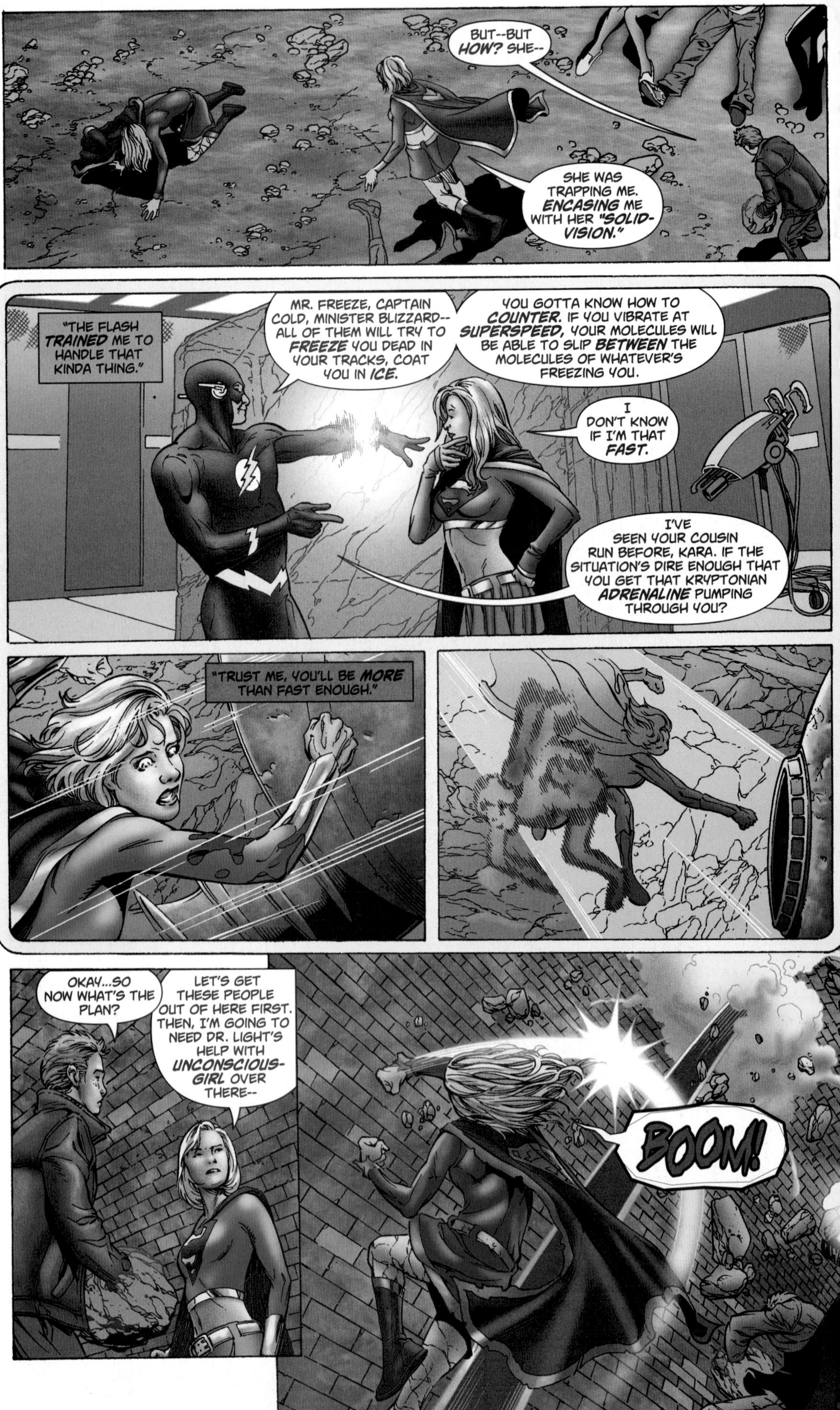

BUT--BUT HOW? SHE--
SHE WAS TRAPPING ME. ENCASING ME WITH HER "SOLID-VISION."
"THE FLASH TRAINED ME TO HANDLE THAT KINDA THING."
MR. FREEZE, CAPTAIN COLD, MINISTER BLIZZARD--ALL OF THEM WILL TRY TO FREEZE YOU DEAD IN YOUR TRACKS, COAT YOU IN ICE.
YOU GOTTA KNOW HOW TO COUNTER. IF YOU VIBRATE AT SUPERSPEED, YOUR MOLECULES WILL BE ABLE TO SLIP BETWEEN THE MOLECULES OF WHATEVER'S FREEZING YOU.
I DON'T KNOW IF I'M THAT FAST.
I'VE SEEN YOUR COUSIN RUN BEFORE, KARA. IF THE SITUATION'S DIRE ENOUGH THAT YOU GET THAT KRYPTONIAN ADRENALINE PUMPING THROUGH YOU?
"TRUST ME, YOU'LL BE MORE THAN FAST ENOUGH."
OKAY...SO NOW WHAT'S THE PLAN?
LET'S GET THESE PEOPLE OUT OF HERE FIRST. THEN, I'M GOING TO NEED DR. LIGHT'S HELP WITH UNCONSCIOUS-GIRL OVER THERE--
BOOM!

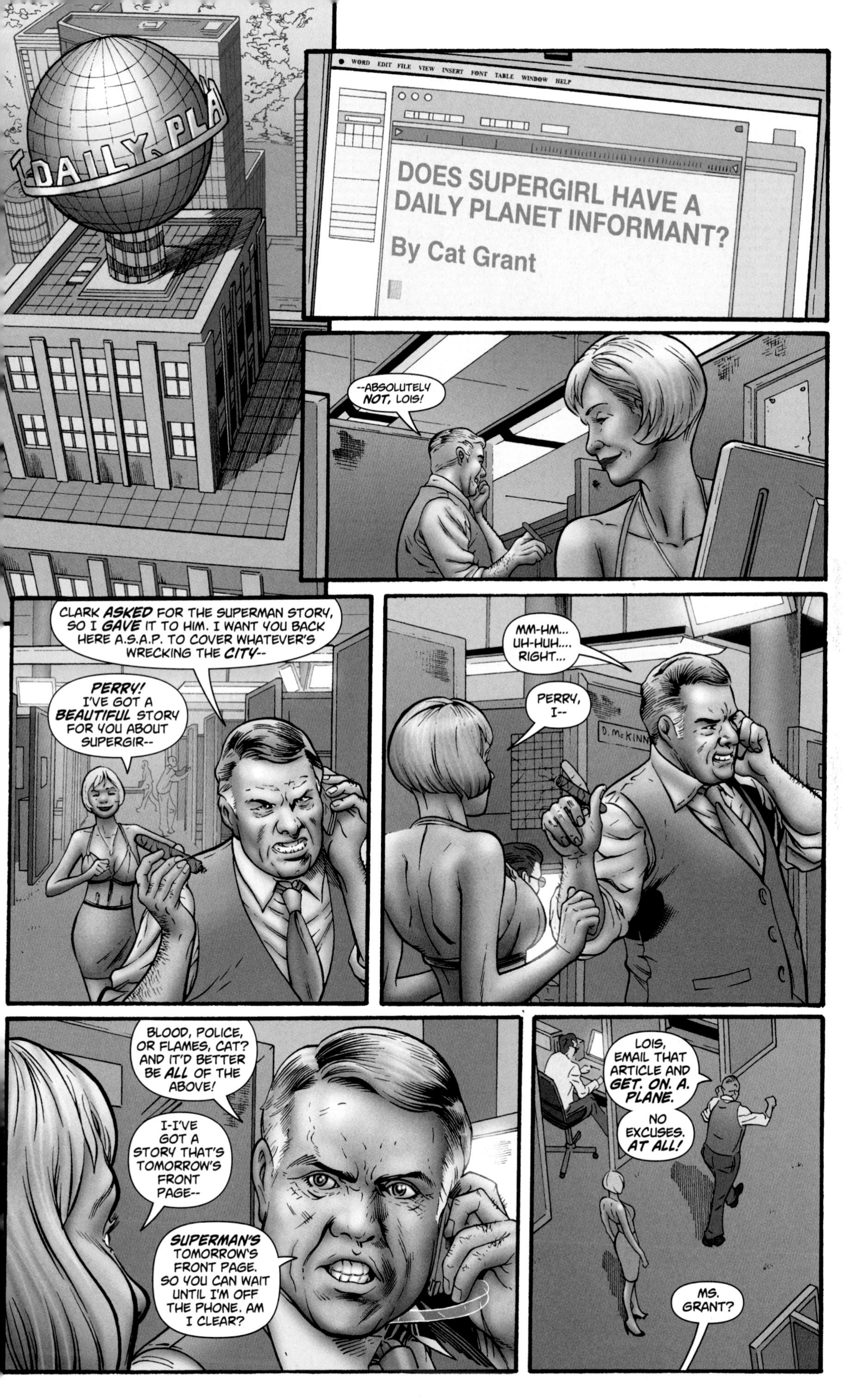
DAILY PLA
WORD EDIT FILE VIEW INSERT FONT TABLE WINDOW HELP
DOES SUPERGIRL HAVE A DAILY PLANET INFORMANT?
By Cat Grant
--ABSOLUTELY NOT, LOIS!
CLARK ASKED FOR THE SUPERMAN STORY, SO I GAVE IT TO HIM. I WANT YOU BACK HERE A.S.A.P. TO COVER WHATEVER'S WRECKING THE CITY--
PERRY! I'VE GOT A BEAUTIFUL STORY FOR YOU ABOUT SUPERGIR--
MM-HM... UH-HUH.... RIGHT...
PERRY, I--
D. McKINN
BLOOD, POLICE, OR FLAMES, CAT? AND IT'D BETTER BE ALL OF THE ABOVE!
I-I'VE GOT A STORY THAT'S TOMORROW'S FRONT PAGE--
SUPERMAN'S TOMORROW'S FRONT PAGE. SO YOU CAN WAIT UNTIL I'M OFF THE PHONE. AM I CLEAR?
LOIS, EMAIL THAT ARTICLE AND GET. ON. A. PLANE.
NO EXCUSES. AT ALL!
MS. GRANT?

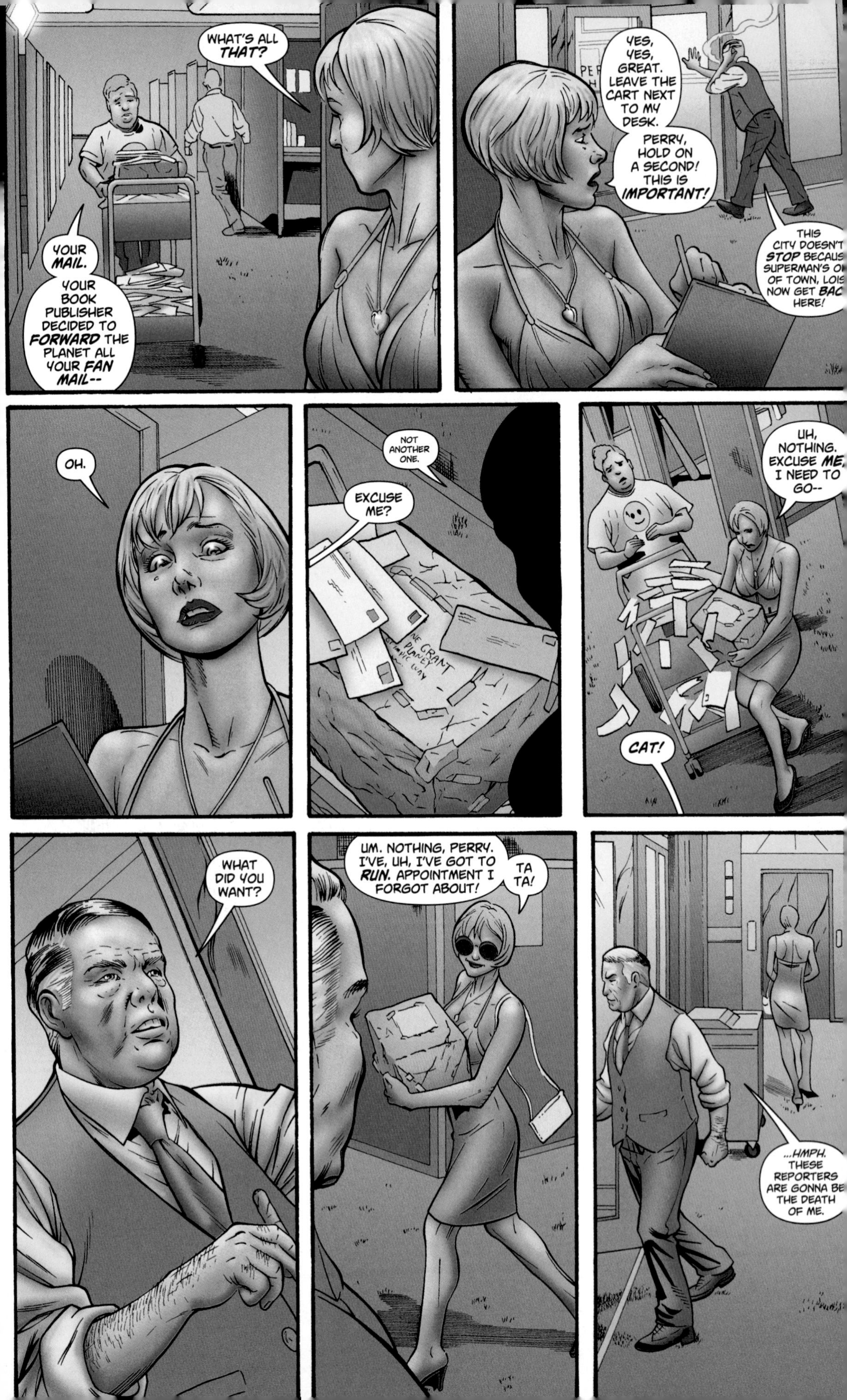
WHAT'S ALL THAT?
YOUR MAIL.
YOUR BOOK PUBLISHER DECIDED TO FORWARD THE PLANET ALL YOUR FAN MAIL--
YES, YES, GREAT. LEAVE THE CART NEXT TO MY DESK.
PERRY, HOLD ON A SECOND! THIS IS IMPORTANT!
THIS CITY DOESN'T STOP BECAUS SUPERMAN'S OU OF TOWN, LOIS NOW GET BAC HERE!
OH.
NOT ANOTHER ONE.
EXCUSE ME?
UH, NOTHING. EXCUSE ME. I NEED TO GO--
CAT!
WHAT DID YOU WANT?
UM. NOTHING, PERRY. I'VE, UH, I'VE GOT TO RUN. APPOINTMENT I FORGOT ABOUT!
TA TA!
...HMPH. THESE REPORTERS ARE GONNA BE THE DEATH OF ME.

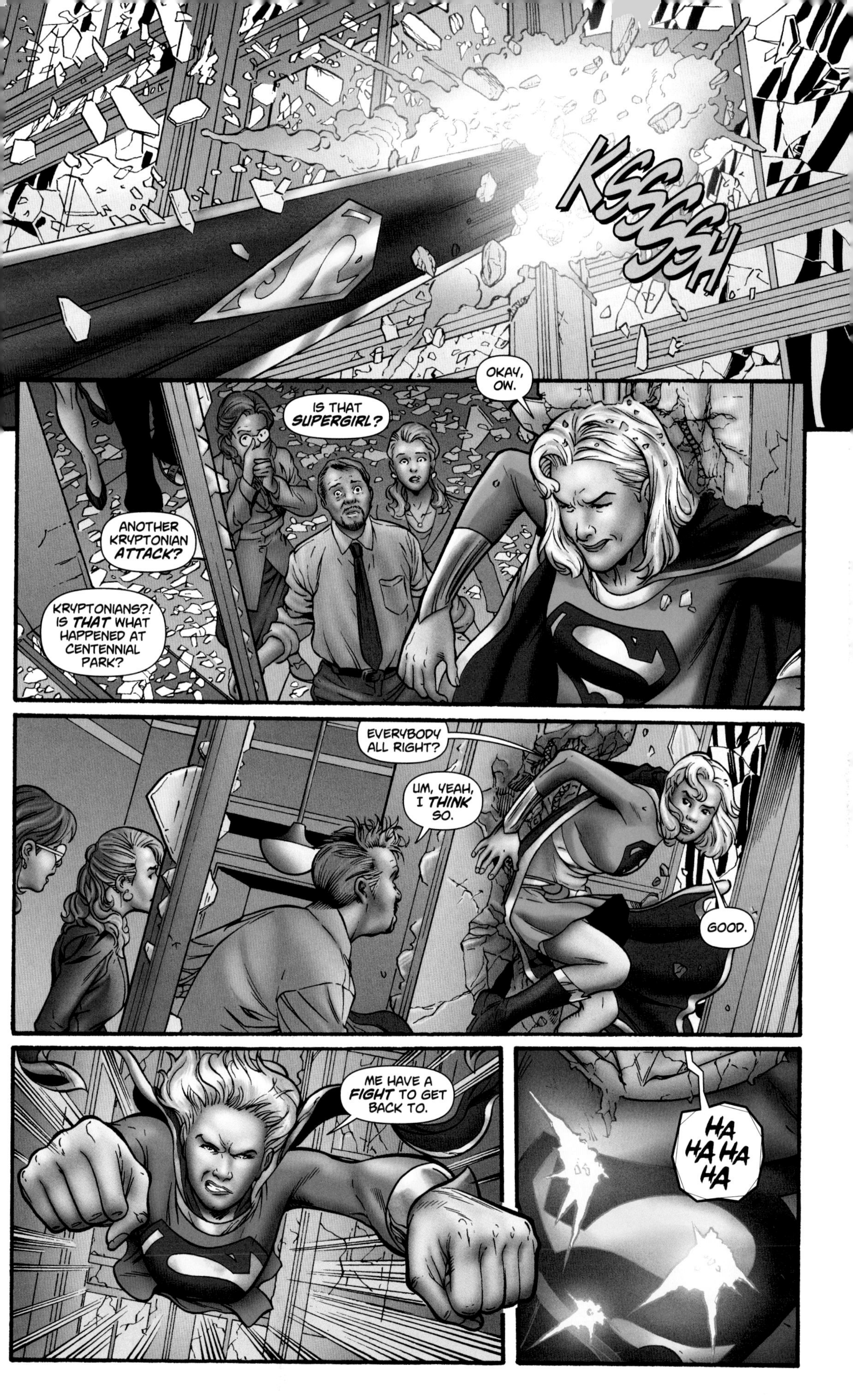
KSSSSH
OKAY, OW.
IS THAT SUPERGIRL?
ANOTHER KRYPTONIAN ATTACK?
KRYPTONIANS?! IS THAT WHAT HAPPENED AT CENTENNIAL PARK?
EVERYBODY ALL RIGHT?
UM, YEAH, I THINK SO.
GOOD.
ME HAVE A FIGHT TO GET BACK TO.
HA HA HA HA HA

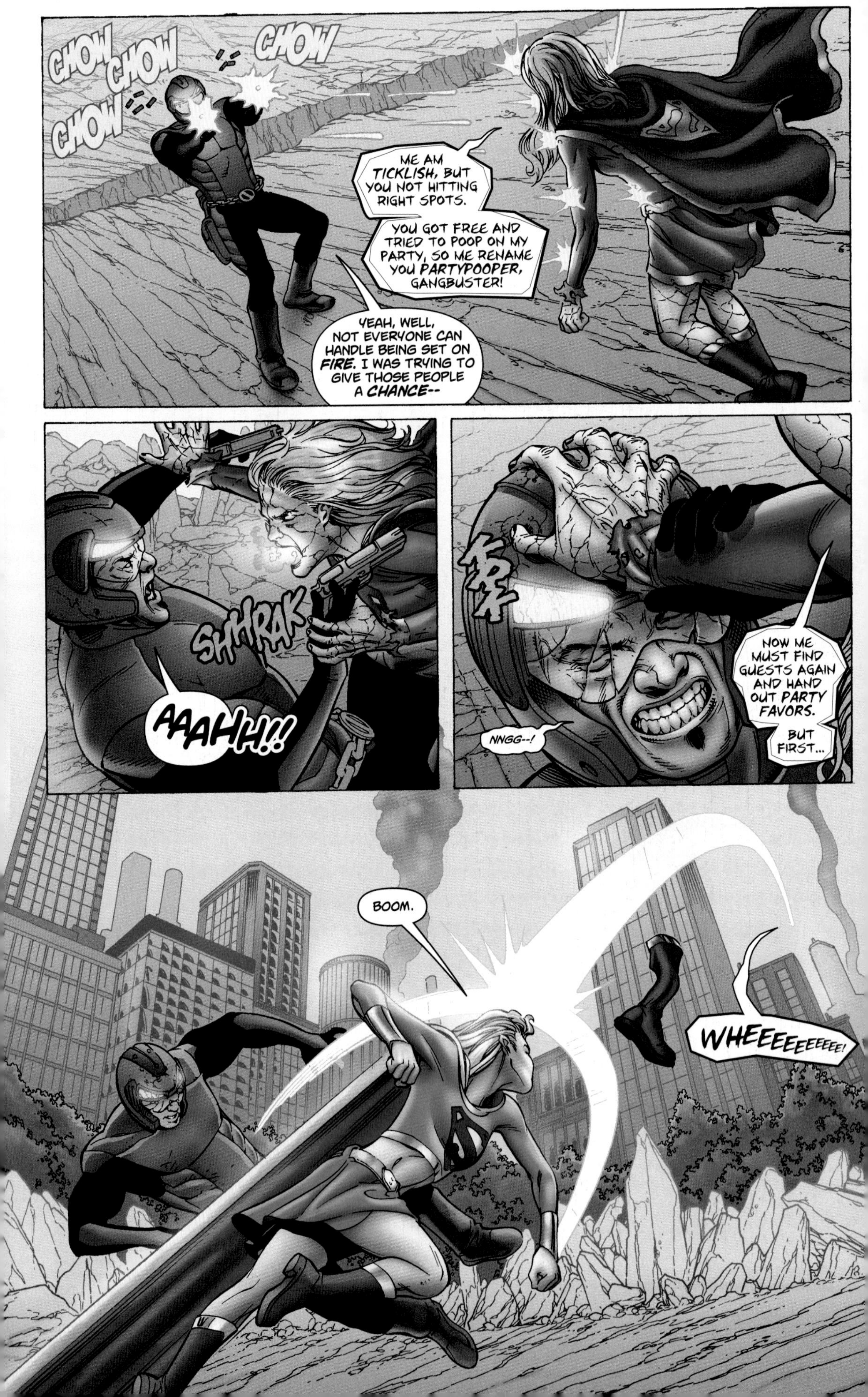
CHOW CHOW
CHOW
CHOW
ME AM TICKLISH, BUT YOU NOT HITTING RIGHT SPOTS.
YOU GOT FREE AND TRIED TO POOP ON MY PARTY, SO ME RENAME YOU PARTYPOOPER, GANGBUSTER!
YEAH, WELL, NOT EVERYONE CAN HANDLE BEING SET ON FIRE. I WAS TRYING TO GIVE THOSE PEOPLE A CHANCE--
SHHRAK
AAAHH!!
NOW ME MUST FIND GUESTS AGAIN AND HAND OUT PARTY FAVORS.
BUT FIRST...
NNGG--!
BOOM.
WHEEEEEEEEEE!

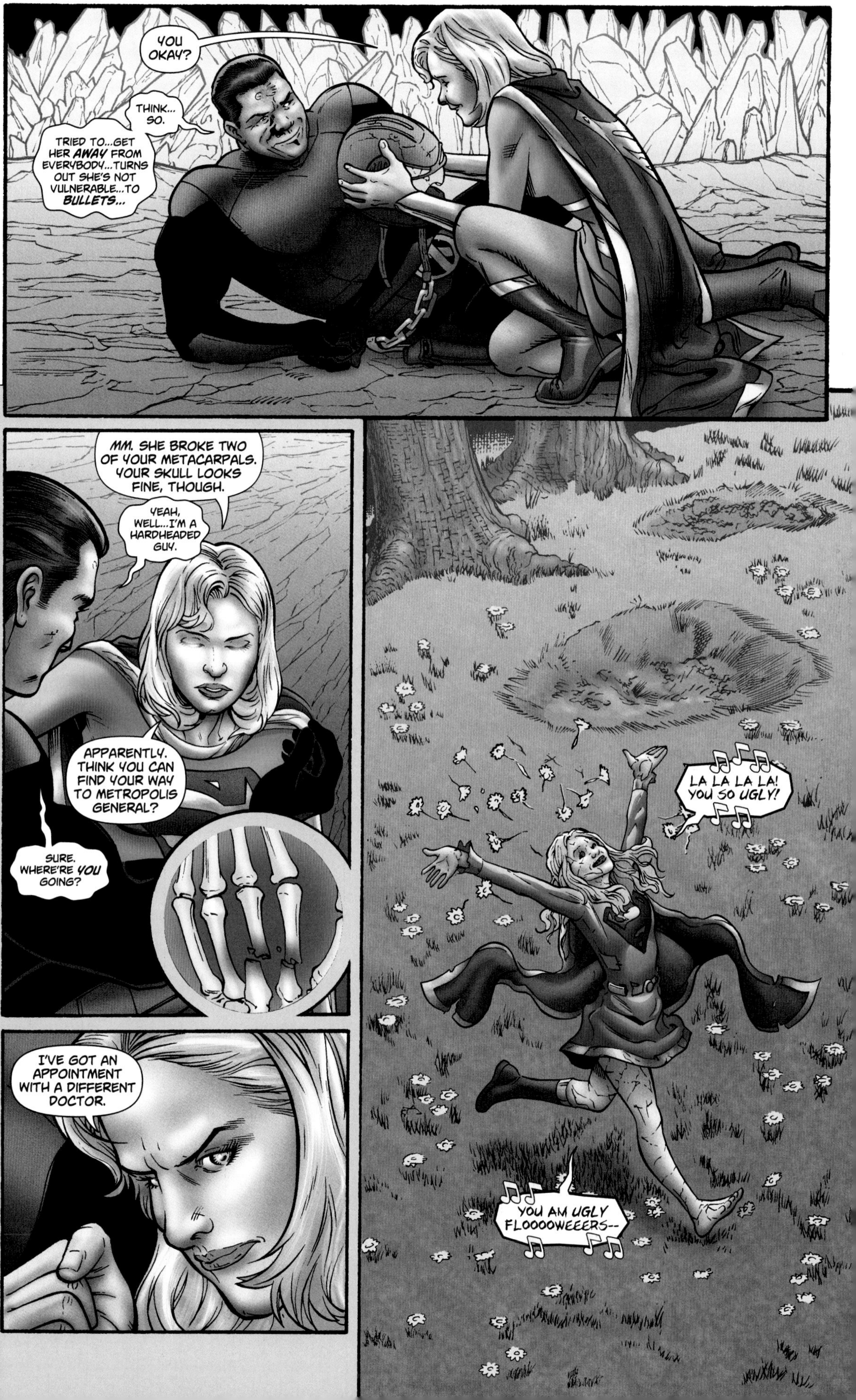

YOU OKAY?
THINK... SO.
TRIED TO...GET HER AWAY FROM EVERYBODY...TURNS OUT SHE'S NOT VULNERABLE...TO BULLETS...
MM. SHE BROKE TWO OF YOUR METACARPALS. YOUR SKULL LOOKS FINE, THOUGH.
YEAH, WELL...I'M A HARDHEADED GUY.
APPARENTLY. THINK YOU CAN FIND YOUR WAY TO METROPOLIS GENERAL?
SURE. WHERE'RE YOU GOING?
I'VE GOT AN APPOINTMENT WITH A DIFFERENT DOCTOR.
LA LA LA LA! YOU SO UGLY!
YOU AM UGLY FLOOOOWEEERS--

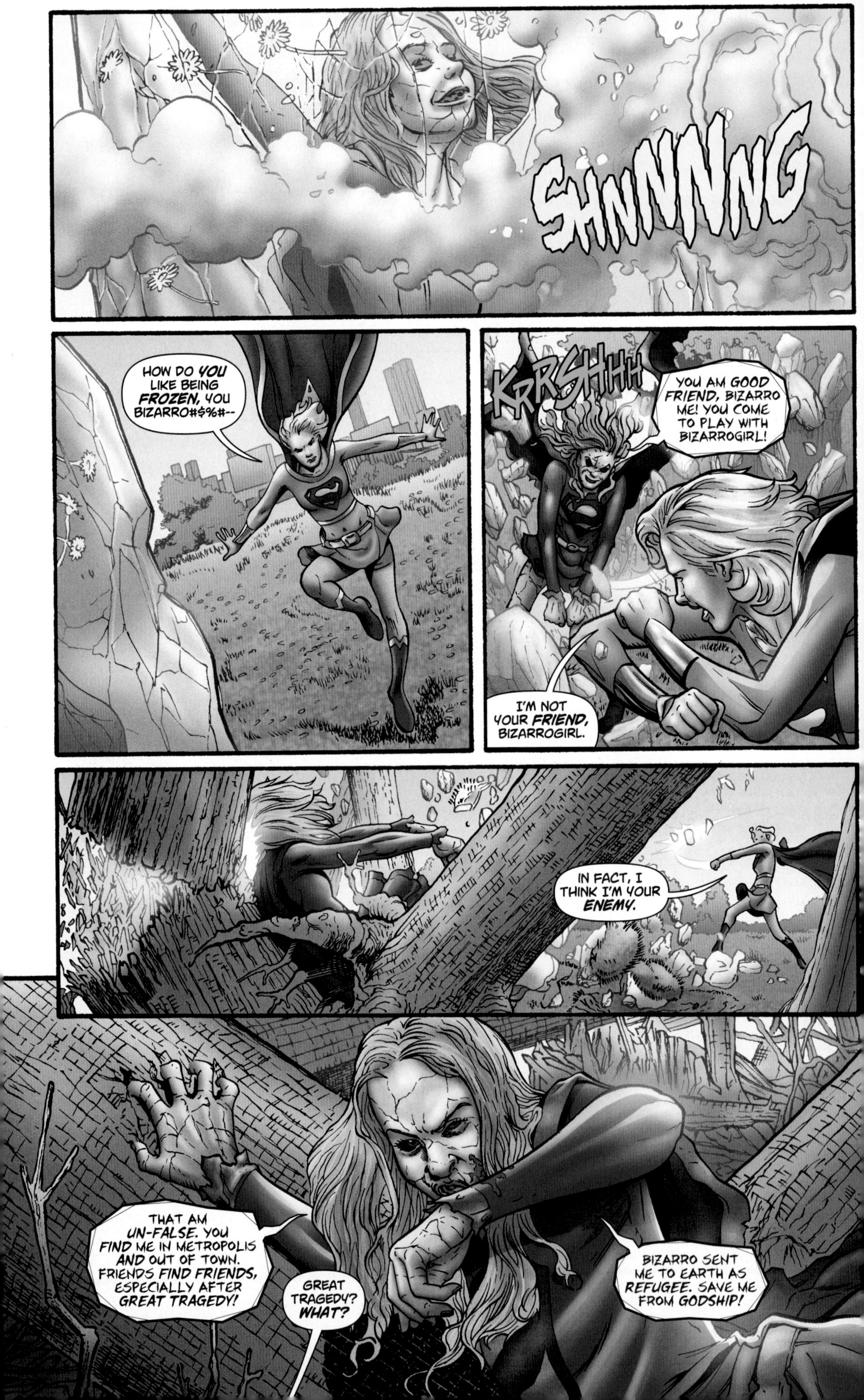
SHNNNNG
HOW DO YOU LIKE BEING FROZEN, YOU BIZARRO#$%#--
KRRSHHH
YOU AM GOOD FRIEND, BIZARRO ME! YOU COME TO PLAY WITH BIZARROGIRL!
I'M NOT YOUR FRIEND, BIZARROGIRL.
IN FACT, I THINK I'M YOUR ENEMY.
THAT AM UN-FALSE. YOU FIND ME IN METROPOLIS AND OUT OF TOWN. FRIENDS FIND FRIENDS, ESPECIALLY AFTER GREAT TRAGEDY!
GREAT TRAGEDY? WHAT?
BIZARRO SENT ME TO EARTH AS REFUGEE. SAVE ME FROM GODSHIP!

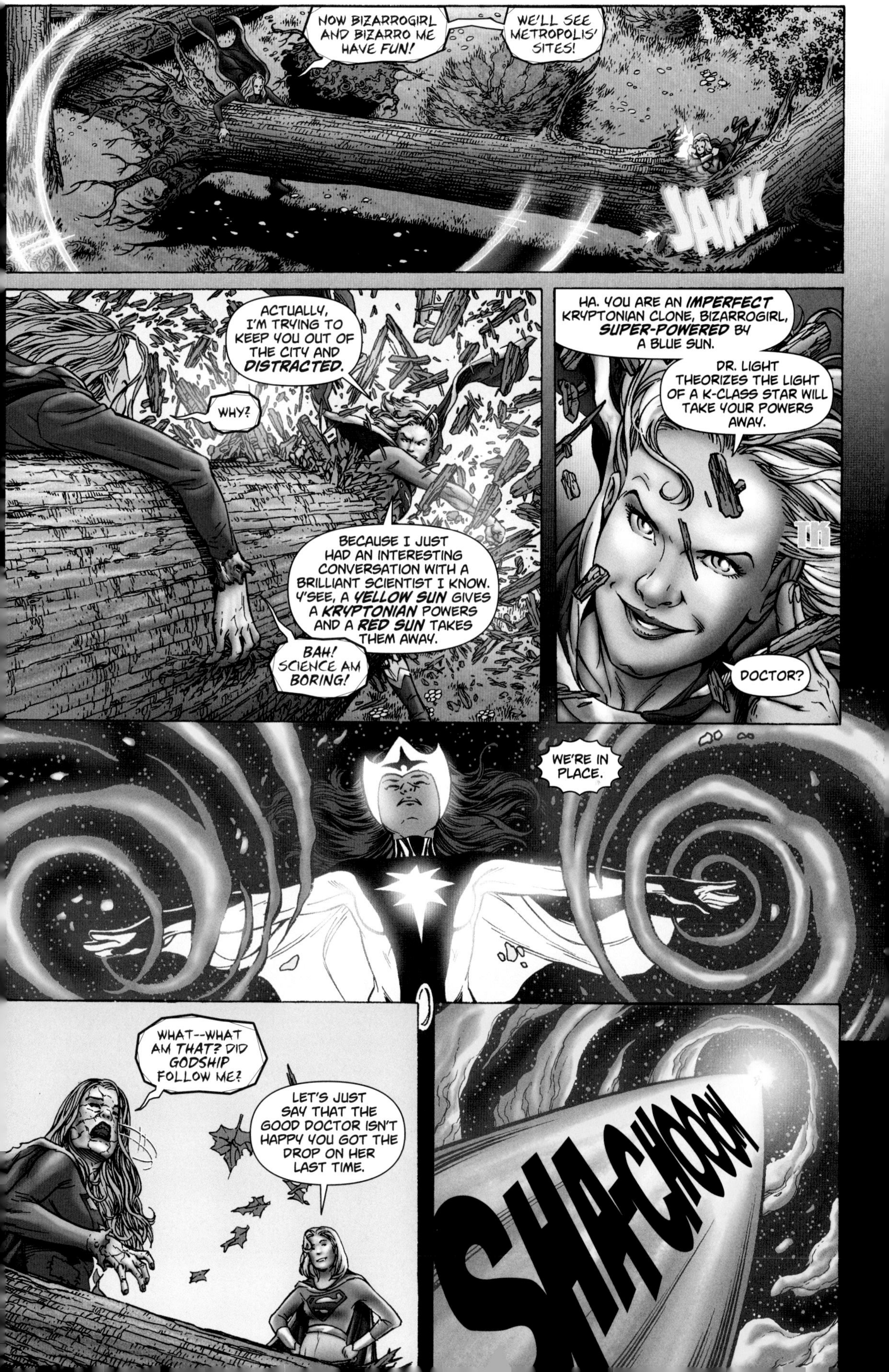
NOW BIZARROGIRL AND BIZARRO ME HAVE FUN!
WE'LL SEE METROPOLIS' SITES!
JAKK
ACTUALLY, I'M TRYING TO KEEP YOU OUT OF THE CITY AND DISTRACTED.
WHY?
BECAUSE I JUST HAD AN INTERESTING CONVERSATION WITH A BRILLIANT SCIENTIST I KNOW. Y'SEE, A YELLOW SUN GIVES A KRYPTONIAN POWERS AND A RED SUN TAKES THEM AWAY.
BAH! SCIENCE AM BORING!
HA. YOU ARE AN IMPERFECT KRYPTONIAN CLONE, BIZARROGIRL, SUPER-POWERED BY A BLUE SUN.
DR. LIGHT THEORIZES THE LIGHT OF A K-CLASS STAR WILL TAKE YOUR POWERS AWAY.
TK
DOCTOR?
WE'RE IN PLACE.
WHAT--WHAT AM THAT? DID GODSHIP FOLLOW ME?
LET'S JUST SAY THAT THE GOOD DOCTOR ISN'T HAPPY YOU GOT THE DROP ON HER LAST TIME.
SHACHOOM

SEE
YA.

UGLY
LIGHT--!

HNH.

FFFSSSSS

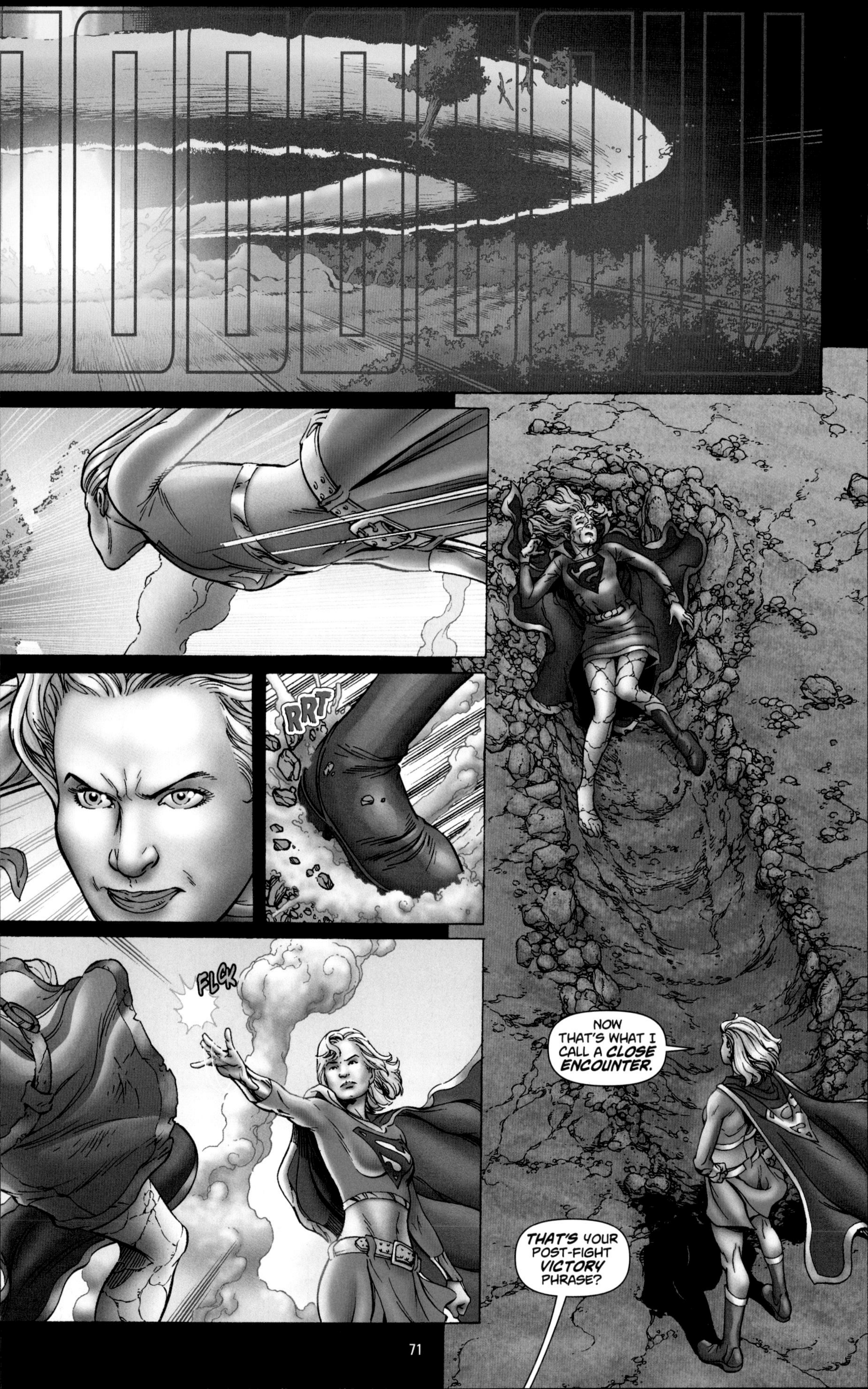
DOOOOOSH
RRRT!
FLCK
NOW THAT'S WHAT I CALL A CLOSE ENCOUNTER.
THAT'S YOUR POST-FIGHT VICTORY PHRASE?

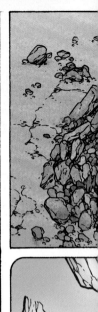

A LINE FROM AN OLD SCI-FI MOVIE?

IT TAKES TIME TO BUILD UP A BEAM THAT *STRONG*, BUT IT HELPS I'M STILL REALLY, REALLY TICKED OFF AT BEING KNOCKED OUT.

SO, SHE'S DEFEATED. WHAT NOW?

OLD? I *JUST* SAW IT. I *WAS* FLYING THROUGH *SPACE* WHEN IT CAME OUT, YOU KNOW.

NICE ORBITAL LASER, BY THE WAY.

WHAT? OH.

BIZARRO HAS BEEN MAKING CLONES OF *HIMSELF* USING A SPECIAL TYPE OF, UH, "CLONE VISION." HE DERIVES THE POWER UNDER BLUE SUNLIGHT. KAL FOUND THAT OUT.

FASCINATING. AND WHY IS SHE DRESSED LIKE YOU?

BIZARRO MADE A *PLANET* FOR HIMSELF, THEN PEOPLED IT ENTIRELY WITH BIZARROS GROWN FROM HIM.*

*AS SEEN IN *SUPERMAN: ESCAPE FROM BIZARRO WORLD!* --BIZARRO MATT

BIZARRO CREATED A *PLANET*? HE BECOMES QUITE POWERFUL UNDER A BLUE SUN, THEN.

AND DID I HEAR HER SAY SOMETHING OVER THE COMM ABOUT BEING A *REFUGEE*?

WAIT, WHAT ARE YOU DOING?

I TOLD YOU, SHE'S GOING BACK TO S.T.A.R. LABS. WE CAN'T LET A DANGEROUS *EXTRATERRESTRIAL* GO UNCHECKED--

YOU MEAN LIKE ME?

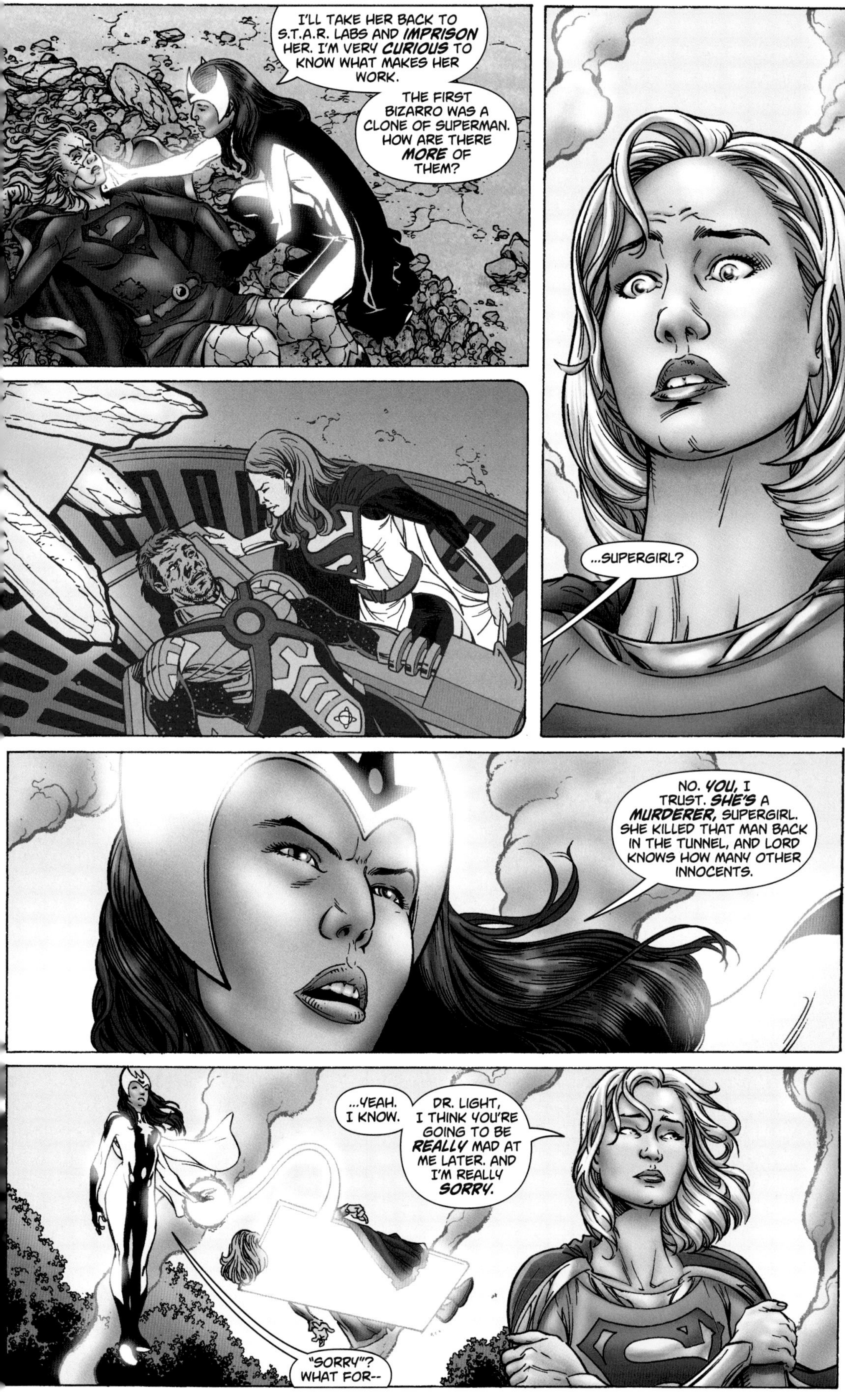
I'LL TAKE HER BACK TO S.T.A.R. LABS AND IMPRISON HER. I'M VERY CURIOUS TO KNOW WHAT MAKES HER WORK.
THE FIRST BIZARRO WAS A CLONE OF SUPERMAN. HOW ARE THERE MORE OF THEM?
...SUPERGIRL?
NO. YOU, I TRUST. SHE'S A MURDERER, SUPERGIRL. SHE KILLED THAT MAN BACK IN THE TUNNEL, AND LORD KNOWS HOW MANY OTHER INNOCENTS.
...YEAH. I KNOW.
DR. LIGHT, I THINK YOU'RE GOING TO BE REALLY MAD AT ME LATER. AND I'M REALLY SORRY.
"SORRY"? WHAT FOR--

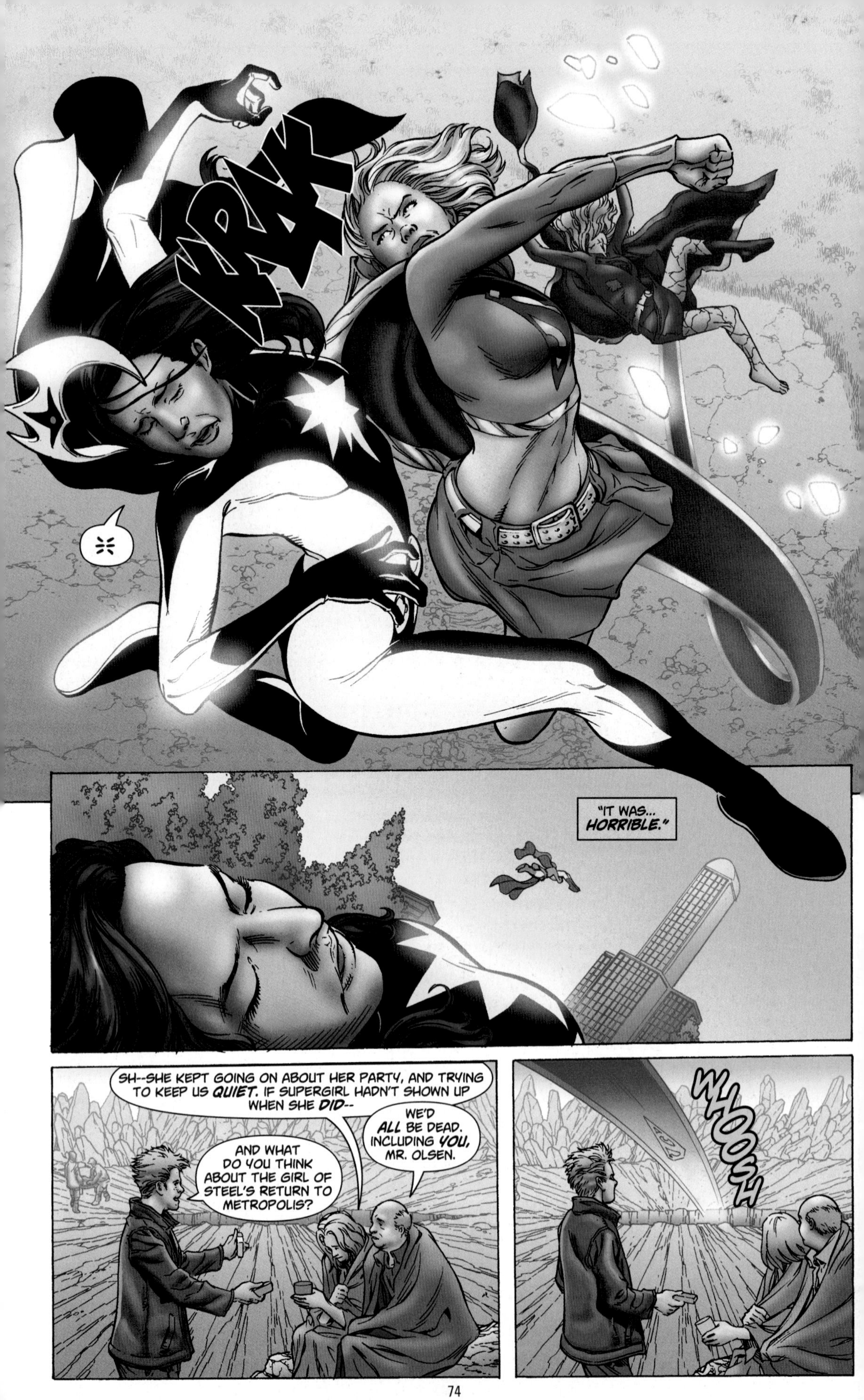
KRAK
"IT WAS... HORRIBLE."
SH--SHE KEPT GOING ON ABOUT HER PARTY, AND TRYING TO KEEP US QUIET. IF SUPERGIRL HADN'T SHOWN UP WHEN SHE DID--
WE'D ALL BE DEAD. INCLUDING YOU, MR. OLSEN.
AND WHAT DO YOU THINK ABOUT THE GIRL OF STEEL'S RETURN TO METROPOLIS?
WHOOSH

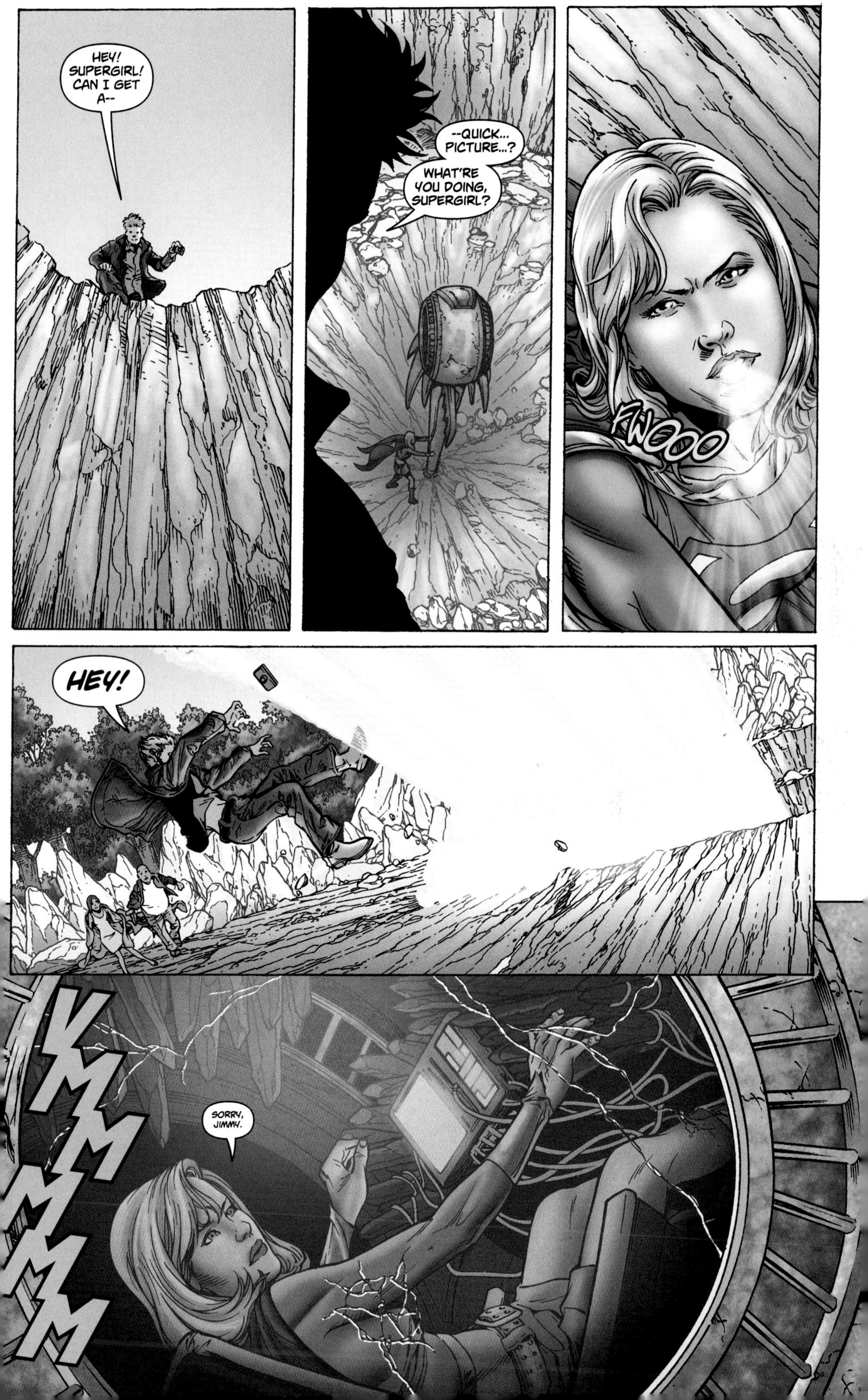
HEY! SUPERGIRL! CAN I GET A--
--QUICK... PICTURE...?
WHAT'RE YOU DOING, SUPERGIRL?
FWOOO
HEY!
KMMMMM
SORRY, JIMMY.

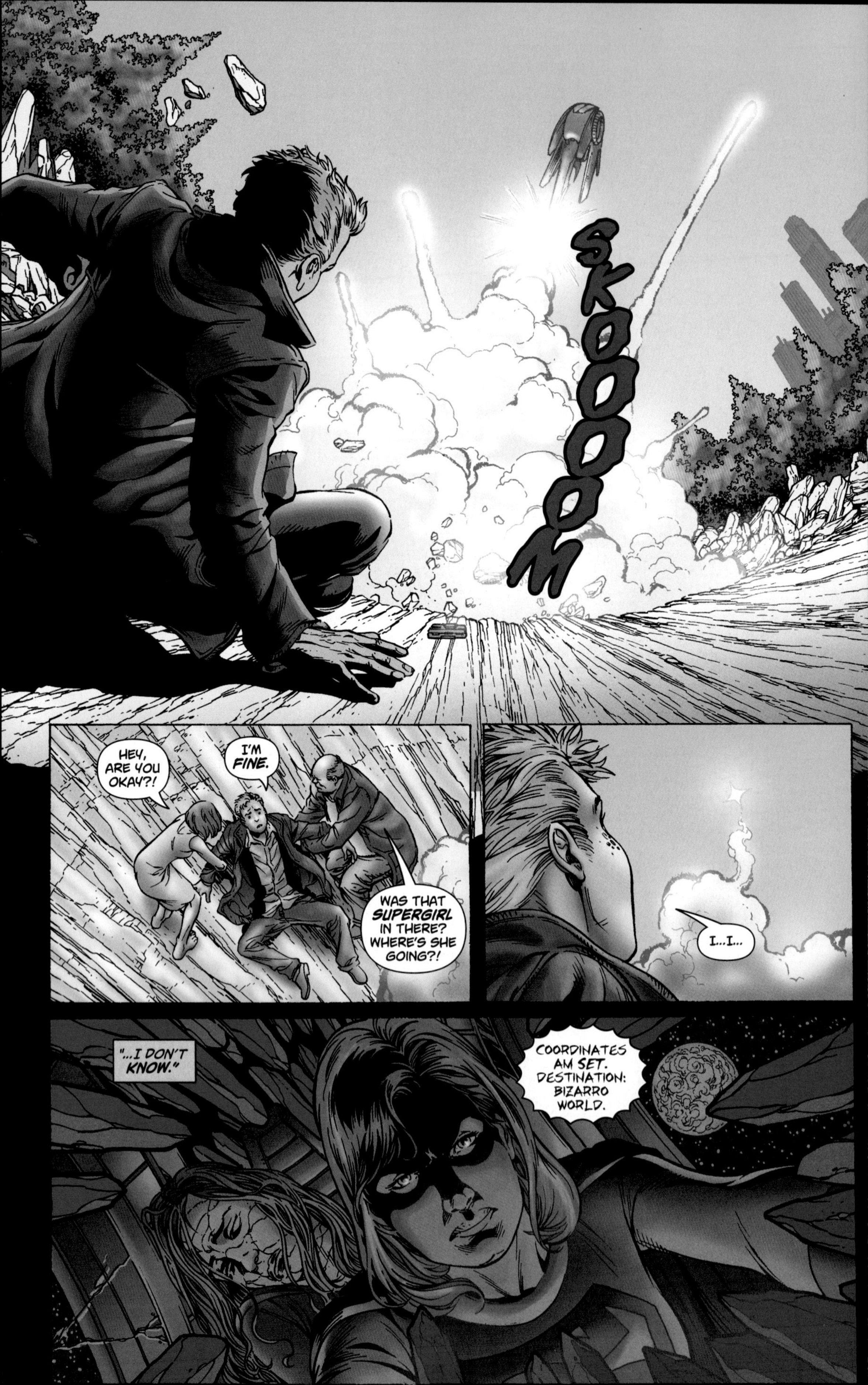
SKOOOOOM
HEY, ARE YOU OKAY?!
I'M FINE.
WAS THAT SUPERGIRL IN THERE? WHERE'S SHE GOING?!
I...I...
"...I DON'T KNOW."
COORDINATES AM SET. DESTINATION: BIZARRO WORLD.

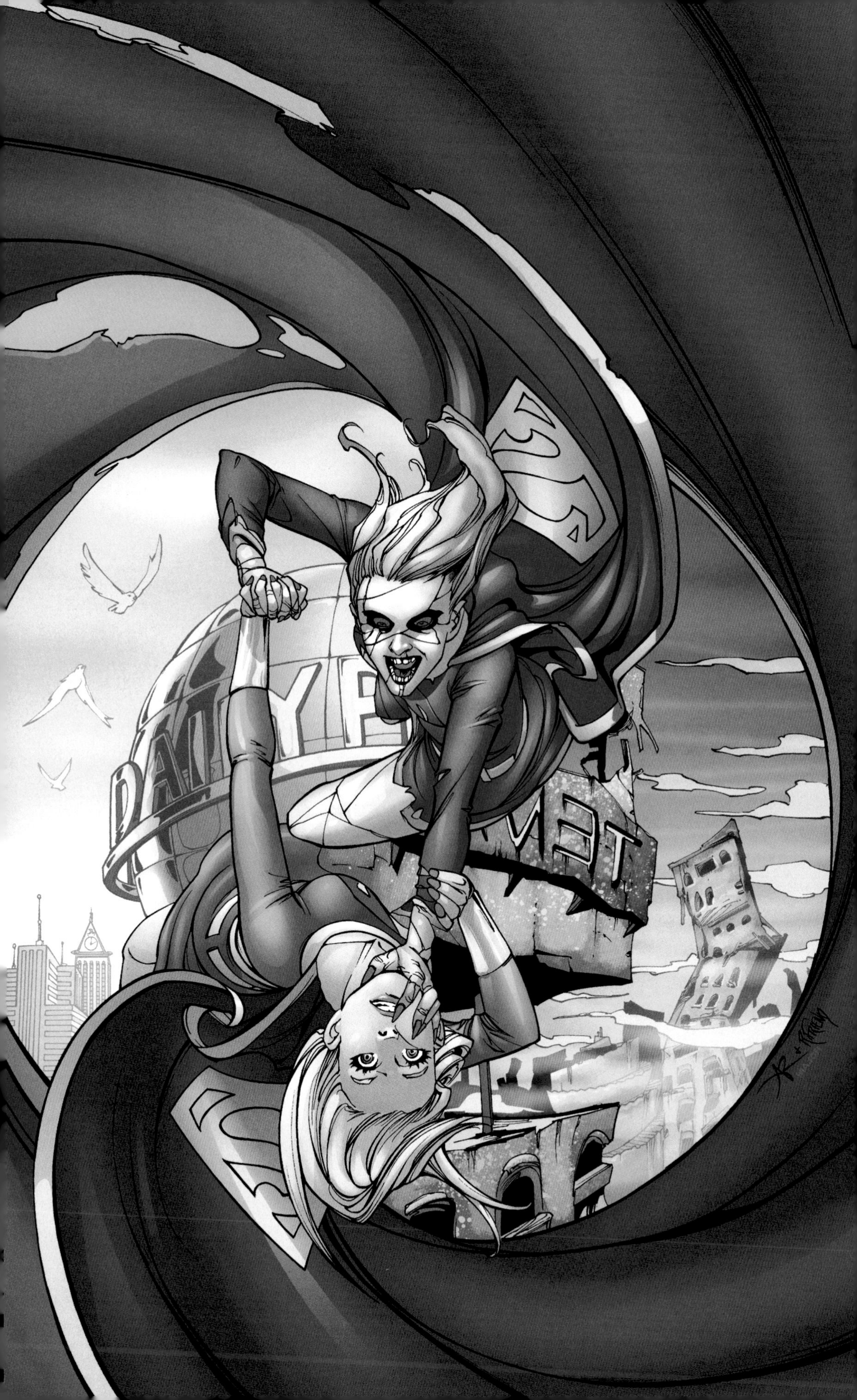

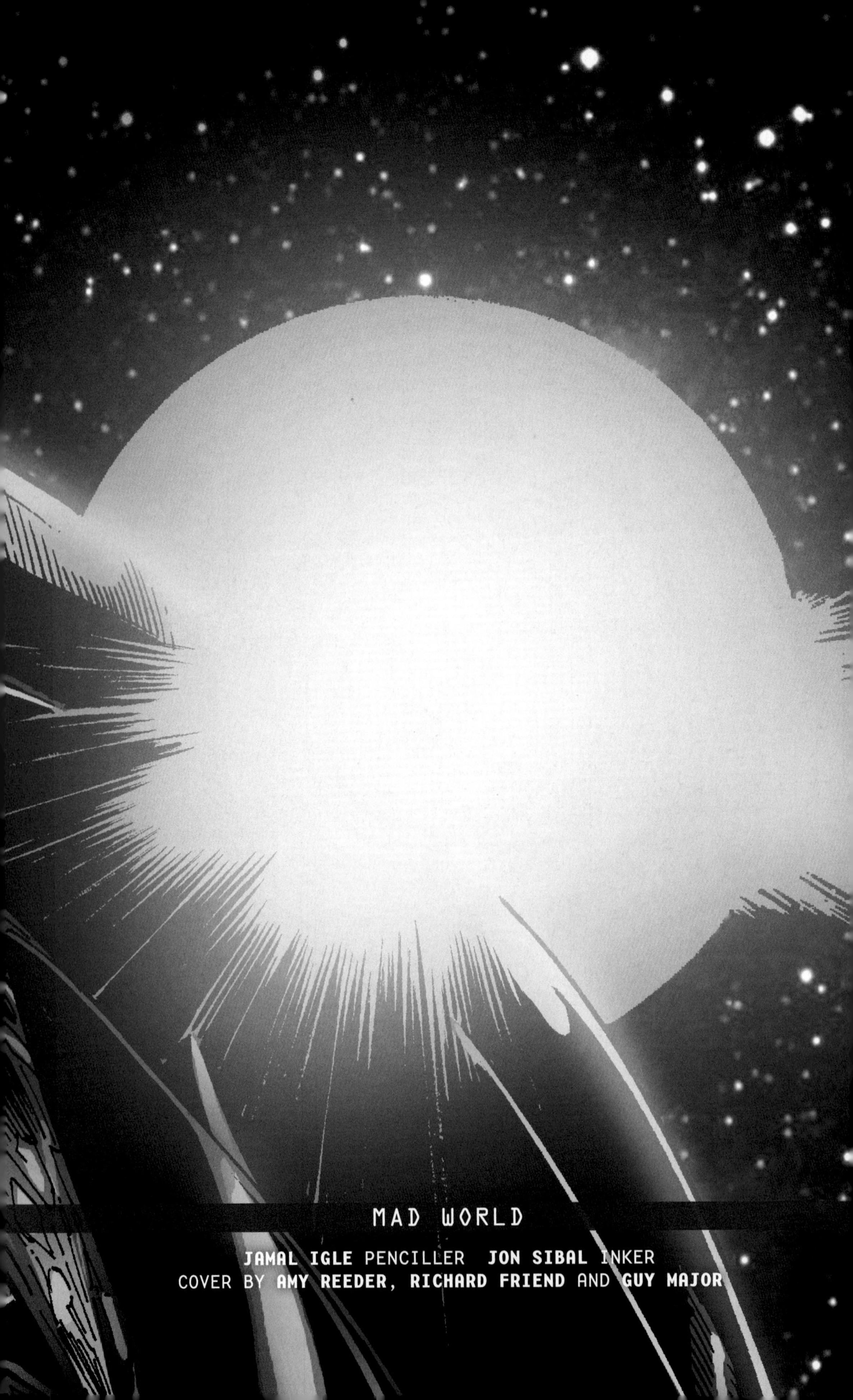
MAD WORLD
JAMAL IGLE PENCILLER JON SIBAL INKER
COVER BY AMY REEDER, RICHARD FRIEND AND GUY MAJOR

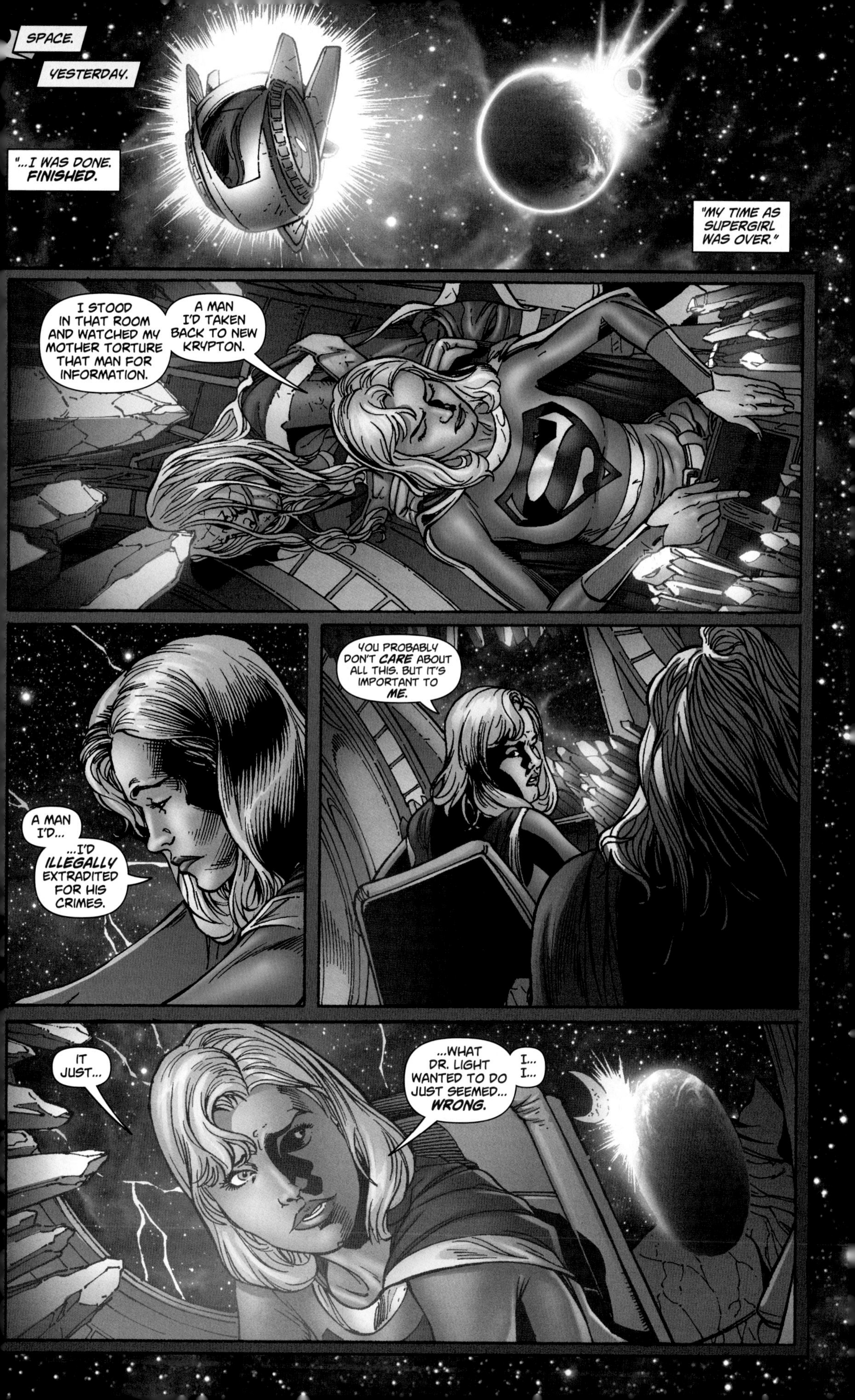
SPACE.
YESTERDAY.
"...I WAS DONE. FINISHED.
"MY TIME AS SUPERGIRL WAS OVER."
I STOOD IN THAT ROOM AND WATCHED MY MOTHER TORTURE THAT MAN FOR INFORMATION.
A MAN I'D TAKEN BACK TO NEW KRYPTON.
A MAN I'D...
...I'D ILLEGALLY EXTRADITED FOR HIS CRIMES.
YOU PROBABLY DON'T CARE ABOUT ALL THIS. BUT IT'S IMPORTANT TO ME.
IT JUST...
...WHAT DR. LIGHT WANTED TO DO JUST SEEMED... WRONG.
I... I...

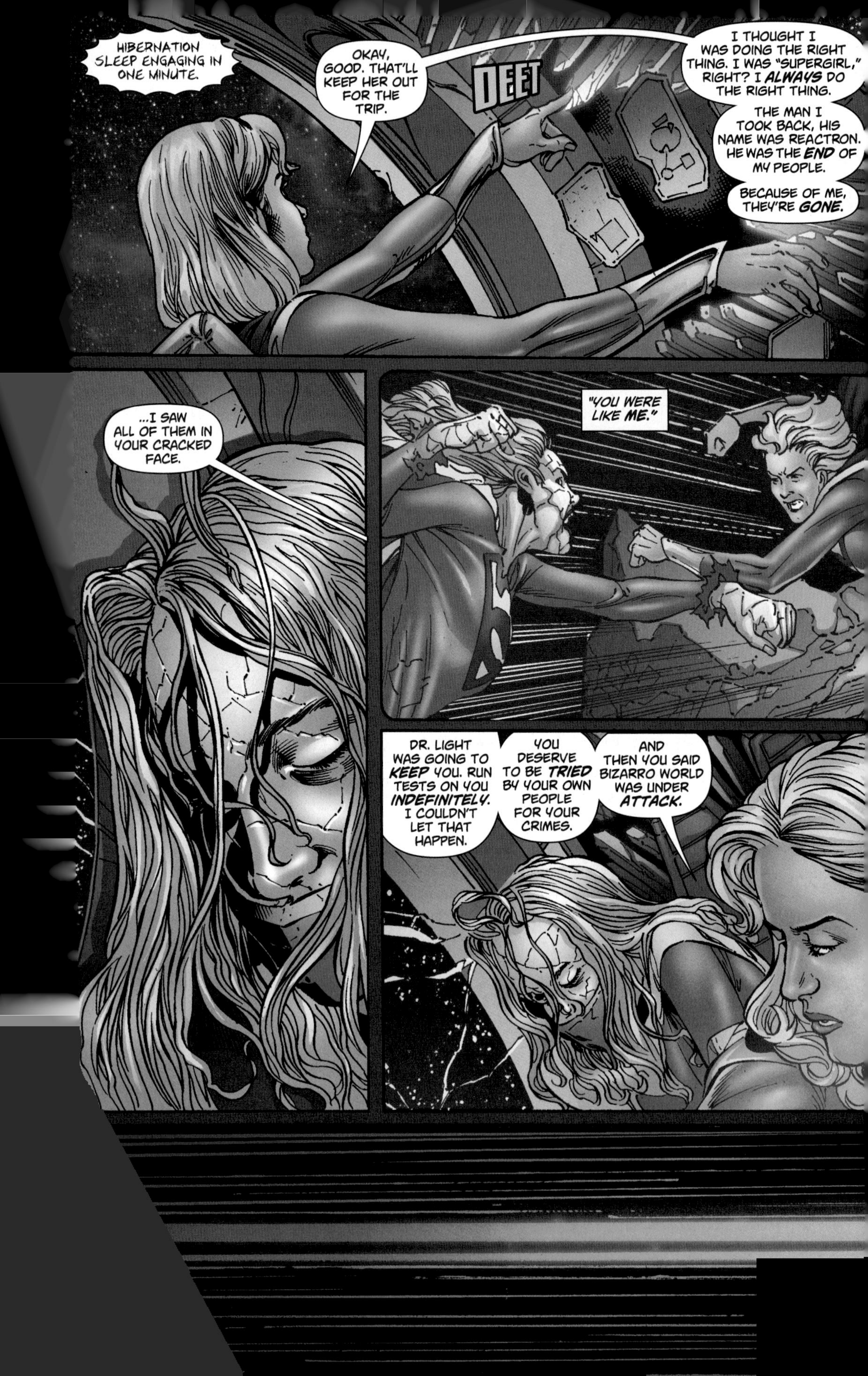
HIBERNATION SLEEP ENGAGING IN ONE MINUTE.
OKAY, GOOD. THAT'LL KEEP HER OUT FOR THE TRIP.
DEET
I THOUGHT I WAS DOING THE RIGHT THING. I WAS "SUPERGIRL," RIGHT? I ALWAYS DO THE RIGHT THING.
THE MAN I TOOK BACK, HIS NAME WAS REACTRON. HE WAS THE END OF MY PEOPLE.
BECAUSE OF ME, THEY'RE GONE.
...I SAW ALL OF THEM IN YOUR CRACKED FACE.
"YOU WERE LIKE ME."
DR. LIGHT WAS GOING TO KEEP YOU. RUN TESTS ON YOU INDEFINITELY. I COULDN'T LET THAT HAPPEN.
YOU DESERVE TO BE TRIED BY YOUR OWN PEOPLE FOR YOUR CRIMES.
AND THEN YOU SAID BIZARRO WORLD WAS UNDER ATTACK.

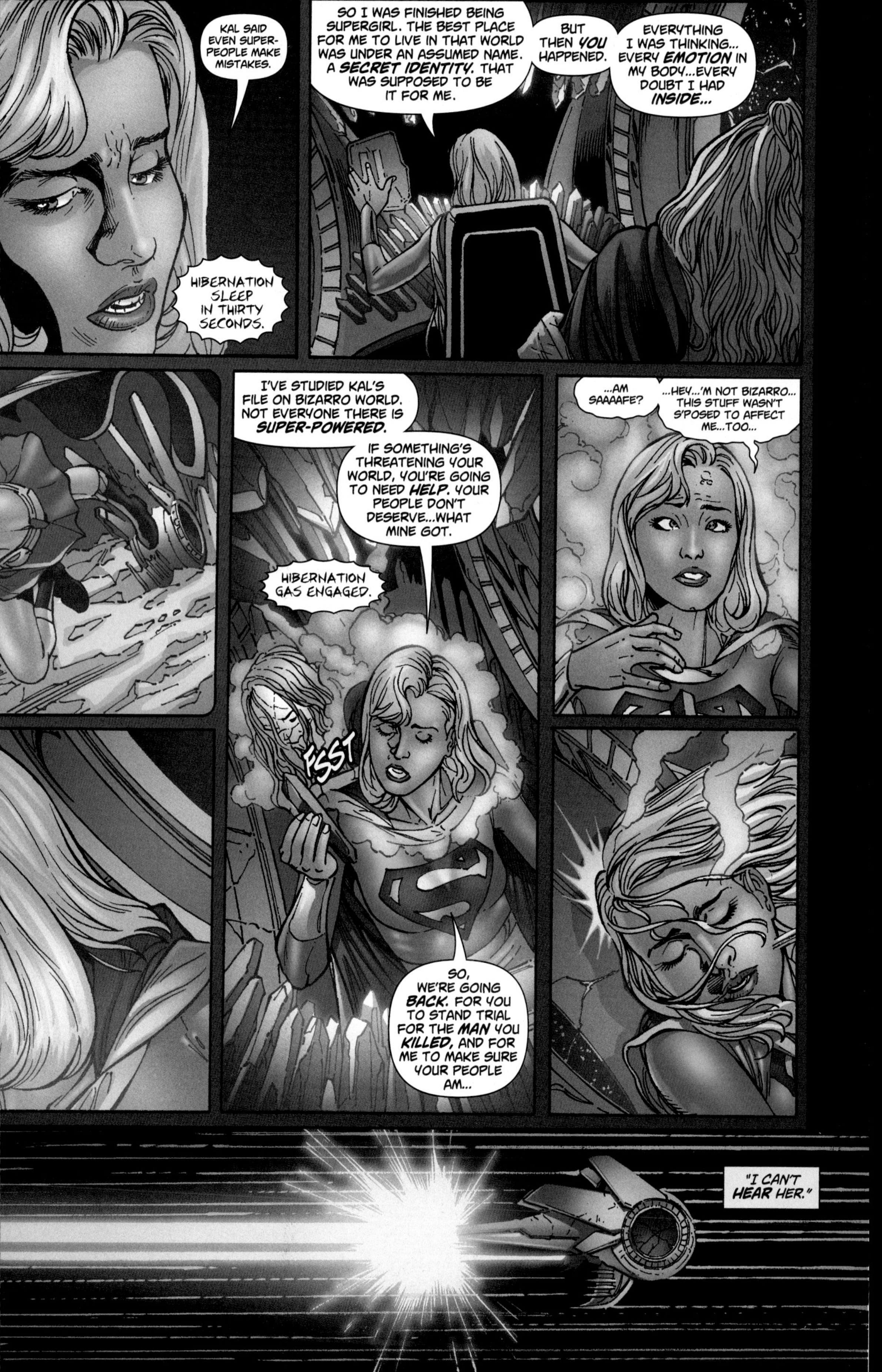
KAL SAID EVEN SUPER-PEOPLE MAKE MISTAKES.
HIBERNATION SLEEP IN THIRTY SECONDS.
SO I WAS FINISHED BEING SUPERGIRL. THE BEST PLACE FOR ME TO LIVE IN THAT WORLD WAS UNDER AN ASSUMED NAME. A SECRET IDENTITY. THAT WAS SUPPOSED TO BE IT FOR ME.
BUT THEN YOU HAPPENED.
EVERYTHING I WAS THINKING... EVERY EMOTION IN MY BODY...EVERY DOUBT I HAD INSIDE...
I'VE STUDIED KAL'S FILE ON BIZARRO WORLD. NOT EVERYONE THERE IS SUPER-POWERED.
IF SOMETHING'S THREATENING YOUR WORLD, YOU'RE GOING TO NEED HELP. YOUR PEOPLE DON'T DESERVE...WHAT MINE GOT.
HIBERNATION GAS ENGAGED.
FSST
SO, WE'RE GOING BACK. FOR YOU TO STAND TRIAL FOR THE MAN YOU KILLED, AND FOR ME TO MAKE SURE YOUR PEOPLE AM...
...AM SAAAAAFE?
...HEY...'M NOT BIZARRO... THIS STUFF WASN'T S'POSED TO AFFECT ME...TOO...
"I CAN'T HEAR HER."

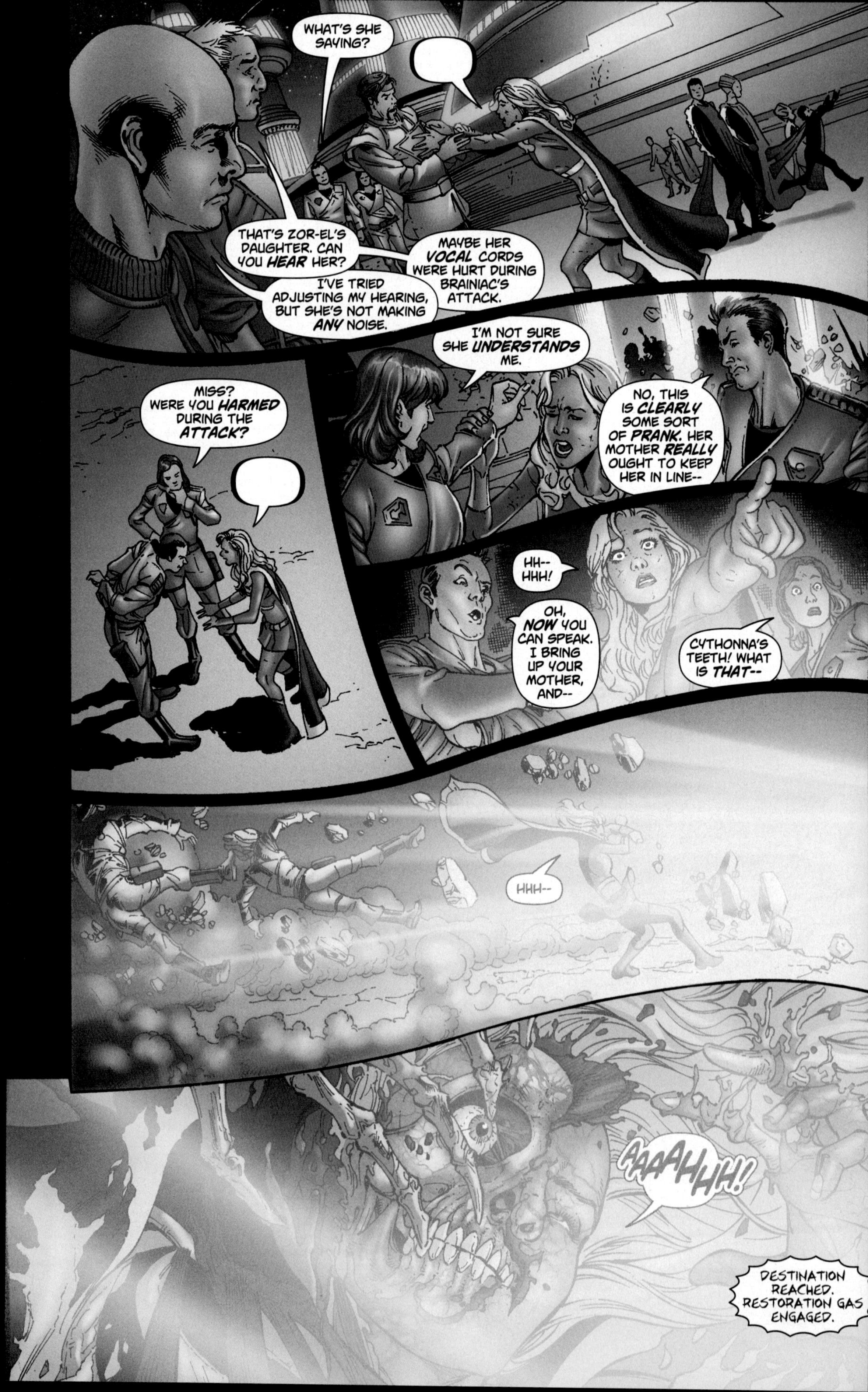
WHAT'S SHE SAYING?
THAT'S ZOR-EL'S DAUGHTER. CAN YOU HEAR HER?
MAYBE HER VOCAL CORDS WERE HURT DURING BRAINIAC'S ATTACK.
I'VE TRIED ADJUSTING MY HEARING, BUT SHE'S NOT MAKING ANY NOISE.
MISS? WERE YOU HARMED DURING THE ATTACK?
I'M NOT SURE SHE UNDERSTANDS ME.
NO, THIS IS CLEARLY SOME SORT OF PRANK. HER MOTHER REALLY OUGHT TO KEEP HER IN LINE--
HH--HHH!
OH, NOW YOU CAN SPEAK. I BRING UP YOUR MOTHER, AND--
CYTHONNA'S TEETH! WHAT IS THAT--
HHH--
AAAAHHH!
DESTINATION REACHED. RESTORATION GAS ENGAGED.

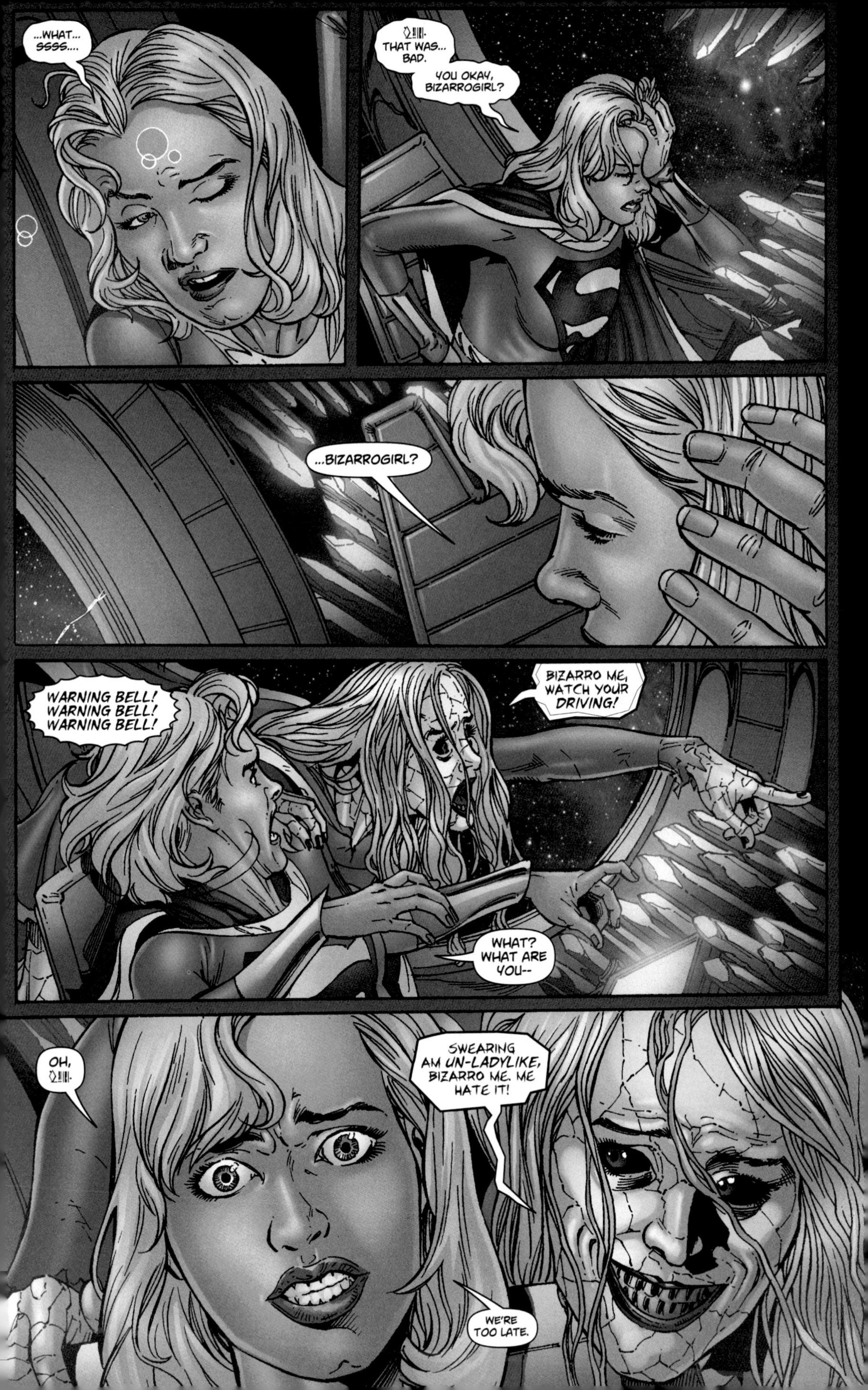
...WHAT... SSSS....
☋!!|!!·. THAT WAS... BAD.
YOU OKAY, BIZARROGIRL?
...BIZARROGIRL?
WARNING BELL! WARNING BELL! WARNING BELL!
BIZARRO ME, WATCH YOUR DRIVING!
WHAT? WHAT ARE YOU--
OH, ☋!!|!!·.
SWEARING AM UN-LADYLIKE, BIZARRO ME. ME HATE IT!
WE'RE TOO LATE.

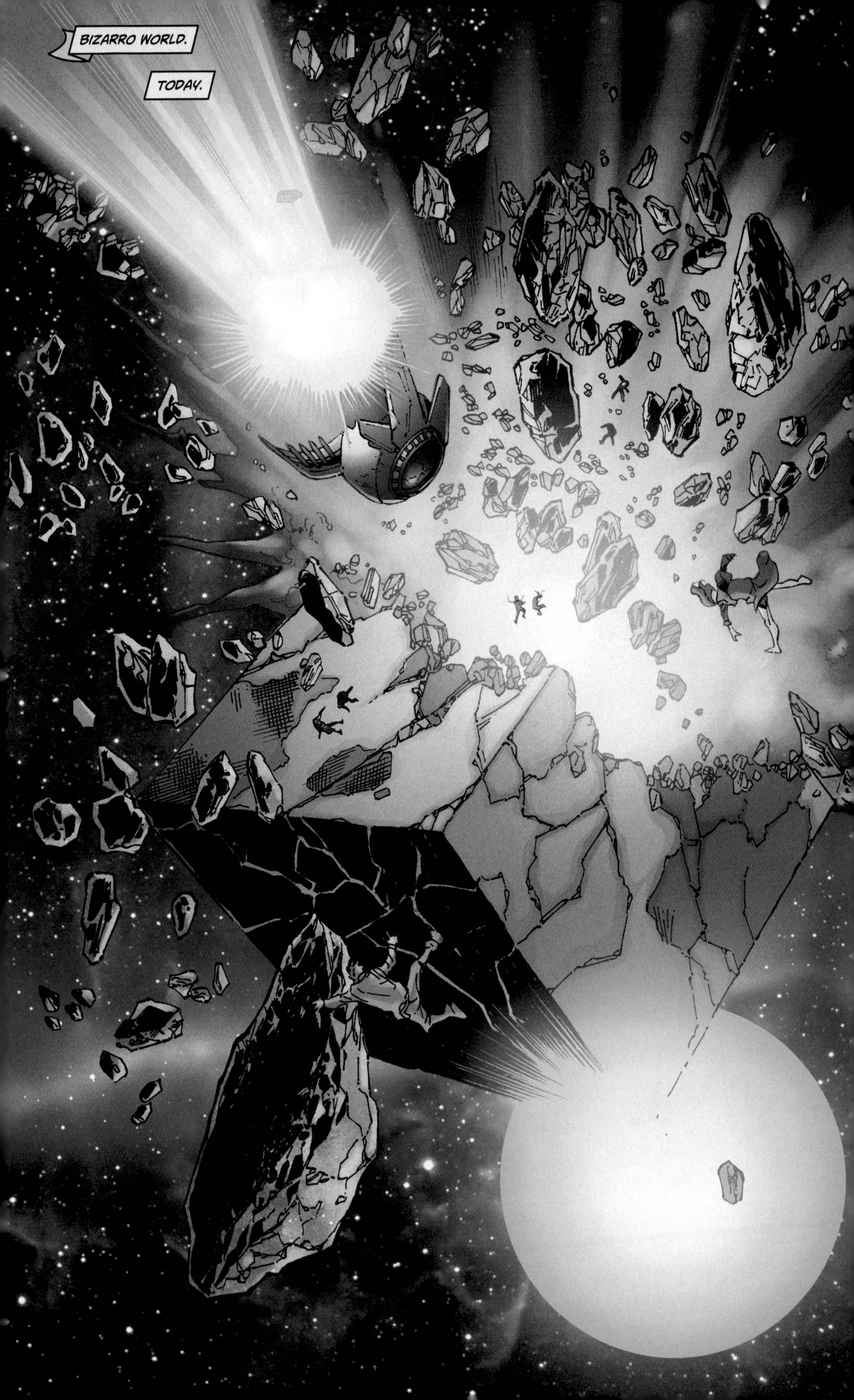
BIZARRO WORLD.
TODAY.

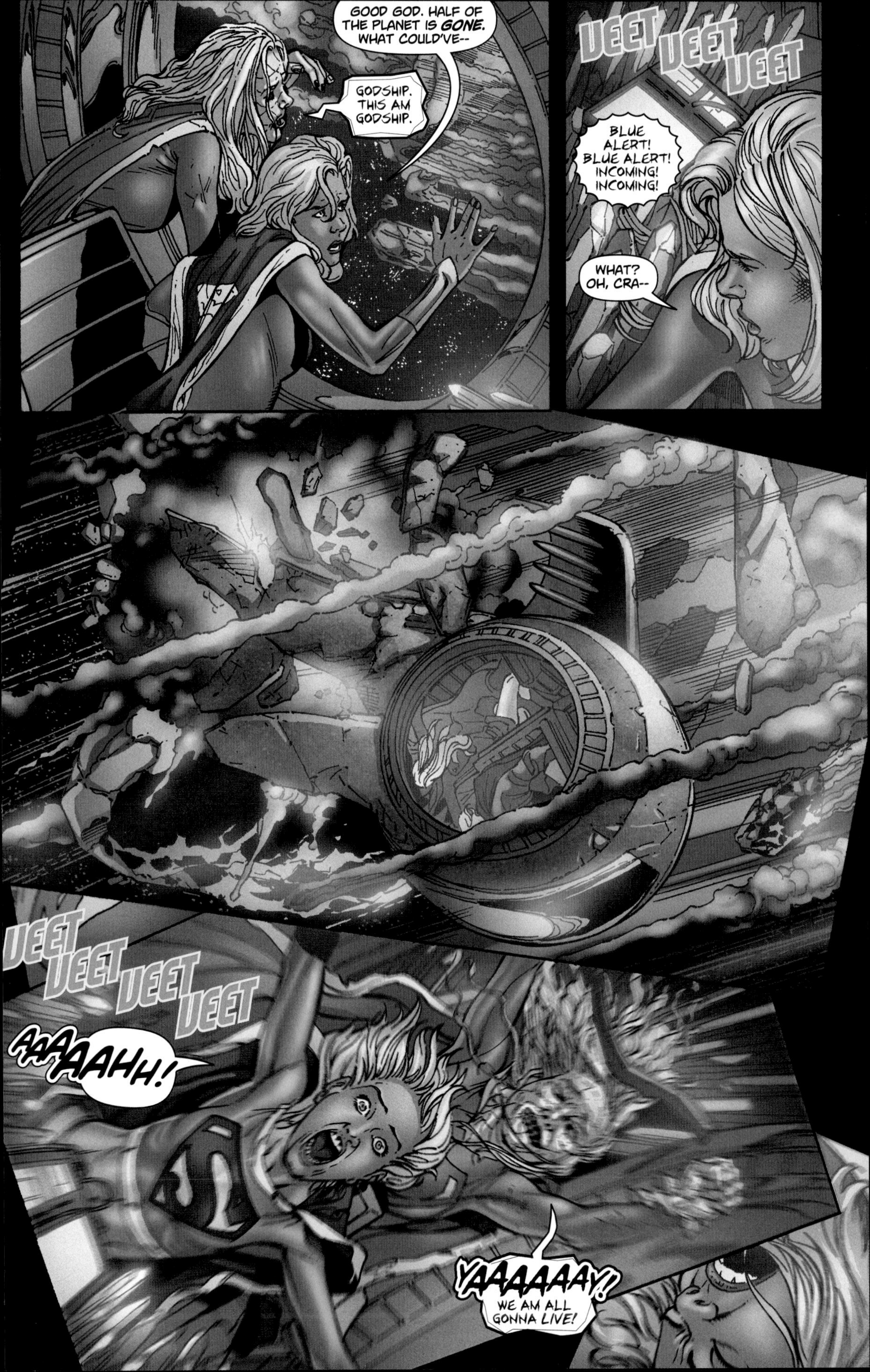
GOOD GOD. HALF OF THE PLANET IS *GONE*. WHAT COULD'VE--
GODSHIP. THIS AM GODSHIP.
VEET VEET VEET
BLUE ALERT! BLUE ALERT! INCOMING! INCOMING!
WHAT? OH, CRA--
VEET VEET VEET VEET
AAAAAHH!
YAAAAAAY! WE AM ALL GONNA LIVE!

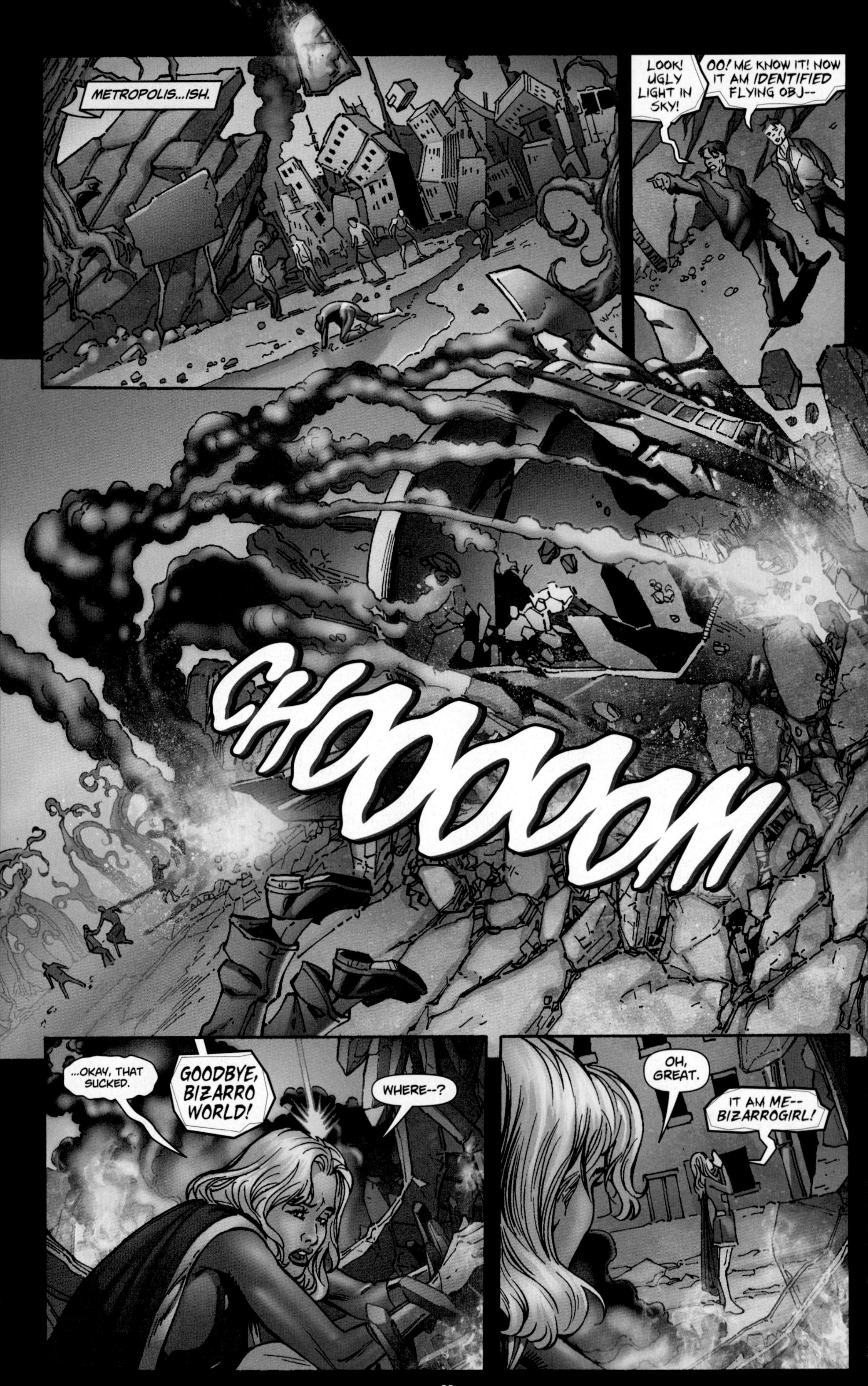
METROPOLIS...ISH.
LOOK! UGLY LIGHT IN SKY!
OO! ME KNOW IT! NOW IT AM IDENTIFIED FLYING OBJ--
CHOOOOOOM
...OKAY, THAT SUCKED.
GOODBYE, BIZARRO WORLD!
WHERE--?
OH, GREAT.
IT AM ME-- BIZARROGIRL!

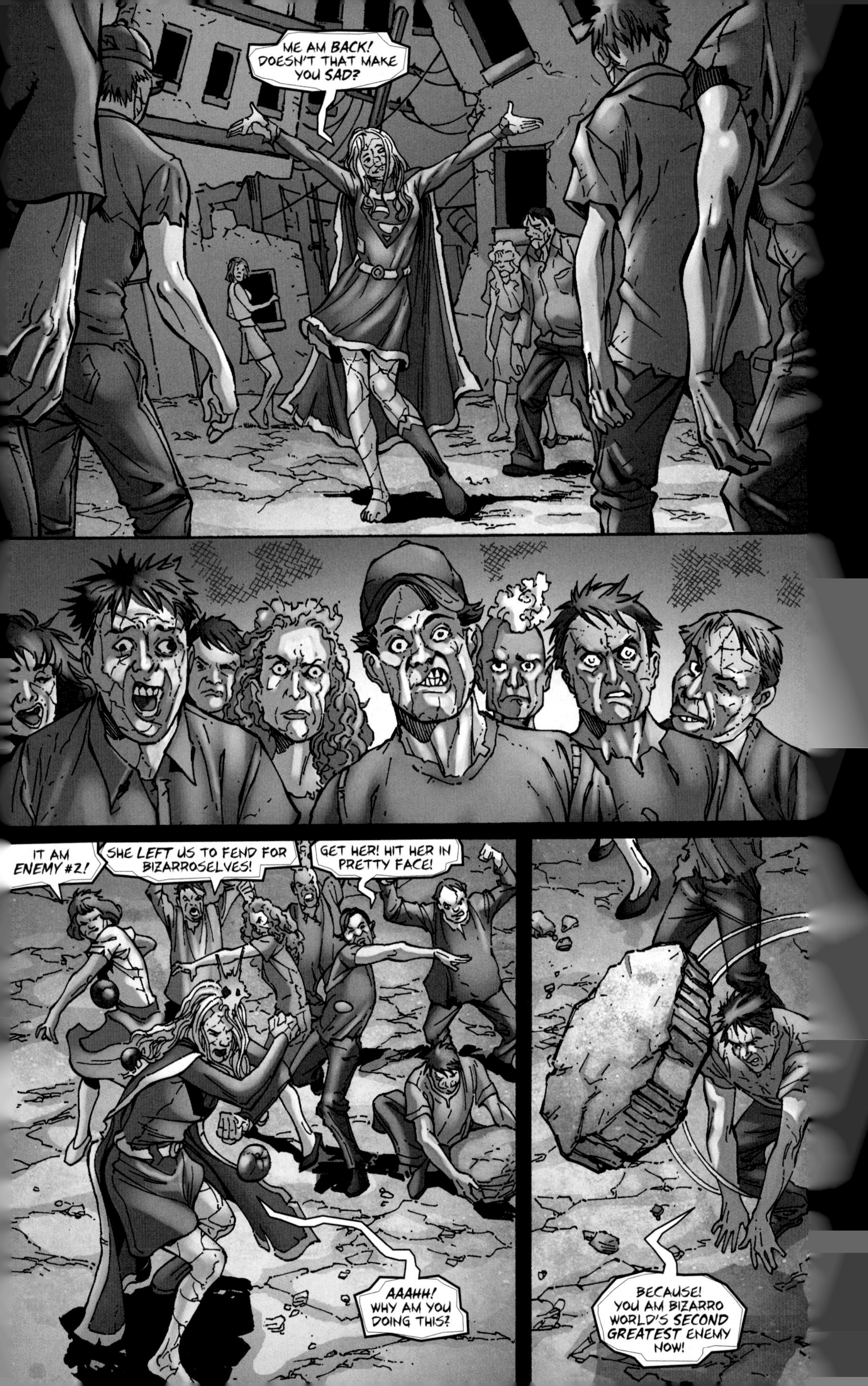
ME AM BACK! DOESN'T THAT MAKE YOU SAD?
IT AM ENEMY #2!
SHE LEFT US TO FEND FOR BIZARROSELVES!
GET HER! HIT HER IN PRETTY FACE!
AAAHH! WHY AM YOU DOING THIS?
BECAUSE! YOU AM BIZARRO WORLD'S SECOND GREATEST ENEMY NOW!

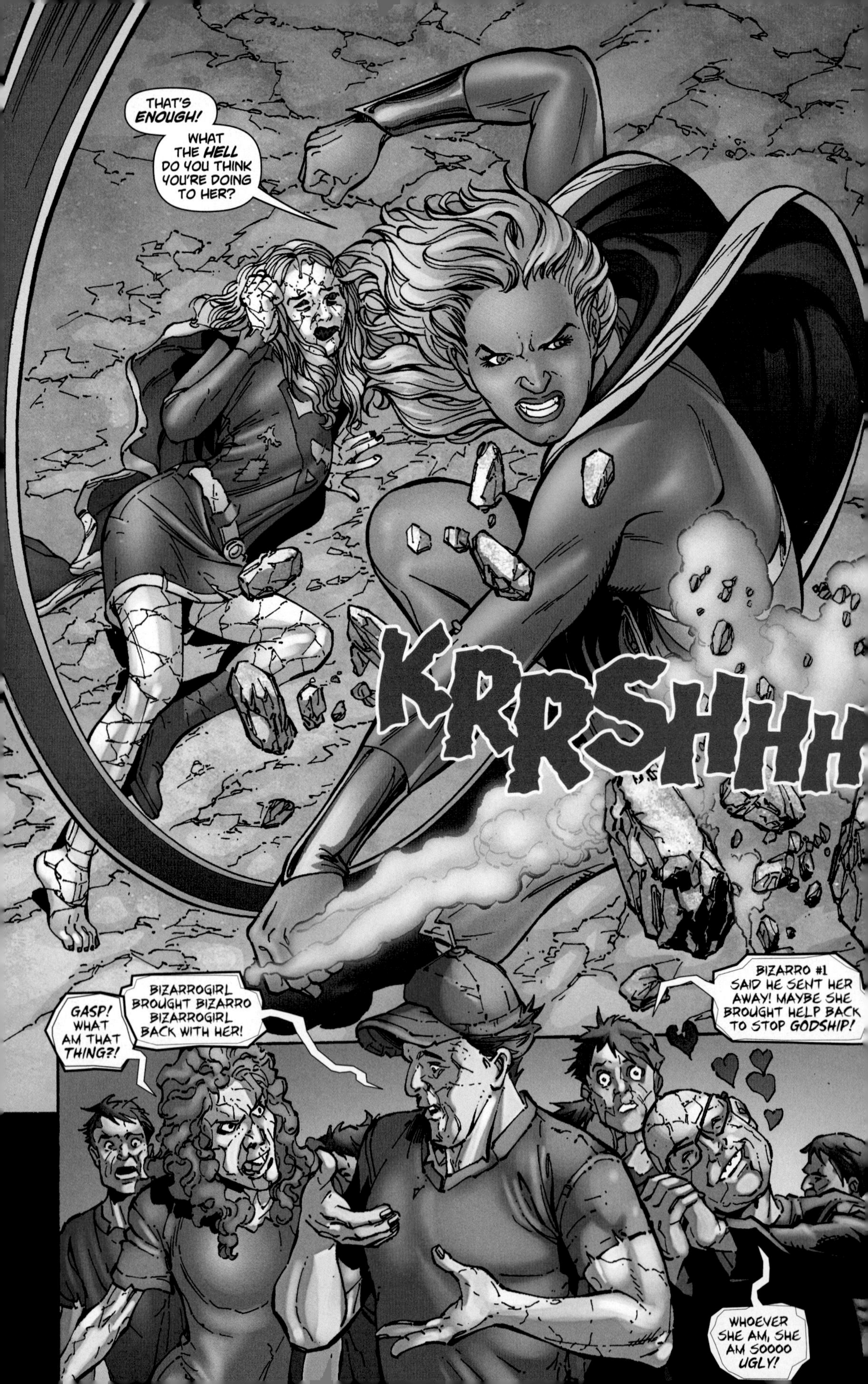
THAT'S ENOUGH!
WHAT THE HELL DO YOU THINK YOU'RE DOING TO HER?
KRRSHHH
GASP! WHAT AM THAT THING?!
BIZARROGIRL BROUGHT BIZARRO BIZARROGIRL BACK WITH HER!
BIZARRO #1 SAID HE SENT HER AWAY! MAYBE SHE BROUGHT HELP BACK TO STOP GODSHIP!
WHOEVER SHE AM, SHE AM SOOOO UGLY!

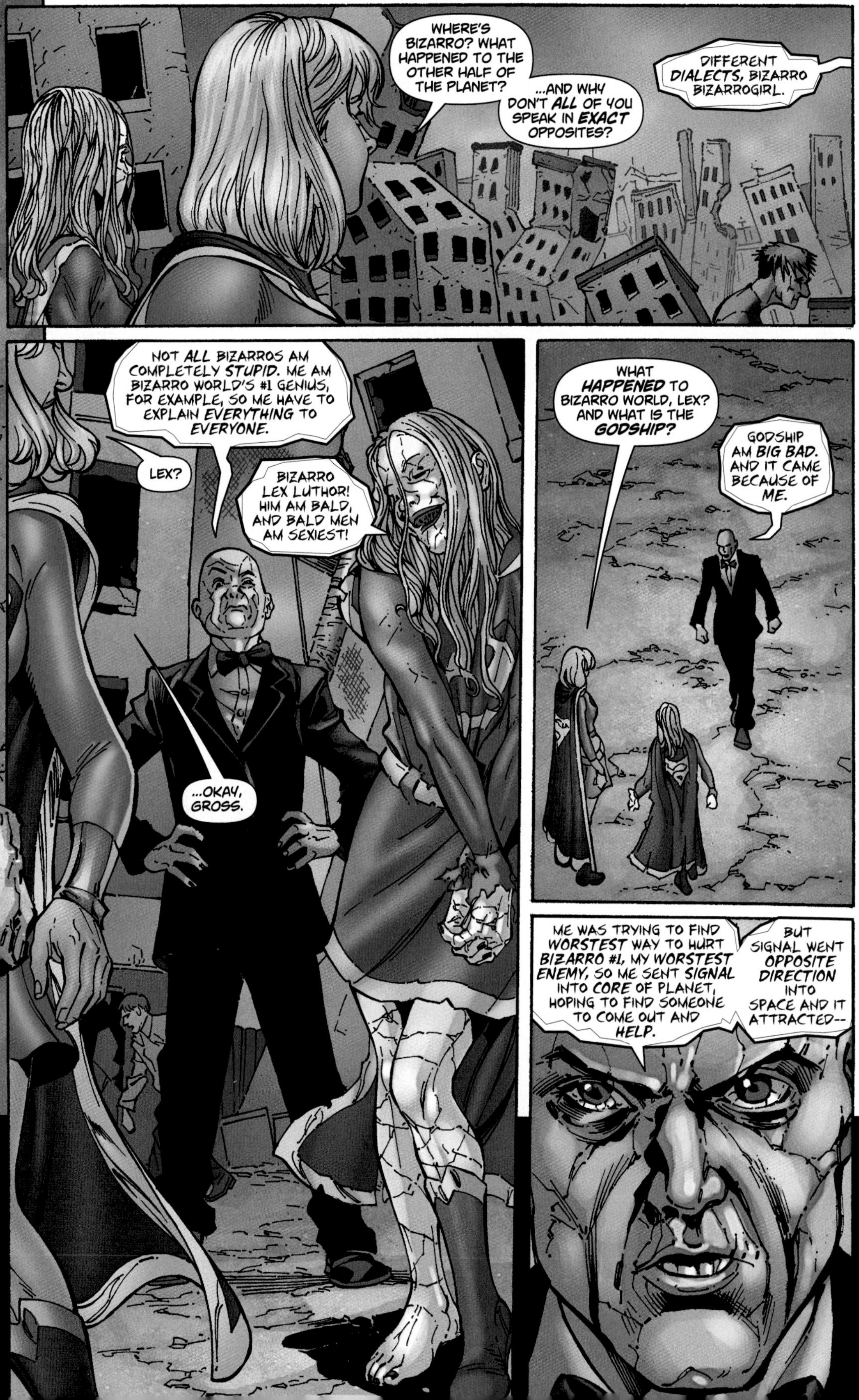
WHERE'S BIZARRO? WHAT HAPPENED TO THE OTHER HALF OF THE PLANET?
...AND WHY DON'T ALL OF YOU SPEAK IN EXACT OPPOSITES?
DIFFERENT DIALECTS, BIZARRO BIZARROGIRL.
NOT ALL BIZARROS AM COMPLETELY STUPID. ME AM BIZARRO WORLD'S #1 GENIUS, FOR EXAMPLE, SO ME HAVE TO EXPLAIN EVERYTHING TO EVERYONE.
LEX?
BIZARRO LEX LUTHOR! HIM AM BALD, AND BALD MEN AM SEXIEST!
...OKAY, GROSS.
WHAT HAPPENED TO BIZARRO WORLD, LEX? AND WHAT IS THE GODSHIP?
GODSHIP AM BIG BAD. AND IT CAME BECAUSE OF ME.
ME WAS TRYING TO FIND WORSTEST WAY TO HURT BIZARRO #1, MY WORSTEST ENEMY, SO ME SENT SIGNAL INTO CORE OF PLANET, HOPING TO FIND SOMEONE TO COME OUT AND HELP.
BUT SIGNAL WENT OPPOSITE DIRECTION INTO SPACE AND IT ATTRACTED--

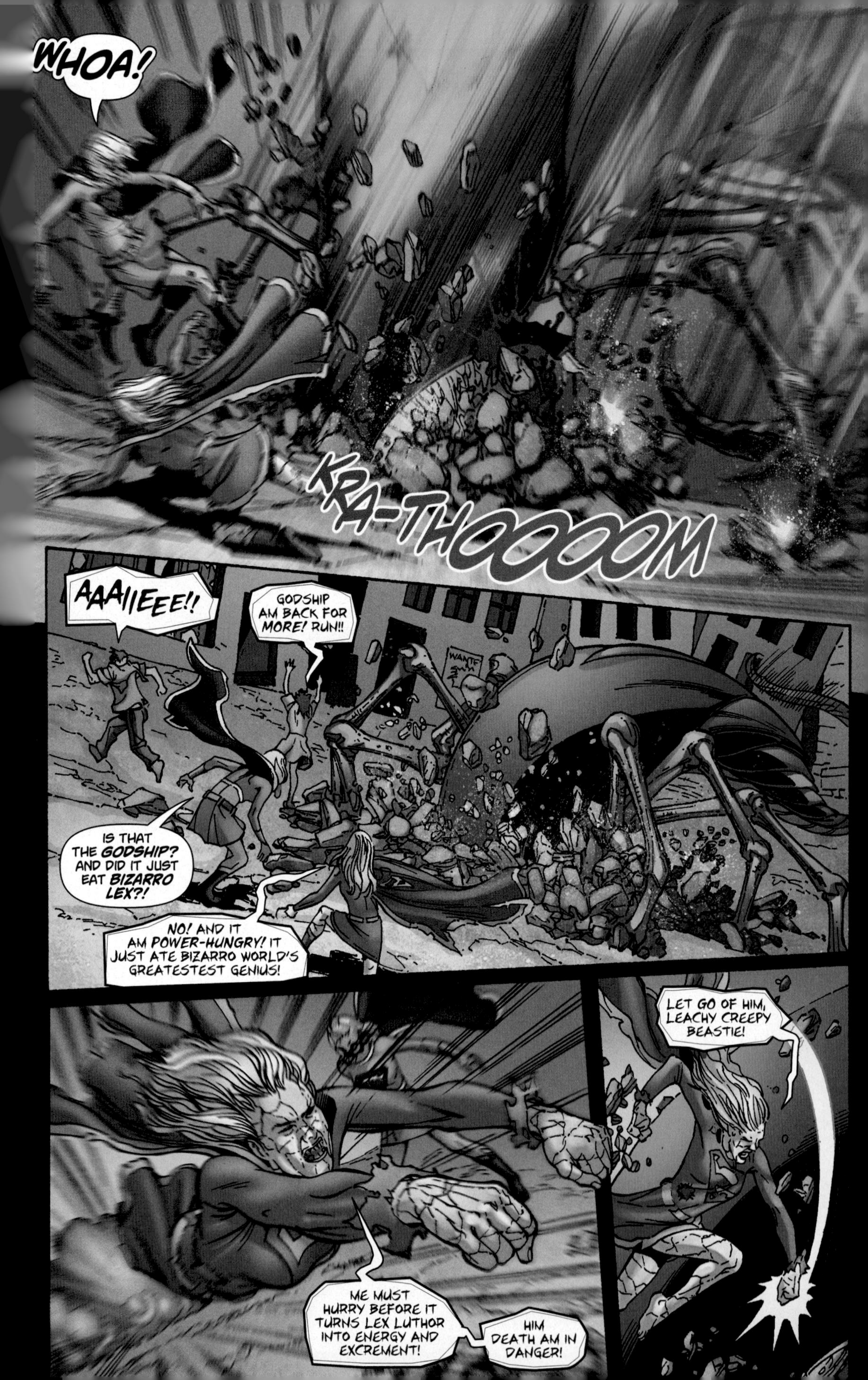
WHOA!
KRA-THOOOOOM
AAAIIEEE!!
GODSHIP AM BACK FOR MORE! RUN!!
IS THAT THE GODSHIP? AND DID IT JUST EAT BIZARRO LEX?!
NO! AND IT AM POWER-HUNGRY! IT JUST ATE BIZARRO WORLD'S GREATESTEST GENIUS!
LET GO OF HIM, LEACHY CREEPY BEASTIE!
ME MUST HURRY BEFORE IT TURNS LEX LUTHOR INTO ENERGY AND EXCREMENT!
HIM DEATH AM IN DANGER!

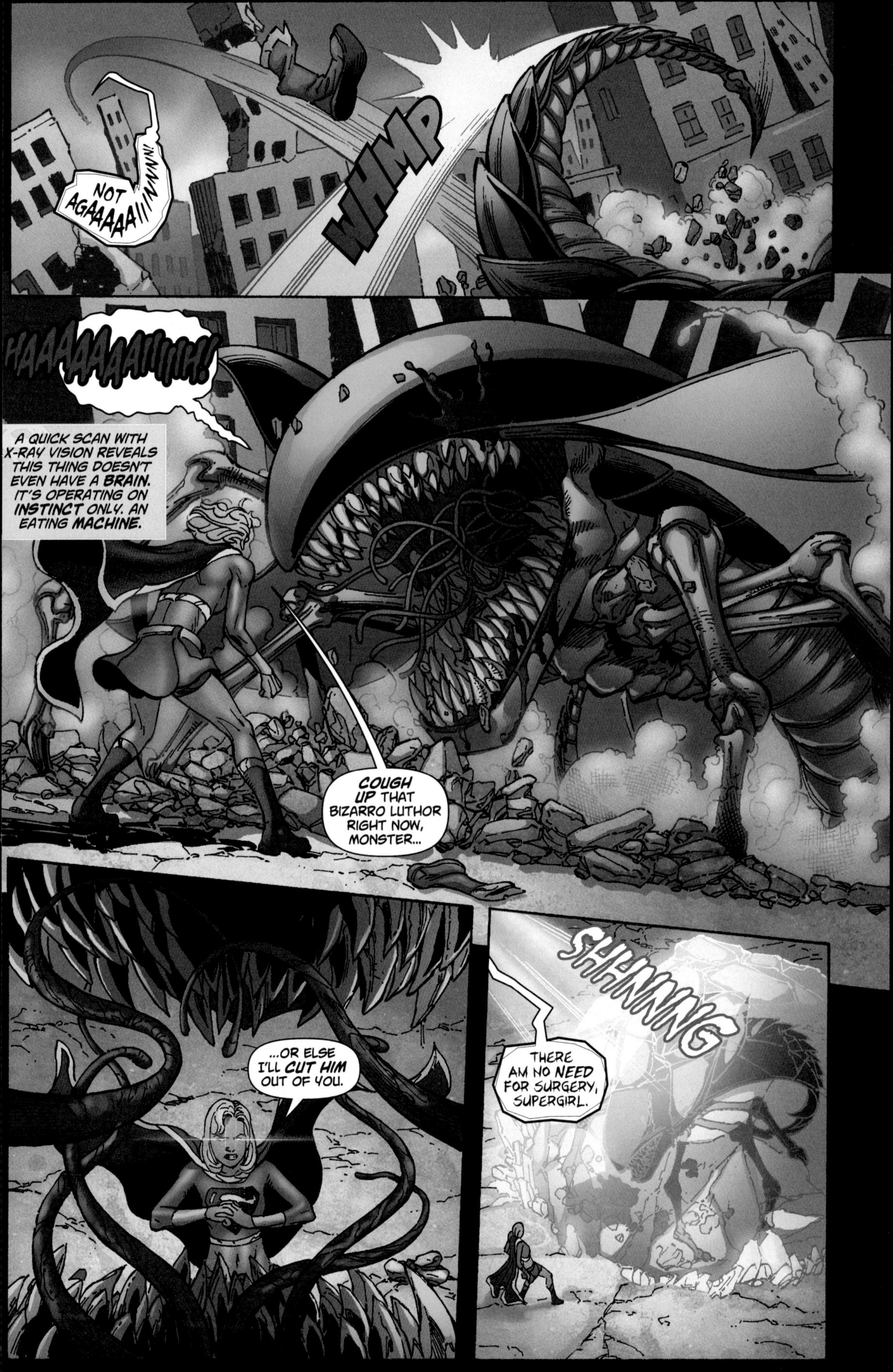
NOT AGAAAAA!!NNNN!
WHMP
HAAAAAAAIIIIIH!
A QUICK SCAN WITH X-RAY VISION REVEALS THIS THING DOESN'T EVEN HAVE A **BRAIN**. IT'S OPERATING ON **INSTINCT** ONLY. AN EATING **MACHINE**.
COUGH UP THAT BIZARRO LUTHOR RIGHT NOW, MONSTER...
...OR ELSE I'LL ***CUT HIM*** OUT OF YOU.
SHHNNNNG
THERE AM NO ***NEED*** FOR SURGERY, SUPERGIRL.

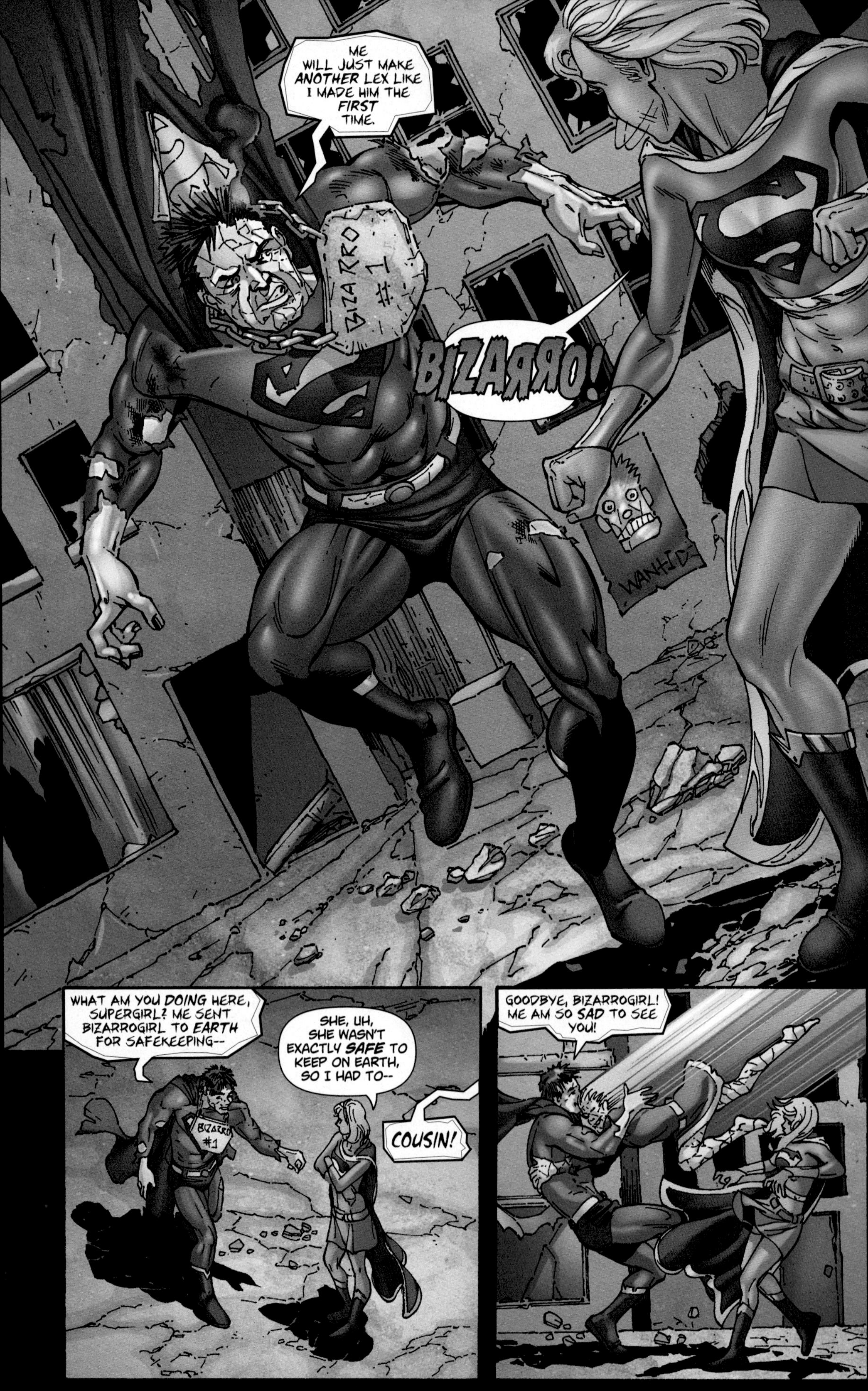
ME WILL JUST MAKE ANOTHER LEX LIKE I MADE HIM THE FIRST TIME.
BIZARRO #1
BIZARRO!
WANTID
WHAT AM YOU DOING HERE, SUPERGIRL? ME SENT BIZARROGIRL TO EARTH FOR SAFEKEEPING--
BIZARRO #1
SHE, UH, SHE WASN'T EXACTLY SAFE TO KEEP ON EARTH, SO I HAD TO--
COUSIN!
GOODBYE, BIZARROGIRL! ME AM SO SAD TO SEE YOU!

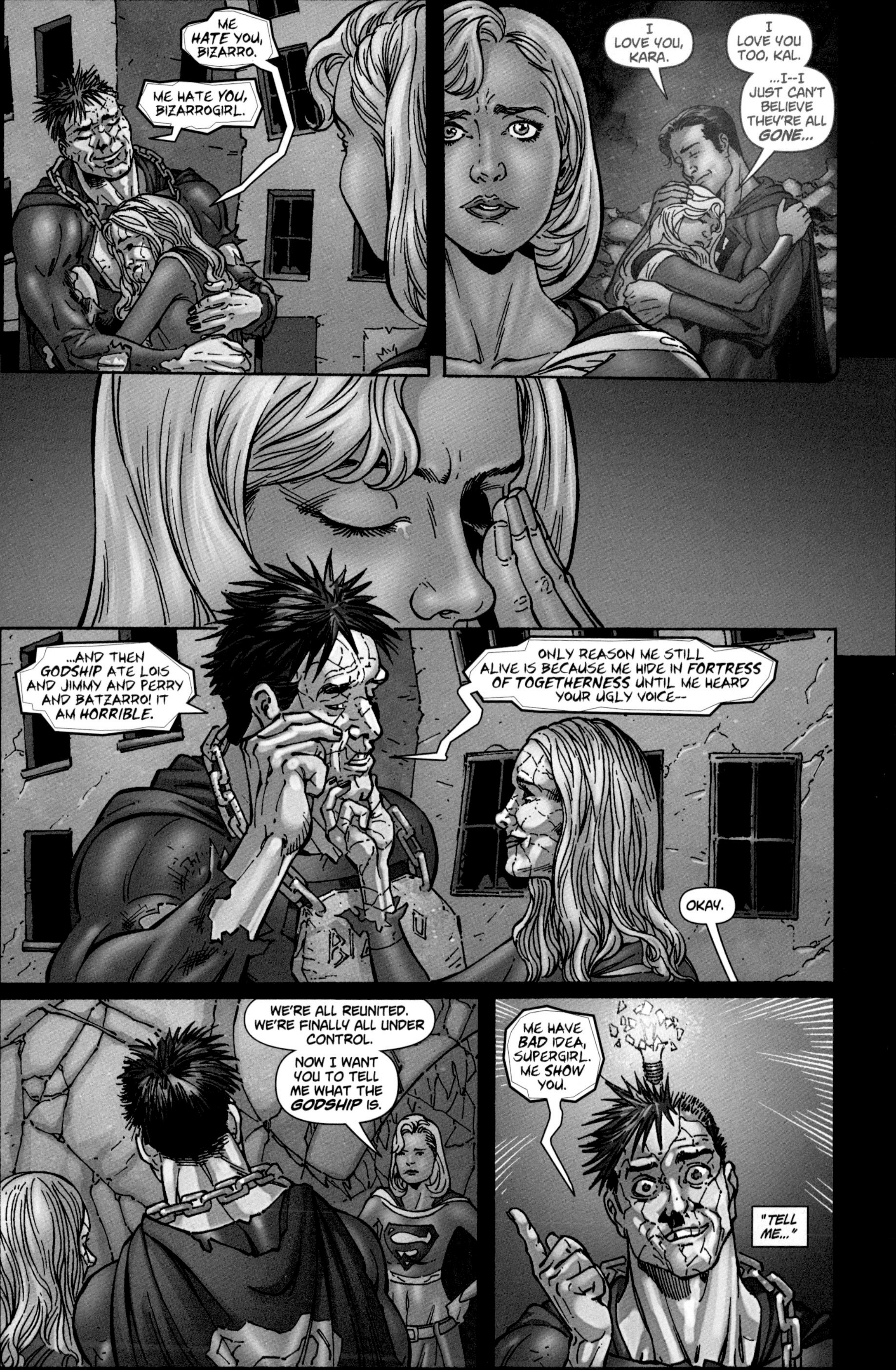

ME HATE YOU, BIZARRO.
ME HATE YOU, BIZARROGIRL.
I LOVE YOU, KARA.
I LOVE YOU TOO, KAL.
...I--I JUST CAN'T BELIEVE THEY'RE ALL GONE...
...AND THEN GODSHIP ATE LOIS AND JIMMY AND PERRY AND BATZARRO! IT AM HORRIBLE.
ONLY REASON ME STILL ALIVE IS BECAUSE ME HIDE IN FORTRESS OF TOGETHERNESS UNTIL ME HEARD YOUR UGLY VOICE--
OKAY.
WE'RE ALL REUNITED. WE'RE FINALLY ALL UNDER CONTROL.
NOW I WANT YOU TO TELL ME WHAT THE GODSHIP IS.
ME HAVE BAD IDEA, SUPERGIRL. ME SHOW YOU.
"TELL ME..."

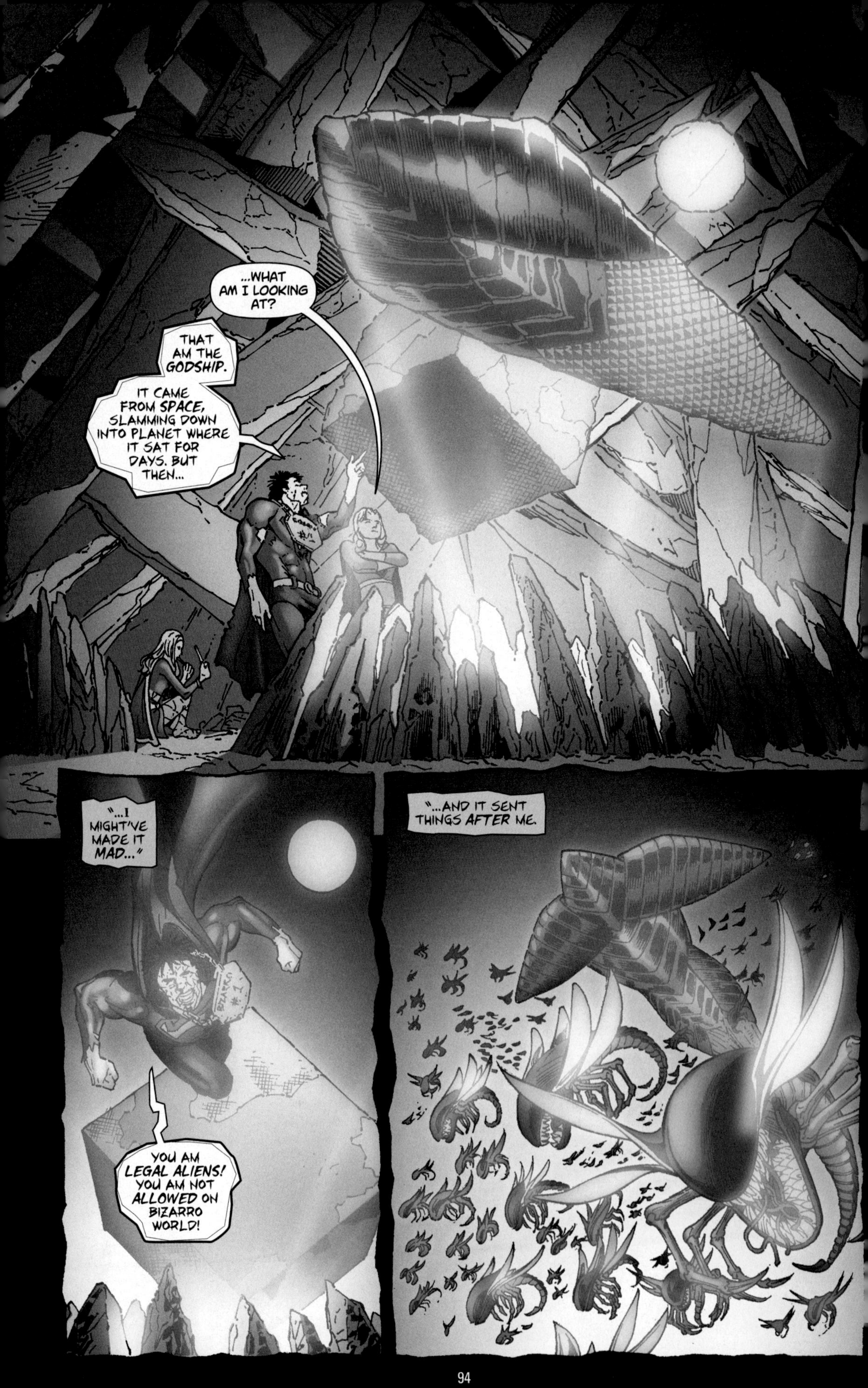
...WHAT AM I LOOKING AT?
THAT AM THE GODSHIP.
IT CAME FROM SPACE, SLAMMING DOWN INTO PLANET WHERE IT SAT FOR DAYS. BUT THEN...
"...I MIGHT'VE MADE IT MAD..."
YOU AM LEGAL ALIENS! YOU AM NOT ALLOWED ON BIZARRO WORLD!
"...AND IT SENT THINGS AFTER ME.

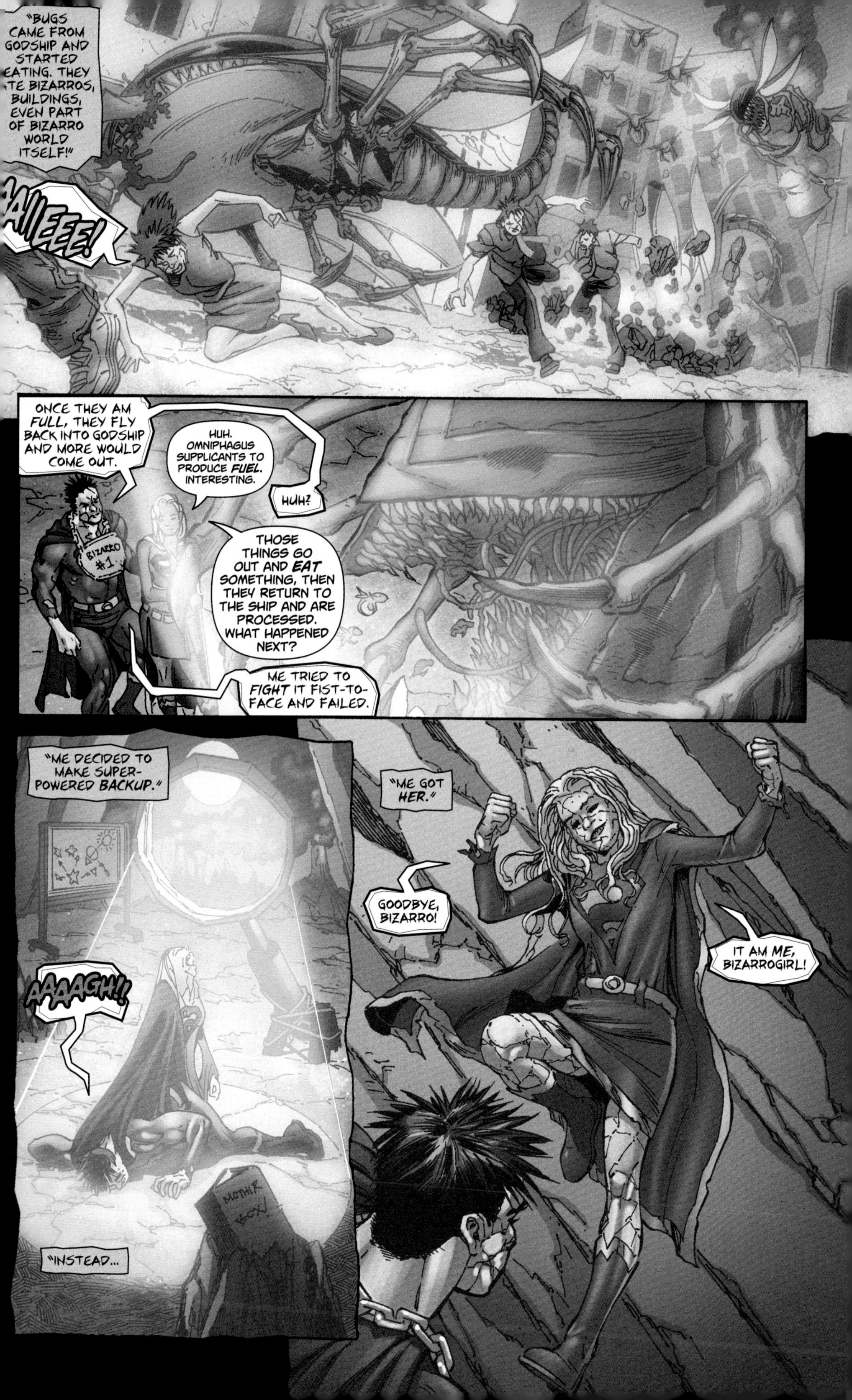
"BUGS CAME FROM GODSHIP AND STARTED EATING. THEY TE BIZARROS, BUILDINGS, EVEN PART OF BIZARRO WORLD ITSELF!"
AIIEEE!
ONCE THEY AM FULL, THEY FLY BACK INTO GODSHIP AND MORE WOULD COME OUT.
HUH. OMNIPHAGUS SUPPLICANTS TO PRODUCE FUEL. INTERESTING.
HUH?
BIZARRO #1
THOSE THINGS GO OUT AND EAT SOMETHING, THEN THEY RETURN TO THE SHIP AND ARE PROCESSED. WHAT HAPPENED NEXT?
ME TRIED TO FIGHT IT FIST-TO-FACE AND FAILED.
"ME DECIDED TO MAKE SUPER-POWERED BACKUP."
AAAAGH!!
MOTHIR BOX!
"INSTEAD...
"ME GOT HER."
GOODBYE, BIZARRO!
IT AM ME, BIZARROGIRL!

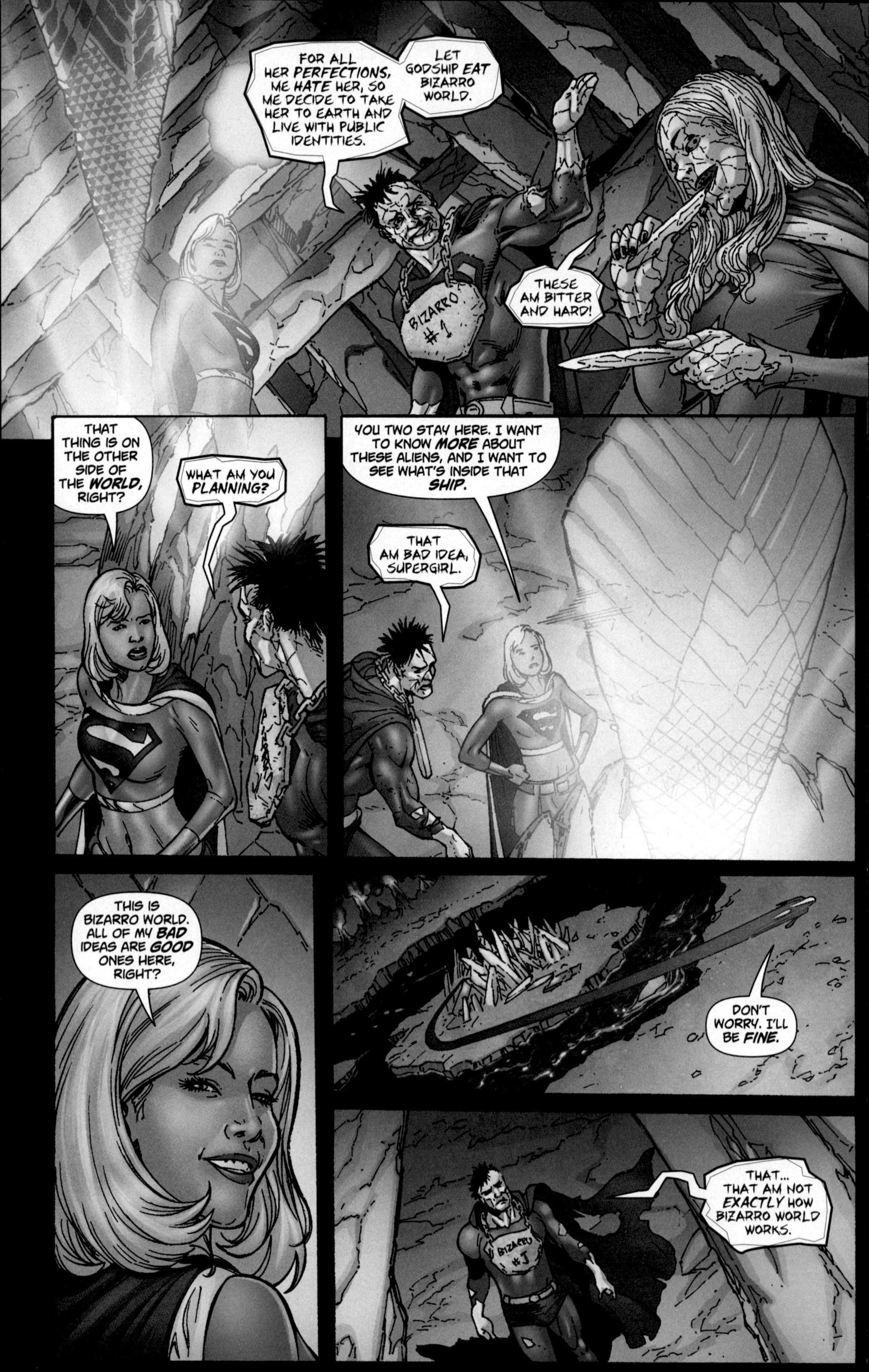

FOR ALL HER PERFECTIONS, ME HATE HER, SO ME DECIDE TO TAKE HER TO EARTH AND LIVE WITH PUBLIC IDENTITIES.
LET GODSHIP EAT BIZARRO WORLD.
THESE AM BITTER AND HARD!
BIZARRO #1
THAT THING IS ON THE OTHER SIDE OF THE WORLD, RIGHT?
WHAT AM YOU PLANNING?
YOU TWO STAY HERE. I WANT TO KNOW MORE ABOUT THESE ALIENS, AND I WANT TO SEE WHAT'S INSIDE THAT SHIP.
THAT AM BAD IDEA, SUPERGIRL.
THIS IS BIZARRO WORLD. ALL OF MY BAD IDEAS ARE GOOD ONES HERE, RIGHT?
DON'T WORRY. I'LL BE FINE.
THAT... THAT AM NOT EXACTLY HOW BIZARRO WORLD WORKS.

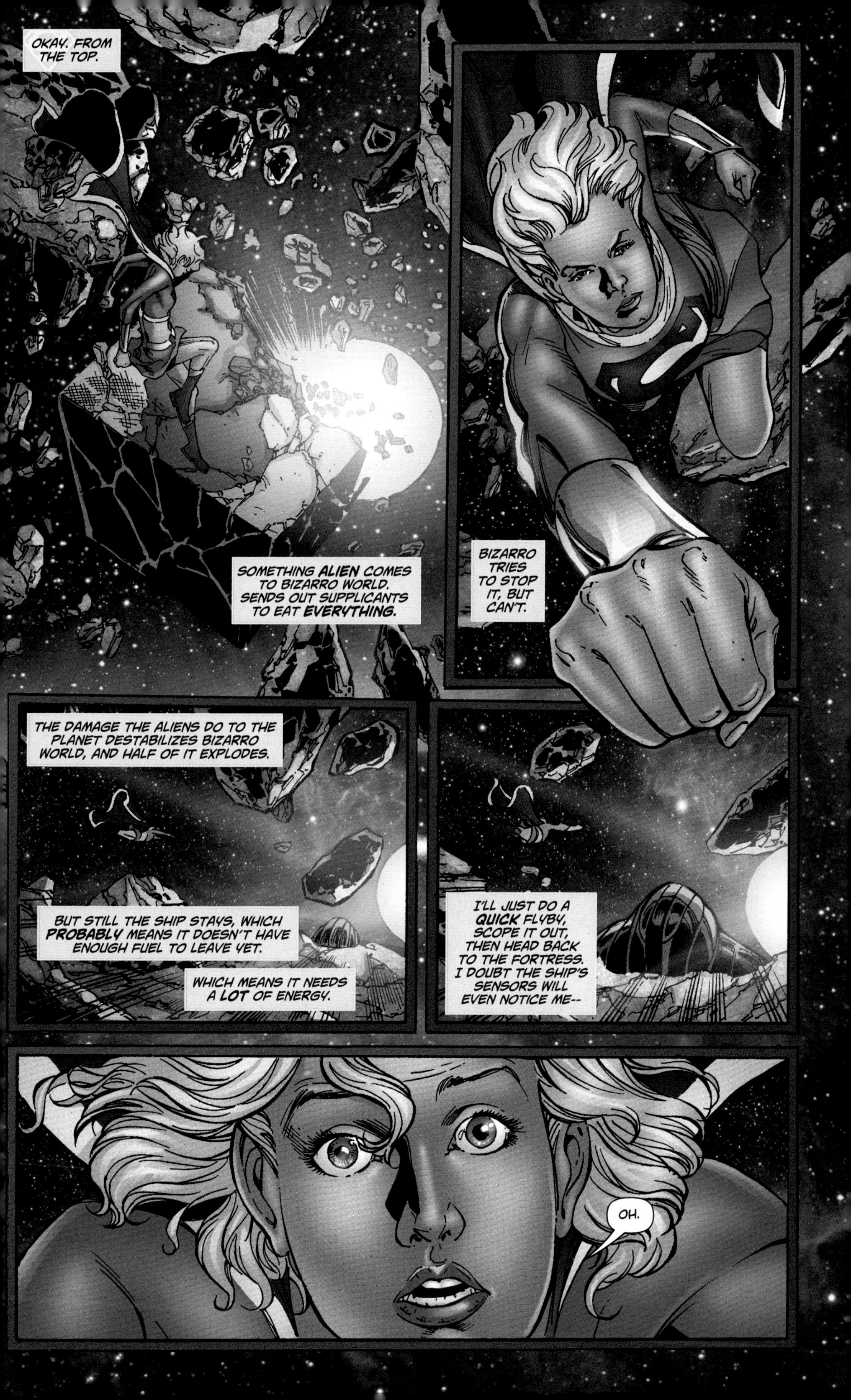

OKAY. FROM THE TOP.
SOMETHING ALIEN COMES TO BIZARRO WORLD. SENDS OUT SUPPLICANTS TO EAT EVERYTHING.
BIZARRO TRIES TO STOP IT, BUT CAN'T.
THE DAMAGE THE ALIENS DO TO THE PLANET DESTABILIZES BIZARRO WORLD, AND HALF OF IT EXPLODES.
BUT STILL THE SHIP STAYS, WHICH PROBABLY MEANS IT DOESN'T HAVE ENOUGH FUEL TO LEAVE YET.
WHICH MEANS IT NEEDS A LOT OF ENERGY.
I'LL JUST DO A QUICK FLYBY, SCOPE IT OUT, THEN HEAD BACK TO THE FORTRESS. I DOUBT THE SHIP'S SENSORS WILL EVEN NOTICE ME--
OH.

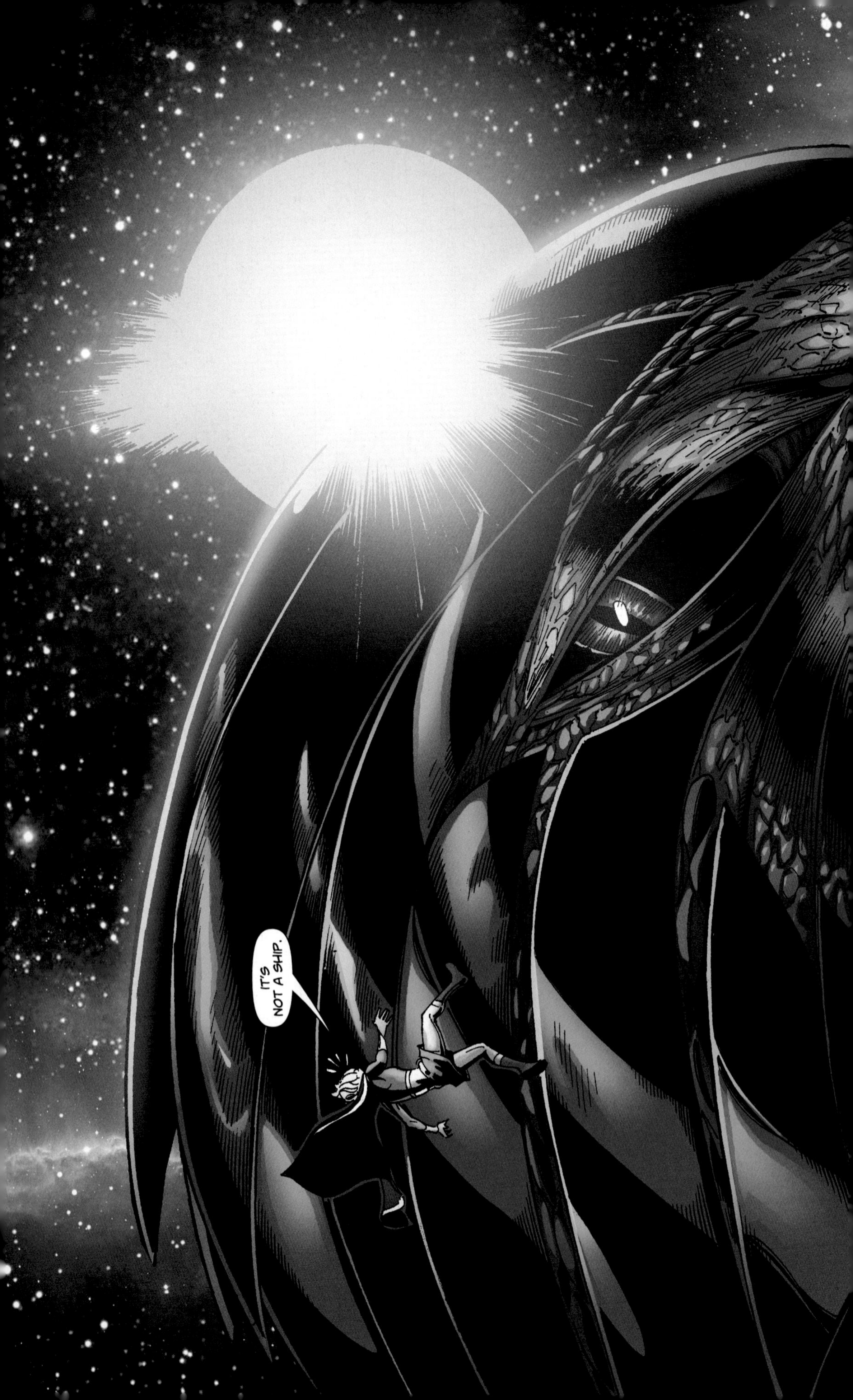
IT'S NOT A SHIP.

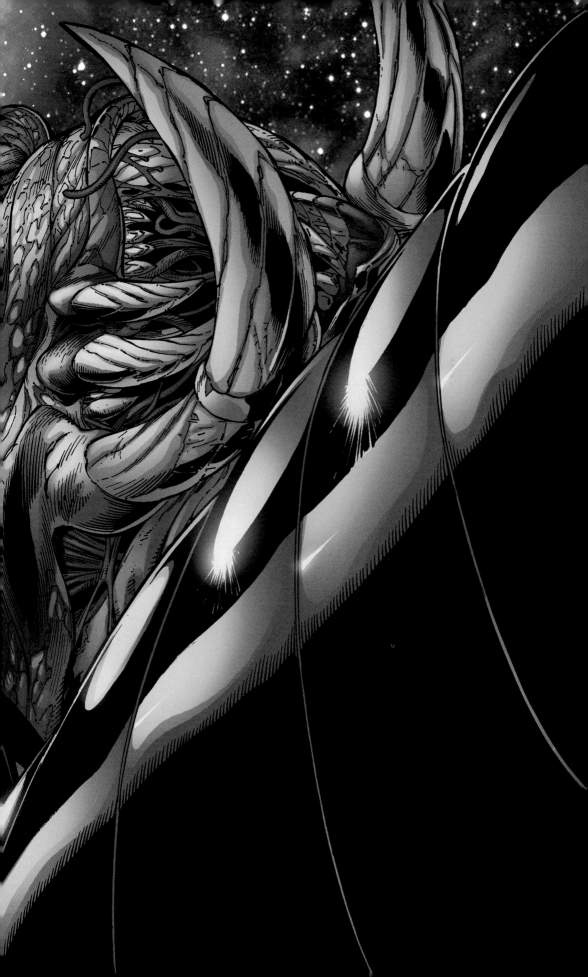

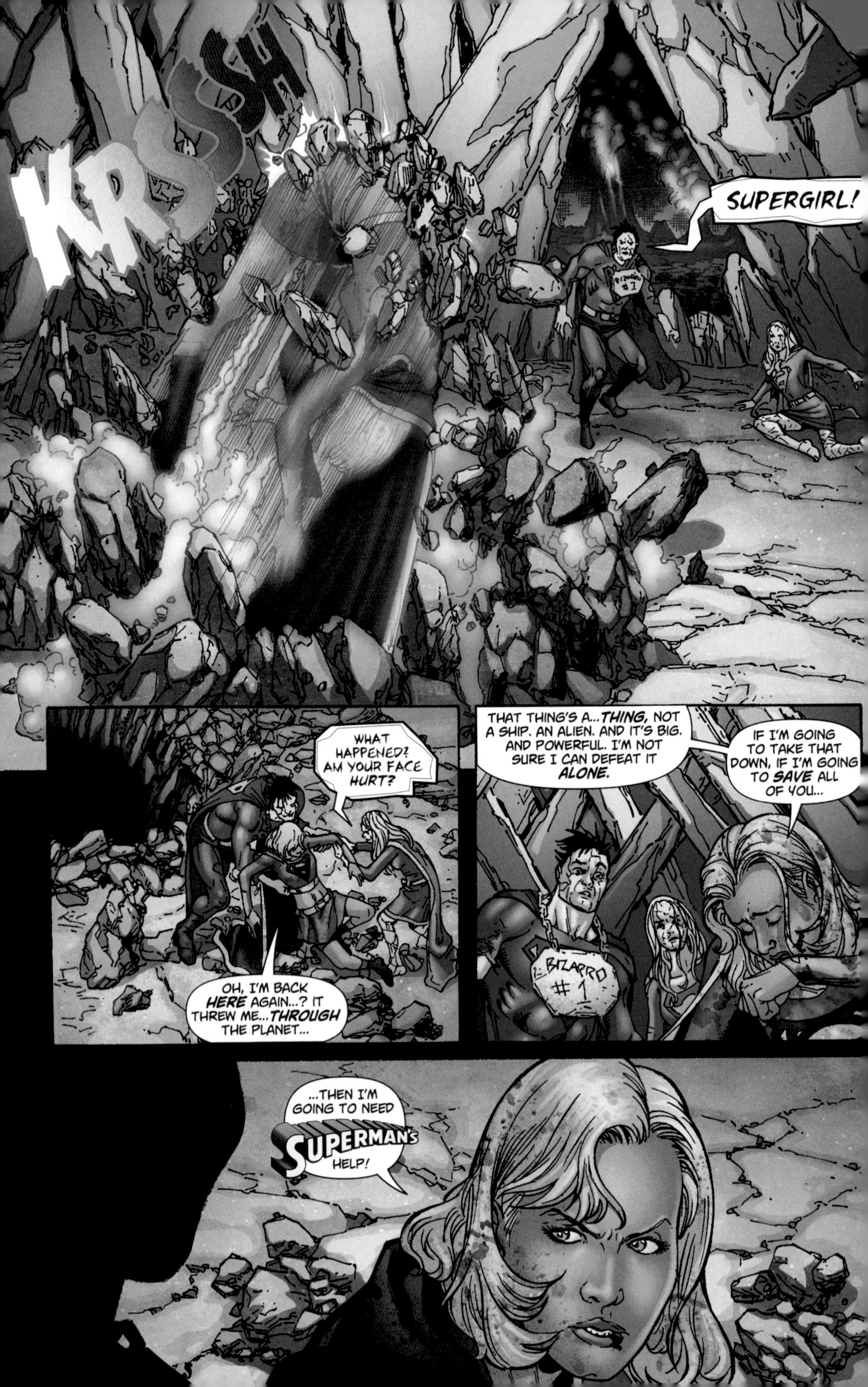
KRSSH
SUPERGIRL!
WHAT HAPPENED? AM YOUR FACE HURT?
OH, I'M BACK HERE AGAIN...? IT THREW ME...THROUGH THE PLANET...
THAT THING'S A...THING, NOT A SHIP. AN ALIEN. AND IT'S BIG. AND POWERFUL. I'M NOT SURE I CAN DEFEAT IT ALONE.
IF I'M GOING TO TAKE THAT DOWN, IF I'M GOING TO SAVE ALL OF YOU...
...THEN I'M GOING TO NEED SUPERMAN'S HELP!

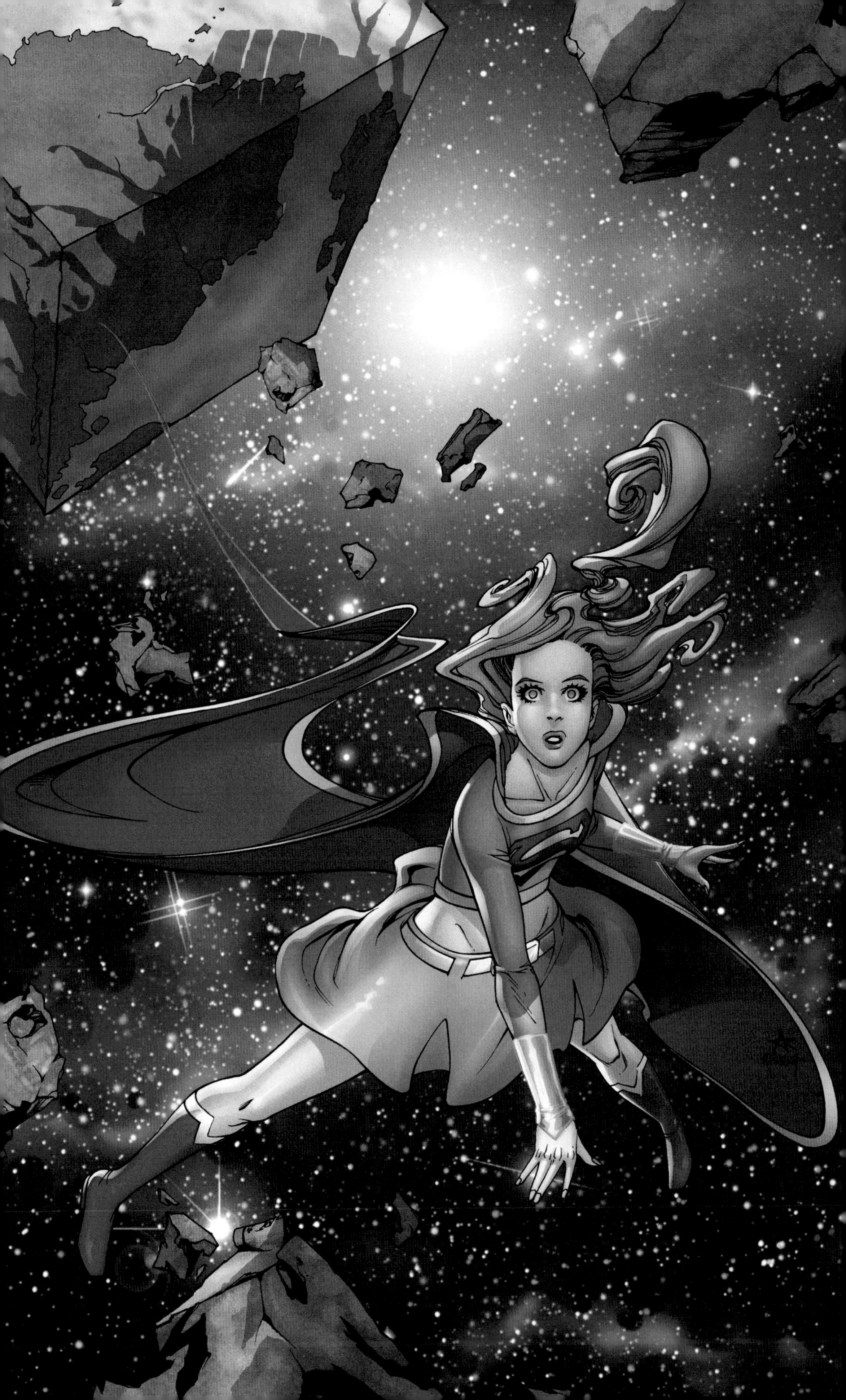

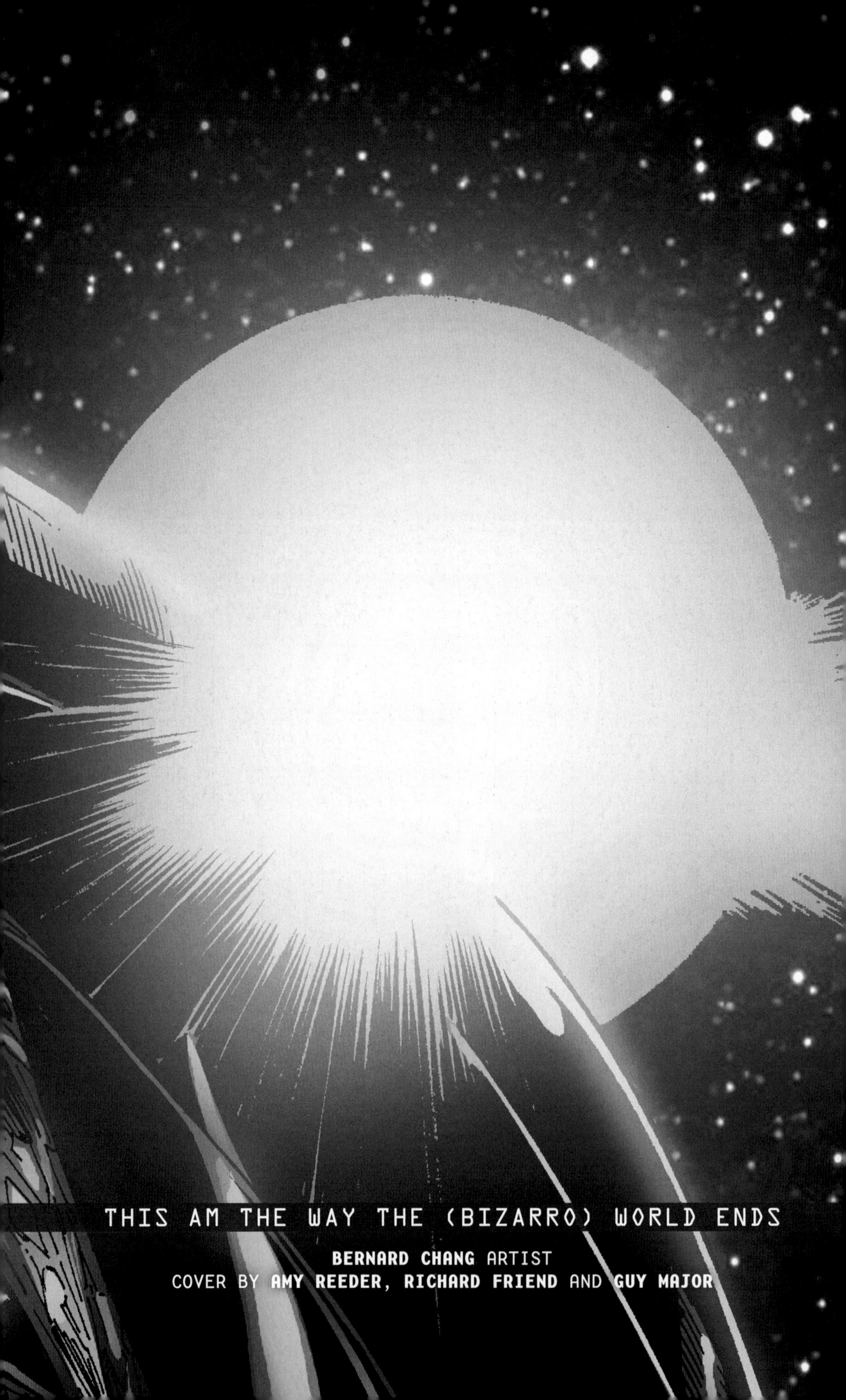

THIS AM THE WAY THE (BIZARRO) WORLD ENDS

BERNARD CHANG ARTIST
COVER BY **AMY REEDER, RICHARD FRIEND** AND **GUY MAJOR**

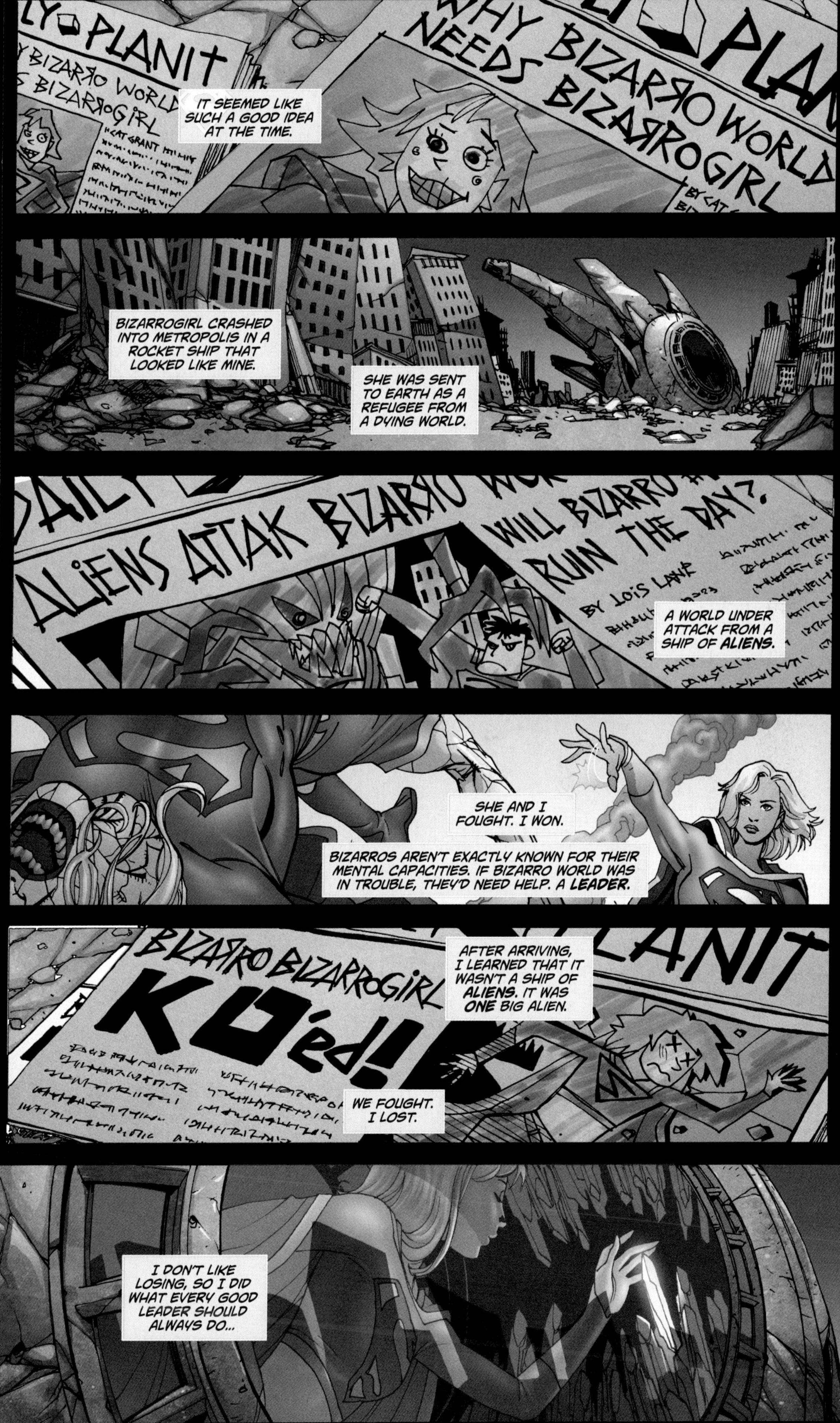
WHY BIZARRO WORLD NEEDS BIZARROGIRL
IT SEEMED LIKE SUCH A GOOD IDEA AT THE TIME.
BIZARROGIRL CRASHED INTO METROPOLIS IN A ROCKET SHIP THAT LOOKED LIKE MINE.
SHE WAS SENT TO EARTH AS A REFUGEE FROM A DYING WORLD.
RUIN THE DAY?
BY LOIS LANE
A WORLD UNDER ATTACK FROM A SHIP OF ALIENS.
SHE AND I FOUGHT. I WON.
BIZARROS AREN'T EXACTLY KNOWN FOR THEIR MENTAL CAPACITIES. IF BIZARRO WORLD WAS IN TROUBLE, THEY'D NEED HELP. A LEADER.
BIZARRO BIZARROGIRL
AFTER ARRIVING, I LEARNED THAT IT WASN'T A SHIP OF ALIENS. IT WAS ONE BIG ALIEN.
WE FOUGHT. I LOST.
I DON'T LIKE LOSING, SO I DID WHAT EVERY GOOD LEADER SHOULD ALWAYS DO...

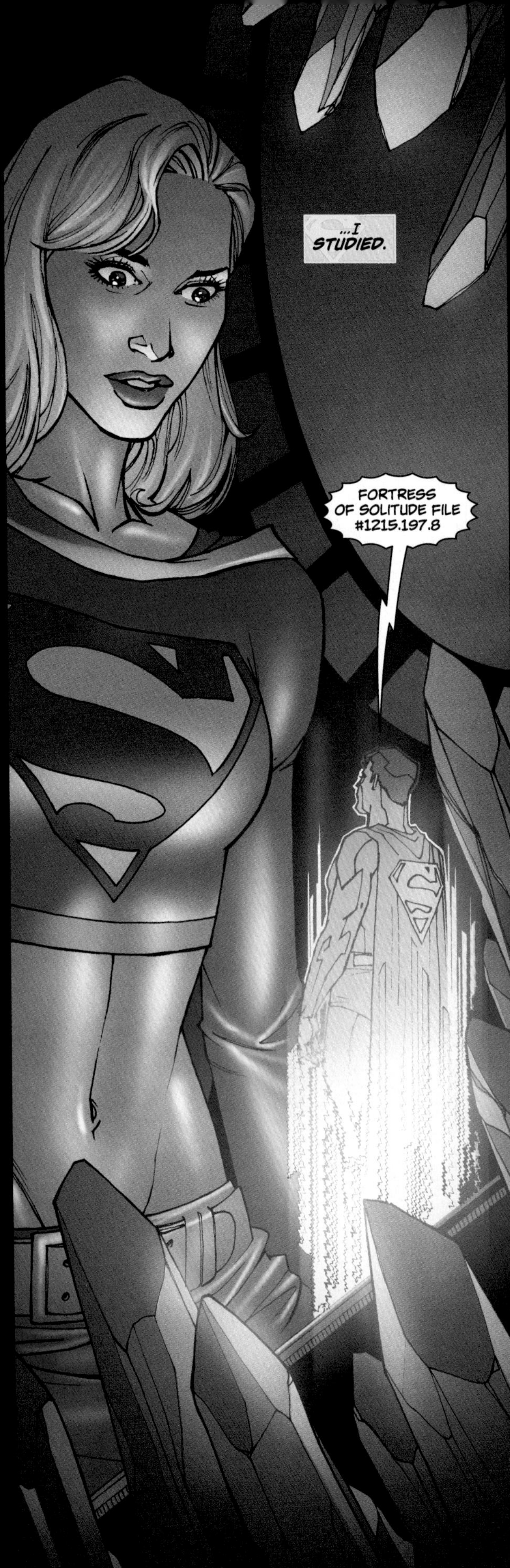
...I STUDIED.
FORTRESS OF SOLITUDE FILE #1215.197.8

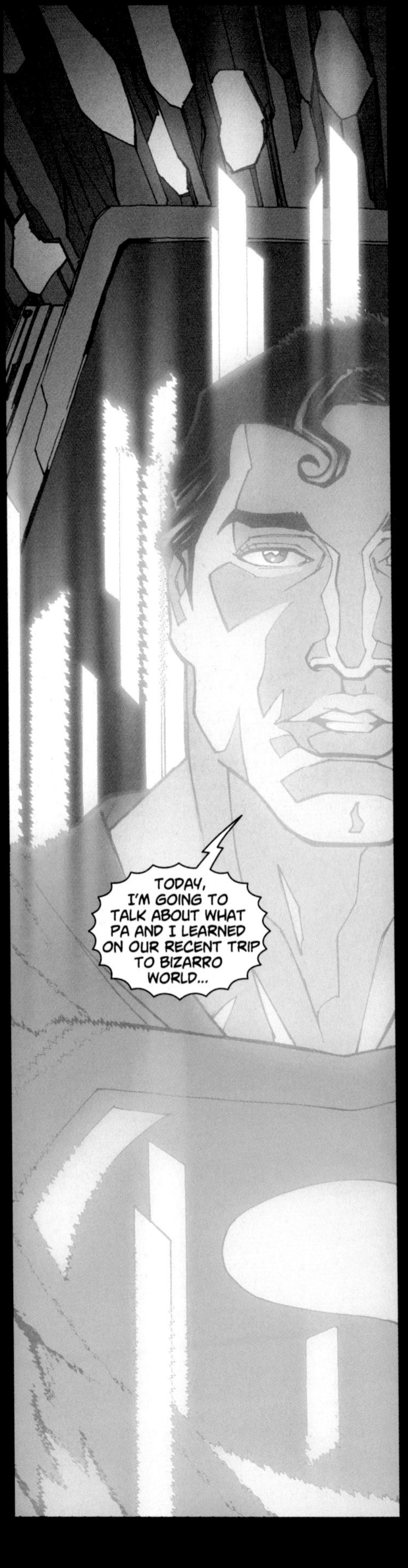
TODAY, I'M GOING TO TALK ABOUT WHAT PA AND I LEARNED ON OUR RECENT TRIP TO BIZARRO WORLD...

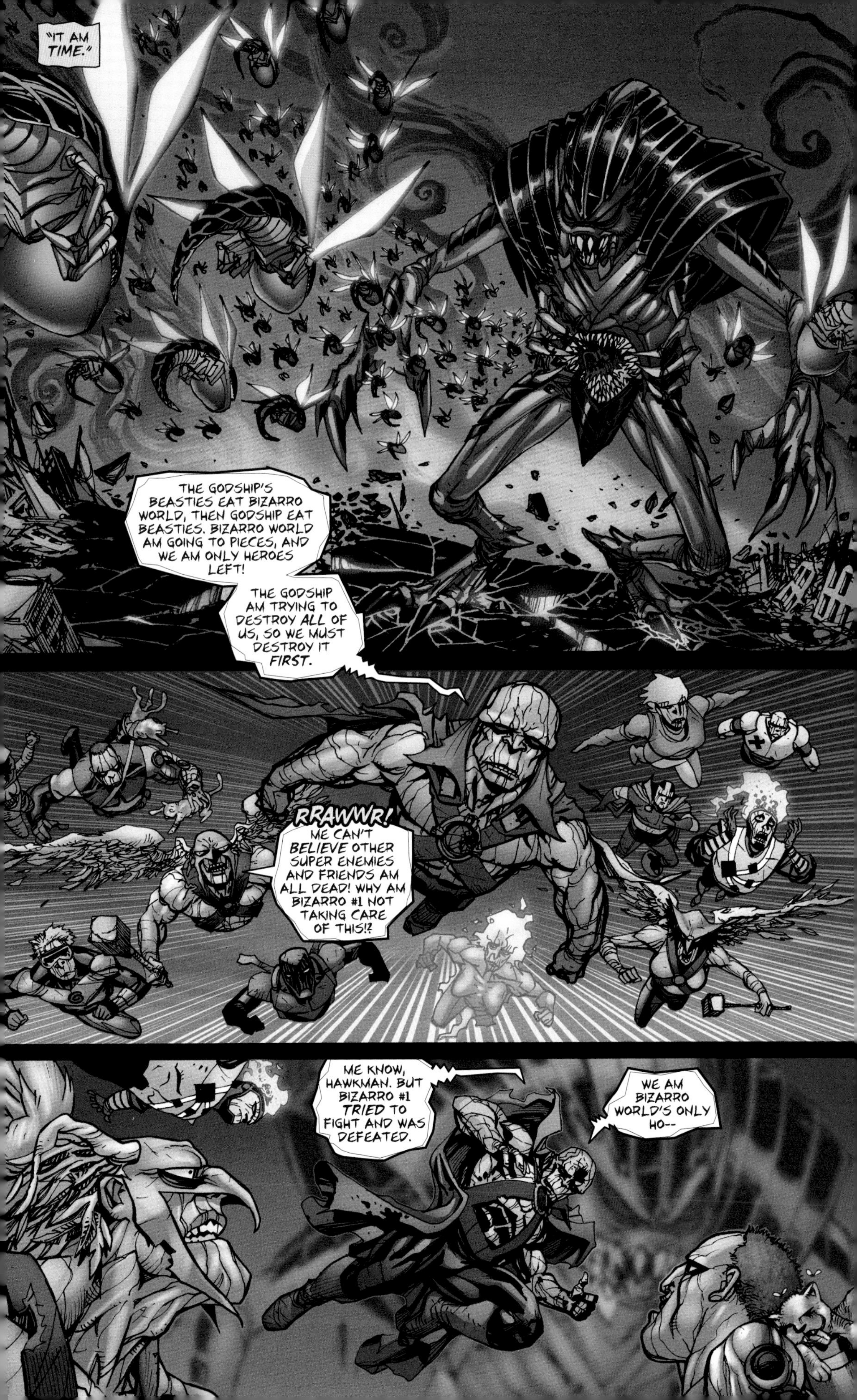
"IT AM TIME."
THE GODSHIP'S BEASTIES EAT BIZARRO WORLD, THEN GODSHIP EAT BEASTIES. BIZARRO WORLD AM GOING TO PIECES, AND WE AM ONLY HEROES LEFT!
THE GODSHIP AM TRYING TO DESTROY ALL OF US, SO WE MUST DESTROY IT FIRST.
RRAWWR!
ME CAN'T BELIEVE OTHER SUPER ENEMIES AND FRIENDS AM ALL DEAD! WHY AM BIZARRO #1 NOT TAKING CARE OF THIS!?
ME KNOW, HAWKMAN. BUT BIZARRO #1 TRIED TO FIGHT AND WAS DEFEATED.
WE AM BIZARRO WORLD'S ONLY HO--

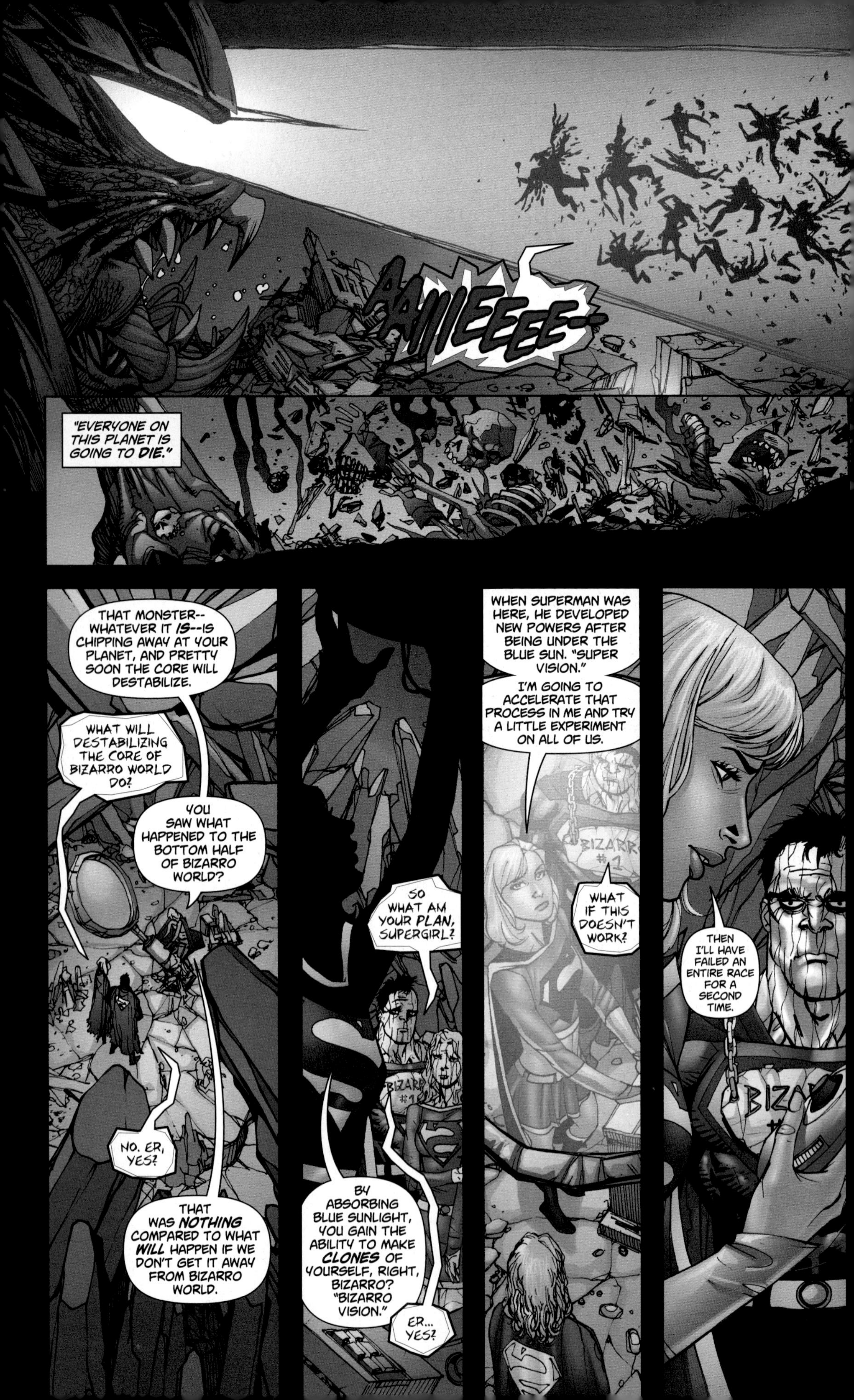
AAIIIEEEEE--
"EVERYONE ON THIS PLANET IS GOING TO DIE."
THAT MONSTER-- WHATEVER IT IS--IS CHIPPING AWAY AT YOUR PLANET, AND PRETTY SOON THE CORE WILL DESTABILIZE.
WHAT WILL DESTABILIZING THE CORE OF BIZARRO WORLD DO?
YOU SAW WHAT HAPPENED TO THE BOTTOM HALF OF BIZARRO WORLD?
NO. ER, YES?
THAT WAS NOTHING COMPARED TO WHAT WILL HAPPEN IF WE DON'T GET IT AWAY FROM BIZARRO WORLD.
SO WHAT AM YOUR PLAN, SUPERGIRL?
BY ABSORBING BLUE SUNLIGHT, YOU GAIN THE ABILITY TO MAKE CLONES OF YOURSELF, RIGHT, BIZARRO? "BIZARRO VISION."
ER... YES?
WHEN SUPERMAN WAS HERE, HE DEVELOPED NEW POWERS AFTER BEING UNDER THE BLUE SUN. "SUPER VISION."
I'M GOING TO ACCELERATE THAT PROCESS IN ME AND TRY A LITTLE EXPERIMENT ON ALL OF US.
WHAT IF THIS DOESN'T WORK?
THEN I'LL HAVE FAILED AN ENTIRE RACE FOR A SECOND TIME.

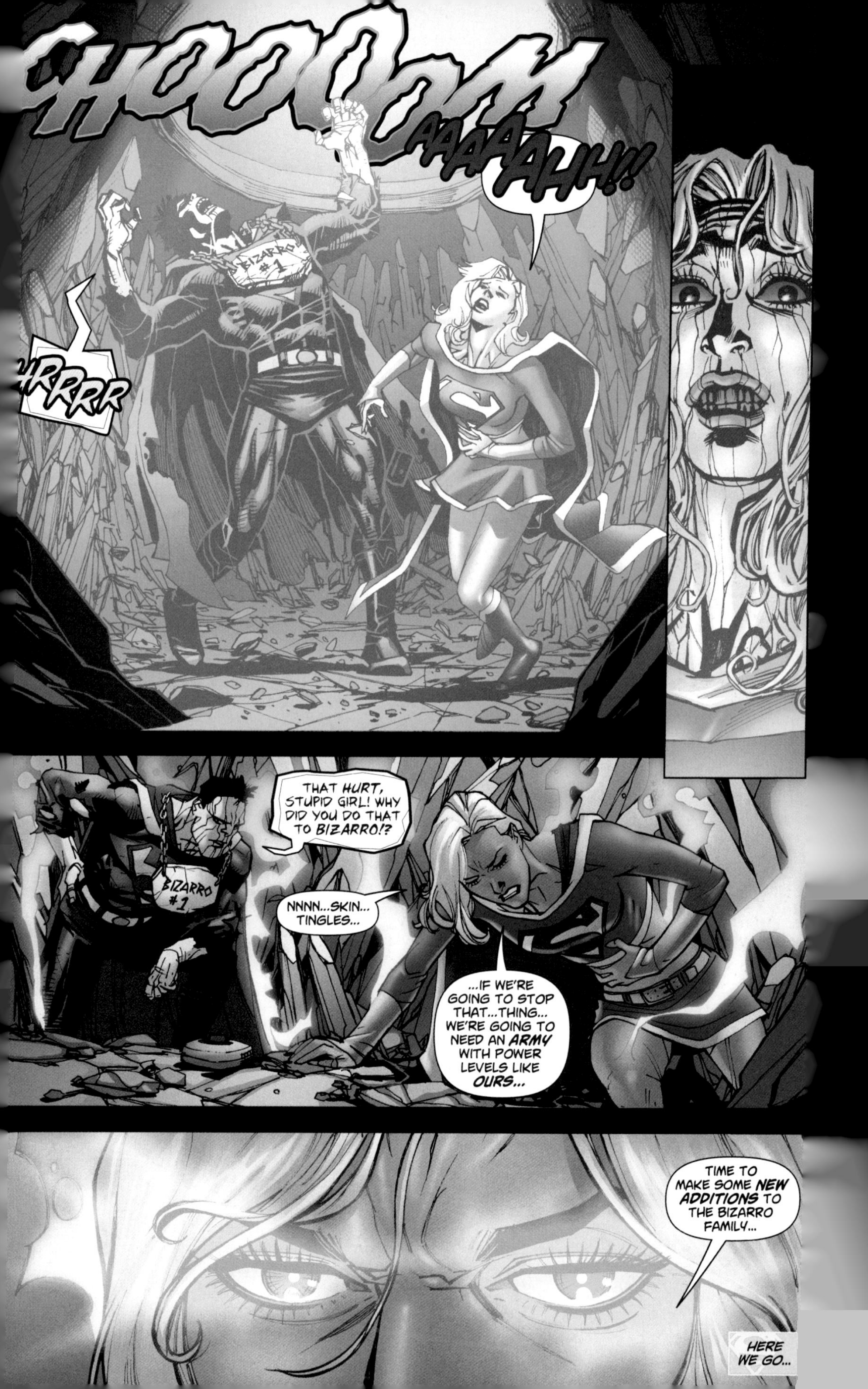
CHOOOOM
AAAAAHH!!
HRRRR
BIZARRO #1
THAT HURT, STUPID GIRL! WHY DID YOU DO THAT TO BIZARRO!?
BIZARRO #1
NNNN...SKIN... TINGLES...
...IF WE'RE GOING TO STOP THAT...THING... WE'RE GOING TO NEED AN ARMY WITH POWER LEVELS LIKE OURS...
TIME TO MAKE SOME NEW ADDITIONS TO THE BIZARRO FAMILY...
HERE WE GO...

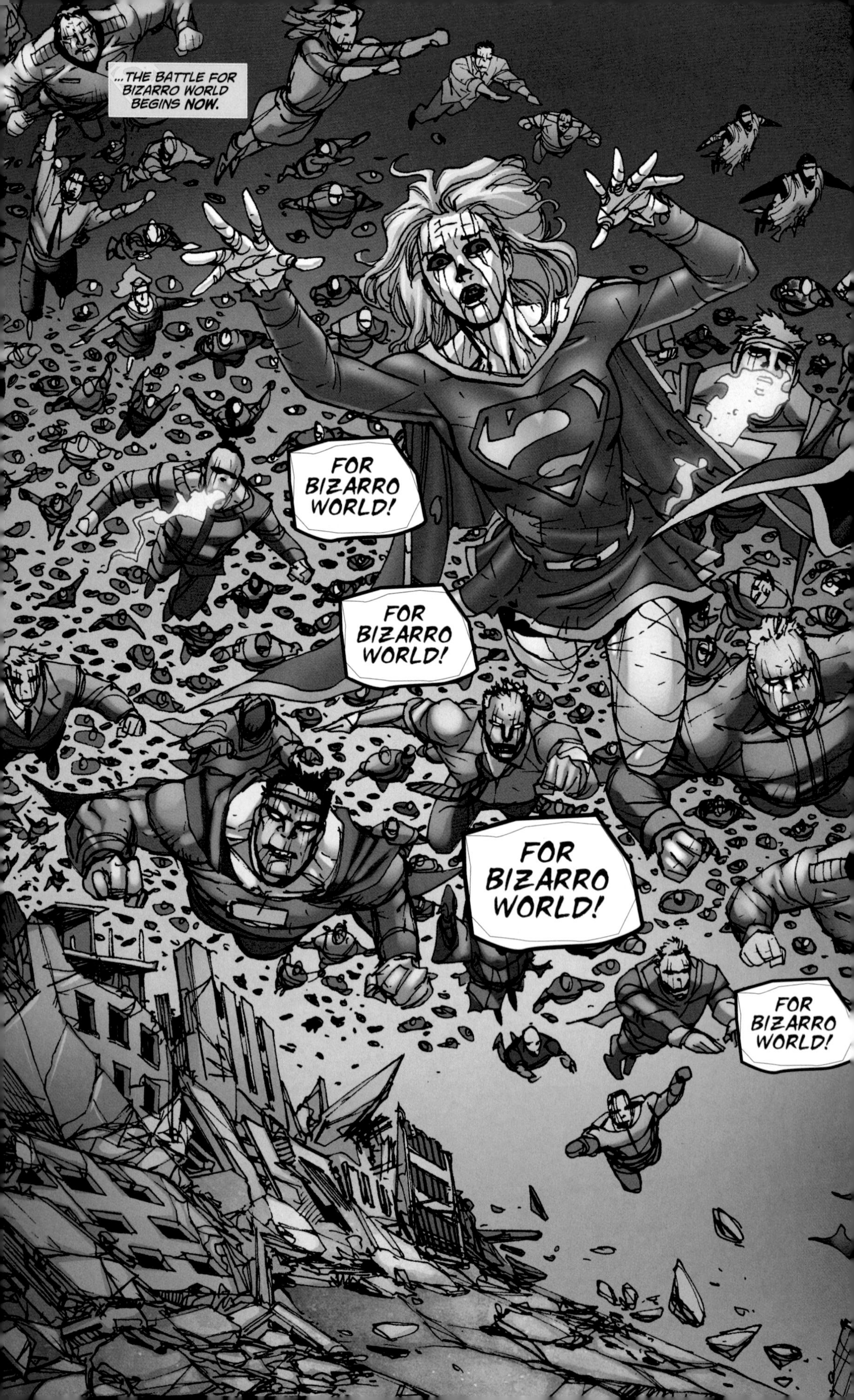
...THE BATTLE FOR BIZARRO WORLD BEGINS NOW.
FOR BIZARRO WORLD!
FOR BIZARRO WORLD!
FOR BIZARRO WORLD!
FOR BIZARRO WORLD!

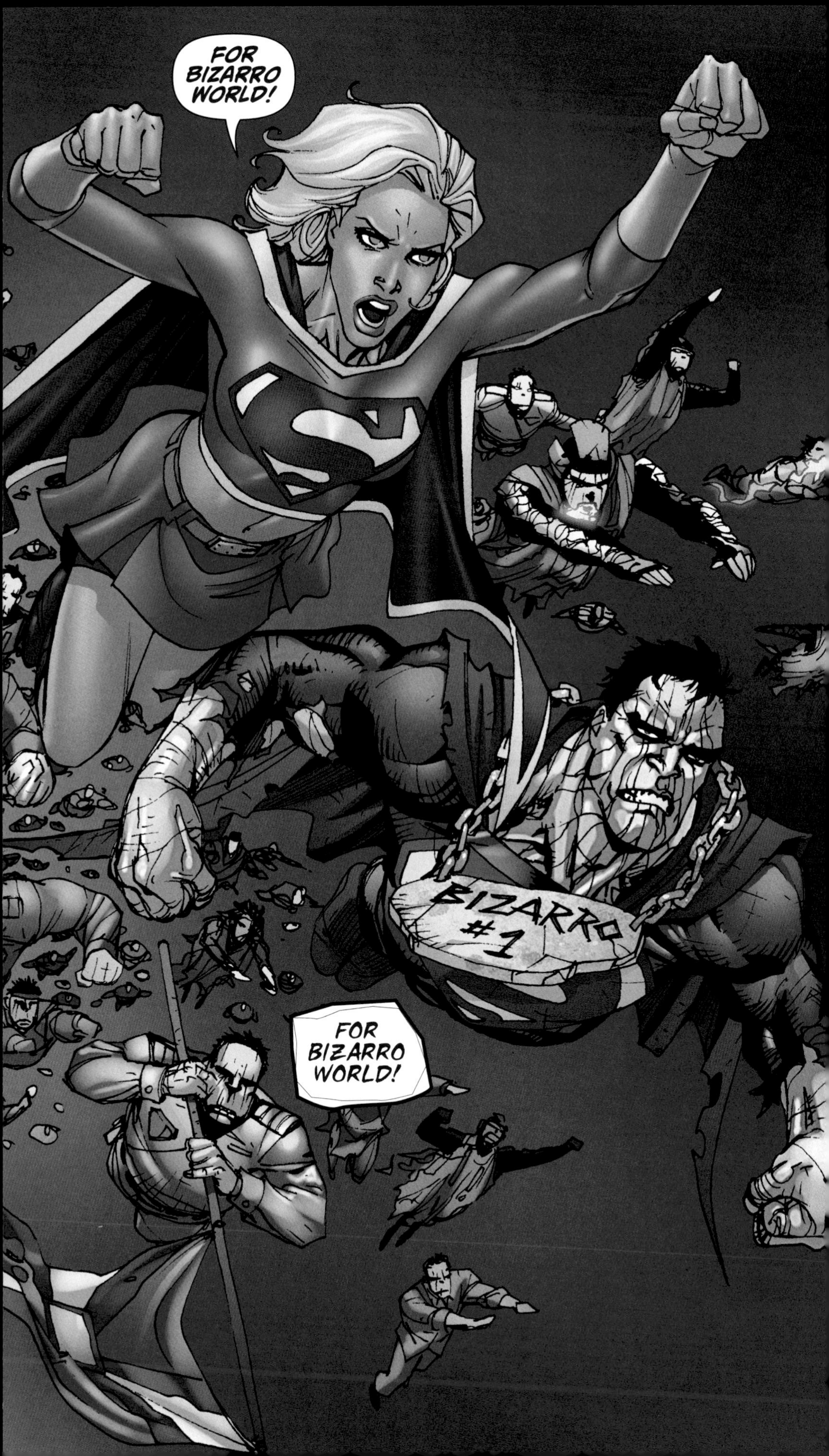
FOR BIZARRO WORLD!
BIZARRO #1
FOR BIZARRO WORLD!

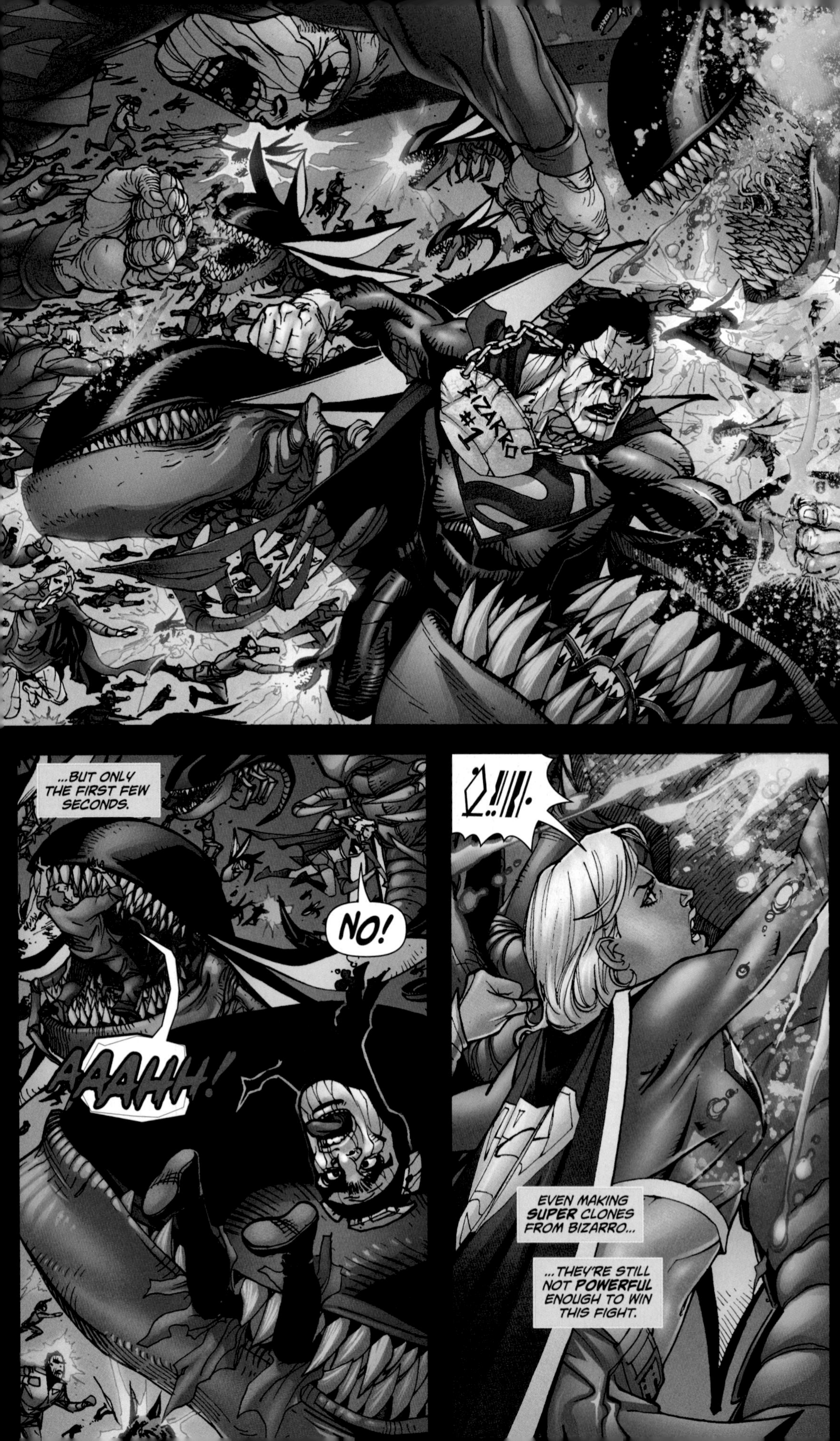
BIZARRO #1
...BUT ONLY THE FIRST FEW SECONDS.
NO!
AAAHH!
EVEN MAKING **SUPER** CLONES FROM BIZARRO...
...THEY'RE STILL NOT **POWERFUL** ENOUGH TO WIN THIS FIGHT.

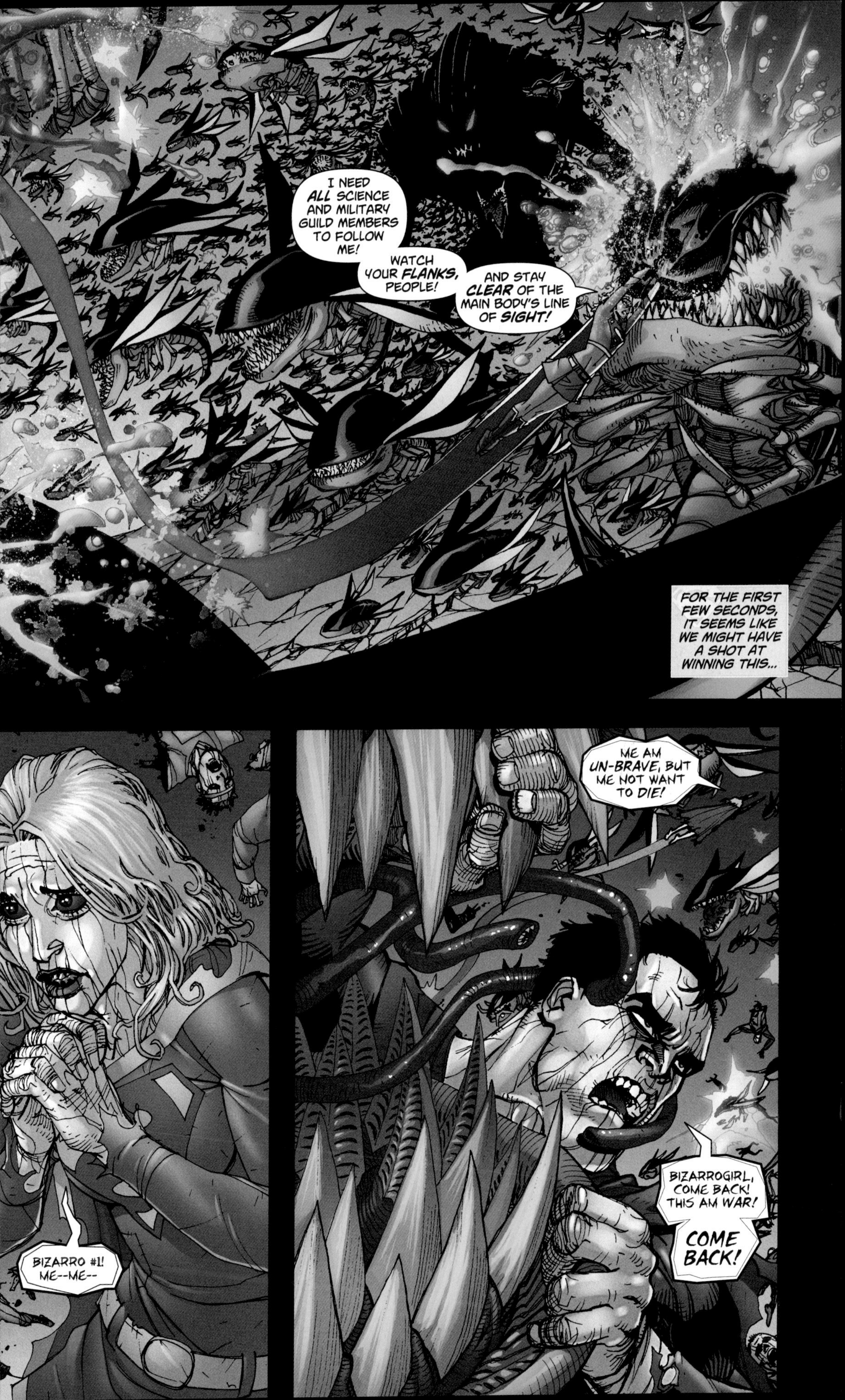
I NEED ALL SCIENCE AND MILITARY GUILD MEMBERS TO FOLLOW ME!
WATCH YOUR FLANKS, PEOPLE!
AND STAY CLEAR OF THE MAIN BODY'S LINE OF SIGHT!
FOR THE FIRST FEW SECONDS, IT SEEMS LIKE WE MIGHT HAVE A SHOT AT WINNING THIS...
BIZARRO #1! ME--ME--
ME AM UN-BRAVE, BUT ME NOT WANT TO DIE!
BIZARROGIRL, COME BACK! THIS AM WAR!
COME BACK!

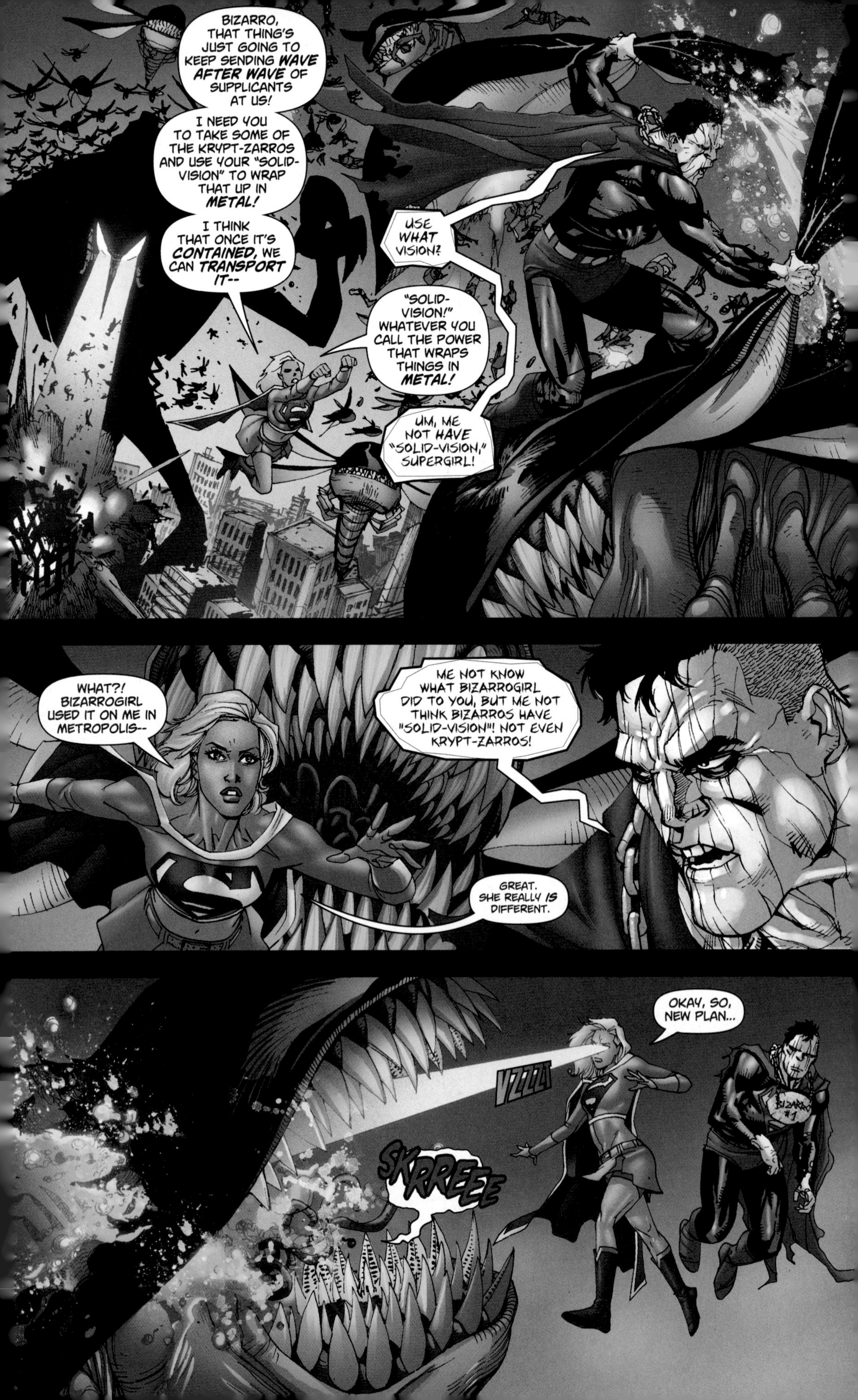
BIZARRO, THAT THING'S JUST GOING TO KEEP SENDING WAVE AFTER WAVE OF SUPPLICANTS AT US!
I NEED YOU TO TAKE SOME OF THE KRYPT-ZARROS AND USE YOUR "SOLID-VISION" TO WRAP THAT UP IN METAL!
I THINK THAT ONCE IT'S CONTAINED, WE CAN TRANSPORT IT--
USE WHAT VISION?
"SOLID-VISION!" WHATEVER YOU CALL THE POWER THAT WRAPS THINGS IN METAL!
UM, ME NOT HAVE "SOLID-VISION," SUPERGIRL!
WHAT?! BIZARROGIRL USED IT ON ME IN METROPOLIS--
ME NOT KNOW WHAT BIZARROGIRL DID TO YOU, BUT ME NOT THINK BIZARROS HAVE "SOLID-VISION"! NOT EVEN KRYPT-ZARROS!
GREAT. SHE REALLY IS DIFFERENT.
OKAY, SO, NEW PLAN...
VZZZT
SKRREEEE
BIZARRO #1

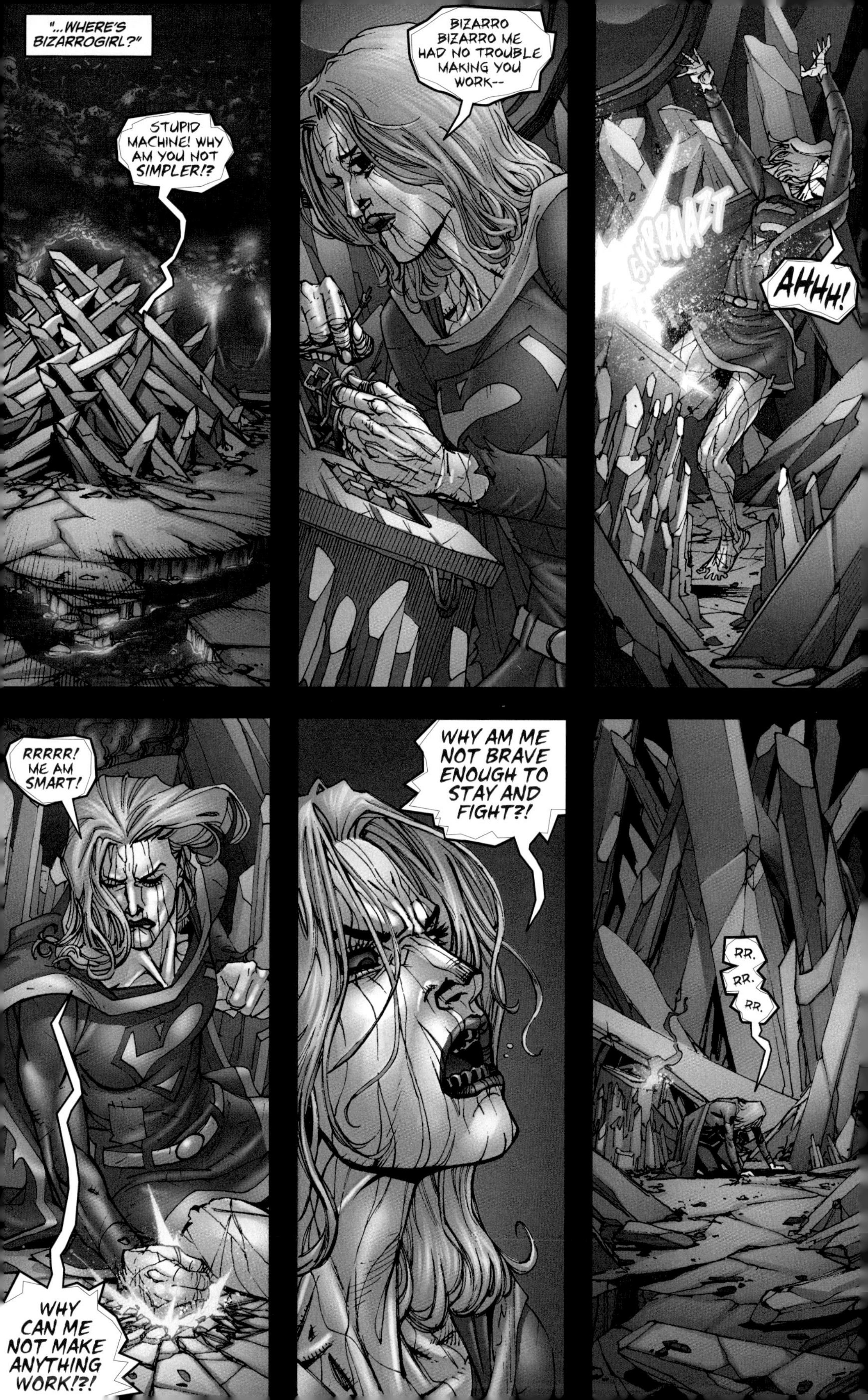
"...WHERE'S BIZARROGIRL?"
STUPID MACHINE! WHY AM YOU NOT SIMPLER!?
BIZARRO BIZARRO ME HAD NO TROUBLE MAKING YOU WORK--
SKRRAAZT
AHHH!
RRRRR! ME AM SMART!
WHY CAN ME NOT MAKE ANYTHING WORK!?!
WHY AM ME NOT BRAVE ENOUGH TO STAY AND FIGHT?!
RR.
RR.
RR.

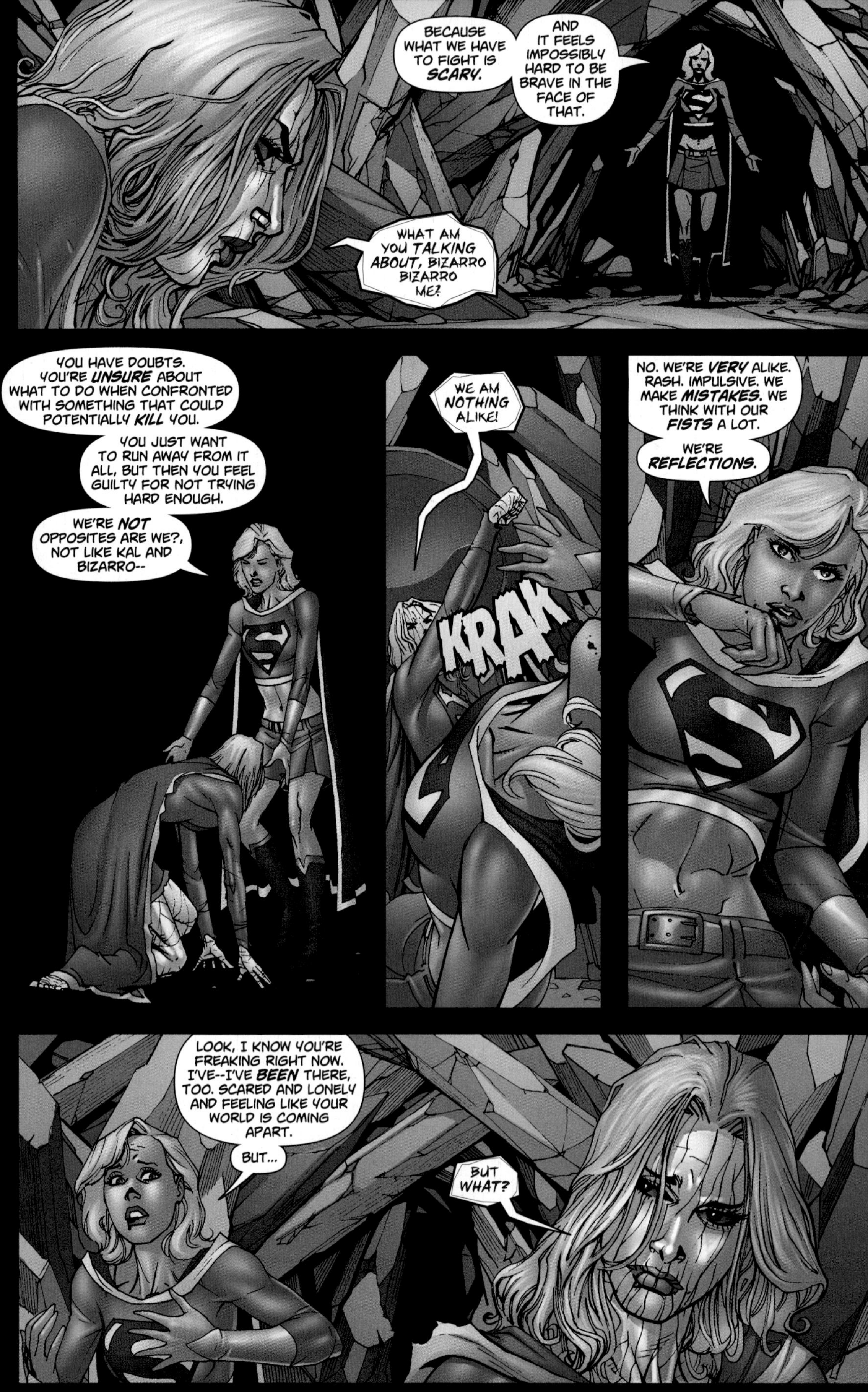
BECAUSE WHAT WE HAVE TO FIGHT IS SCARY.
AND IT FEELS IMPOSSIBLY HARD TO BE BRAVE IN THE FACE OF THAT.
WHAT AM YOU TALKING ABOUT, BIZARRO BIZARRO ME?
YOU HAVE DOUBTS. YOU'RE UNSURE ABOUT WHAT TO DO WHEN CONFRONTED WITH SOMETHING THAT COULD POTENTIALLY KILL YOU.
YOU JUST WANT TO RUN AWAY FROM IT ALL, BUT THEN YOU FEEL GUILTY FOR NOT TRYING HARD ENOUGH.
WE'RE NOT OPPOSITES ARE WE?, NOT LIKE KAL AND BIZARRO--
WE AM NOTHING ALIKE!
KRAK
NO. WE'RE VERY ALIKE. RASH. IMPULSIVE. WE MAKE MISTAKES. WE THINK WITH OUR FISTS A LOT.
WE'RE REFLECTIONS.
LOOK, I KNOW YOU'RE FREAKING RIGHT NOW. I'VE--I'VE BEEN THERE, TOO. SCARED AND LONELY AND FEELING LIKE YOUR WORLD IS COMING APART.
BUT...
BUT WHAT?

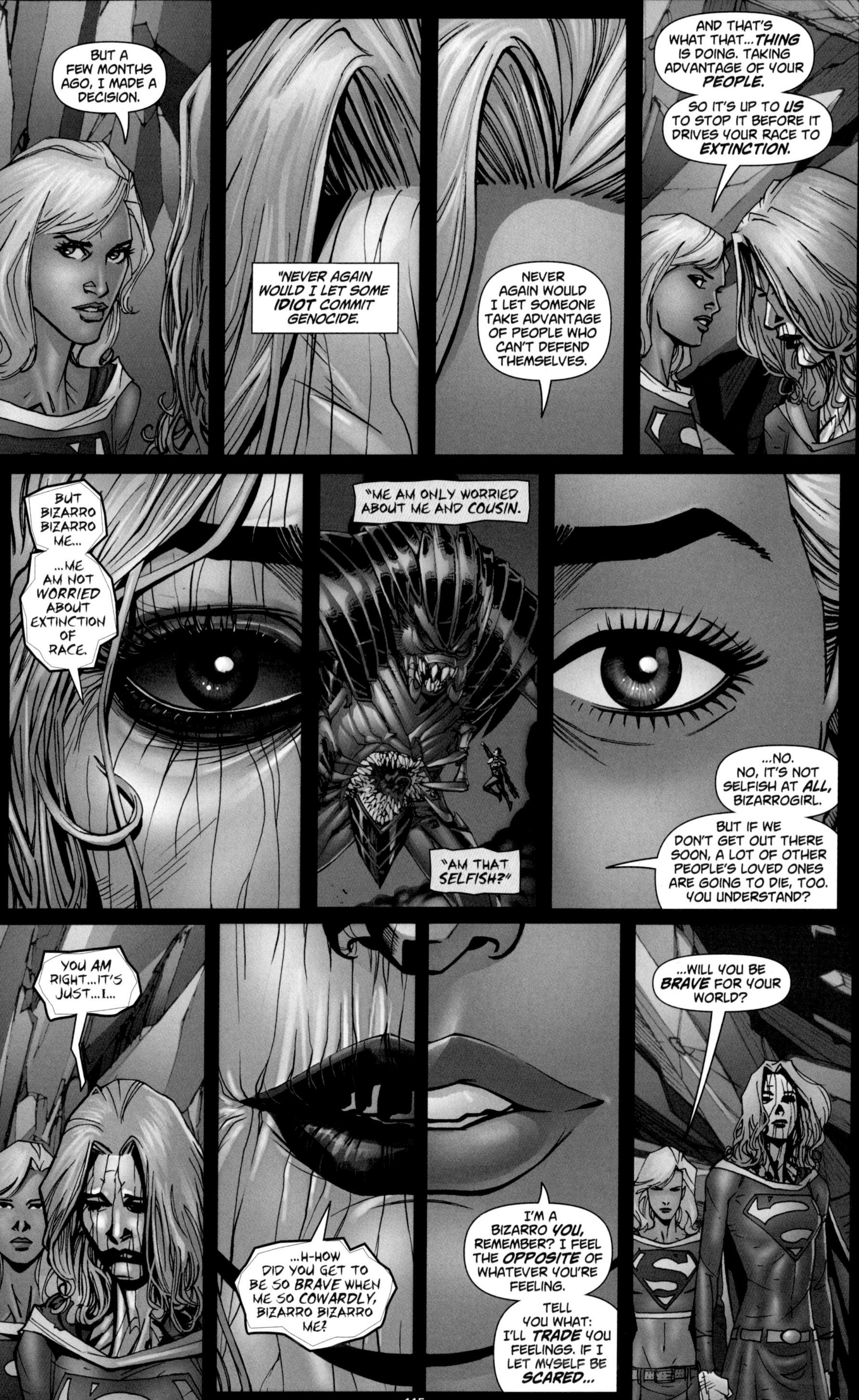
BUT A FEW MONTHS AGO, I MADE A DECISION.
"NEVER AGAIN WOULD I LET SOME IDIOT COMMIT GENOCIDE.
NEVER AGAIN WOULD I LET SOMEONE TAKE ADVANTAGE OF PEOPLE WHO CAN'T DEFEND THEMSELVES.
AND THAT'S WHAT THAT...THING IS DOING. TAKING ADVANTAGE OF YOUR PEOPLE.
SO IT'S UP TO US TO STOP IT BEFORE IT DRIVES YOUR RACE TO EXTINCTION.
BUT BIZARRO BIZARRO ME...
...ME AM NOT WORRIED ABOUT EXTINCTION OF RACE.
"ME AM ONLY WORRIED ABOUT ME AND COUSIN.
"AM THAT SELFISH?"
...NO. NO, IT'S NOT SELFISH AT ALL, BIZARROGIRL.
BUT IF WE DON'T GET OUT THERE SOON, A LOT OF OTHER PEOPLE'S LOVED ONES ARE GOING TO DIE, TOO. YOU UNDERSTAND?
YOU AM RIGHT...IT'S JUST...I...
...H-HOW DID YOU GET TO BE SO BRAVE WHEN ME SO COWARDLY, BIZARRO BIZARRO ME?
I'M A BIZARRO YOU, REMEMBER? I FEEL THE OPPOSITE OF WHATEVER YOU'RE FEELING.
TELL YOU WHAT: I'LL TRADE YOU FEELINGS. IF I LET MYSELF BE SCARED...
...WILL YOU BE BRAVE FOR YOUR WORLD?

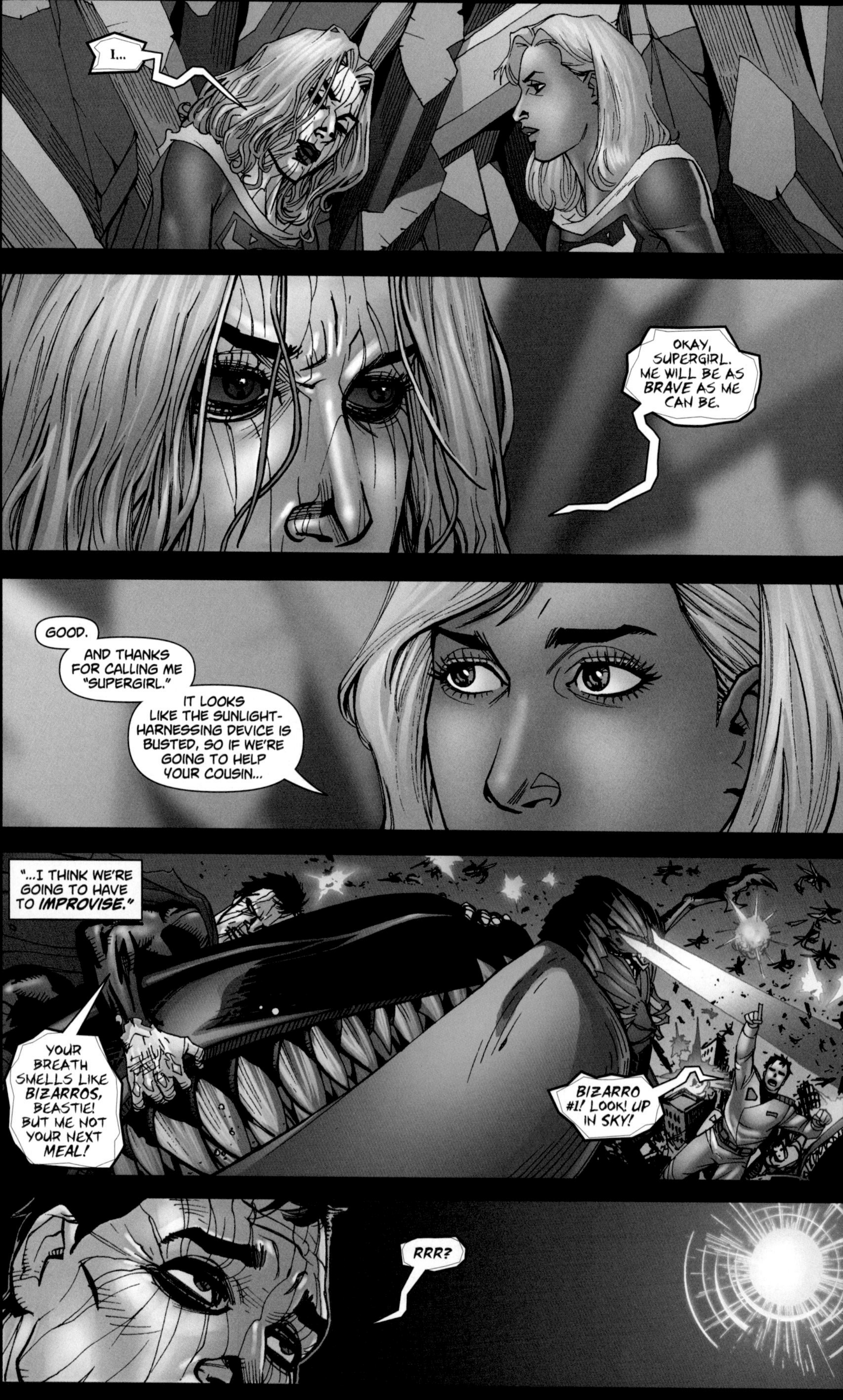
I...
OKAY, SUPERGIRL. ME WILL BE AS BRAVE AS ME CAN BE.
GOOD.
AND THANKS FOR CALLING ME "SUPERGIRL."
IT LOOKS LIKE THE SUNLIGHT-HARNESSING DEVICE IS BUSTED, SO IF WE'RE GOING TO HELP YOUR COUSIN...
"...I THINK WE'RE GOING TO HAVE TO IMPROVISE."
YOUR BREATH SMELLS LIKE BIZARROS, BEASTIE! BUT ME NOT YOUR NEXT MEAL!
BIZARRO #1! LOOK! UP IN SKY!
RRR?

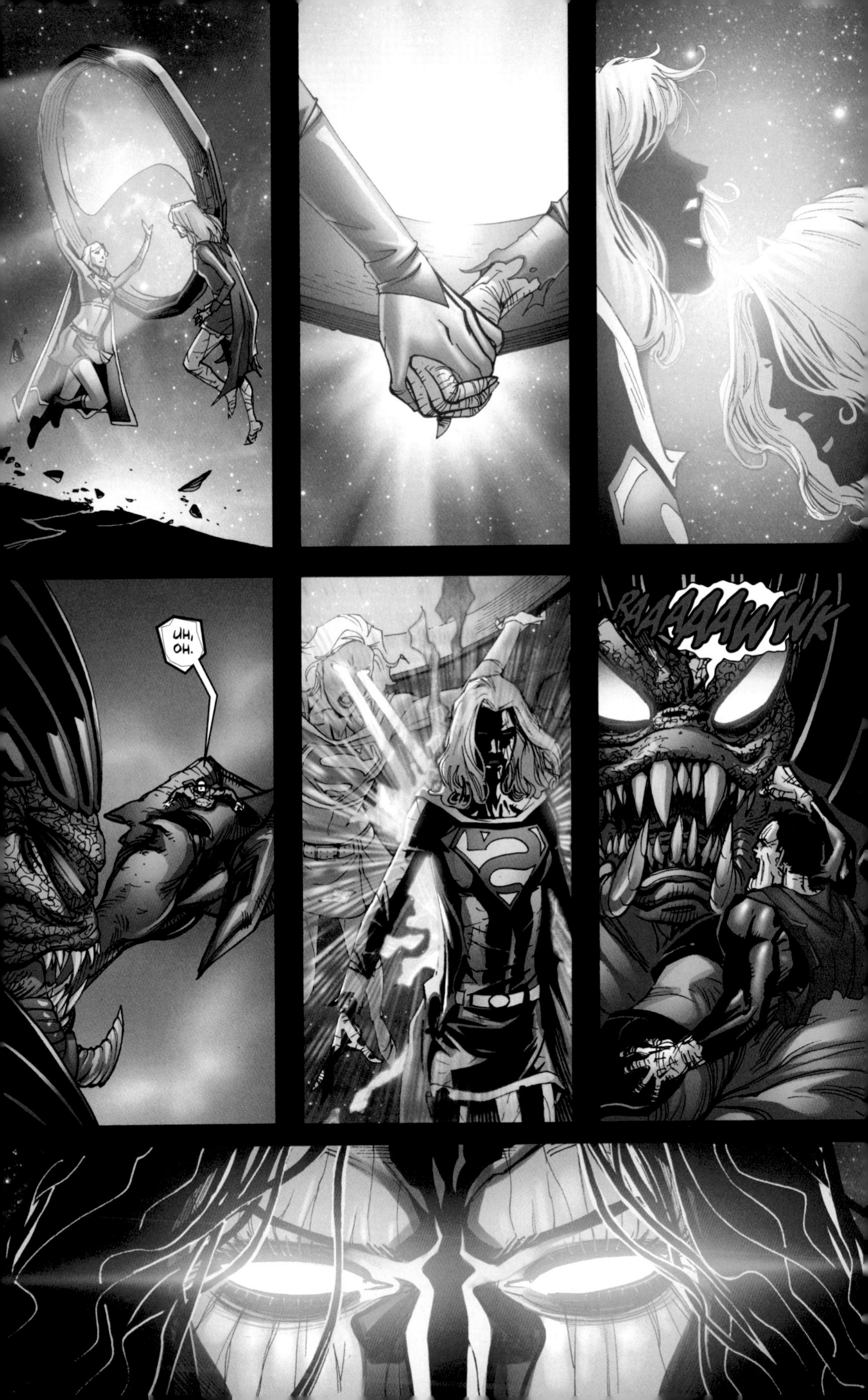
UH, OH.
RAAAAAAWWK

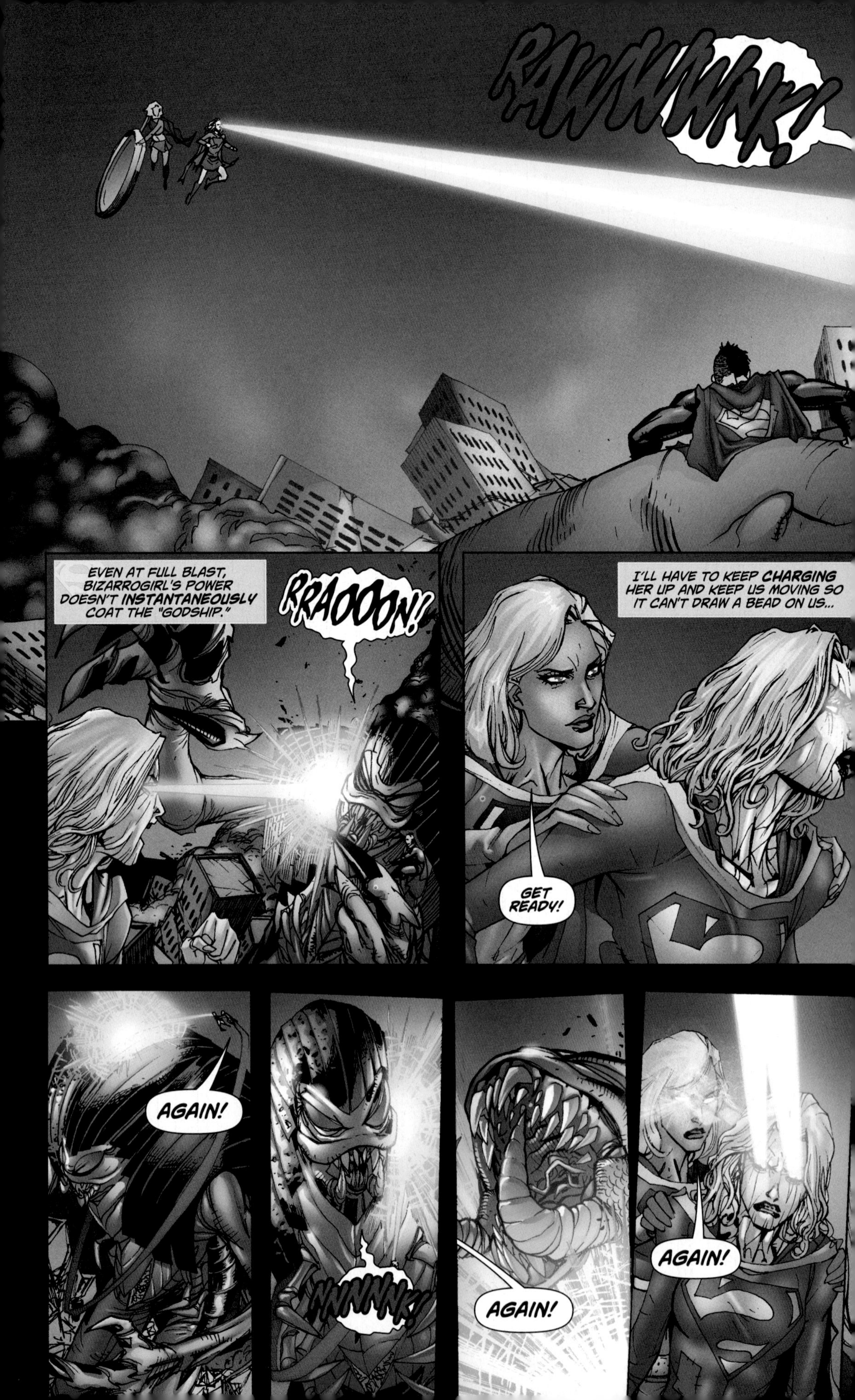
RAWWWWNK!
EVEN AT FULL BLAST, BIZARROGIRL'S POWER DOESN'T INSTANTANEOUSLY COAT THE "GODSHIP."
RRAOOOON!
I'LL HAVE TO KEEP CHARGING HER UP AND KEEP US MOVING SO IT CAN'T DRAW A BEAD ON US...
GET READY!
AGAIN!
NNNNNK!
AGAIN!
AGAIN!

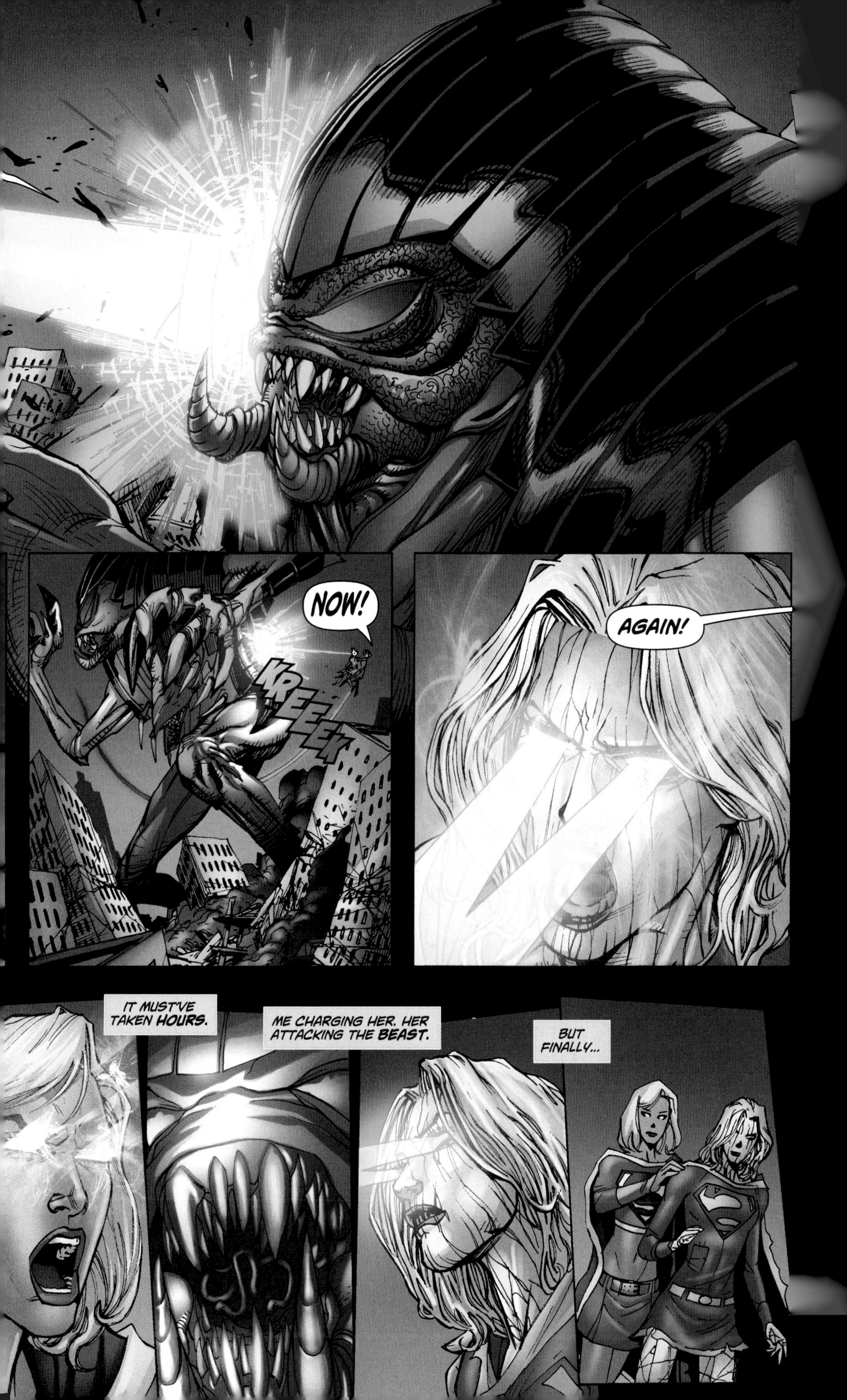
NOW!
KREEEK
AGAIN!
IT MUST'VE TAKEN HOURS.
ME CHARGING HER. HER ATTACKING THE BEAST.
BUT FINALLY...

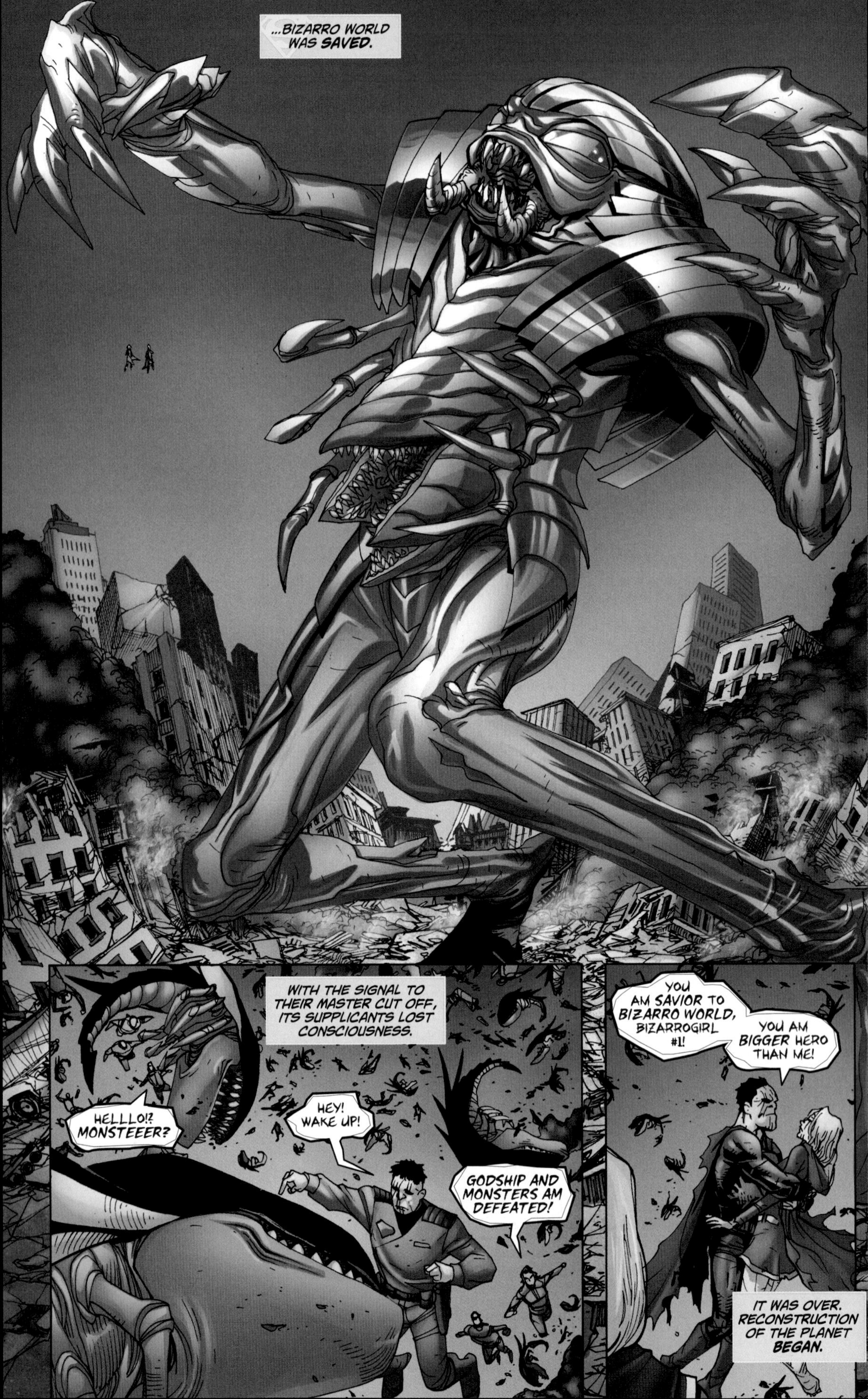
...BIZARRO WORLD WAS SAVED.
WITH THE SIGNAL TO THEIR MASTER CUT OFF, ITS SUPPLICANTS LOST CONSCIOUSNESS.
HELLLO!? MONSTEEER?
HEY! WAKE UP!
GODSHIP AND MONSTERS AM DEFEATED!
YOU AM SAVIOR TO BIZARRO WORLD, BIZARROGIRL #1!
YOU AM BIGGER HERO THAN ME!
IT WAS OVER. RECONSTRUCTION OF THE PLANET BEGAN.

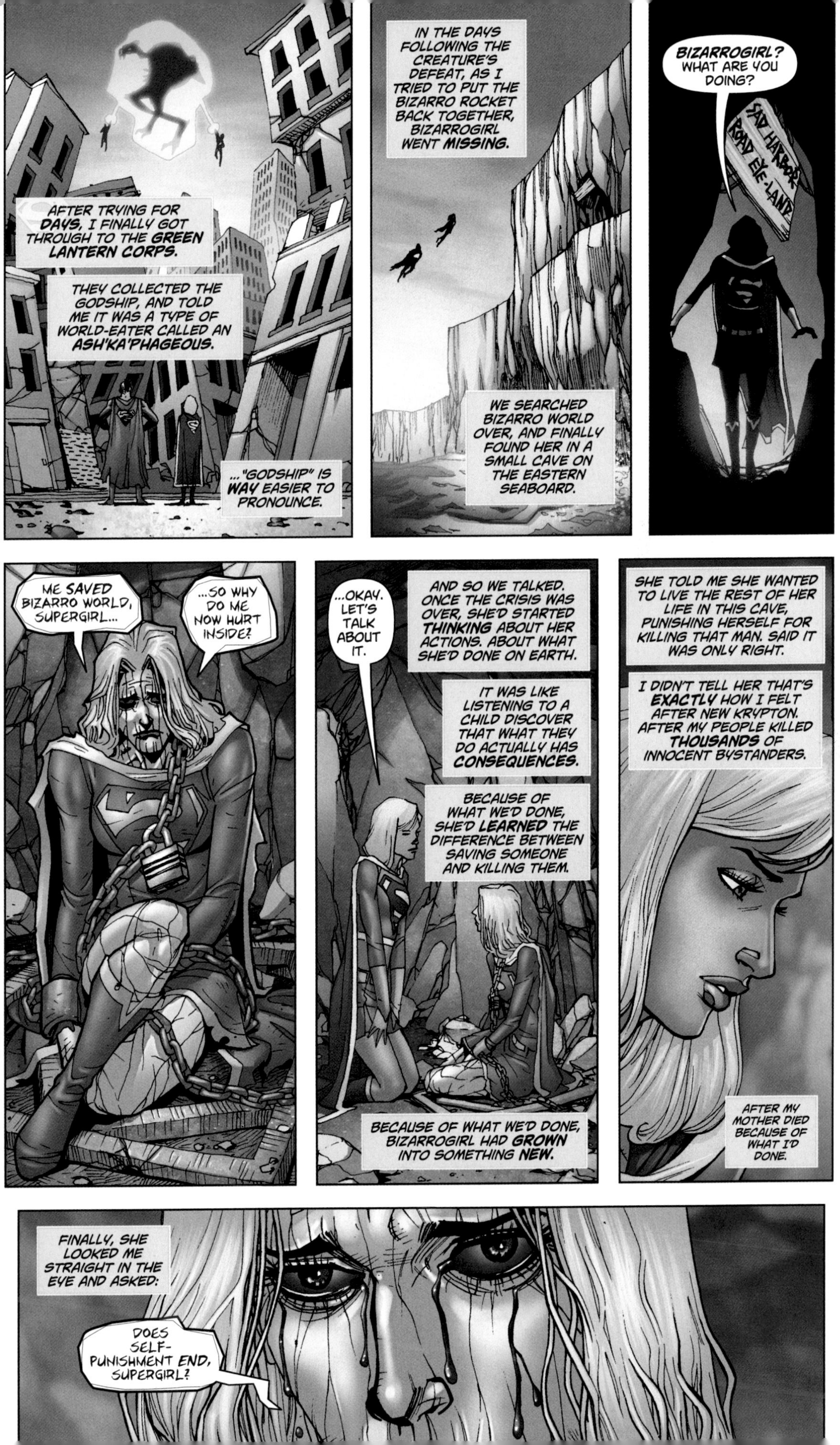
AFTER TRYING FOR DAYS, I FINALLY GOT THROUGH TO THE GREEN LANTERN CORPS.
THEY COLLECTED THE GODSHIP, AND TOLD ME IT WAS A TYPE OF WORLD-EATER CALLED AN ASH'KA'PHAGEOUS.
..."GODSHIP" IS WAY EASIER TO PRONOUNCE.
IN THE DAYS FOLLOWING THE CREATURE'S DEFEAT, AS I TRIED TO PUT THE BIZARRO ROCKET BACK TOGETHER, BIZARROGIRL WENT MISSING.
WE SEARCHED BIZARRO WORLD OVER, AND FINALLY FOUND HER IN A SMALL CAVE ON THE EASTERN SEABOARD.
BIZARROGIRL? WHAT ARE YOU DOING?
SAD HARBOR ROAD EYE-LAND
ME SAVED BIZARRO WORLD, SUPERGIRL...
...SO WHY DO ME NOW HURT INSIDE?
...OKAY. LET'S TALK ABOUT IT.
AND SO WE TALKED. ONCE THE CRISIS WAS OVER, SHE'D STARTED THINKING ABOUT HER ACTIONS. ABOUT WHAT SHE'D DONE ON EARTH.
IT WAS LIKE LISTENING TO A CHILD DISCOVER THAT WHAT THEY DO ACTUALLY HAS CONSEQUENCES.
BECAUSE OF WHAT WE'D DONE, SHE'D LEARNED THE DIFFERENCE BETWEEN SAVING SOMEONE AND KILLING THEM.
BECAUSE OF WHAT WE'D DONE, BIZARROGIRL HAD GROWN INTO SOMETHING NEW.
SHE TOLD ME SHE WANTED TO LIVE THE REST OF HER LIFE IN THIS CAVE, PUNISHING HERSELF FOR KILLING THAT MAN. SAID IT WAS ONLY RIGHT.
I DIDN'T TELL HER THAT'S EXACTLY HOW I FELT AFTER NEW KRYPTON. AFTER MY PEOPLE KILLED THOUSANDS OF INNOCENT BYSTANDERS.
AFTER MY MOTHER DIED BECAUSE OF WHAT I'D DONE.
FINALLY, SHE LOOKED ME STRAIGHT IN THE EYE AND ASKED:
DOES SELF-PUNISHMENT END, SUPERGIRL?

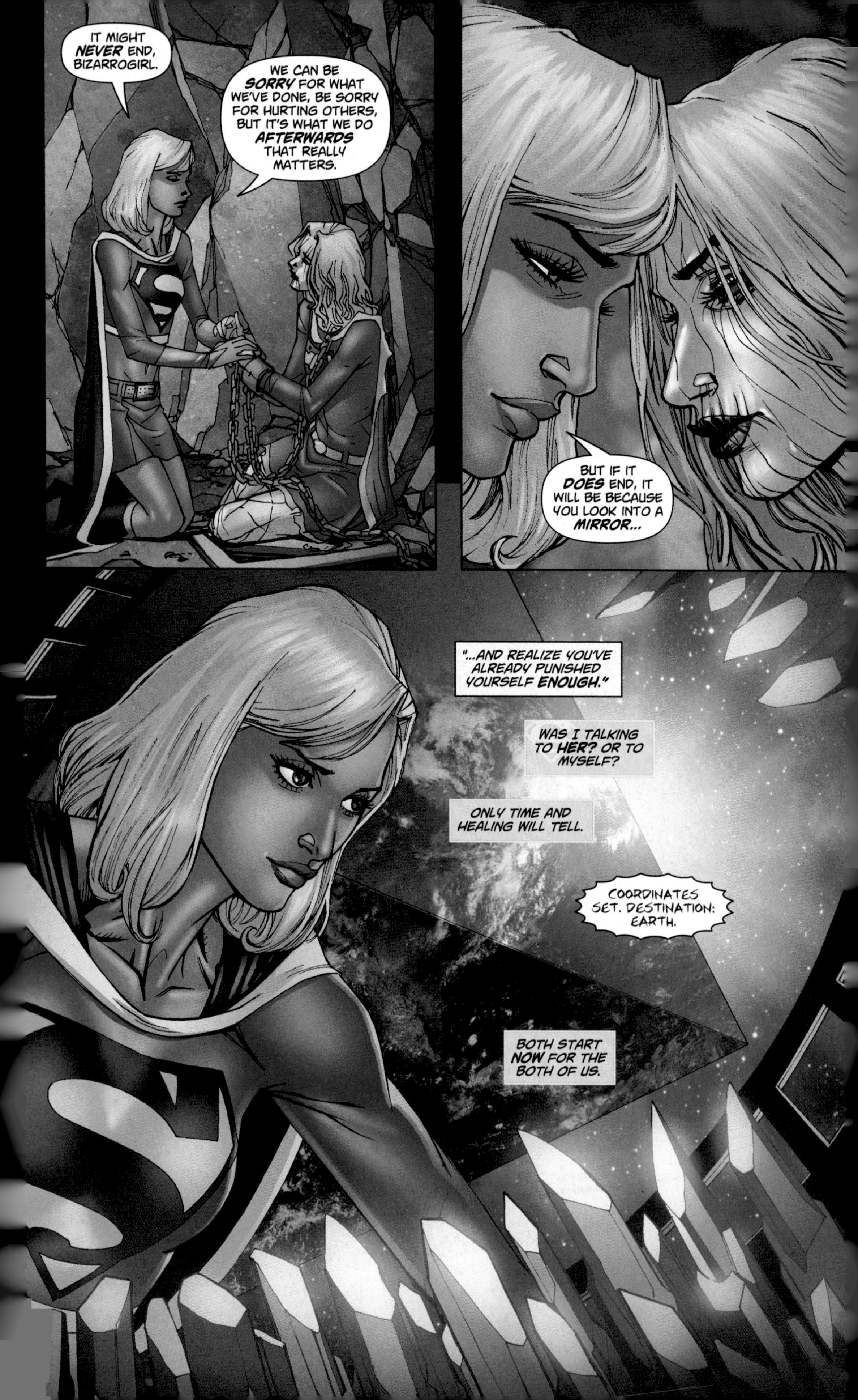
IT MIGHT NEVER END, BIZARROGIRL.
WE CAN BE SORRY FOR WHAT WE'VE DONE, BE SORRY FOR HURTING OTHERS, BUT IT'S WHAT WE DO AFTERWARDS THAT REALLY MATTERS.
BUT IF IT DOES END, IT WILL BE BECAUSE YOU LOOK INTO A MIRROR...
"...AND REALIZE YOU'VE ALREADY PUNISHED YOURSELF ENOUGH."
WAS I TALKING TO HER? OR TO MYSELF?
ONLY TIME AND HEALING WILL TELL.
COORDINATES SET. DESTINATION: EARTH.
BOTH START NOW FOR THE BOTH OF US.

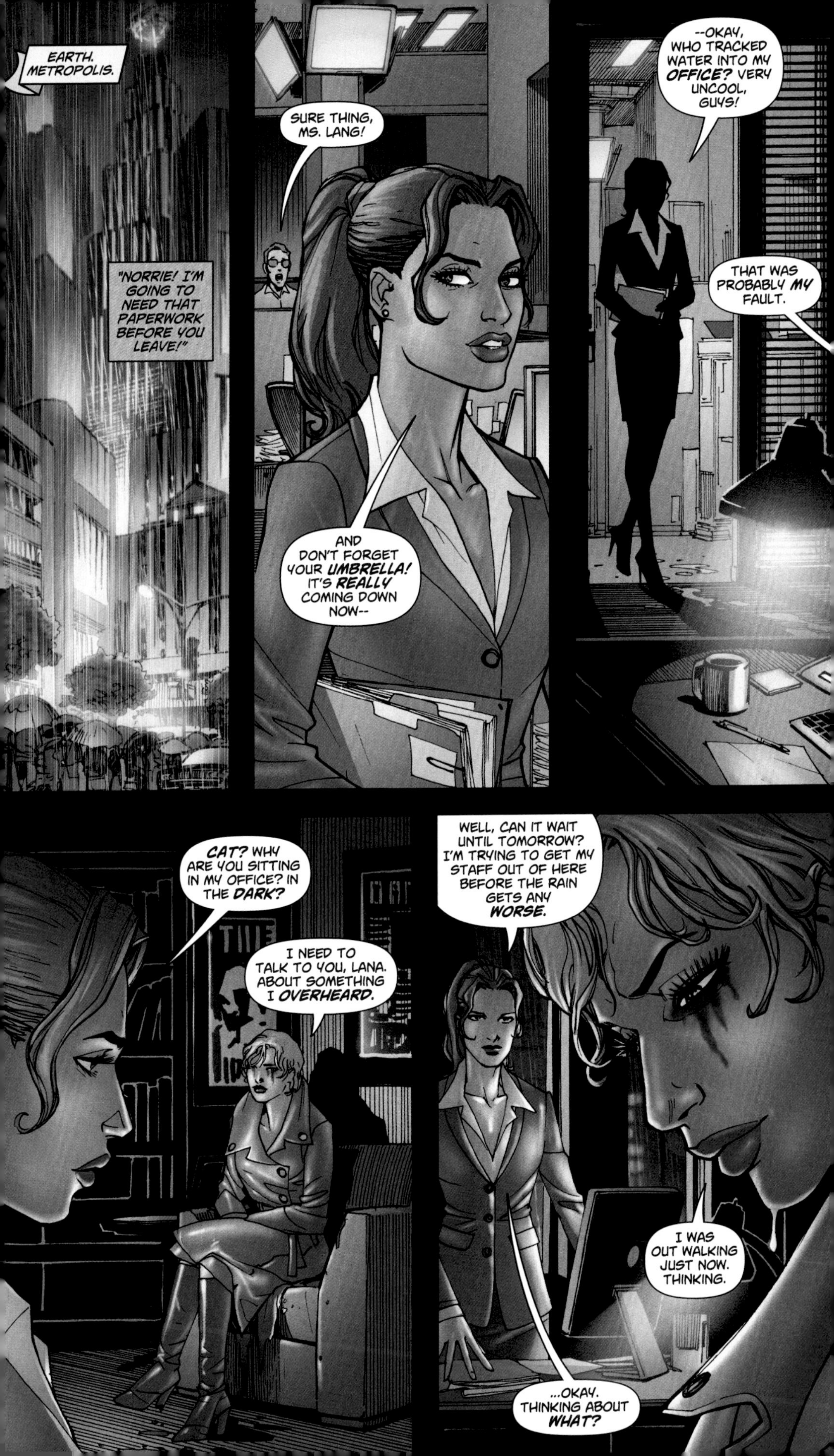
EARTH. METROPOLIS.
"NORRIE! I'M GOING TO NEED THAT PAPERWORK BEFORE YOU LEAVE!"
SURE THING, MS. LANG!
AND DON'T FORGET YOUR **UMBRELLA!** IT'S **REALLY** COMING DOWN NOW--
--OKAY, WHO TRACKED WATER INTO MY **OFFICE?** VERY UNCOOL, GUYS!
THAT WAS PROBABLY **MY** FAULT.
CAT? WHY ARE YOU SITTING IN MY OFFICE? IN THE **DARK?**
I NEED TO TALK TO YOU, LANA. ABOUT SOMETHING I **OVERHEARD**.
WELL, CAN IT WAIT UNTIL TOMORROW? I'M TRYING TO GET MY STAFF OUT OF HERE BEFORE THE RAIN GETS ANY **WORSE**.
I WAS OUT WALKING JUST NOW. THINKING.
...OKAY. THINKING ABOUT **WHAT?**

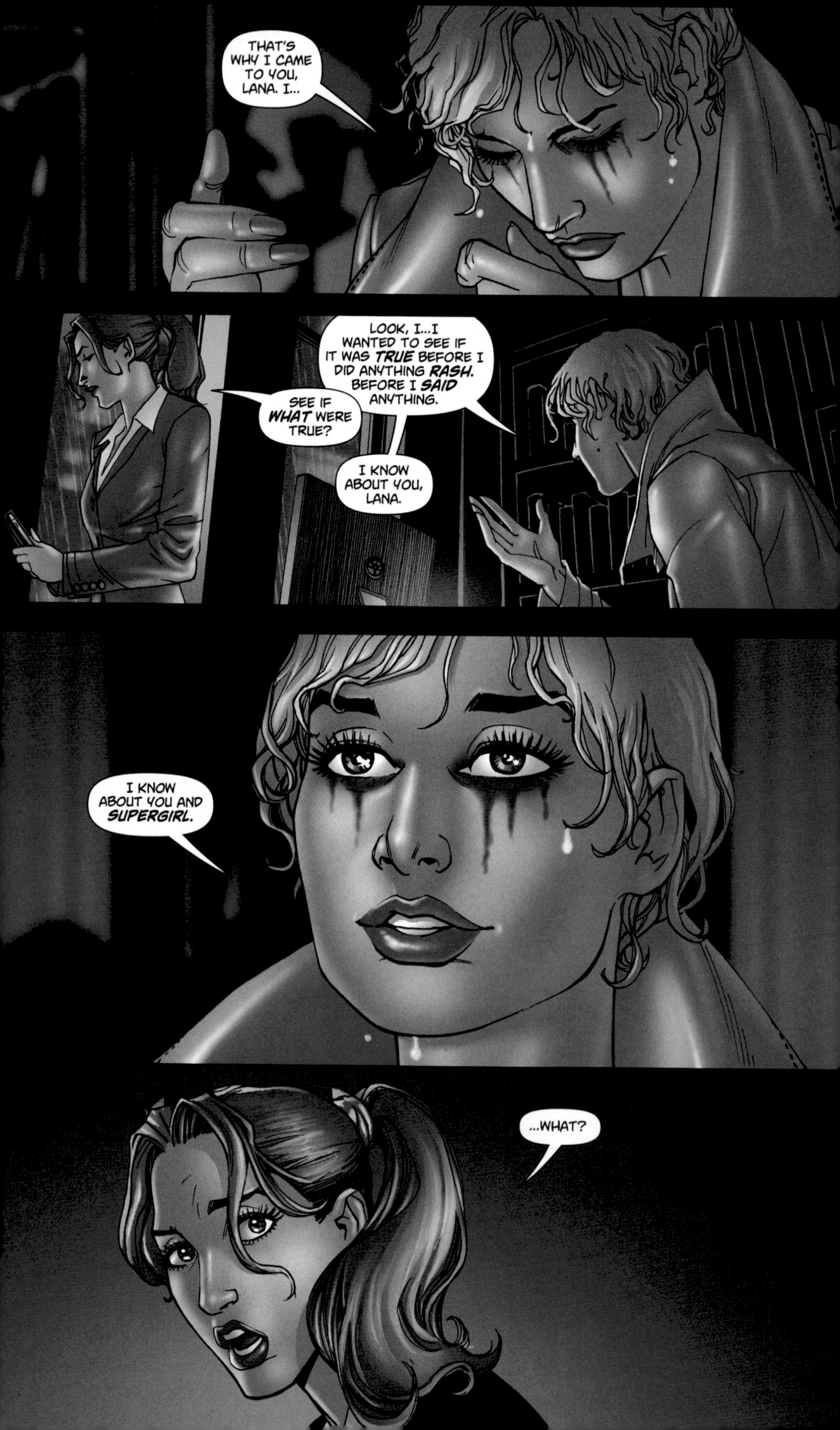
THAT'S WHY I CAME TO YOU, LANA. I...
SEE IF *WHAT* WERE TRUE?
LOOK, I...I WANTED TO SEE IF IT WAS *TRUE* BEFORE I DID ANYTHING *RASH*. BEFORE I *SAID* ANYTHING.
I KNOW ABOUT YOU, LANA.
I KNOW ABOUT YOU AND *SUPERGIRL*.
...WHAT?

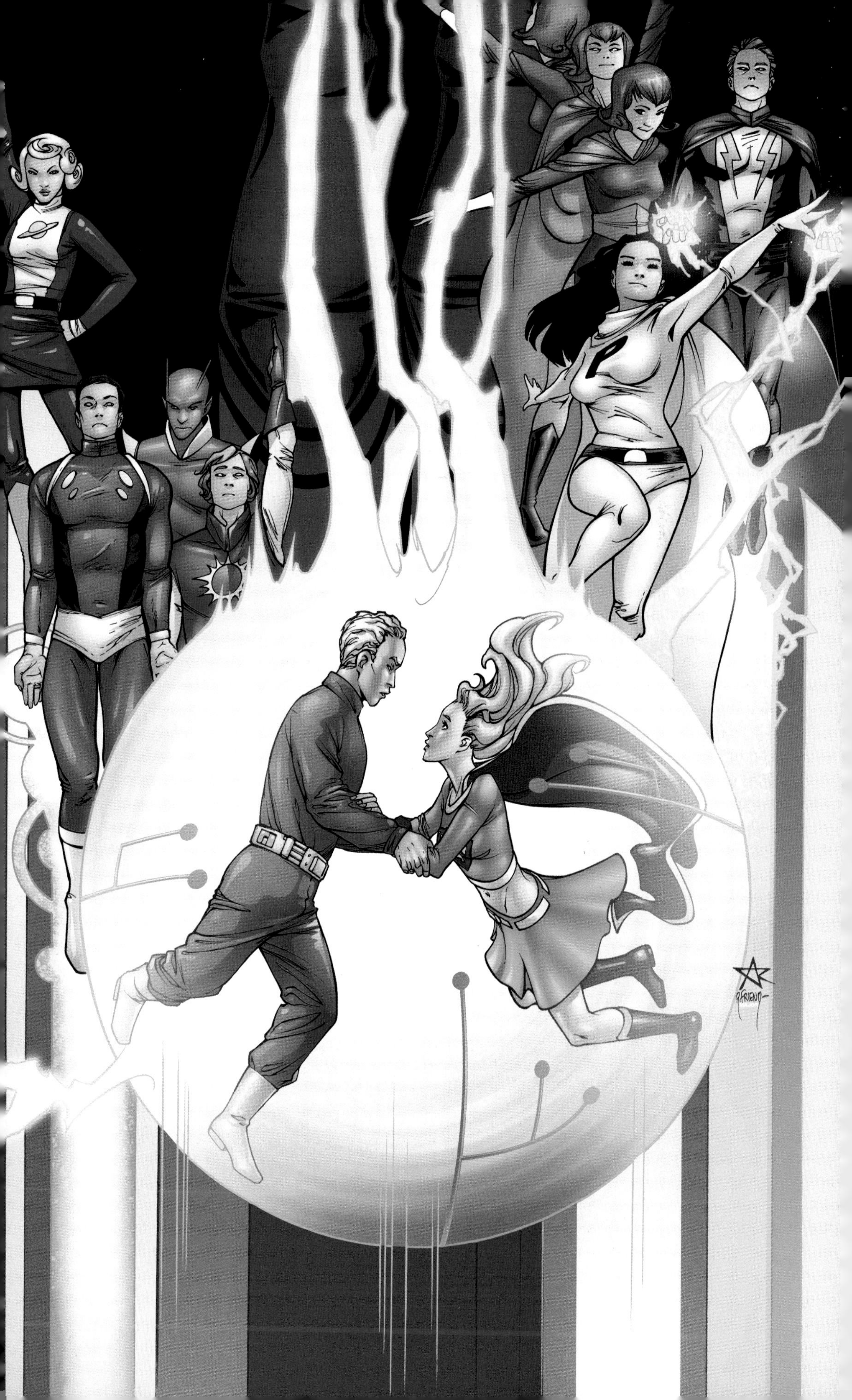

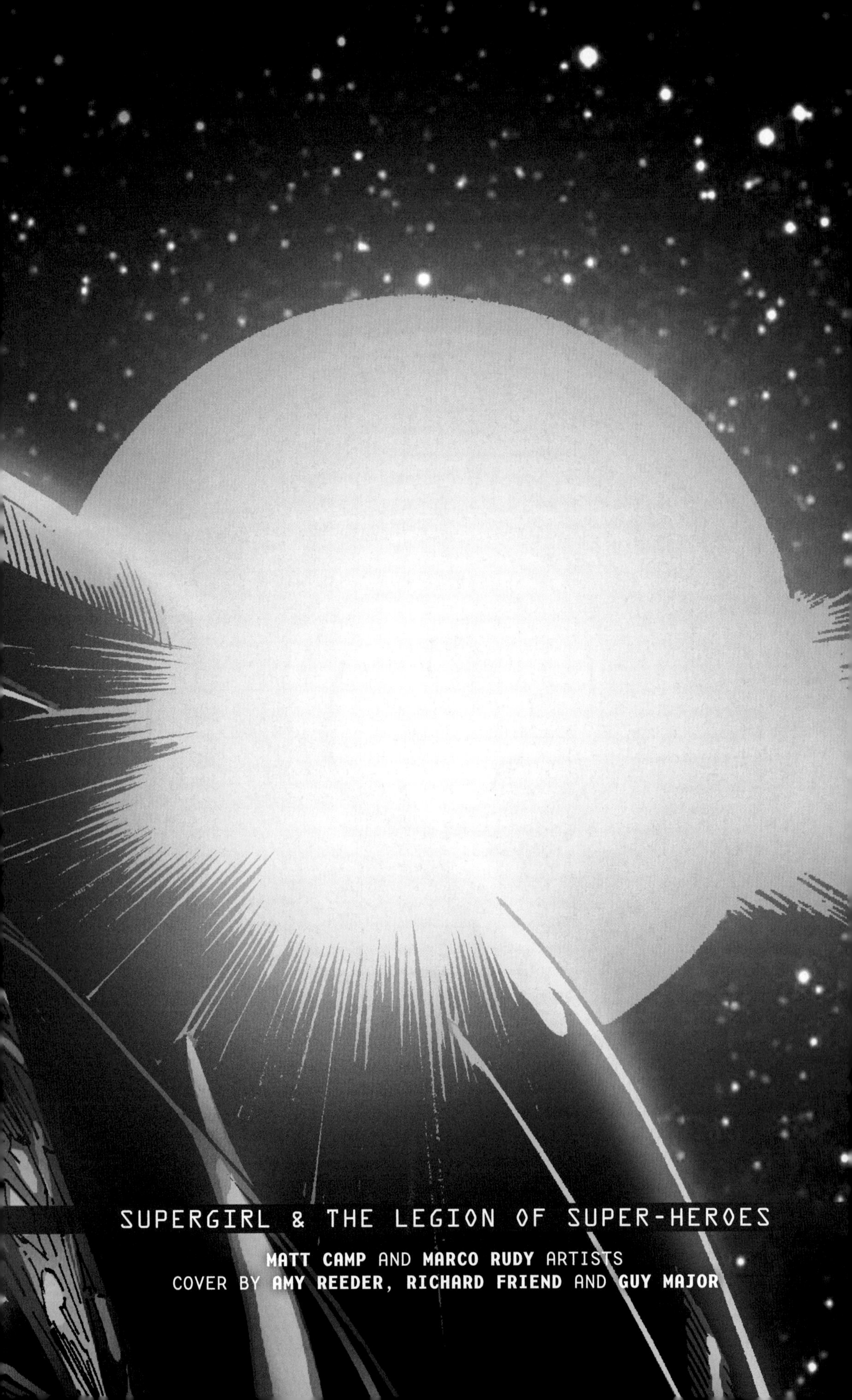

SUPERGIRL & THE LEGION OF SUPER-HEROES

MATT CAMP AND **MARCO RUDY** ARTISTS
COVER BY **AMY REEDER, RICHARD FRIEND** AND **GUY MAJOR**

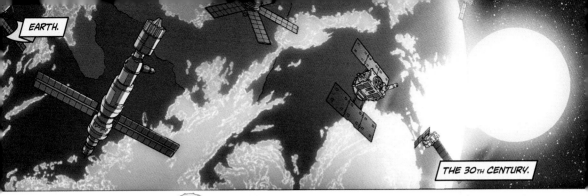

EARTH.

THE 30TH CENTURY.

METROPOLIS.

--I *KNOW* HE IS. BUT IF I CAN'T KEEP HER ON, WHERE *ELSE* CAN I FIND INEXPENSIVE *HELP?*

MOM?

THEY CAN'T KEEP MAKING LAWS LIKE THAT... NO, I DON'T *EXPECT* THEM TO, IT'S JUST THAT--

...MOM?

WHAT *IS* IT, CARTAR?!

LOOK!!! UP IN THE SKY!

WHAT IS IT?

IT'S A BIRD!

BIRDS DON'T LOOK LIKE THAT. *MUST* BE A SKYBUS.

NO, IT'S NOT. IT'S...

...IT'S COMING THIS *WAY!*

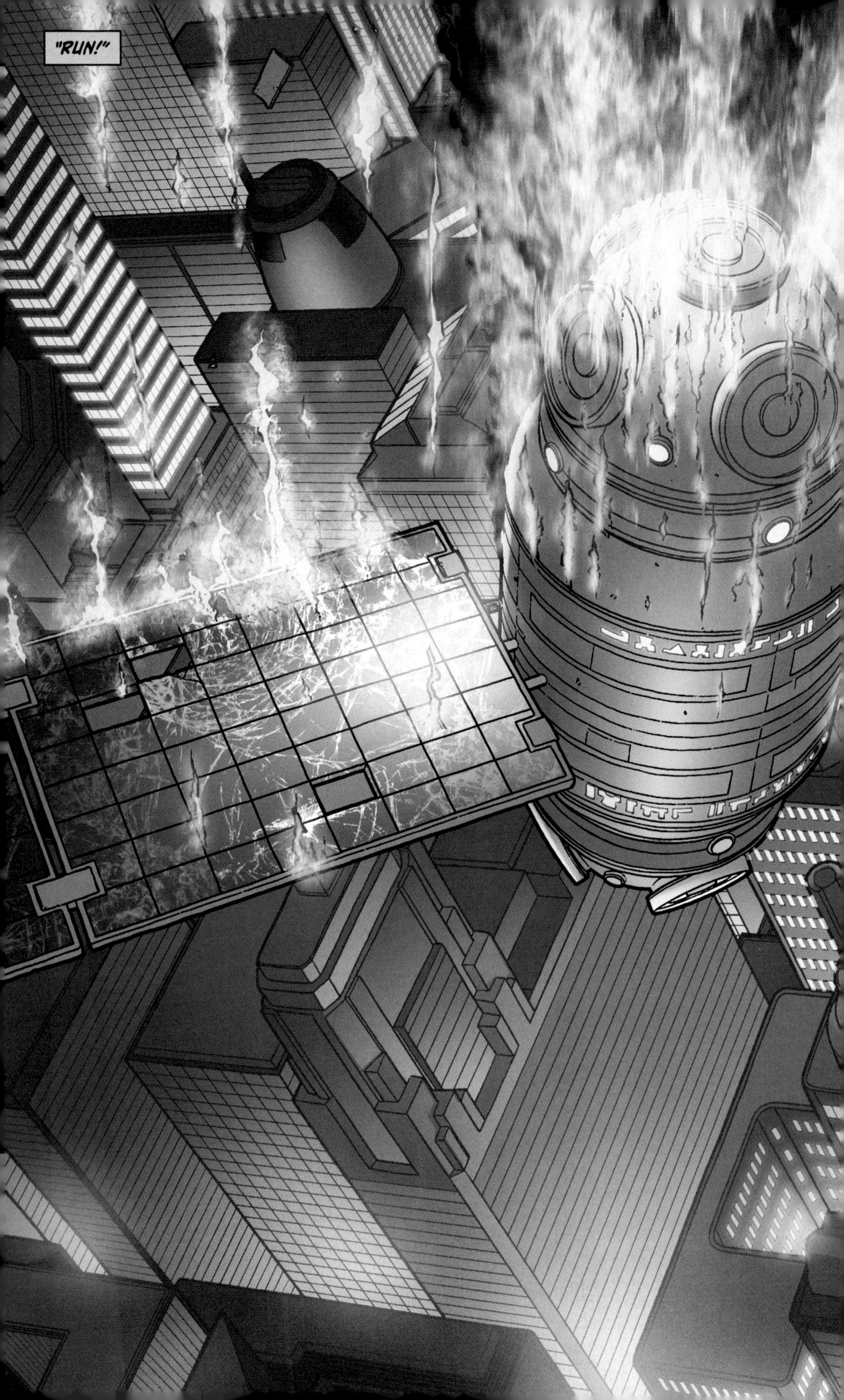
"RUN!"

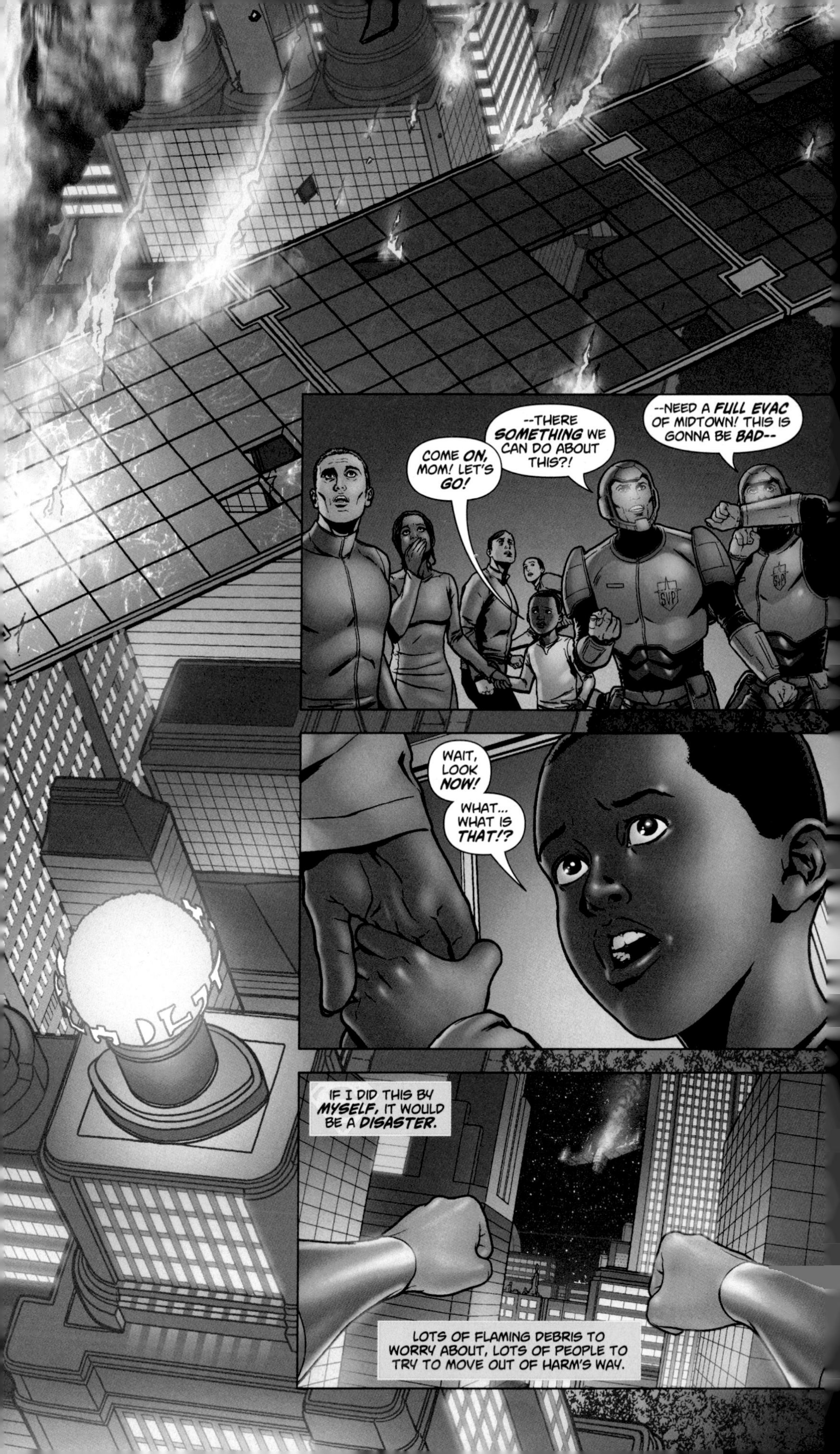
--NEED A FULL EVAC OF MIDTOWN! THIS IS GONNA BE BAD--
--THERE SOMETHING WE CAN DO ABOUT THIS?!
COME ON, MOM! LET'S GO!
WAIT, LOOK NOW!
WHAT... WHAT IS THAT!?
IF I DID THIS BY MYSELF, IT WOULD BE A DISASTER.
LOTS OF FLAMING DEBRIS TO WORRY ABOUT, LOTS OF PEOPLE TO TRY TO MOVE OUT OF HARM'S WAY.

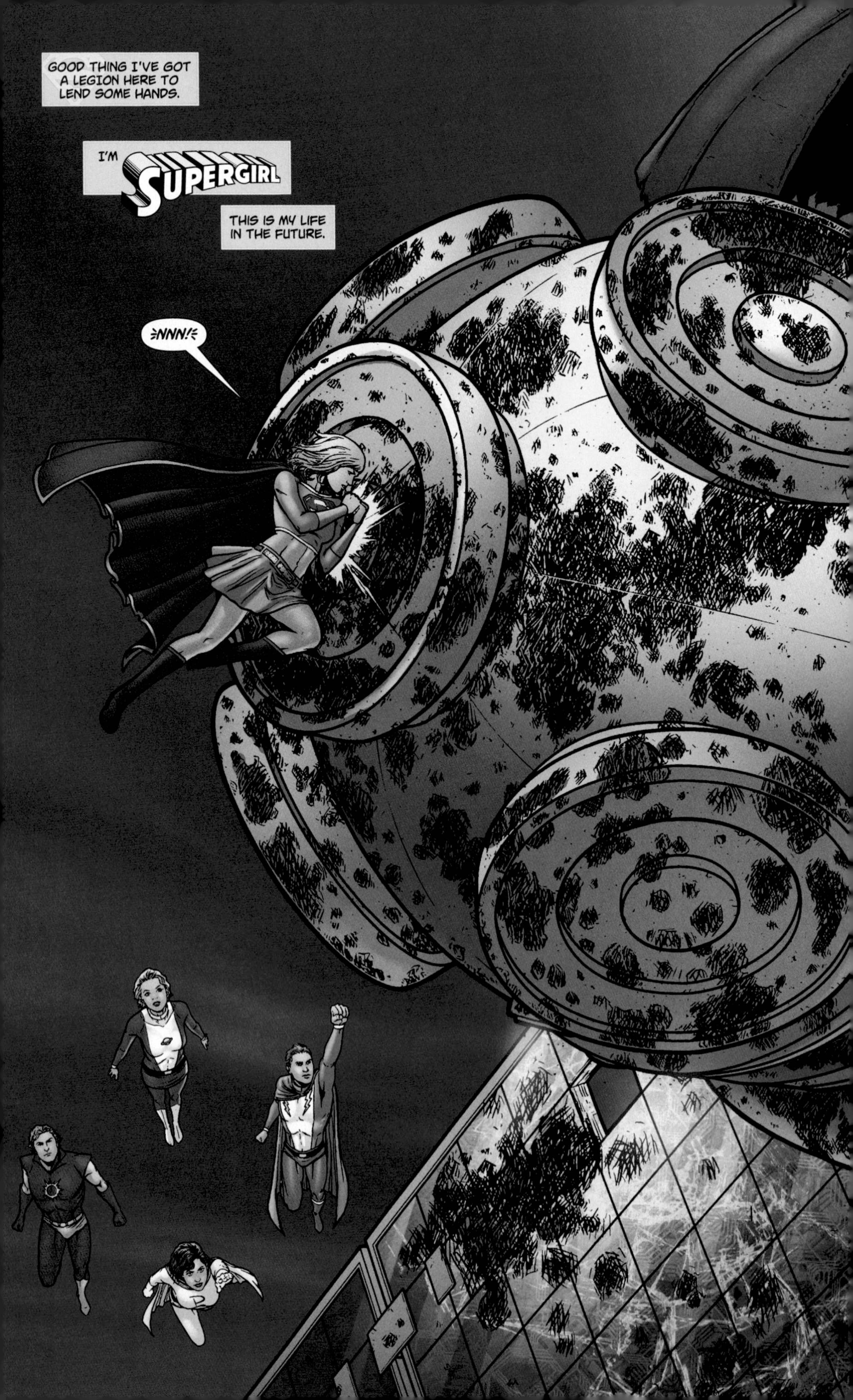
GOOD THING I'VE GOT A LEGION HERE TO LEND SOME HANDS.
I'M SUPERGIRL
THIS IS MY LIFE IN THE FUTURE.
NNN!

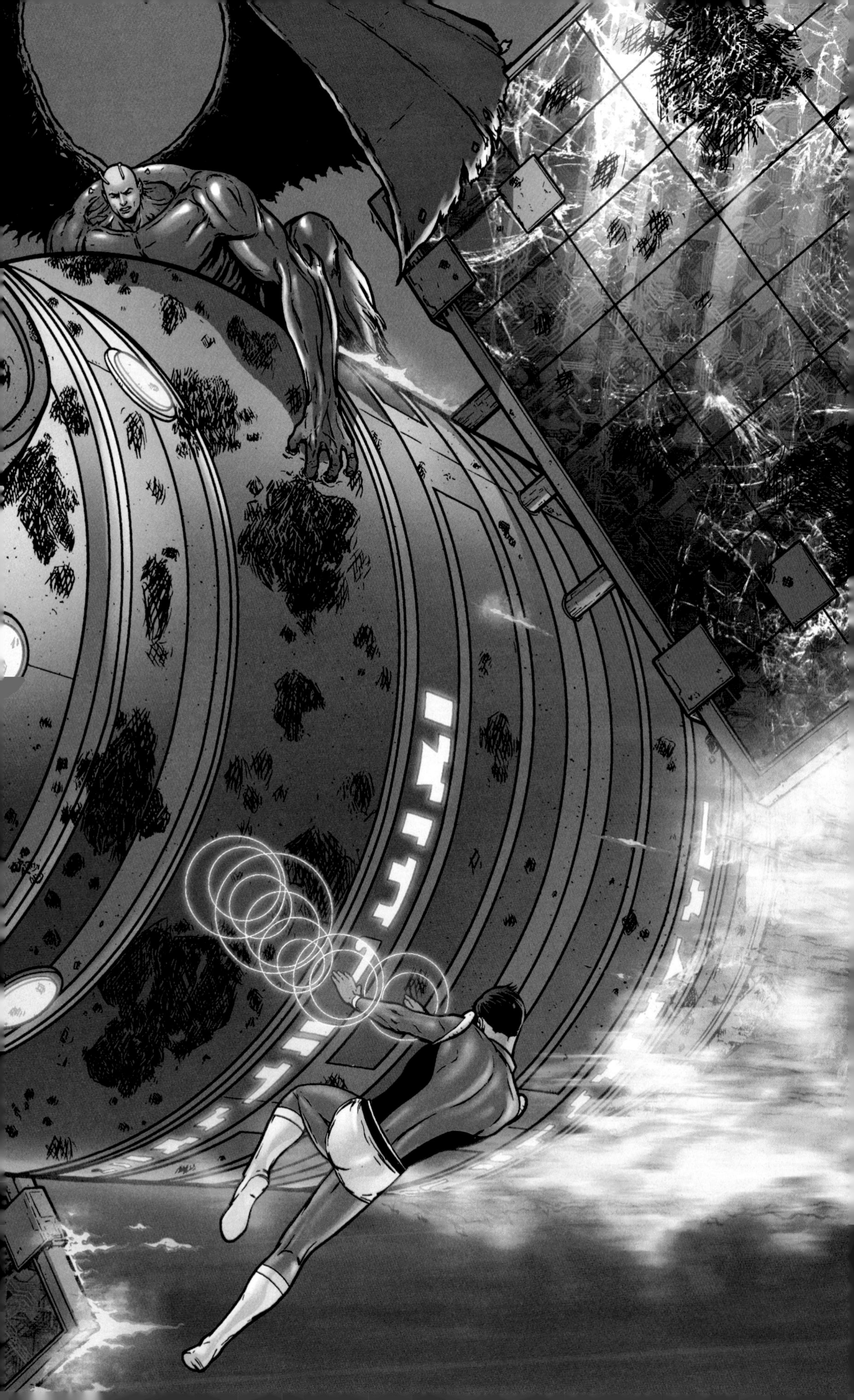

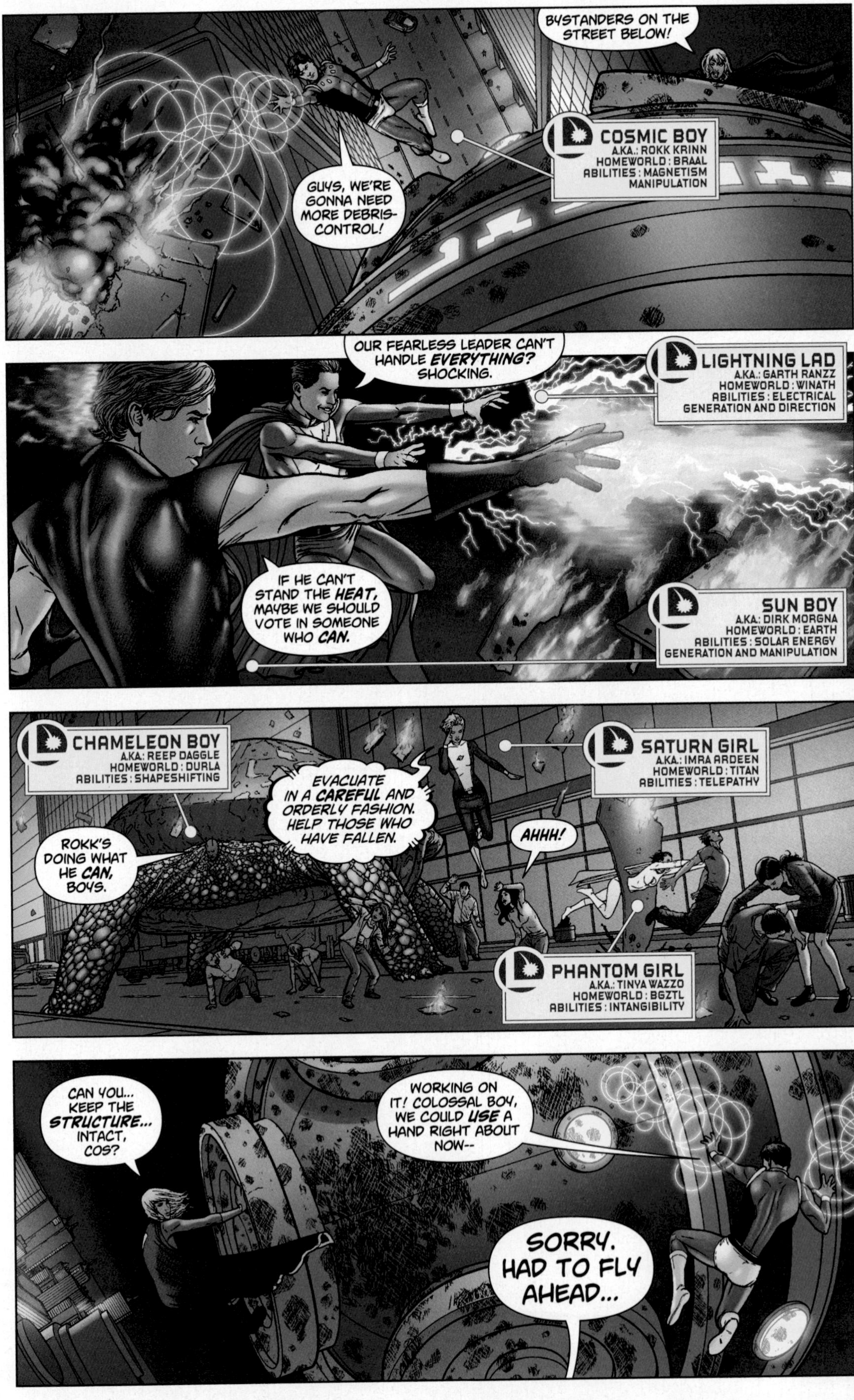
BYSTANDERS ON THE STREET BELOW!
COSMIC BOY A.K.A.: ROKK KRINN HOMEWORLD: BRAAL ABILITIES: MAGNETISM MANIPULATION
GUYS, WE'RE GONNA NEED MORE DEBRIS-CONTROL!
OUR FEARLESS LEADER CAN'T HANDLE EVERYTHING? SHOCKING.
LIGHTNING LAD A.KA.: GARTH RANZZ HOMEWORLD: WINATH ABILITIES: ELECTRICAL GENERATION AND DIRECTION
IF HE CAN'T STAND THE HEAT, MAYBE WE SHOULD VOTE IN SOMEONE WHO CAN.
SUN BOY A.KA.: DIRK MORGNA HOMEWORLD: EARTH ABILITIES: SOLAR ENERGY GENERATION AND MANIPULATION
CHAMELEON BOY A.K.A.: REEP DAGGLE HOMEWORLD: DURLA ABILITIES: SHAPESHIFTING
EVACUATE IN A CAREFUL AND ORDERLY FASHION. HELP THOSE WHO HAVE FALLEN.
SATURN GIRL A.KA.: IMRA ARDEEN HOMEWORLD: TITAN ABILITIES: TELEPATHY
ROKK'S DOING WHAT HE CAN, BOYS.
AHHH!
PHANTOM GIRL A.KA.: TINYA WAZZO HOMEWORLD: BGZTL ABILITIES: INTANGIBILITY
CAN YOU... KEEP THE STRUCTURE... INTACT, COS?
WORKING ON IT! COLOSSAL BOY, WE COULD USE A HAND RIGHT ABOUT NOW--
SORRY. HAD TO FLY AHEAD...

...IT TAKES *TIME* TO GET UP TO THIS SIZE.

CHROOOM

COLOSSAL BOY
A.K.A: GIM ALLON
HOMEWORLD: EARTH
ABILITIES: GIANT GROWTH

CAN YOU HOLD ON TO ALL OF THAT? IT'S PRETTY HEAVY.

I *GOT* IT, S.G.

NICE WORK, LEGIONNAIRES. SUPERGIRL, THANK YOU AGAIN FOR *HELPING*.

JUST TRYING TO PULL MY OWN *WEIGHT* WHILE I'M HERE.

FALLING SATELLITE? *EASY* FOR US. ANY IDEA WHAT BROUGHT THIS HUNKA JUNK DOWN--

WAIT. DO YOU HEAR THAT?

HEAR WHA--

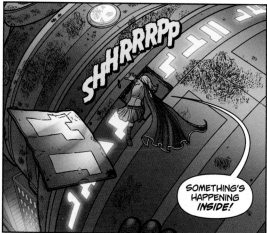

SHHRRRPP

SOMETHING'S HAPPENING *INSIDE!*

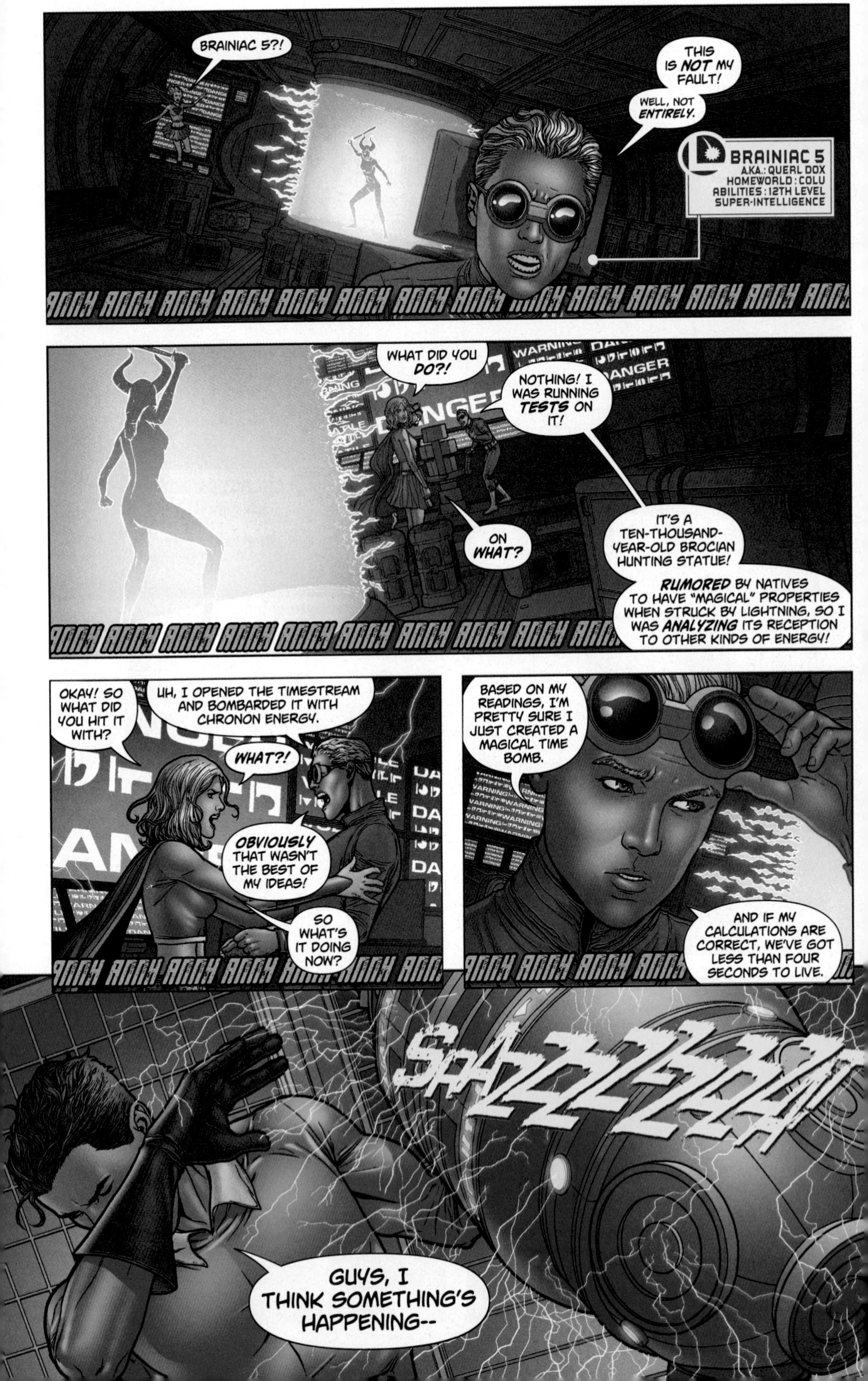
BRAINIAC 5?!
THIS IS NOT MY FAULT!
WELL, NOT ENTIRELY.
BRAINIAC 5
A.KA.: QUERL DOX
HOMEWORLD : COLU
ABILITIES : 12TH LEVEL SUPER-INTELLIGENCE
ANNK ANNK ANNK ANNK ANNK ANNK ANNK ANNK ANNK ANNK ANNK
WHAT DID YOU DO?!
NOTHING! I WAS RUNNING TESTS ON IT!
ON WHAT?
IT'S A TEN-THOUSAND-YEAR-OLD BROCIAN HUNTING STATUE!
RUMORED BY NATIVES TO HAVE "MAGICAL" PROPERTIES WHEN STRUCK BY LIGHTNING, SO I WAS ANALYZING ITS RECEPTION TO OTHER KINDS OF ENERGY!
ANNK ANNK ANNK ANNK ANNK ANNK ANNK ANNK
OKAY! SO WHAT DID YOU HIT IT WITH?
UH, I OPENED THE TIMESTREAM AND BOMBARDED IT WITH CHRONON ENERGY.
WHAT?!
OBVIOUSLY THAT WASN'T THE BEST OF MY IDEAS!
SO WHAT'S IT DOING NOW?
ANNK ANNK ANNK ANNK ANNK ANNK ANNK
BASED ON MY READINGS, I'M PRETTY SURE I JUST CREATED A MAGICAL TIME BOMB.
AND IF MY CALCULATIONS ARE CORRECT, WE'VE GOT LESS THAN FOUR SECONDS TO LIVE.
ANNK ANNK ANNK
GUYS, I THINK SOMETHING'S HAPPENING--

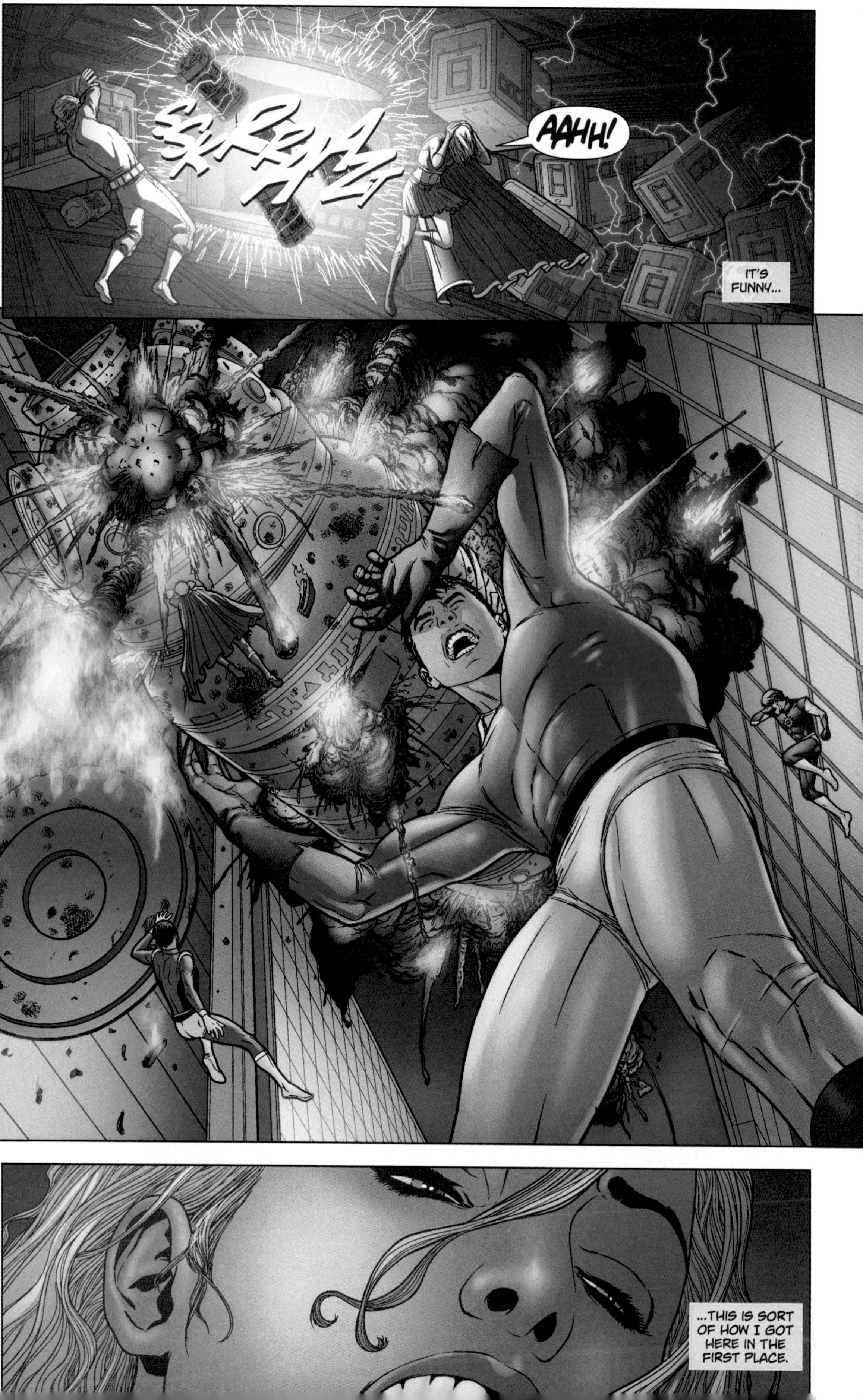
SKRRRAM!
AAHH!
IT'S FUNNY...
...THIS IS SORT OF HOW I GOT HERE IN THE FIRST PLACE.

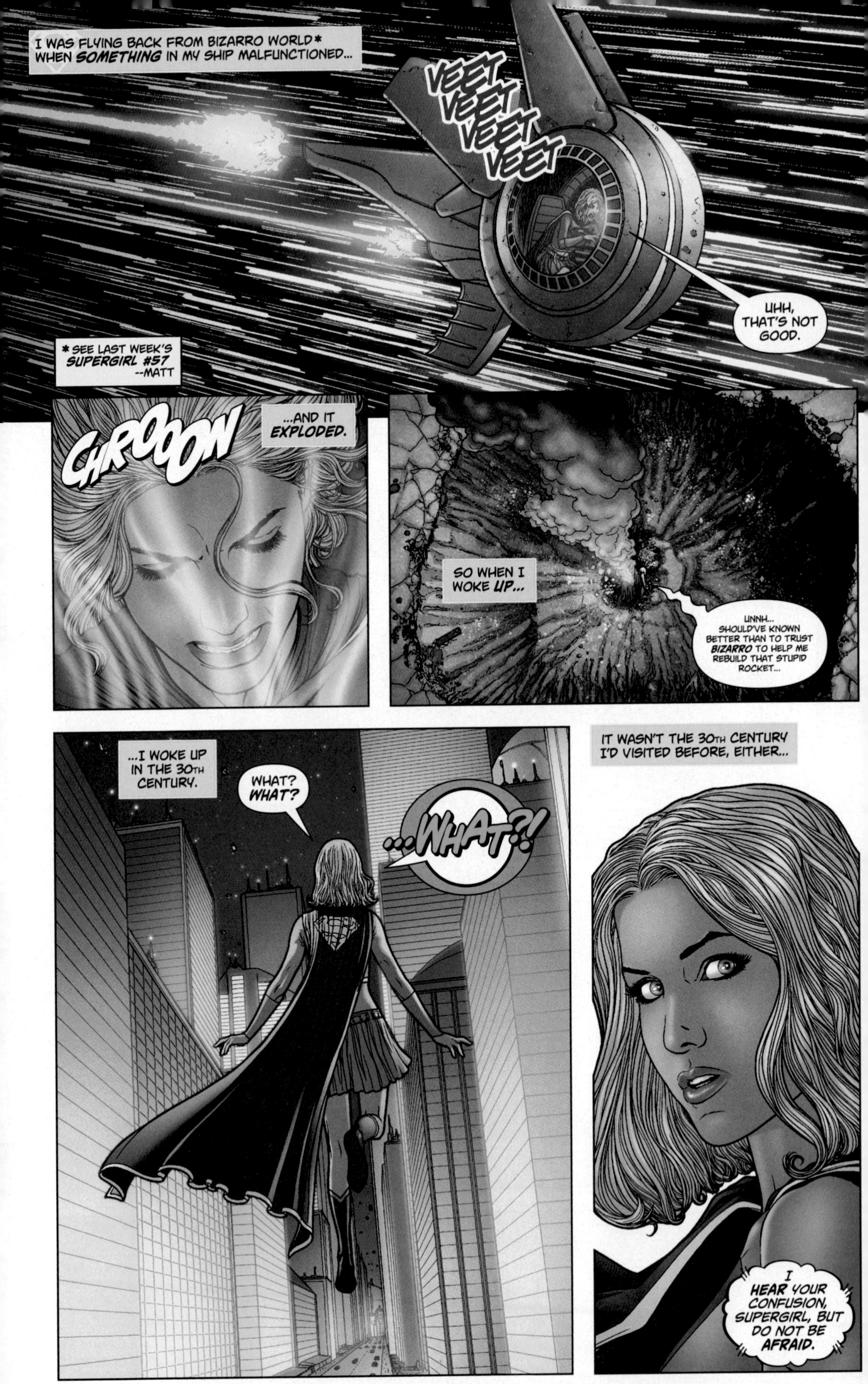
I WAS FLYING BACK FROM BIZARRO WORLD* WHEN SOMETHING IN MY SHIP MALFUNCTIONED...
VEEET VEEET VEEET VEEET
UHH, THAT'S NOT GOOD.
* SEE LAST WEEK'S SUPERGIRL #57 --MATT
CHROOOOM
...AND IT EXPLODED.
SO WHEN I WOKE UP...
UNNH... SHOULD'VE KNOWN BETTER THAN TO TRUST BIZARRO TO HELP ME REBUILD THAT STUPID ROCKET...
...I WOKE UP IN THE 30TH CENTURY.
WHAT? WHAT?
...WHAT?!
IT WASN'T THE 30TH CENTURY I'D VISITED BEFORE, EITHER...
I HEAR YOUR CONFUSION, SUPERGIRL, BUT DO NOT BE AFRAID.

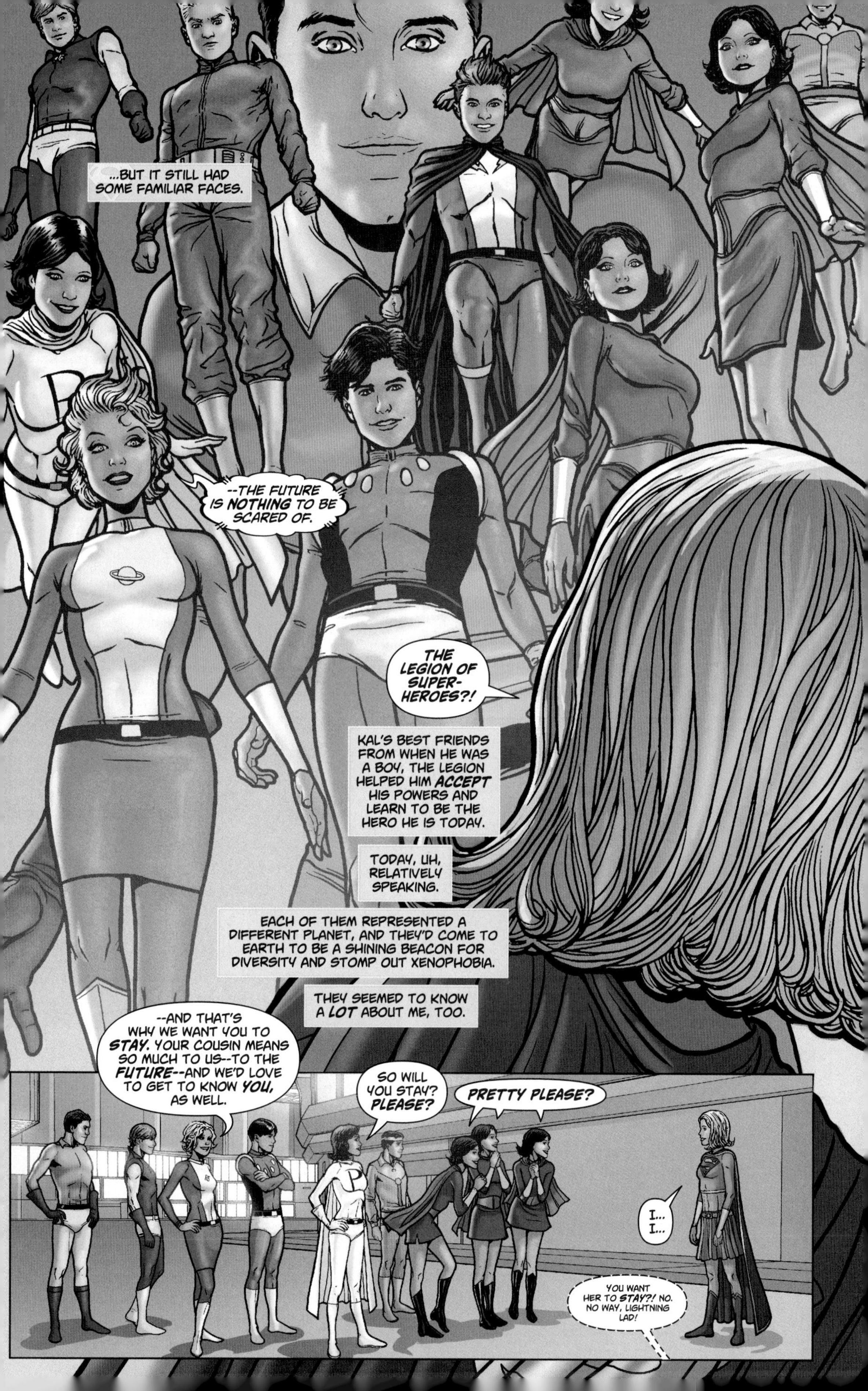
...BUT IT STILL HAD SOME FAMILIAR FACES.
--THE FUTURE IS NOTHING TO BE SCARED OF.
THE LEGION OF SUPER-HEROES?!
KAL'S BEST FRIENDS FROM WHEN HE WAS A BOY, THE LEGION HELPED HIM ACCEPT HIS POWERS AND LEARN TO BE THE HERO HE IS TODAY.
TODAY, UH, RELATIVELY SPEAKING.
EACH OF THEM REPRESENTED A DIFFERENT PLANET, AND THEY'D COME TO EARTH TO BE A SHINING BEACON FOR DIVERSITY AND STOMP OUT XENOPHOBIA.
THEY SEEMED TO KNOW A LOT ABOUT ME, TOO.
--AND THAT'S WHY WE WANT YOU TO STAY. YOUR COUSIN MEANS SO MUCH TO US--TO THE FUTURE--AND WE'D LOVE TO GET TO KNOW YOU, AS WELL.
SO WILL YOU STAY? PLEASE?
PRETTY PLEASE?
I... I...
YOU WANT HER TO STAY?! NO. NO WAY, LIGHTNING LAD!

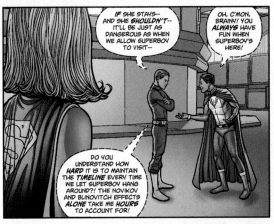

IF SHE STAYS--AND SHE *SHOULDN'T*--IT'LL BE JUST AS DANGEROUS AS WHEN WE ALLOW SUPERBOY TO VISIT--

OH, C'MON, BRAINY! YOU *ALWAYS* HAVE FUN WHEN SUPERBOY'S HERE!

DO YOU UNDERSTAND HOW *HARD* IT IS TO MAINTAIN THE *TIMELINE* EVERY TIME WE LET SUPERBOY HANG AROUND?! THE NOVIKOV AND BLINOVITCH EFFECTS *ALONE* TAKE ME *HOURS* TO ACCOUNT FOR!

AND WHAT IF SHE GETS LOOSE IN THE *SUPERMAN MUSEUM* AND LEARNS ABOUT HER OWN *FUTURE*, GARTH?!

IF SHE LEARNS IN *ADVANCE* ABOUT "THE SCION OF SUPERWOMAN" OR "THE DEADLY DAY OF THE DOLLMAKER" OR "LEX LUTHOR'S *OTHER* SON," THOSE THINGS MIGHT NOT HAPPEN. AND THEY *HAVE* TO HAPPEN!

THEY'RE *SET* EVENTS IN THE TIMESTREAM, AND IF WE *DISRUPT* THAT--

EASY. WE GET IMRA TO DO THE MEMORY TRICK THAT SHE DOES ON KAL, AND ALL OF THIS WILL JUST SEEM LIKE A *DREAM* TO HER.

AND I THOUGHT *YOU* WERE SUPPOSED TO BE THE *GENIUS* ON THIS TEAM.

NO, LIGHTNING LAD, THAT'S NOT *GOOD* ENOUGH. WE NEED TO SEND HER BACK *RIGHT NOW*, BEFORE THIS GETS ANY *WORSE*!

AND WHO *KNOWS* IF SHE EVEN *WANTS* TO STAY HERE--

ACTUALLY...

...I'D LIKE TO.

BUT *ONLY* IF IT'S OKAY WITH YOU, BRAINIAC 5.

UM... I...I... UH...

FINE.

BUT SUPERBOY *CANNOT* COME TO THE FUTURE WHILE *YOU'RE* HERE.

ONE POTENTIAL THREAT TO THE SPACE/TIME CONTINUUM AT A TIME.

I *KNEW* HIM, THOUGH. BRAINIAC 5. I'D MET HIM BEFORE...

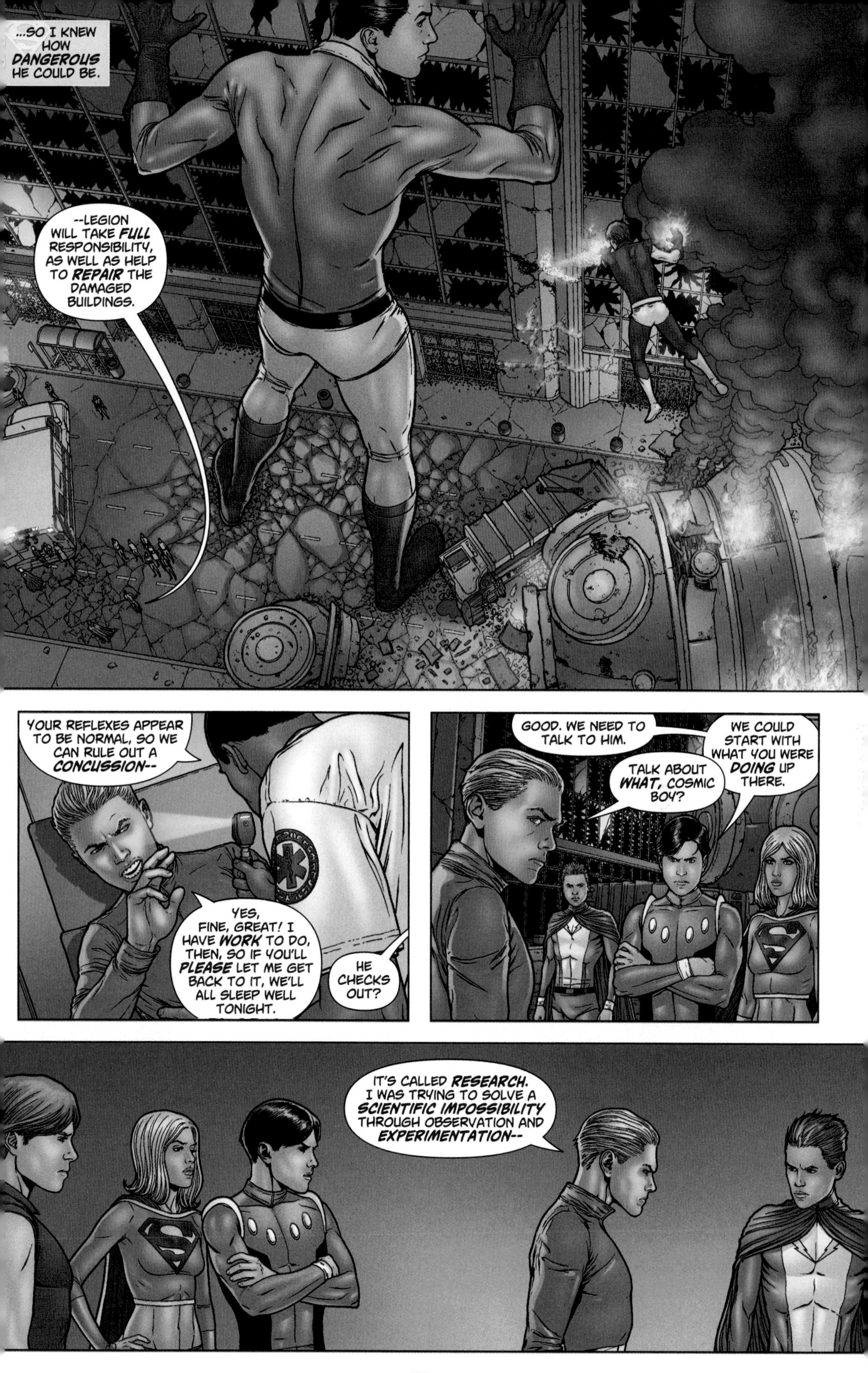
...SO I KNEW HOW DANGEROUS HE COULD BE.
--LEGION WILL TAKE FULL RESPONSIBILITY, AS WELL AS HELP TO REPAIR THE DAMAGED BUILDINGS.
YOUR REFLEXES APPEAR TO BE NORMAL, SO WE CAN RULE OUT A CONCUSSION--
YES, FINE, GREAT! I HAVE WORK TO DO, THEN, SO IF YOU'LL PLEASE LET ME GET BACK TO IT, WE'LL ALL SLEEP WELL TONIGHT.
HE CHECKS OUT?
GOOD. WE NEED TO TALK TO HIM.
TALK ABOUT WHAT, COSMIC BOY?
WE COULD START WITH WHAT YOU WERE DOING UP THERE.
IT'S CALLED RESEARCH. I WAS TRYING TO SOLVE A SCIENTIFIC IMPOSSIBILITY THROUGH OBSERVATION AND EXPERIMENTATION--

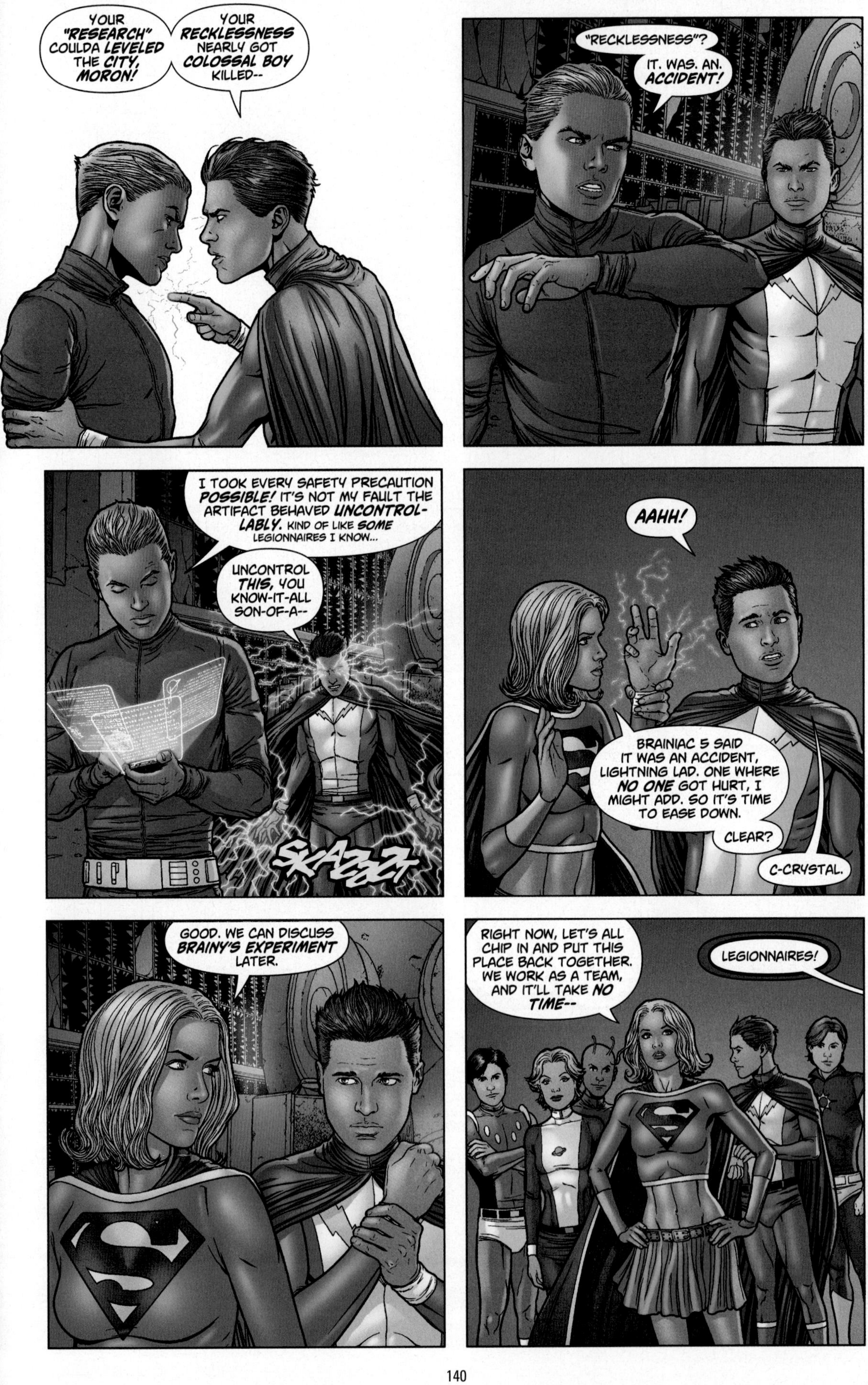
YOUR "RESEARCH" COULDA LEVELED THE CITY, MORON!
YOUR RECKLESSNESS NEARLY GOT COLOSSAL BOY KILLED--
"RECKLESSNESS"?
IT. WAS. AN. ACCIDENT!
I TOOK EVERY SAFETY PRECAUTION POSSIBLE! IT'S NOT MY FAULT THE ARTIFACT BEHAVED UNCONTROL-LABLY. KIND OF LIKE SOME LEGIONNAIRES I KNOW...
UNCONTROL THIS, YOU KNOW-IT-ALL SON-OF-A--
SKAZZZZK
AAHH!
BRAINIAC 5 SAID IT WAS AN ACCIDENT, LIGHTNING LAD. ONE WHERE NO ONE GOT HURT, I MIGHT ADD. SO IT'S TIME TO EASE DOWN.
CLEAR?
C-CRYSTAL.
GOOD. WE CAN DISCUSS BRAINY'S EXPERIMENT LATER.
RIGHT NOW, LET'S ALL CHIP IN AND PUT THIS PLACE BACK TOGETHER. WE WORK AS A TEAM, AND IT'LL TAKE NO TIME--
LEGIONNAIRES!

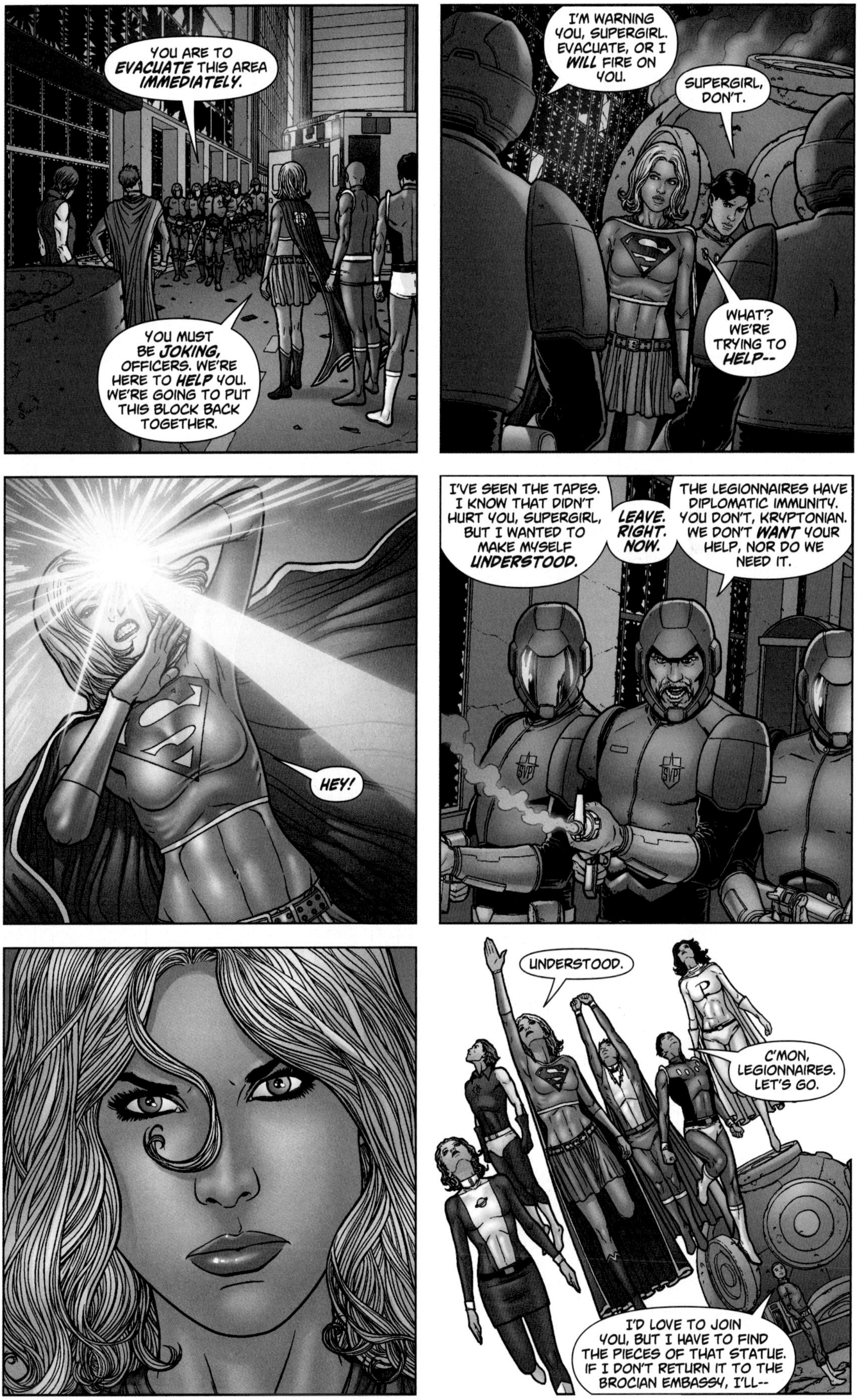
YOU ARE TO EVACUATE THIS AREA IMMEDIATELY.
YOU MUST BE JOKING, OFFICERS. WE'RE HERE TO HELP YOU. WE'RE GOING TO PUT THIS BLOCK BACK TOGETHER.
I'M WARNING YOU, SUPERGIRL. EVACUATE, OR I WILL FIRE ON YOU.
SUPERGIRL, DON'T.
WHAT? WE'RE TRYING TO HELP--
HEY!
I'VE SEEN THE TAPES. I KNOW THAT DIDN'T HURT YOU, SUPERGIRL, BUT I WANTED TO MAKE MYSELF UNDERSTOOD.
LEAVE. RIGHT. NOW.
THE LEGIONNAIRES HAVE DIPLOMATIC IMMUNITY. YOU DON'T, KRYPTONIAN. WE DON'T WANT YOUR HELP, NOR DO WE NEED IT.
UNDERSTOOD.
C'MON, LEGIONNAIRES. LET'S GO.
I'D LOVE TO JOIN YOU, BUT I HAVE TO FIND THE PIECES OF THAT STATUE. IF I DON'T RETURN IT TO THE BROCIAN EMBASSY, I'LL--

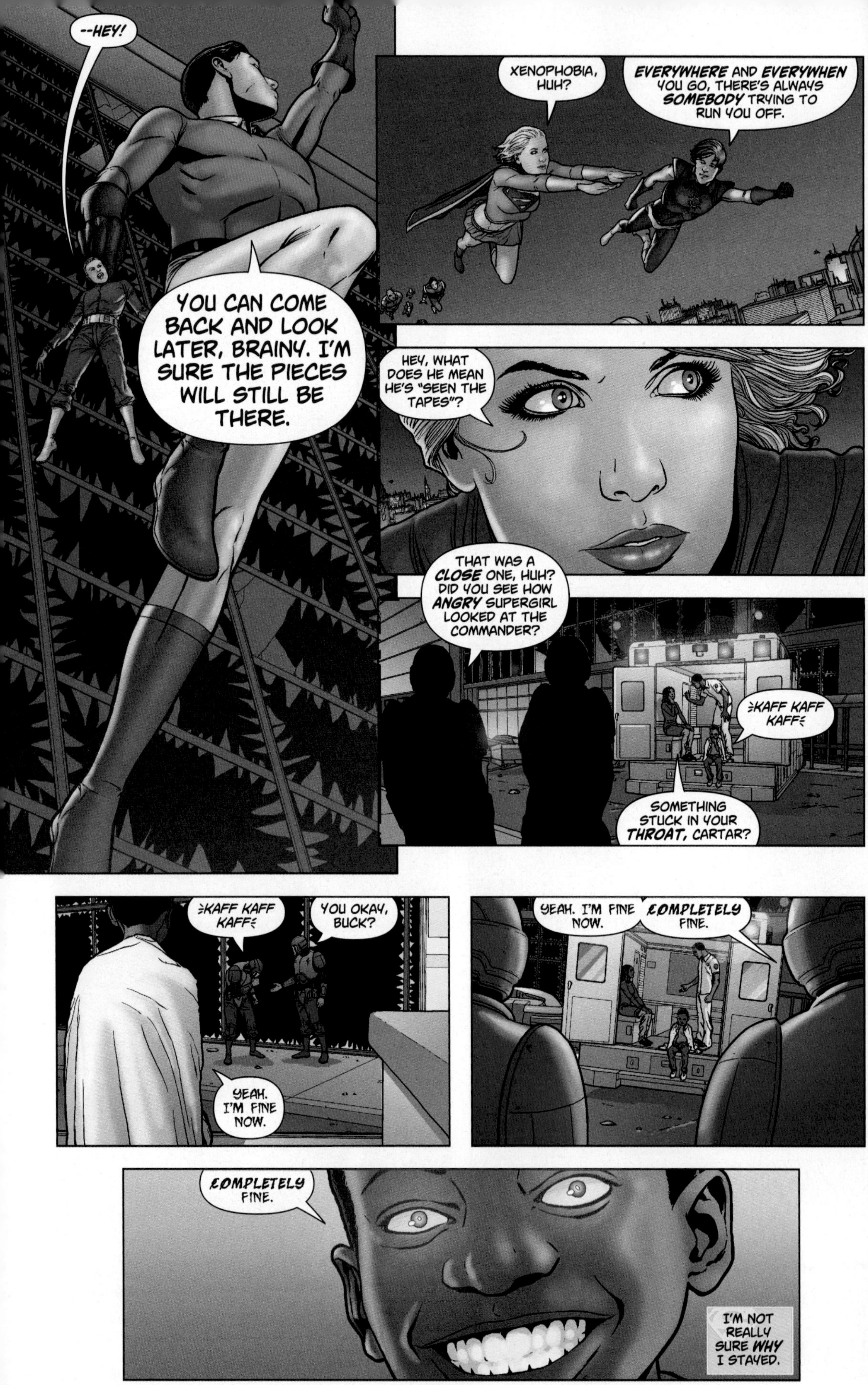
--HEY!
YOU CAN COME BACK AND LOOK LATER, BRAINY. I'M SURE THE PIECES WILL STILL BE THERE.
XENOPHOBIA, HUH?
EVERYWHERE AND EVERYWHEN YOU GO, THERE'S ALWAYS SOMEBODY TRYING TO RUN YOU OFF.
HEY, WHAT DOES HE MEAN HE'S "SEEN THE TAPES"?
THAT WAS A CLOSE ONE, HUH? DID YOU SEE HOW ANGRY SUPERGIRL LOOKED AT THE COMMANDER?
KAFF KAFF KAFF
SOMETHING STUCK IN YOUR THROAT, CARTAR?
KAFF KAFF KAFF
YOU OKAY, BUCK?
YEAH. I'M FINE NOW.
YEAH. I'M FINE NOW.
COMPLETELY FINE.
COMPLETELY FINE.
I'M NOT REALLY SURE WHY I STAYED.

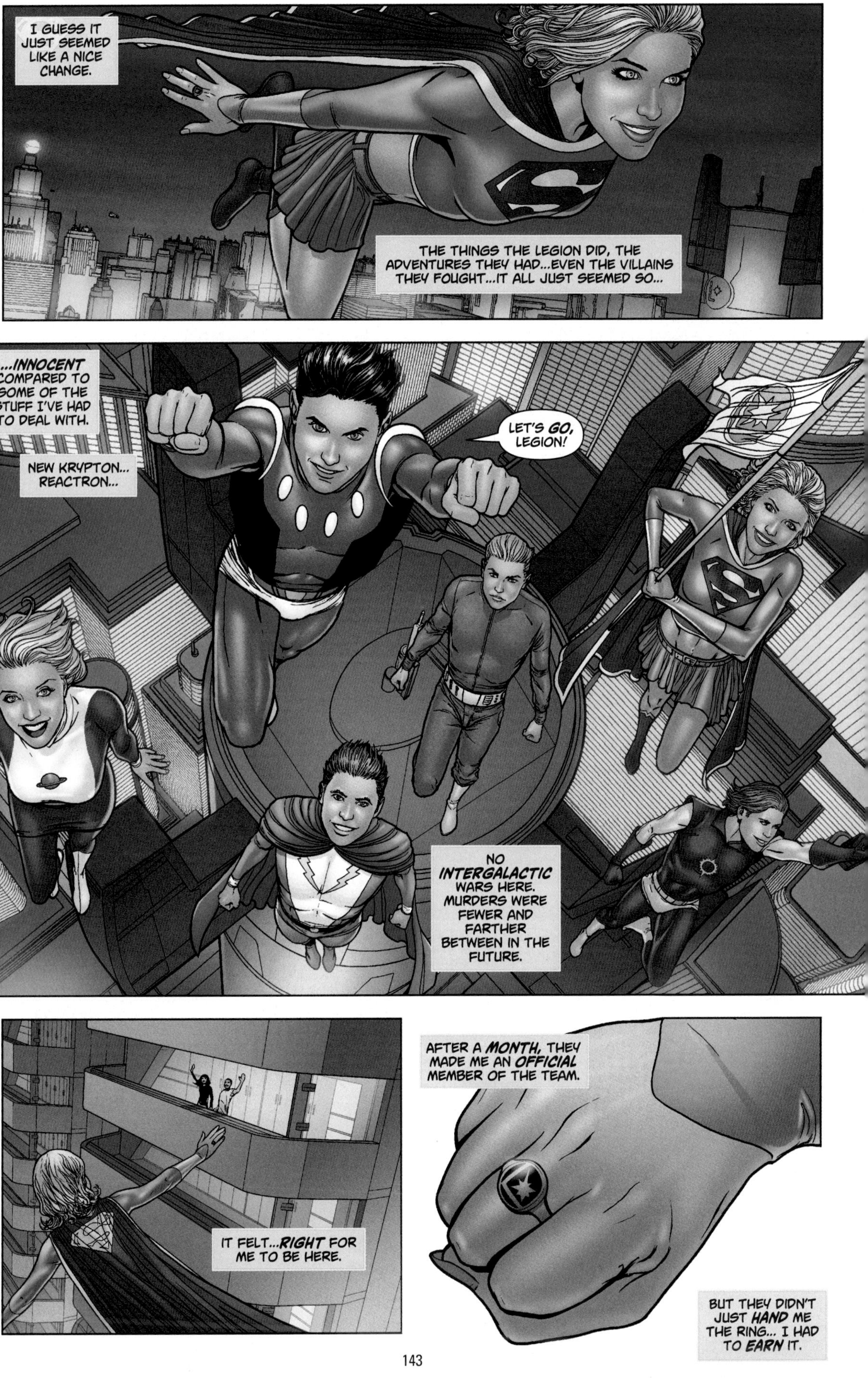
I GUESS IT JUST SEEMED LIKE A NICE CHANGE.
THE THINGS THE LEGION DID, THE ADVENTURES THEY HAD...EVEN THE VILLAINS THEY FOUGHT...IT ALL JUST SEEMED SO...
...INNOCENT COMPARED TO SOME OF THE STUFF I'VE HAD TO DEAL WITH.
NEW KRYPTON... REACTRON...
LET'S GO, LEGION!
NO INTERGALACTIC WARS HERE. MURDERS WERE FEWER AND FARTHER BETWEEN IN THE FUTURE.
IT FELT...RIGHT FOR ME TO BE HERE.
AFTER A MONTH, THEY MADE ME AN OFFICIAL MEMBER OF THE TEAM.
BUT THEY DIDN'T JUST HAND ME THE RING... I HAD TO EARN IT.

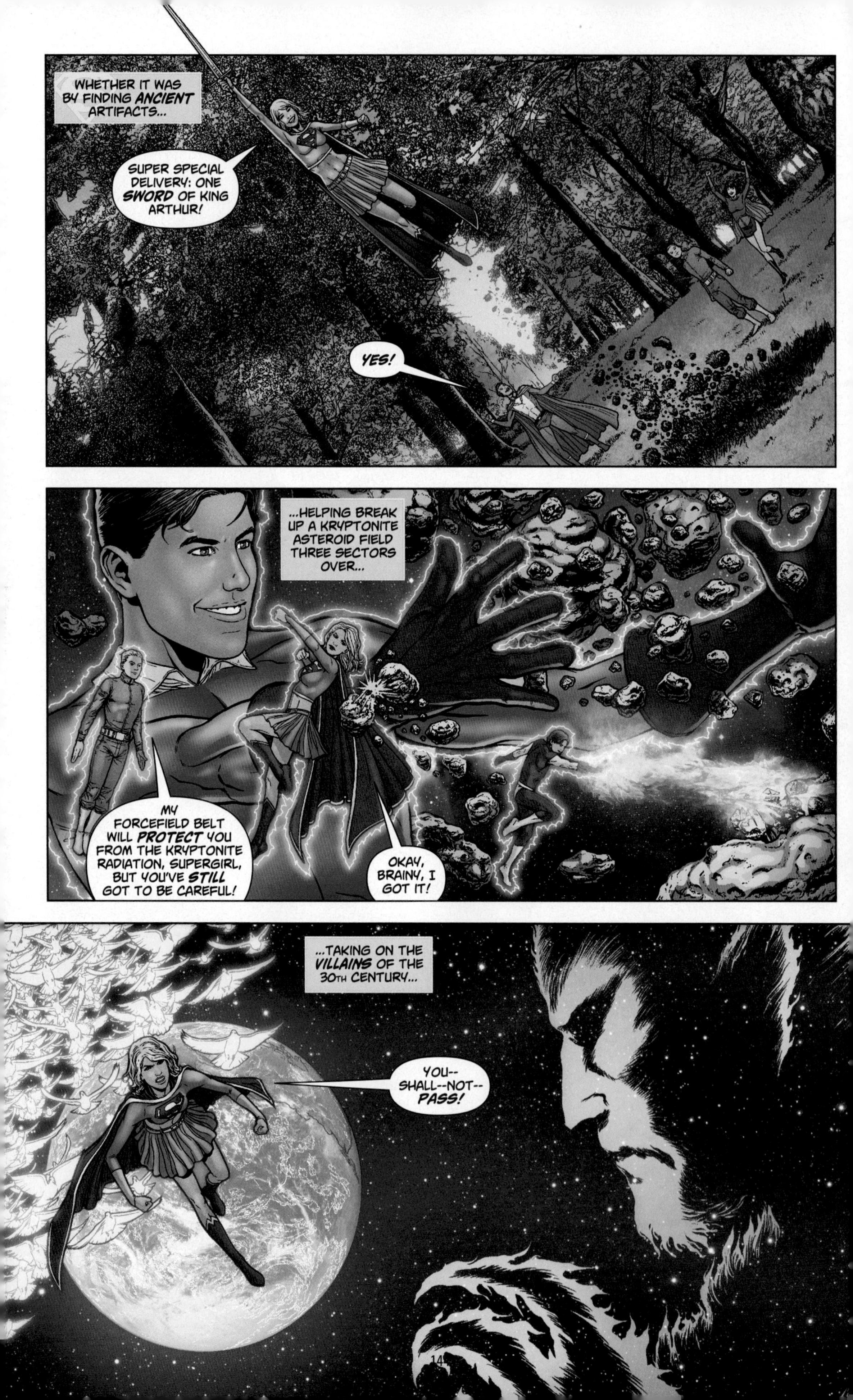
WHETHER IT WAS BY FINDING ANCIENT ARTIFACTS...
SUPER SPECIAL DELIVERY: ONE SWORD OF KING ARTHUR!
YES!
...HELPING BREAK UP A KRYPTONITE ASTEROID FIELD THREE SECTORS OVER...
MY FORCEFIELD BELT WILL PROTECT YOU FROM THE KRYPTONITE RADIATION, SUPERGIRL, BUT YOU'VE STILL GOT TO BE CAREFUL!
OKAY, BRAINY, I GOT IT!
...TAKING ON THE VILLAINS OF THE 30TH CENTURY...
YOU-- SHALL--NOT-- PASS!

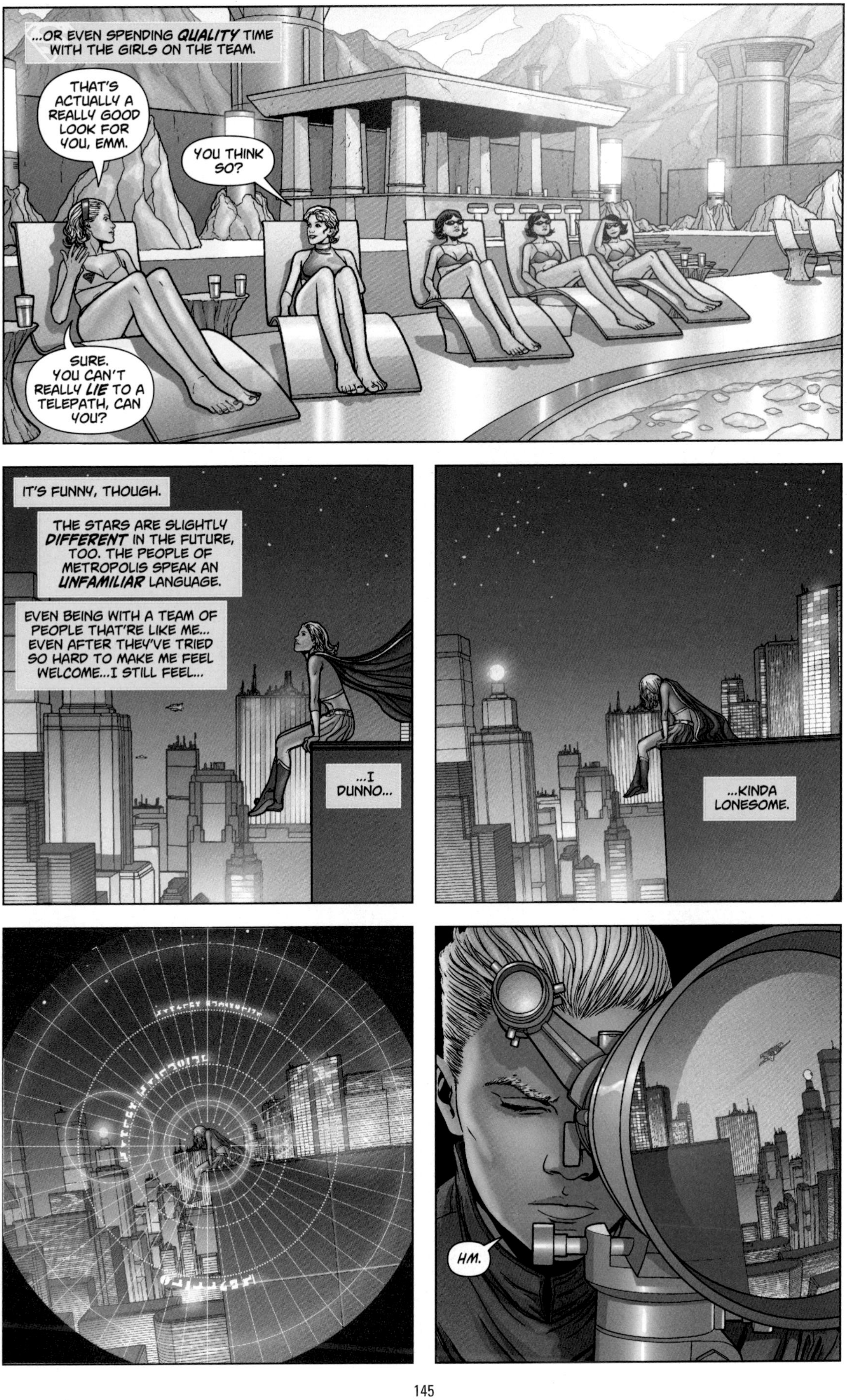
...OR EVEN SPENDING QUALITY TIME WITH THE GIRLS ON THE TEAM.
THAT'S ACTUALLY A REALLY GOOD LOOK FOR YOU, EMM.
YOU THINK SO?
SURE. YOU CAN'T REALLY LIE TO A TELEPATH, CAN YOU?
IT'S FUNNY, THOUGH.
THE STARS ARE SLIGHTLY DIFFERENT IN THE FUTURE, TOO. THE PEOPLE OF METROPOLIS SPEAK AN UNFAMILIAR LANGUAGE.
EVEN BEING WITH A TEAM OF PEOPLE THAT'RE LIKE ME... EVEN AFTER THEY'VE TRIED SO HARD TO MAKE ME FEEL WELCOME...I STILL FEEL...
...I DUNNO...
...KINDA LONESOME.
HM.

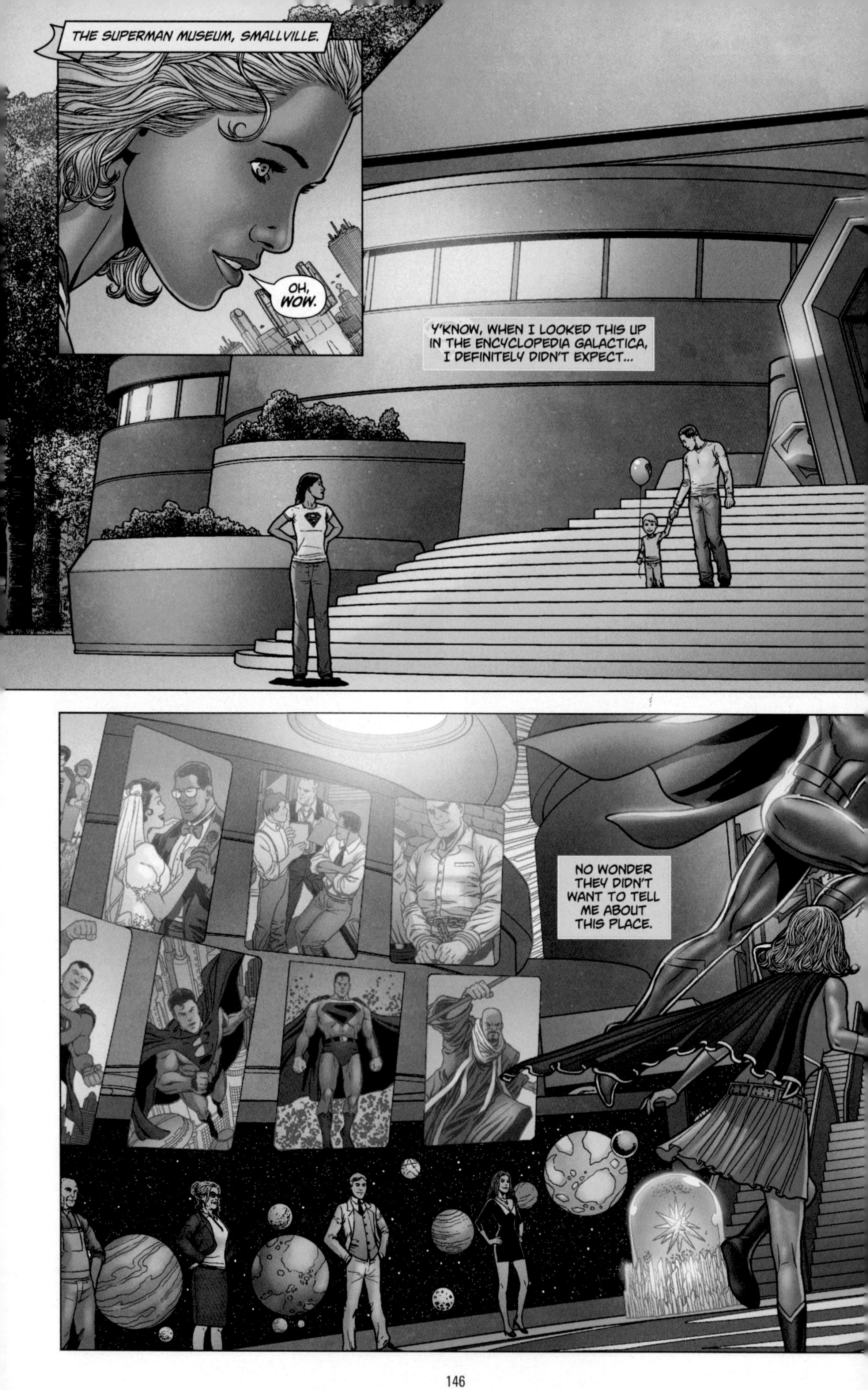
THE SUPERMAN MUSEUM, SMALLVILLE.
OH, WOW.
Y'KNOW, WHEN I LOOKED THIS UP IN THE ENCYCLOPEDIA GALACTICA, I DEFINITELY DIDN'T EXPECT...
NO WONDER THEY DIDN'T WANT TO TELL ME ABOUT THIS PLACE.

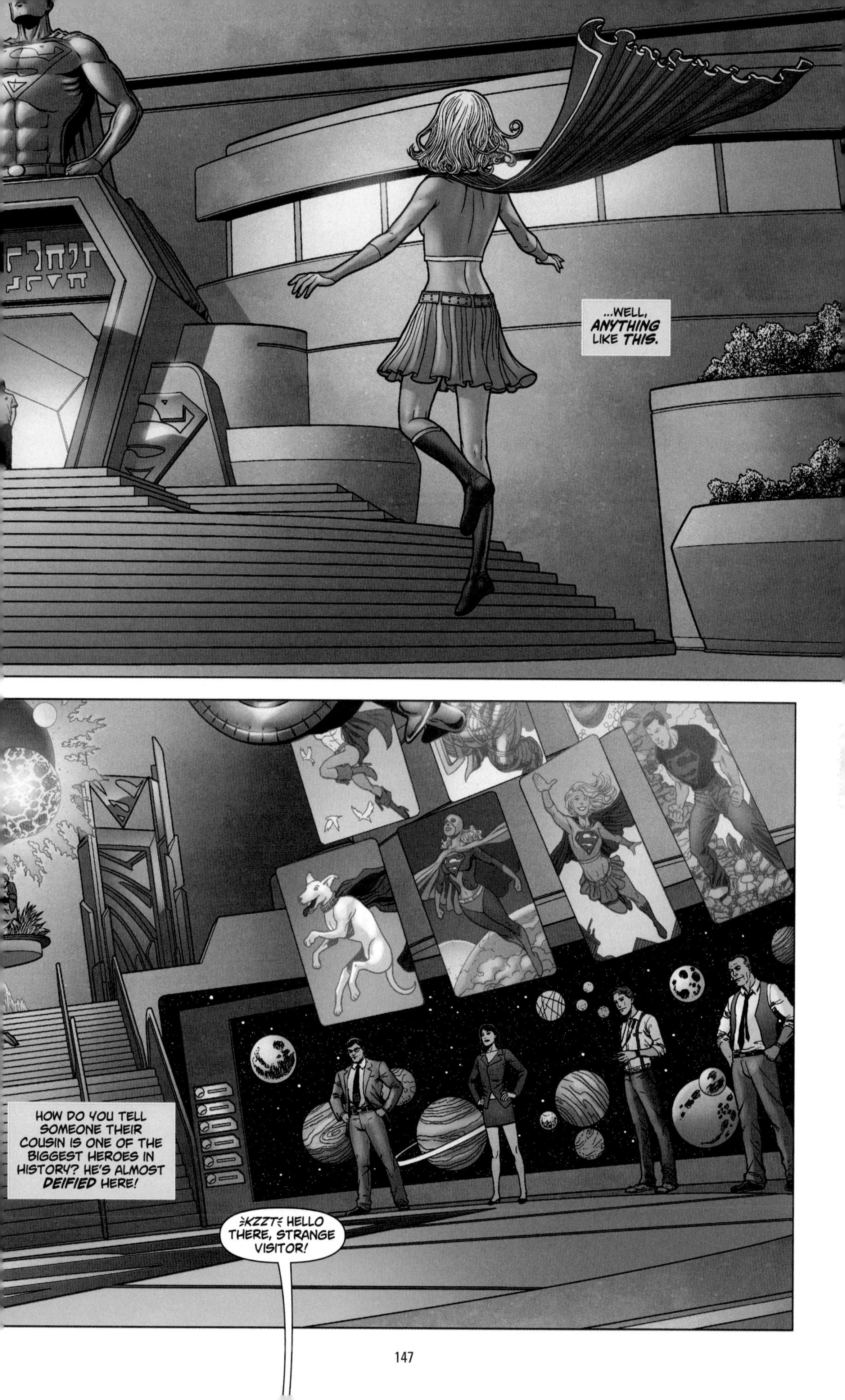
...WELL, ANYTHING LIKE THIS.
HOW DO YOU TELL SOMEONE THEIR COUSIN IS ONE OF THE BIGGEST HEROES IN HISTORY? HE'S ALMOST DEIFIED HERE!
KZZT HELLO THERE, STRANGE VISITOR!

WELCOME TO THE *SUPERMAN MUSEUM!* I'M JIMMY OLSEN.

A THOUSAND YEARS AGO, I WAS SUPERMAN'S *CONFIDANT* AND *BEST FRIEND.*

REALLY? I NEVER GOT THAT FROM THE TWO OF YOU.

HA HA! YOU'RE A JOKESTER. I'LL BE YOUR *HOLOGRAPHIC GUIDE* THIS MORNING. YOU GOT ANY QUESTIONS, ALL YOU GOTTA DO IS *ASK.* WHAT WOULD YOU LIKE TO SEE *FIRST?*

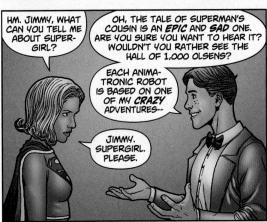

HM. JIMMY, WHAT CAN YOU TELL ME ABOUT SUPER-GIRL?

OH, THE TALE OF SUPERMAN'S COUSIN IS AN *EPIC* AND *SAD* ONE. ARE YOU SURE YOU WANT TO HEAR IT? WOULDN'T YOU RATHER SEE THE HALL OF 1,000 OLSENS?

EACH ANIMA-TRONIC ROBOT IS BASED ON ONE OF MY *CRAZY* ADVENTURES--

JIMMY. SUPERGIRL. PLEASE.

I CAN SEE YOU'RE SET ON THIS. OKAY, THEN.

FOLLOW ME.

--PARENTS SENT HER AWAY FROM ARGO CITY IN A ROCKET SO SHE WOULDN'T BE CAPTURED BY BRAINIAC LIKE THE REST OF THE KANDORIANS.

SHE CAME TO EARTH AND ALSO BECAME A HERO, STRIVING TO LIVE UP TO THE SYMBOL OF THE HOUSE OF EL--ONE THAT SUPERMAN HAD MADE INTO A SYMBOL OF HOPE.

TRAGICALLY, DURING ONE OF THE GREATEST BATTLES IN HISTORY, SHE WAS KILLED STOPPING THE WORST THREAT THE EARTH HAD EVER KNOWN, GIVING HER LIFE TO SAVE HER ADOPTED PLANET.

THAT'S WHY THE SUPERMAN MUSEUM COMMEMORATES HER COURAGE AND HEROISM IN LIFE WITH THE *"SUPERGIRL MEMORIAL HALL."*

...WHAT?

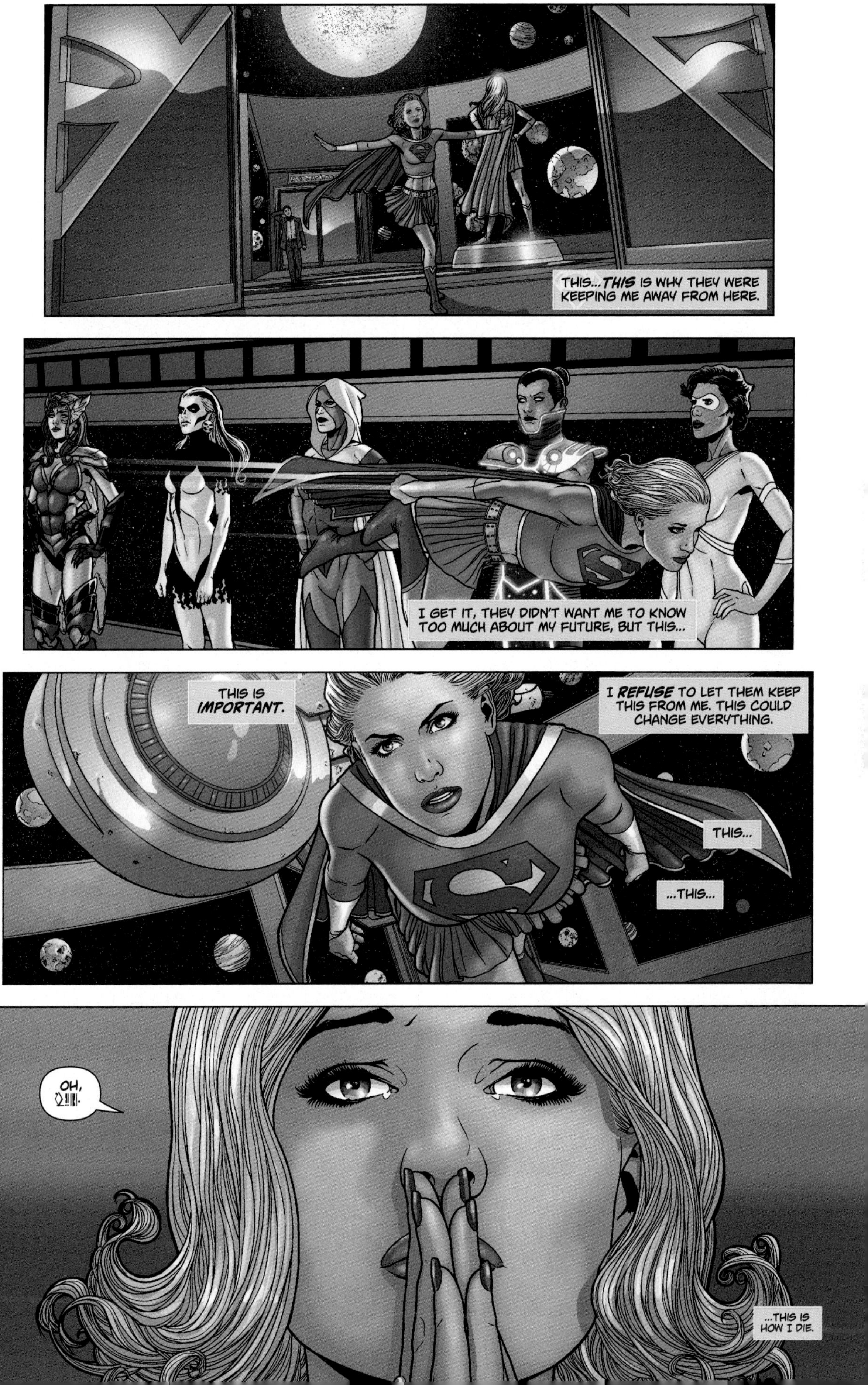
THIS...THIS IS WHY THEY WERE KEEPING ME AWAY FROM HERE.
I GET IT, THEY DIDN'T WANT ME TO KNOW TOO MUCH ABOUT MY FUTURE, BUT THIS...
THIS IS IMPORTANT.
I REFUSE TO LET THEM KEEP THIS FROM ME. THIS COULD CHANGE EVERYTHING.
THIS...
...THIS...
OH,
...THIS IS HOW I DIE.

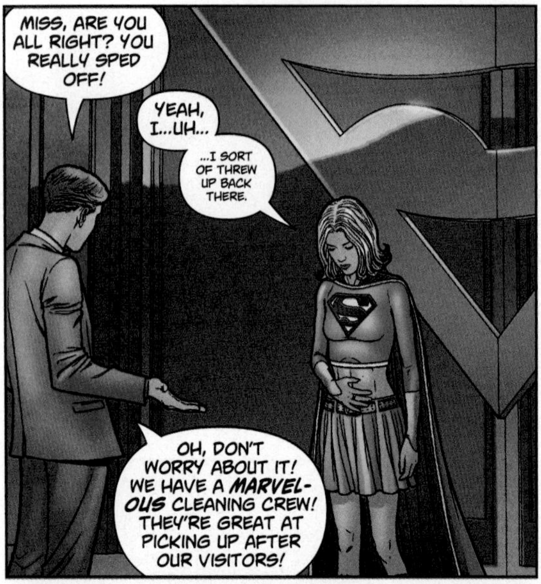
MISS, ARE YOU ALL RIGHT? YOU REALLY SPED OFF!
YEAH, I...UH...
...I SORT OF THREW UP BACK THERE.
OH, DON'T WORRY ABOUT IT! WE HAVE A MARVEL-OUS CLEANING CREW! THEY'RE GREAT AT PICKING UP AFTER OUR VISITORS!

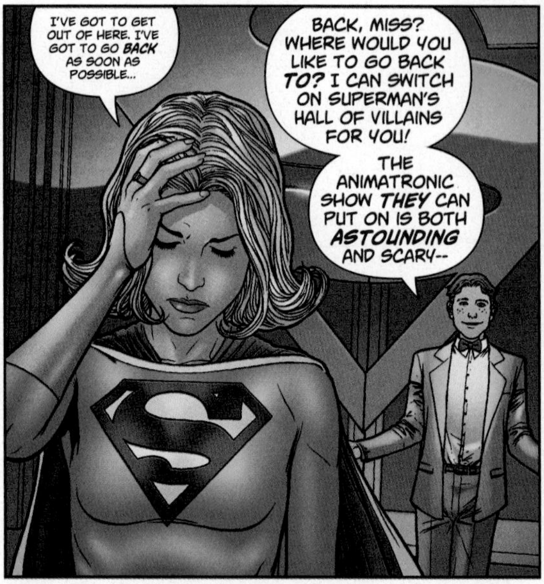
I'VE GOT TO GET OUT OF HERE. I'VE GOT TO GO BACK AS SOON AS POSSIBLE...
BACK, MISS? WHERE WOULD YOU LIKE TO GO BACK TO? I CAN SWITCH ON SUPERMAN'S HALL OF VILLAINS FOR YOU!
THE ANIMATRONIC SHOW THEY CAN PUT ON IS BOTH ASTOUNDING AND SCARY--

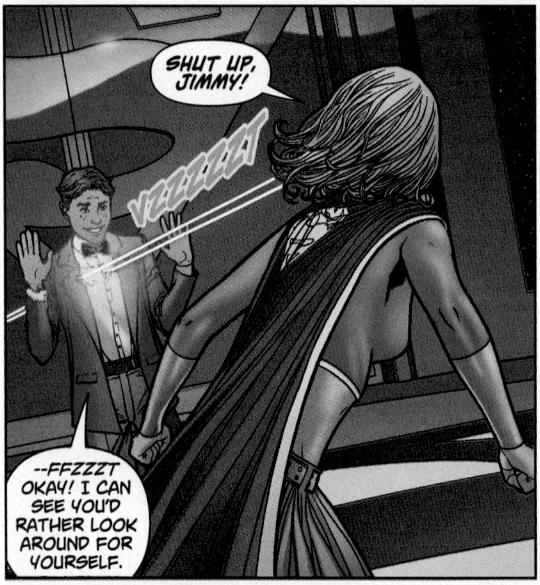
SHUT UP, JIMMY!
VZZZZZT
--FFZZZT OKAY! I CAN SEE YOU'D RATHER LOOK AROUND FOR YOURSELF.

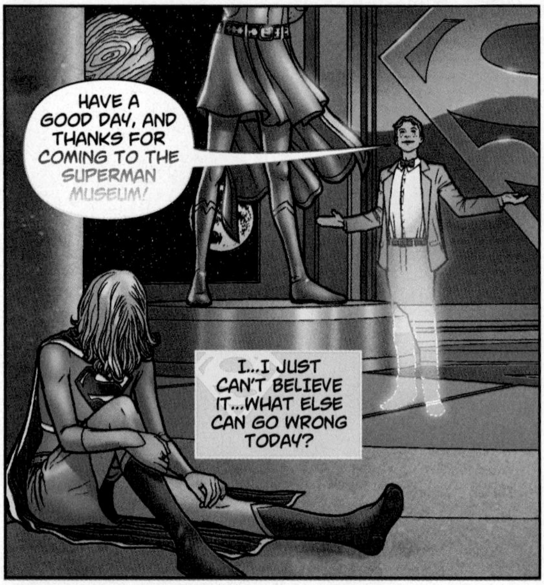
HAVE A GOOD DAY, AND THANKS FOR COMING TO THE SUPERMAN MUSEUM!
I...I JUST CAN'T BELIEVE IT...WHAT ELSE CAN GO WRONG TODAY?

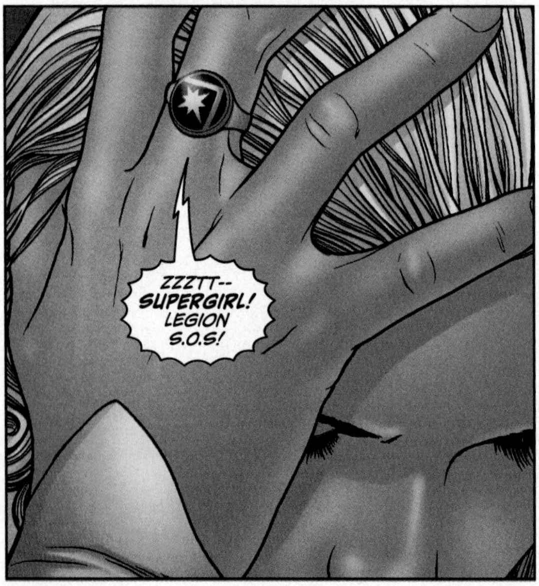
ZZZTT--SUPERGIRL! LEGION S.O.S!

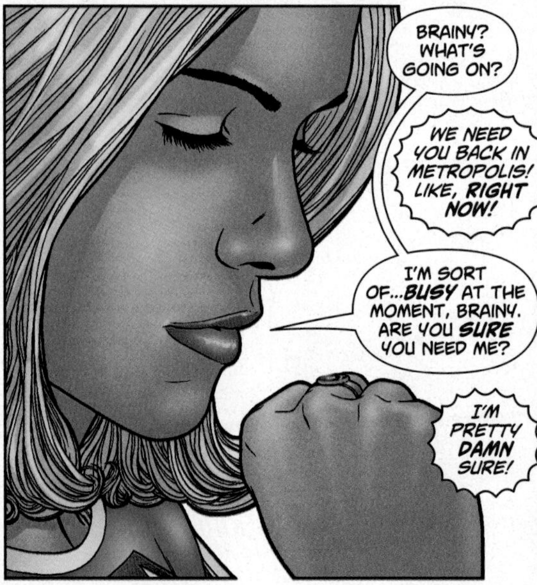
BRAINY? WHAT'S GOING ON?
WE NEED YOU BACK IN METROPOLIS! LIKE, RIGHT NOW!
I'M SORT OF...BUSY AT THE MOMENT, BRAINY. ARE YOU SURE YOU NEED ME?
I'M PRETTY DAMN SURE!

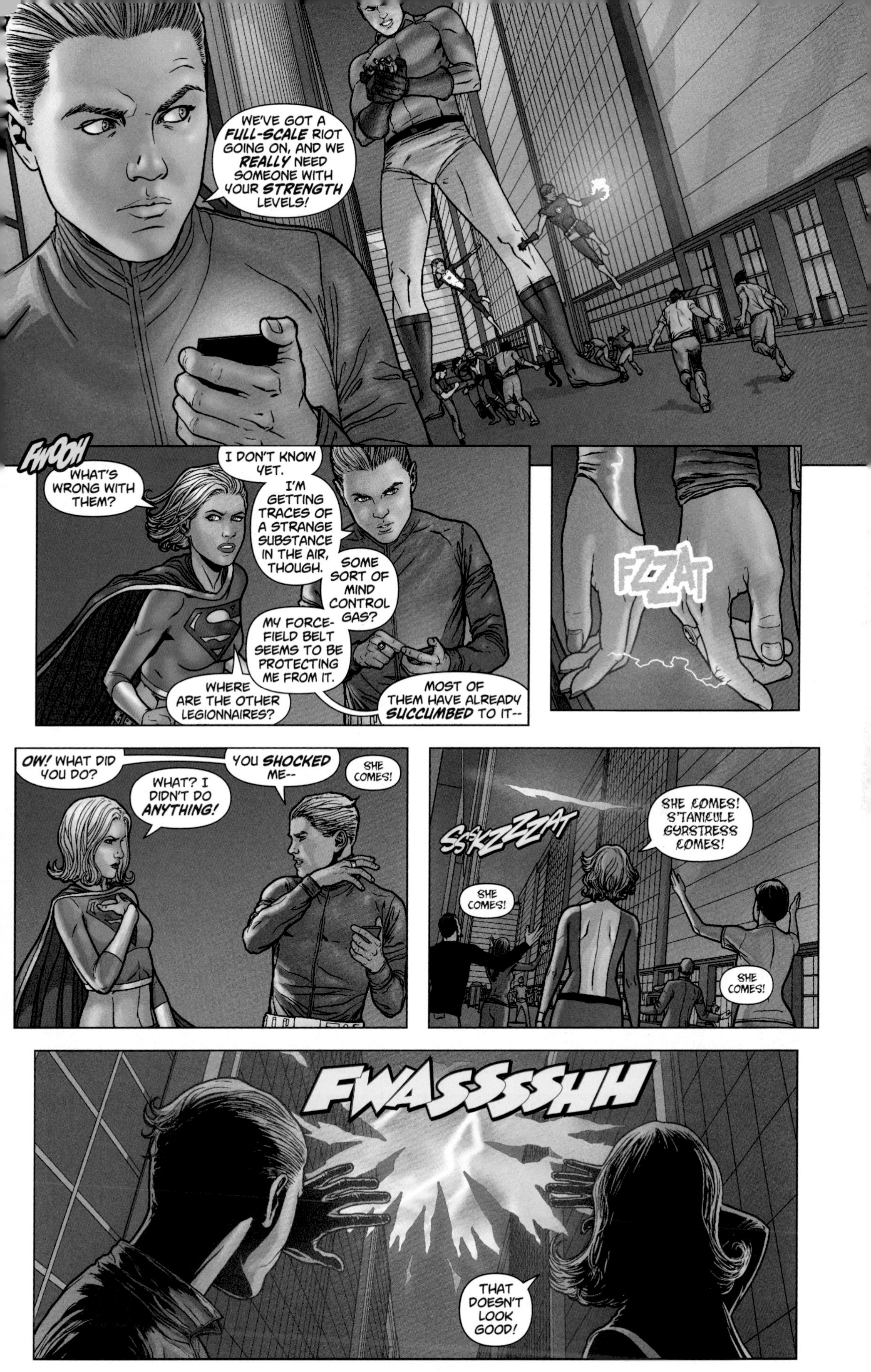

WE'VE GOT A FULL-SCALE RIOT GOING ON, AND WE REALLY NEED SOMEONE WITH YOUR STRENGTH LEVELS!
FWOOH
WHAT'S WRONG WITH THEM?
I DON'T KNOW YET.
I'M GETTING TRACES OF A STRANGE SUBSTANCE IN THE AIR, THOUGH.
SOME SORT OF MIND CONTROL GAS?
MY FORCE-FIELD BELT SEEMS TO BE PROTECTING ME FROM IT.
WHERE ARE THE OTHER LEGIONNAIRES?
MOST OF THEM HAVE ALREADY SUCCUMBED TO IT--
FZZAT
OW! WHAT DID YOU DO?
YOU SHOCKED ME--
WHAT? I DIDN'T DO ANYTHING!
SHE COMES!
SSKZZZZAT
SHE COMES! S'TANICULE GYRSTRESS COMES!
SHE COMES!
SHE COMES!
FWASSSSHH
THAT DOESN'T LOOK GOOD!

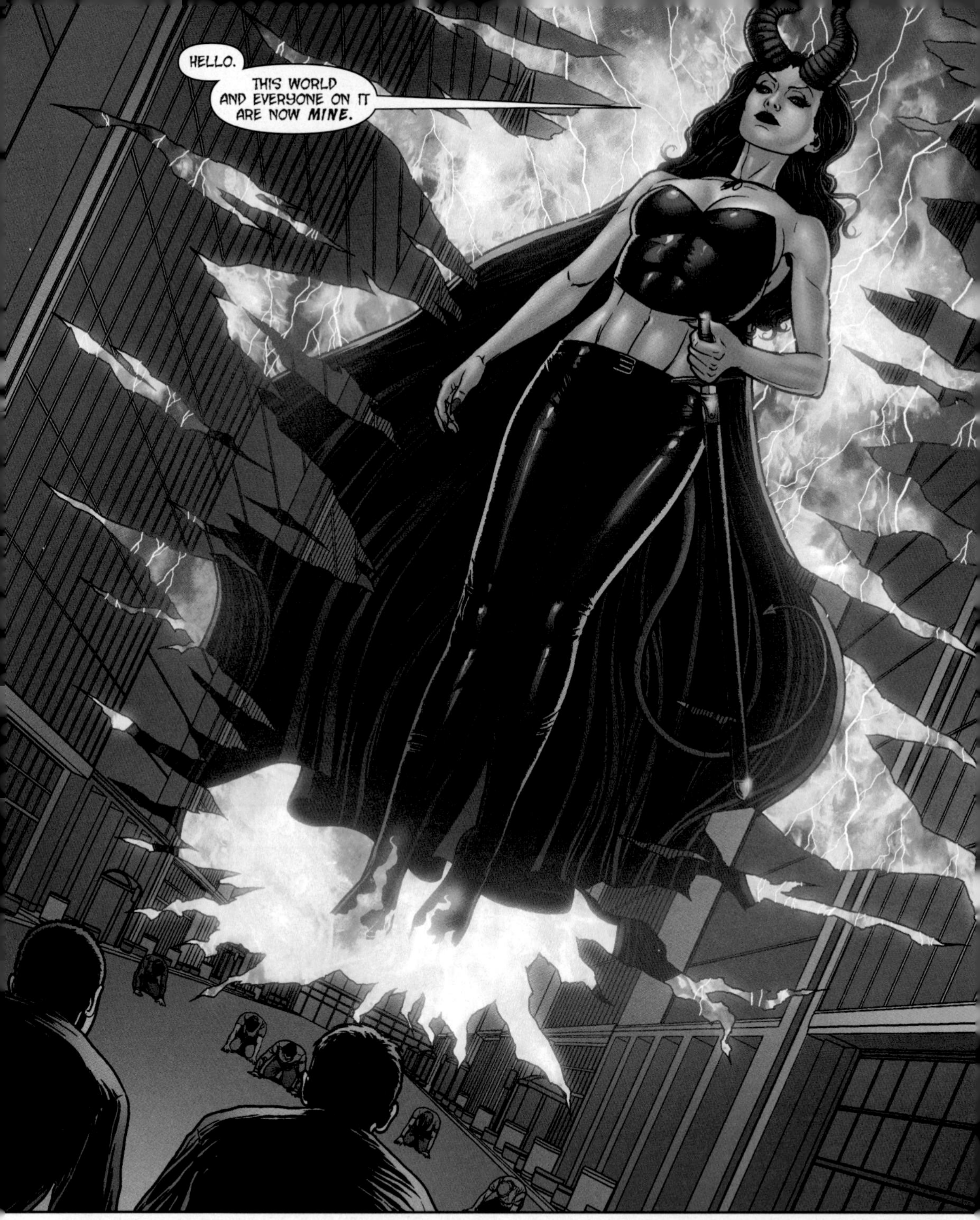
HELLO.
THIS WORLD AND EVERYONE ON IT ARE NOW MINE.

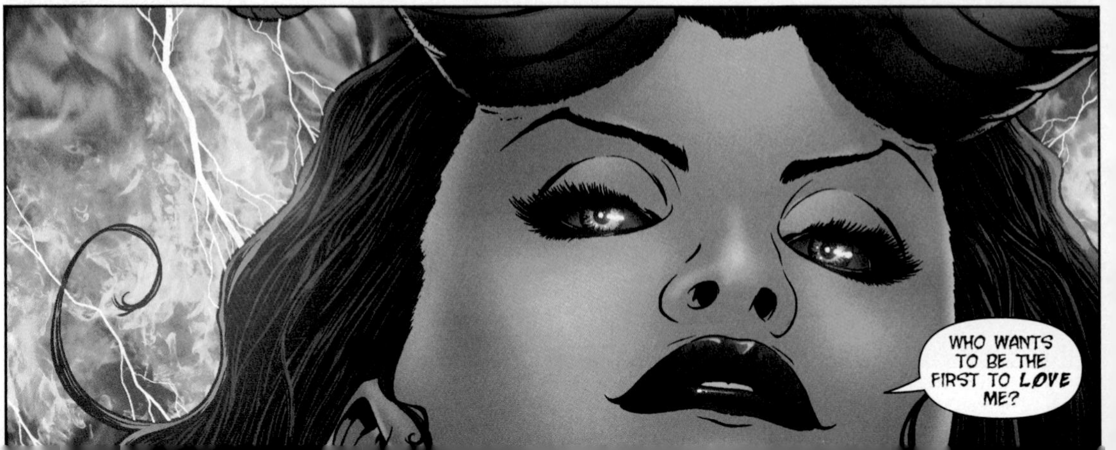
WHO WANTS TO BE THE FIRST TO LOVE ME?

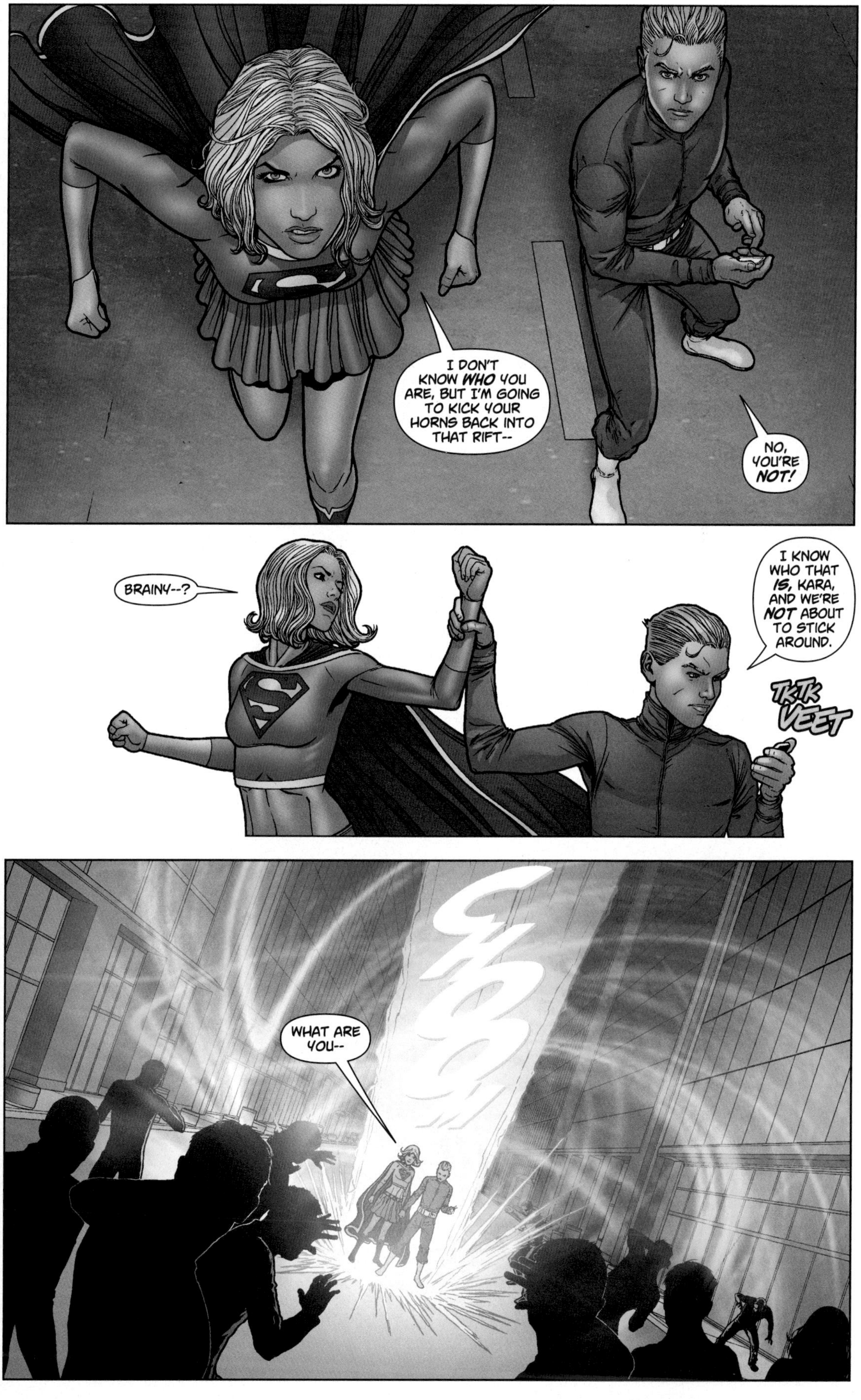
I DON'T KNOW **WHO** YOU ARE, BUT I'M GOING TO KICK YOUR HORNS BACK INTO THAT RIFT--
NO, YOU'RE **NOT!**
BRAINY--?
I KNOW WHO THAT **IS**, KARA, AND WE'RE **NOT** ABOUT TO STICK AROUND.
TKTK VEET
WHAT ARE YOU--

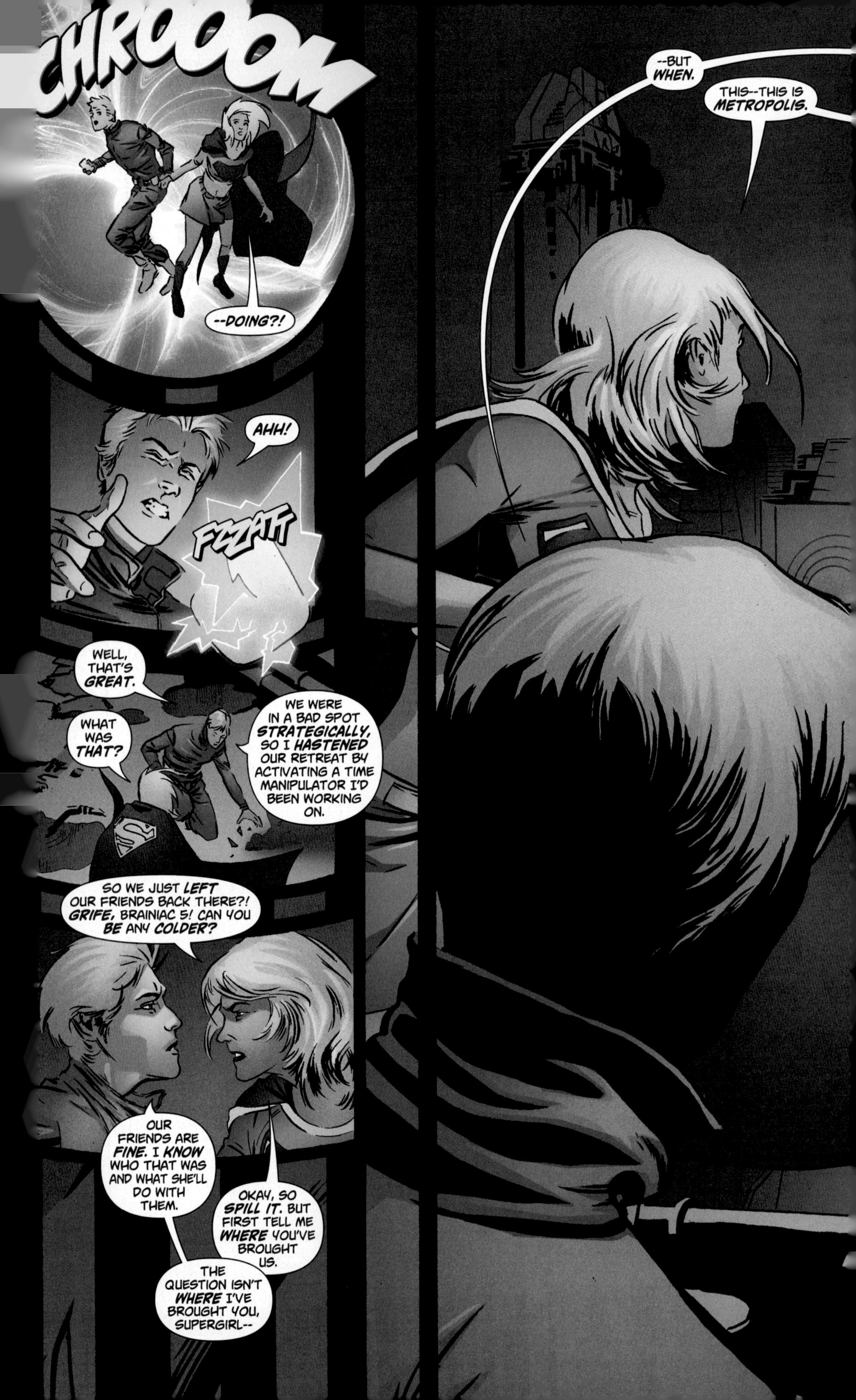
CHROOOM
--DOING?!
AHH!
FZZATT
WELL, THAT'S GREAT.
WHAT WAS THAT?
WE WERE IN A BAD SPOT STRATEGICALLY, SO I HASTENED OUR RETREAT BY ACTIVATING A TIME MANIPULATOR I'D BEEN WORKING ON.
SO WE JUST LEFT OUR FRIENDS BACK THERE?! GRIFE, BRAINIAC 5! CAN YOU BE ANY COLDER?
OUR FRIENDS ARE FINE. I KNOW WHO THAT WAS AND WHAT SHE'LL DO WITH THEM.
OKAY, SO SPILL IT. BUT FIRST TELL ME WHERE YOU'VE BROUGHT US.
THE QUESTION ISN'T WHERE I'VE BROUGHT YOU, SUPERGIRL--
--BUT WHEN.
THIS--THIS IS METROPOLIS.

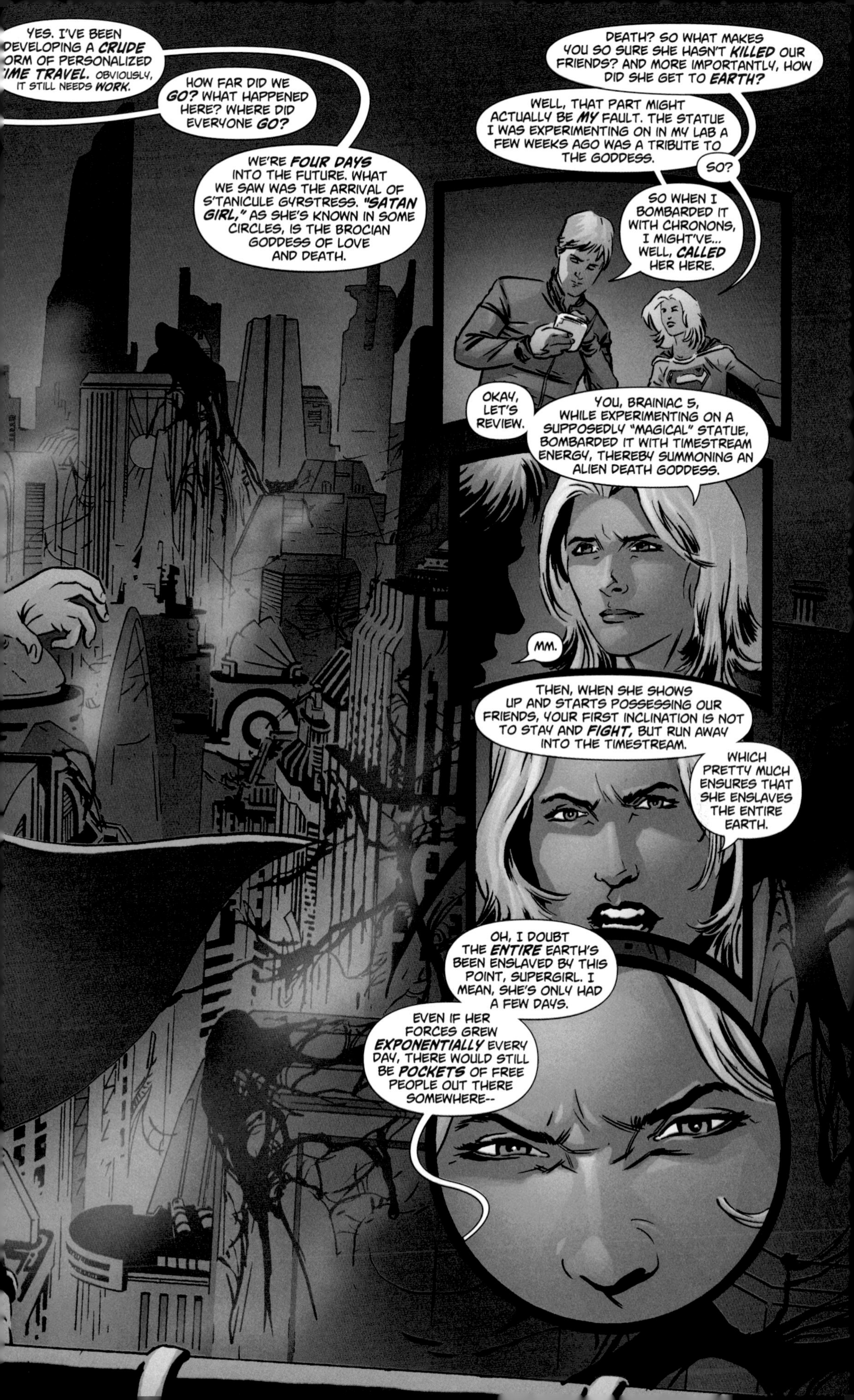
YES. I'VE BEEN DEVELOPING A CRUDE FORM OF PERSONALIZED TIME TRAVEL. OBVIOUSLY, IT STILL NEEDS WORK.
HOW FAR DID WE GO? WHAT HAPPENED HERE? WHERE DID EVERYONE GO?
WE'RE FOUR DAYS INTO THE FUTURE. WHAT WE SAW WAS THE ARRIVAL OF S'TANICULE GYRSTRESS. "SATAN GIRL," AS SHE'S KNOWN IN SOME CIRCLES, IS THE BROCIAN GODDESS OF LOVE AND DEATH.
DEATH? SO WHAT MAKES YOU SO SURE SHE HASN'T KILLED OUR FRIENDS? AND MORE IMPORTANTLY, HOW DID SHE GET TO EARTH?
WELL, THAT PART MIGHT ACTUALLY BE MY FAULT. THE STATUE I WAS EXPERIMENTING ON IN MY LAB A FEW WEEKS AGO WAS A TRIBUTE TO THE GODDESS.
SO?
SO WHEN I BOMBARDED IT WITH CHRONONS, I MIGHT'VE... WELL, CALLED HER HERE.
OKAY, LET'S REVIEW.
YOU, BRAINIAC 5, WHILE EXPERIMENTING ON A SUPPOSEDLY "MAGICAL" STATUE, BOMBARDED IT WITH TIMESTREAM ENERGY, THEREBY SUMMONING AN ALIEN DEATH GODDESS.
MM.
THEN, WHEN SHE SHOWS UP AND STARTS POSSESSING OUR FRIENDS, YOUR FIRST INCLINATION IS NOT TO STAY AND FIGHT, BUT RUN AWAY INTO THE TIMESTREAM.
WHICH PRETTY MUCH ENSURES THAT SHE ENSLAVES THE ENTIRE EARTH.
OH, I DOUBT THE ENTIRE EARTH'S BEEN ENSLAVED BY THIS POINT, SUPERGIRL. I MEAN, SHE'S ONLY HAD A FEW DAYS.
EVEN IF HER FORCES GREW EXPONENTIALLY EVERY DAY, THERE WOULD STILL BE POCKETS OF FREE PEOPLE OUT THERE SOMEWHERE--

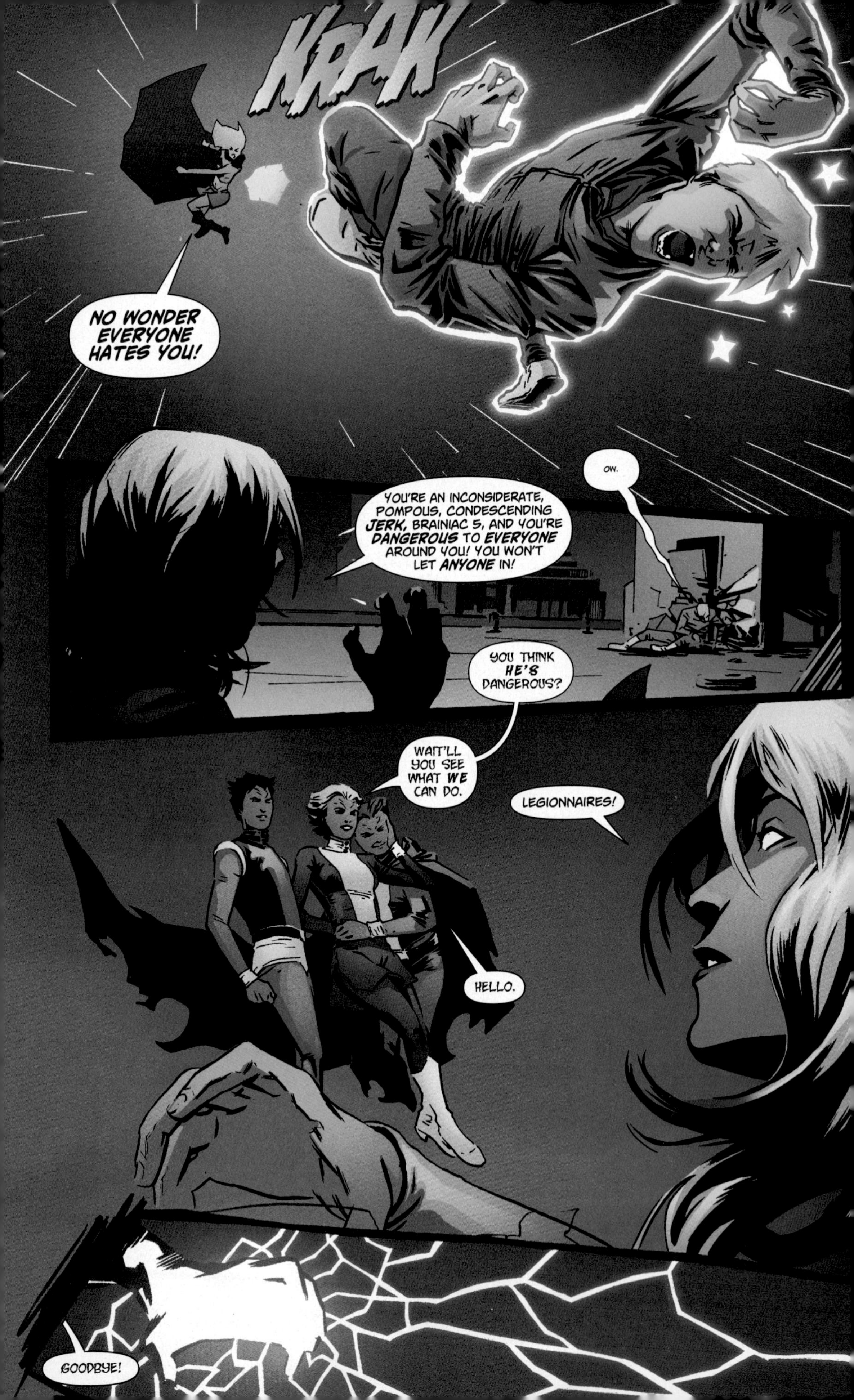
KRAK
NO WONDER EVERYONE HATES YOU!
YOU'RE AN INCONSIDERATE, POMPOUS, CONDESCENDING JERK, BRAINIAC 5, AND YOU'RE DANGEROUS TO EVERYONE AROUND YOU! YOU WON'T LET ANYONE IN!
OW.
YOU THINK HE'S DANGEROUS?
WAIT'LL YOU SEE WHAT WE CAN DO.
LEGIONNAIRES!
HELLO.
GOODBYE!

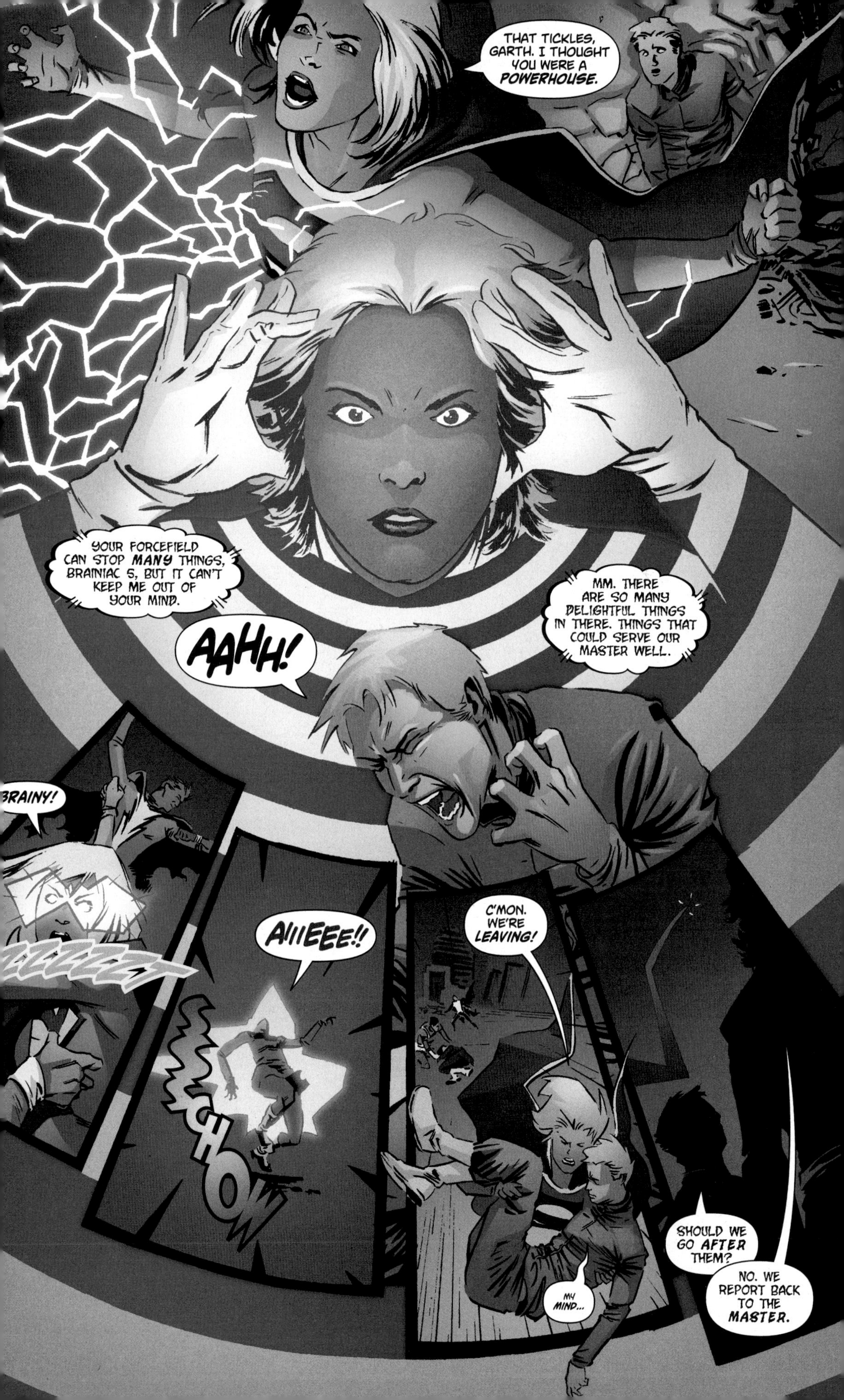

THAT TICKLES, GARTH. I THOUGHT YOU WERE A POWERHOUSE.
YOUR FORCEFIELD CAN STOP MANY THINGS, BRAINIAC 5, BUT IT CAN'T KEEP ME OUT OF YOUR MIND.
MM. THERE ARE SO MANY DELIGHTFUL THINGS IN THERE. THINGS THAT COULD SERVE OUR MASTER WELL.
AAHH!
BRAINY!
AIIIEEE!!
WHCHOW
C'MON. WE'RE LEAVING!
MY MIND...
SHOULD WE GO AFTER THEM?
NO. WE REPORT BACK TO THE MASTER.

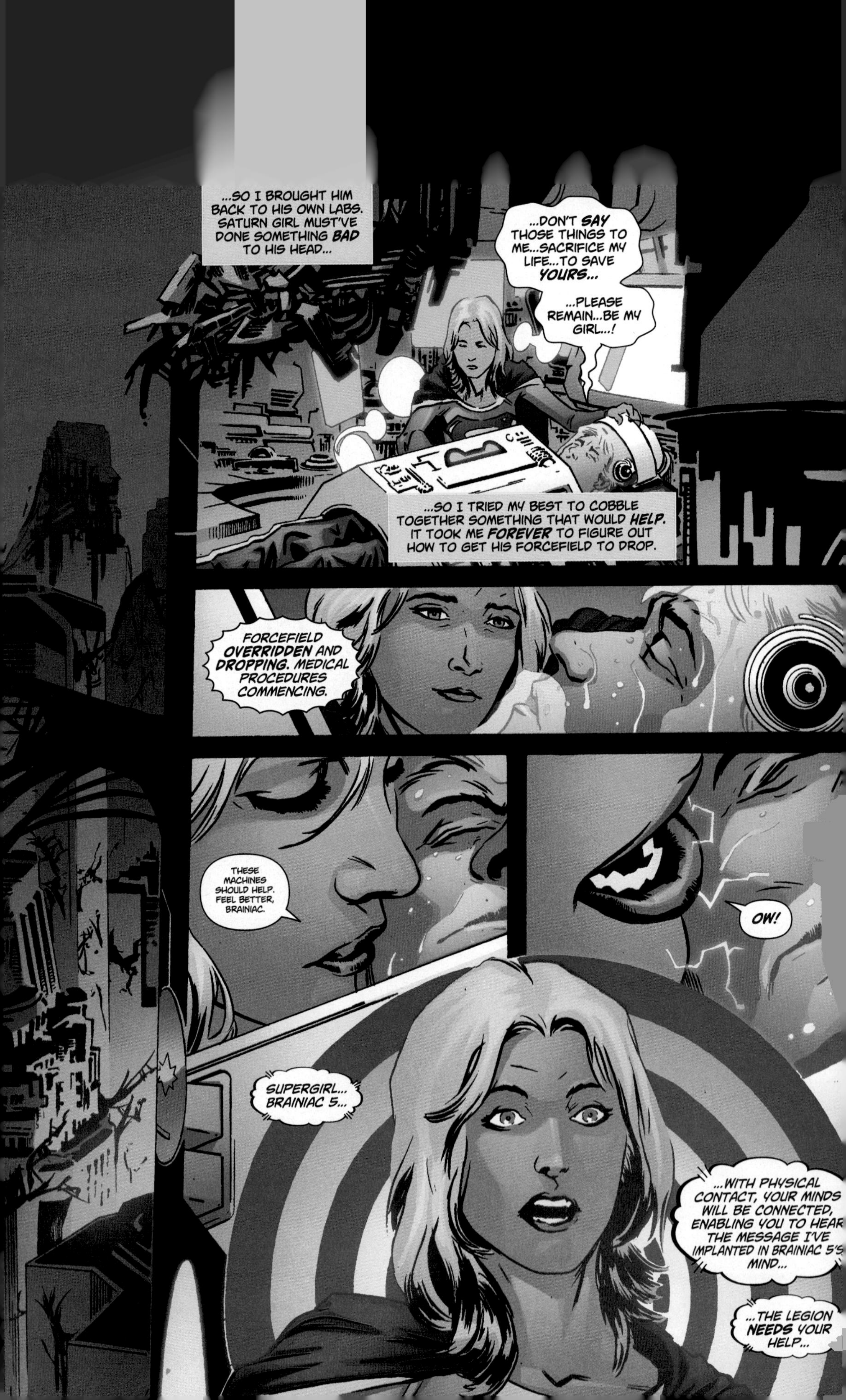

...SO I BROUGHT HIM BACK TO HIS OWN LABS. SATURN GIRL MUST'VE DONE SOMETHING BAD TO HIS HEAD...
...DON'T SAY THOSE THINGS TO ME...SACRIFICE MY LIFE...TO SAVE YOURS...
...PLEASE REMAIN...BE MY GIRL...!
...SO I TRIED MY BEST TO COBBLE TOGETHER SOMETHING THAT WOULD HELP. IT TOOK ME FOREVER TO FIGURE OUT HOW TO GET HIS FORCEFIELD TO DROP.
FORCEFIELD OVERRIDDEN AND DROPPING. MEDICAL PROCEDURES COMMENCING.
THESE MACHINES SHOULD HELP. FEEL BETTER, BRAINIAC.
OW!
SUPERGIRL... BRAINIAC 5...
...WITH PHYSICAL CONTACT, YOUR MINDS WILL BE CONNECTED, ENABLING YOU TO HEAR THE MESSAGE I'VE IMPLANTED IN BRAINIAC 5'S MIND...
...THE LEGION NEEDS YOUR HELP...

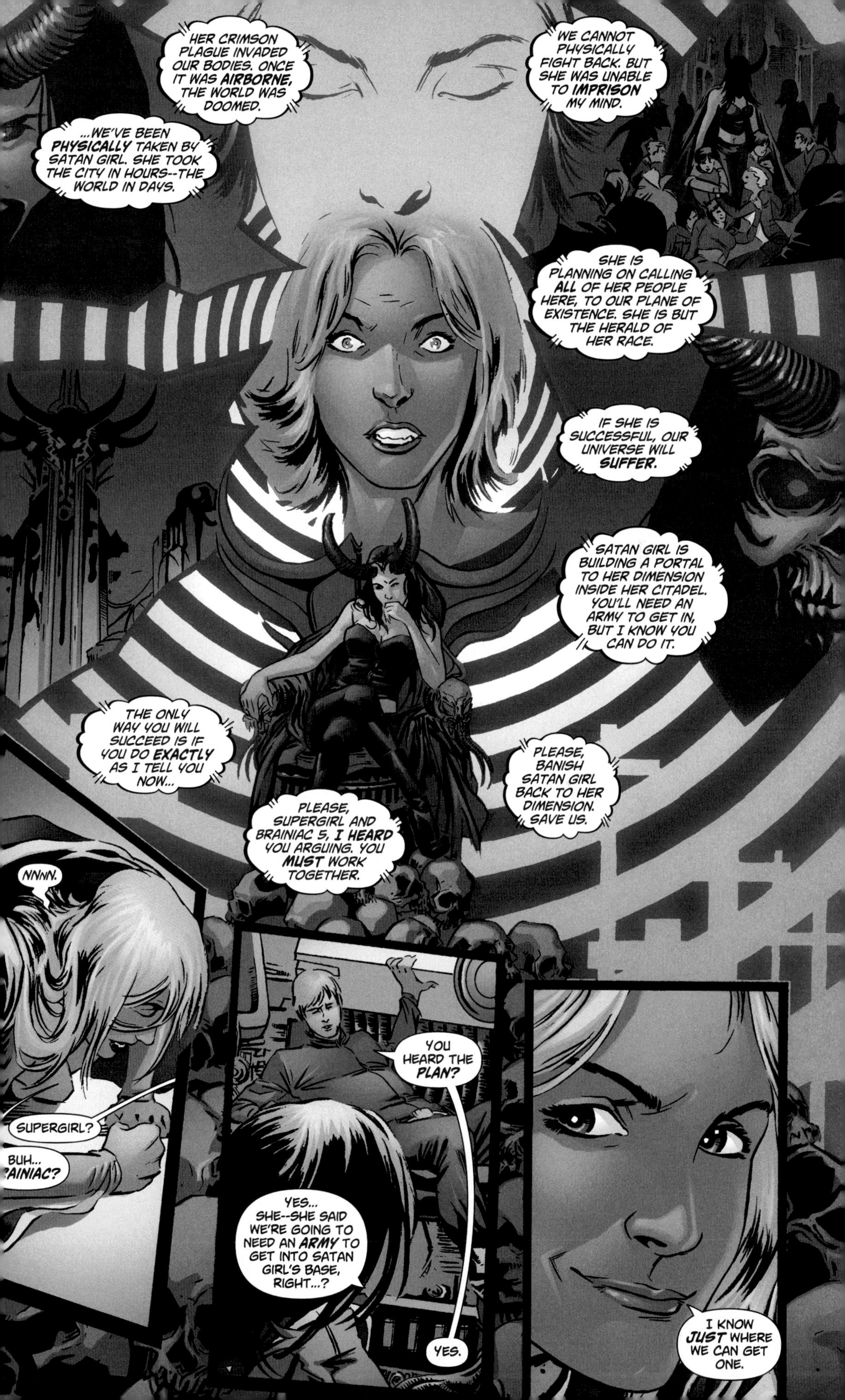
HER CRIMSON PLAGUE INVADED OUR BODIES. ONCE IT WAS AIRBORNE, THE WORLD WAS DOOMED.
...WE'VE BEEN PHYSICALLY TAKEN BY SATAN GIRL. SHE TOOK THE CITY IN HOURS--THE WORLD IN DAYS.
WE CANNOT PHYSICALLY FIGHT BACK. BUT SHE WAS UNABLE TO IMPRISON MY MIND.
SHE IS PLANNING ON CALLING ALL OF HER PEOPLE HERE, TO OUR PLANE OF EXISTENCE. SHE IS BUT THE HERALD OF HER RACE.
IF SHE IS SUCCESSFUL, OUR UNIVERSE WILL SUFFER.
SATAN GIRL IS BUILDING A PORTAL TO HER DIMENSION INSIDE HER CITADEL. YOU'LL NEED AN ARMY TO GET IN, BUT I KNOW YOU CAN DO IT.
THE ONLY WAY YOU WILL SUCCEED IS IF YOU DO EXACTLY AS I TELL YOU NOW...
PLEASE, BANISH SATAN GIRL BACK TO HER DIMENSION. SAVE US.
PLEASE, SUPERGIRL AND BRAINIAC 5, I HEARD YOU ARGUING. YOU MUST WORK TOGETHER.
NNNN.
SUPERGIRL?
BUH... RAINIAC?
YOU HEARD THE PLAN?
YES... SHE--SHE SAID WE'RE GOING TO NEED AN ARMY TO GET INTO SATAN GIRL'S BASE, RIGHT...?
YES.
I KNOW JUST WHERE WE CAN GET ONE.

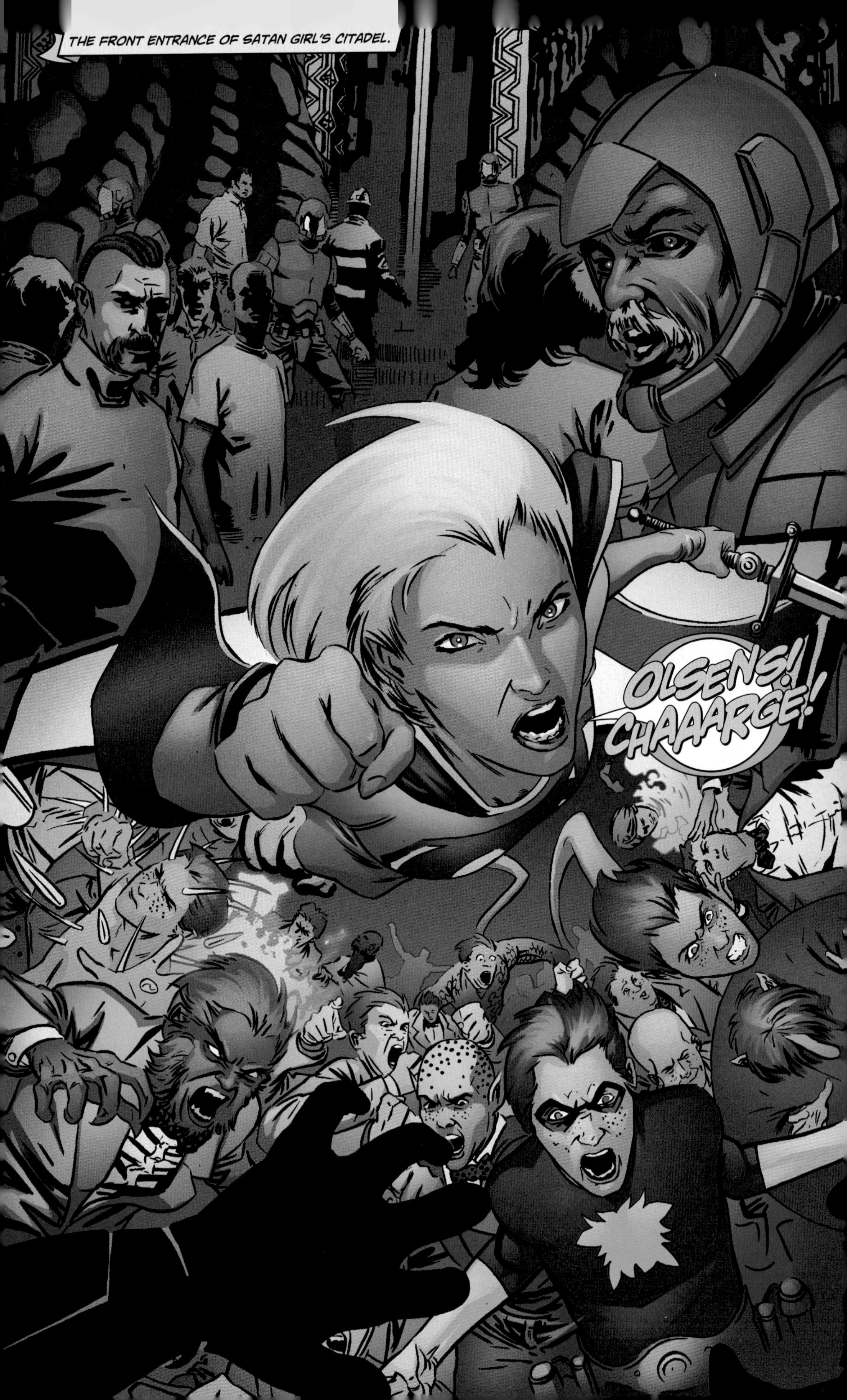
THE FRONT ENTRANCE OF SATAN GIRL'S CITADEL.
OLSENS! CHAAARGE!

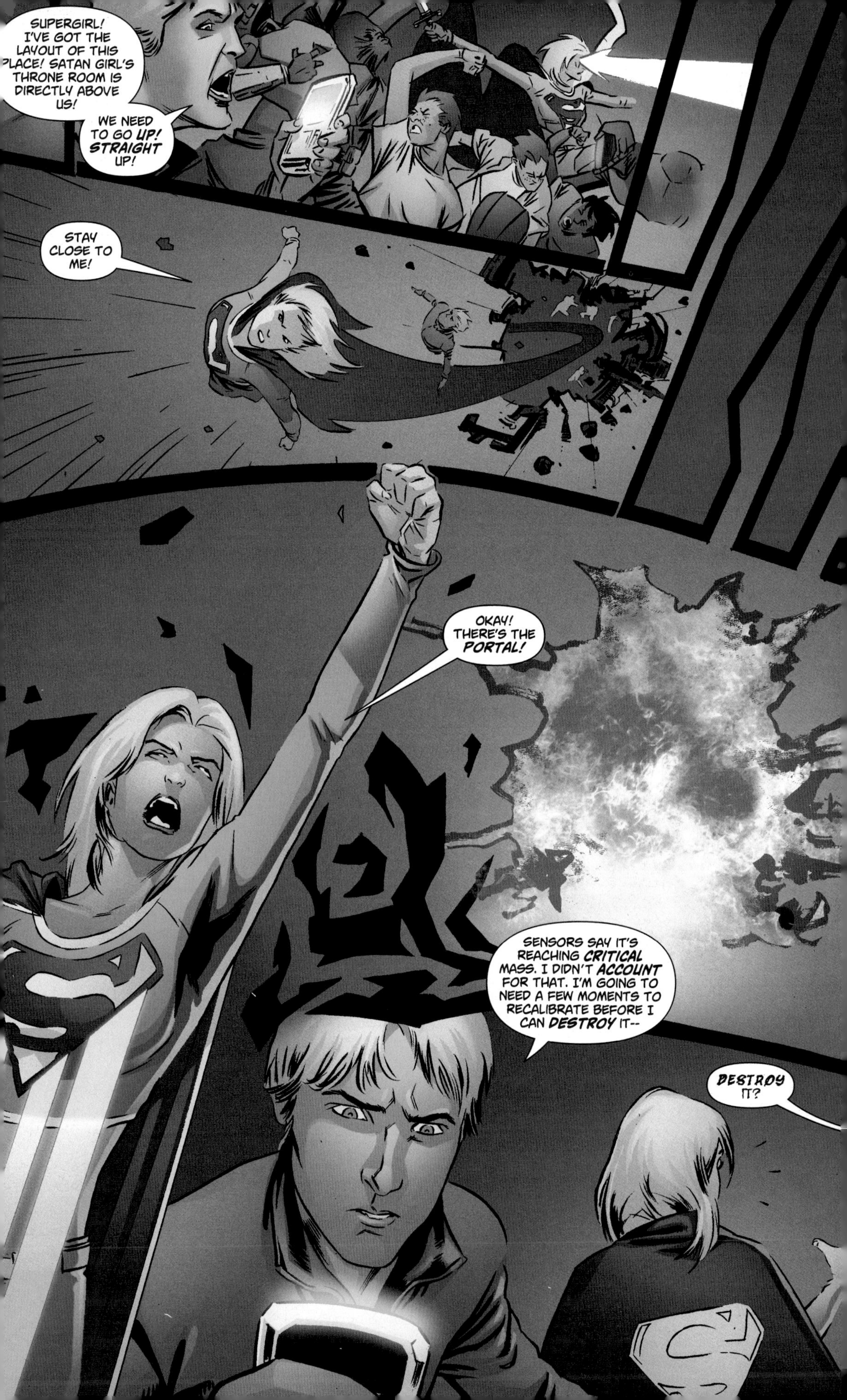
SUPERGIRL! I'VE GOT THE LAYOUT OF THIS PLACE! SATAN GIRL'S THRONE ROOM IS DIRECTLY ABOVE US!
WE NEED TO GO UP! STRAIGHT UP!
STAY CLOSE TO ME!
OKAY! THERE'S THE PORTAL!
SENSORS SAY IT'S REACHING CRITICAL MASS. I DIDN'T ACCOUNT FOR THAT. I'M GOING TO NEED A FEW MOMENTS TO RECALIBRATE BEFORE I CAN DESTROY IT--
DESTROY IT?

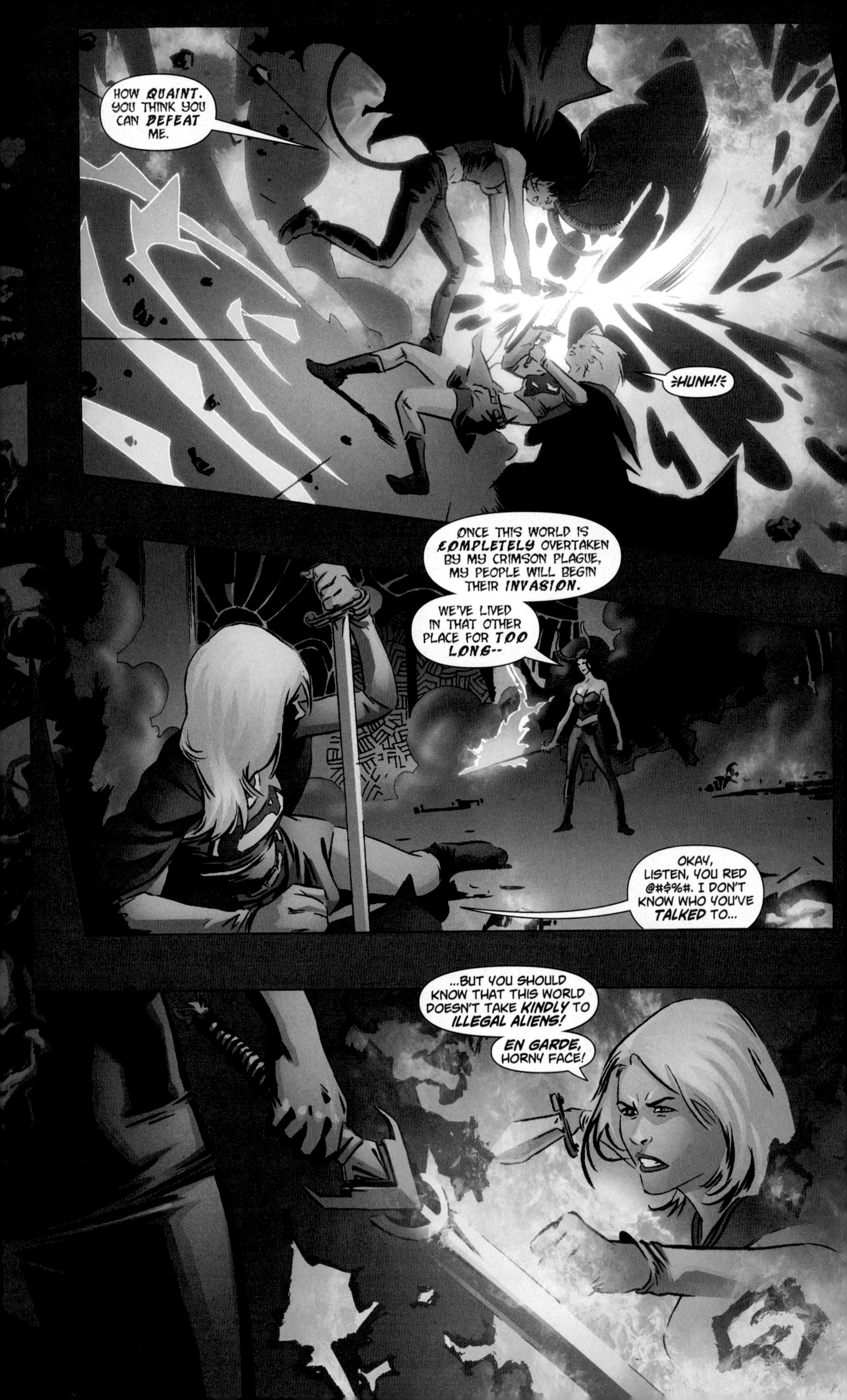
HOW QUAINT. YOU THINK YOU CAN DEFEAT ME.
HUNH!
ONCE THIS WORLD IS COMPLETELY OVERTAKEN BY MY CRIMSON PLAGUE, MY PEOPLE WILL BEGIN THEIR INVASION.
WE'VE LIVED IN THAT OTHER PLACE FOR TOO LONG--
OKAY, LISTEN, YOU RED @#$%#. I DON'T KNOW WHO YOU'VE TALKED TO...
...BUT YOU SHOULD KNOW THAT THIS WORLD DOESN'T TAKE KINDLY TO ILLEGAL ALIENS!
EN GARDE, HORNY FACE!

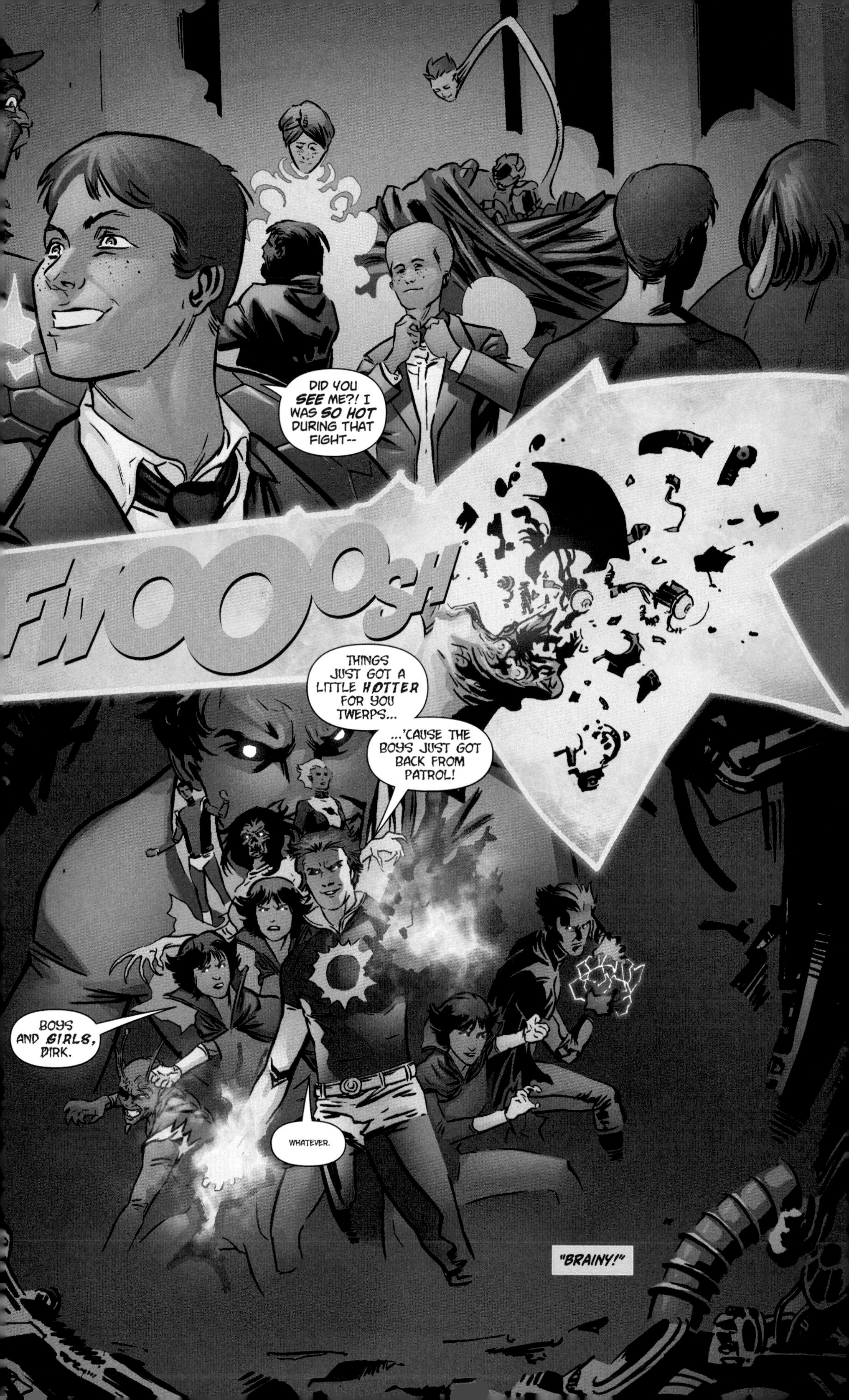
DID YOU SEE ME?! I WAS SO HOT DURING THAT FIGHT--
FWOOOSH
THINGS JUST GOT A LITTLE HOTTER FOR YOU TWERPS...
...'CAUSE THE BOYS JUST GOT BACK FROM PATROL!
BOYS AND GIRLS, DIRK.
WHATEVER.
"BRAINY!"

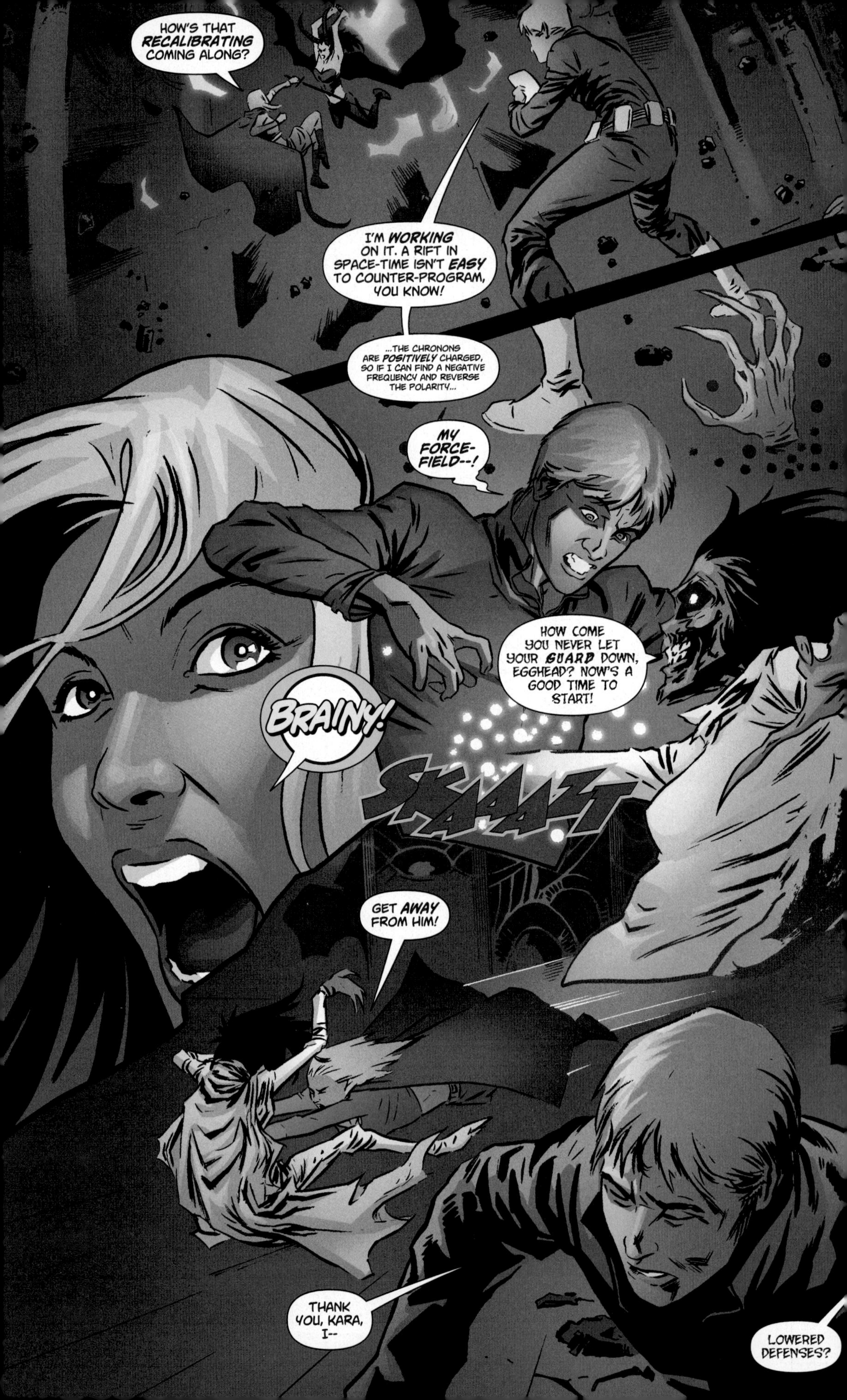
HOW'S THAT RECALIBRATING COMING ALONG?
I'M WORKING ON IT. A RIFT IN SPACE-TIME ISN'T EASY TO COUNTER-PROGRAM, YOU KNOW!
...THE CHRONONS ARE POSITIVELY CHARGED, SO IF I CAN FIND A NEGATIVE FREQUENCY AND REVERSE THE POLARITY...
MY FORCE-FIELD--!
HOW COME YOU NEVER LET YOUR GUARD DOWN, EGGHEAD? NOW'S A GOOD TIME TO START!
BRAINY!
SKAAAZT
GET AWAY FROM HIM!
THANK YOU, KARA, I--
LOWERED DEFENSES?

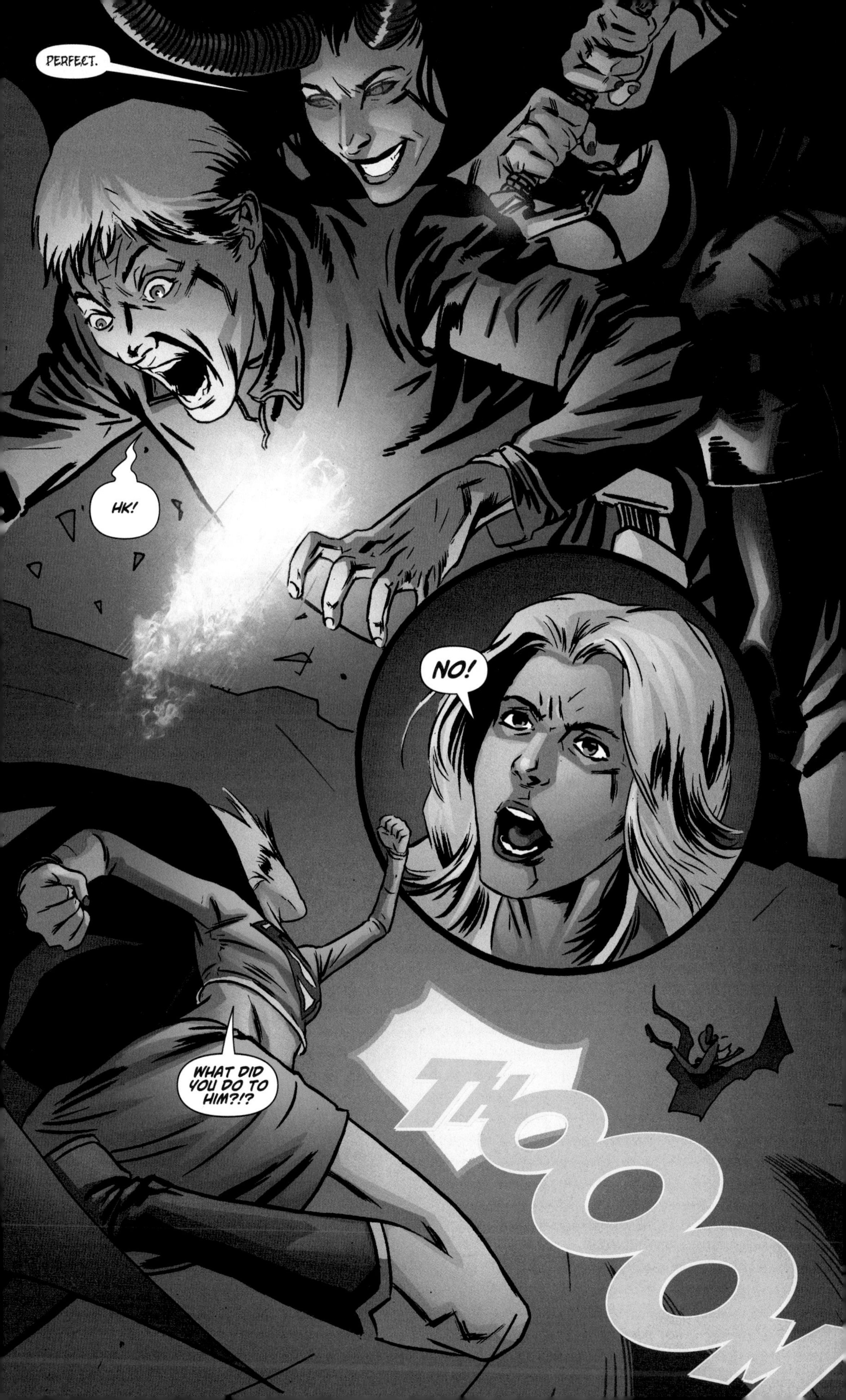
PERFECT.
HK!
NO!
WHAT DID YOU DO TO HIM?!?
THOOOM

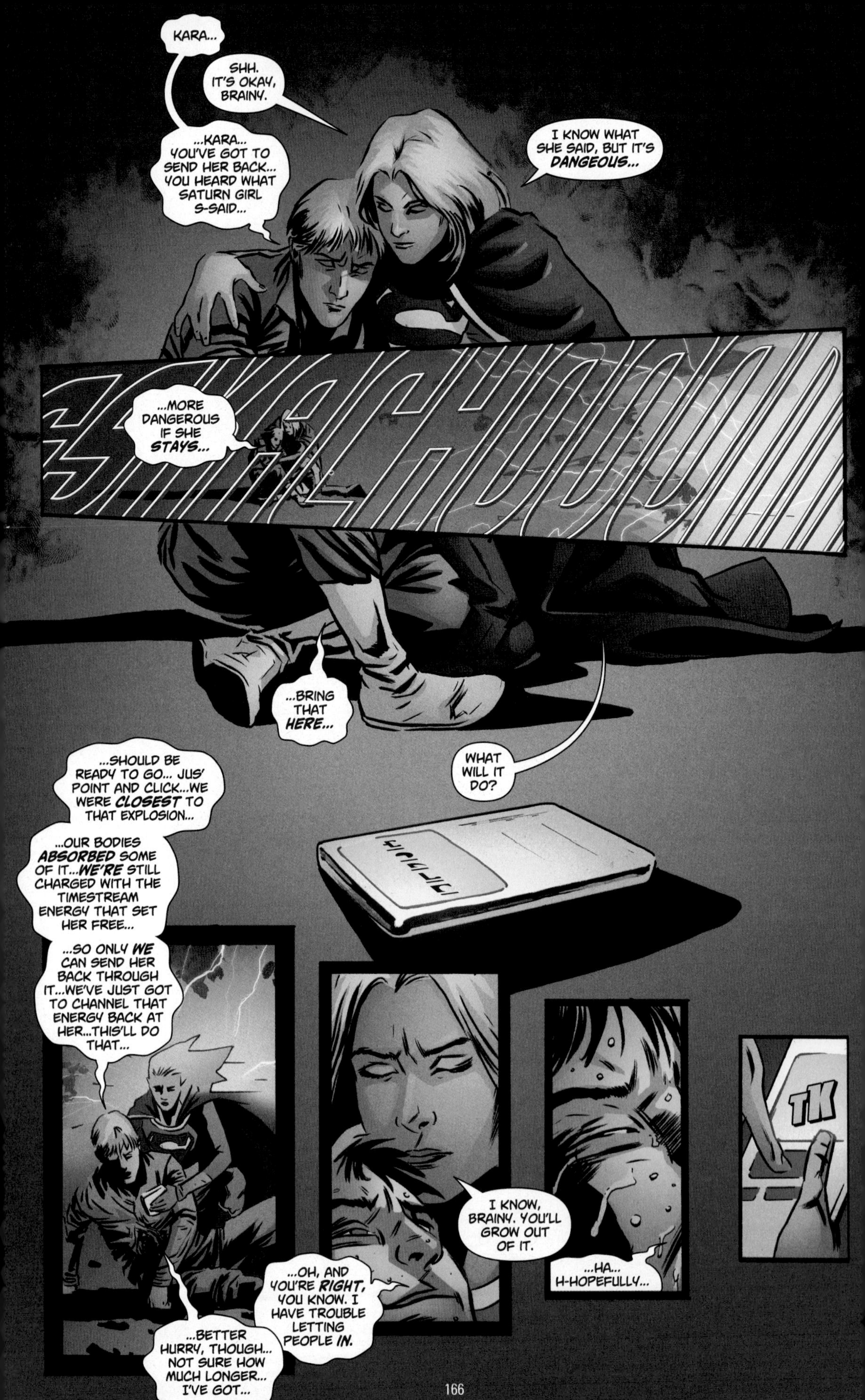
KARA...
SHH. IT'S OKAY, BRAINY.
...KARA... YOU'VE GOT TO SEND HER BACK... YOU HEARD WHAT SATURN GIRL S-SAID...
I KNOW WHAT SHE SAID, BUT IT'S DANGEOUS...
...MORE DANGEROUS IF SHE STAYS...
...BRING THAT HERE...
WHAT WILL IT DO?
...SHOULD BE READY TO GO... JUS' POINT AND CLICK...WE WERE CLOSEST TO THAT EXPLOSION...
...OUR BODIES ABSORBED SOME OF IT...WE'RE STILL CHARGED WITH THE TIMESTREAM ENERGY THAT SET HER FREE...
...SO ONLY WE CAN SEND HER BACK THROUGH IT...WE'VE JUST GOT TO CHANNEL THAT ENERGY BACK AT HER...THIS'LL DO THAT...
...BETTER HURRY, THOUGH... NOT SURE HOW MUCH LONGER... I'VE GOT...
...OH, AND YOU'RE RIGHT, YOU KNOW. I HAVE TROUBLE LETTING PEOPLE IN.
I KNOW, BRAINY. YOU'LL GROW OUT OF IT.
...HA... H-HOPEFULLY...
TK

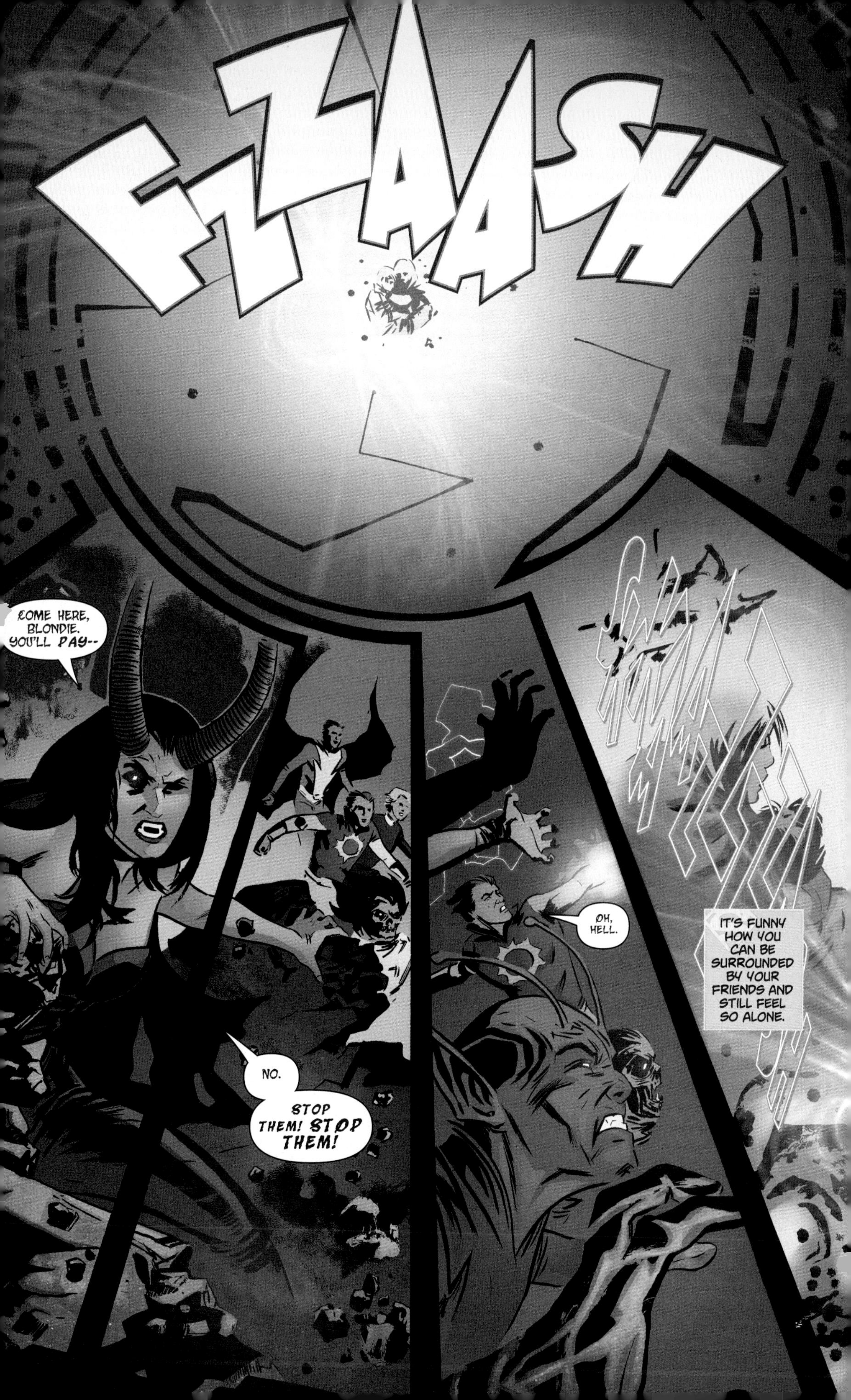
FZZAASH
COME HERE, BLONDIE. YOU'LL PAY--
NO.
STOP THEM! STOP THEM!
OH, HELL.
IT'S FUNNY HOW YOU CAN BE SURROUNDED BY YOUR FRIENDS AND STILL FEEL SO ALONE.

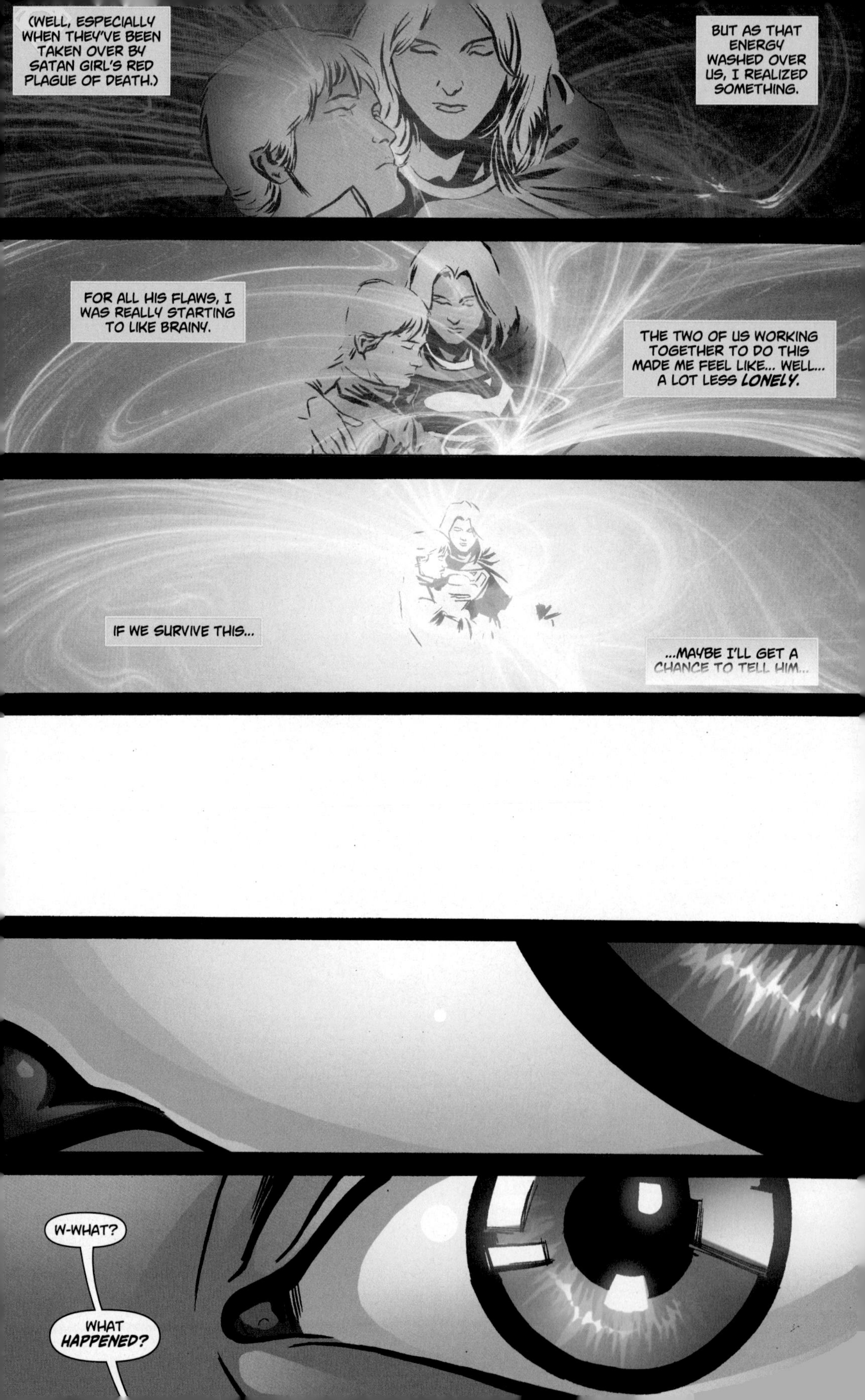
(WELL, ESPECIALLY WHEN THEY'VE BEEN TAKEN OVER BY SATAN GIRL'S RED PLAGUE OF DEATH.)
BUT AS THAT ENERGY WASHED OVER US, I REALIZED SOMETHING.
FOR ALL HIS FLAWS, I WAS REALLY STARTING TO LIKE BRAINY.
THE TWO OF US WORKING TOGETHER TO DO THIS MADE ME FEEL LIKE... WELL... A LOT LESS *LONELY.*
IF WE SURVIVE THIS...
...MAYBE I'LL GET A CHANCE TO TELL HIM...
W-WHAT?
WHAT *HAPPENED?*

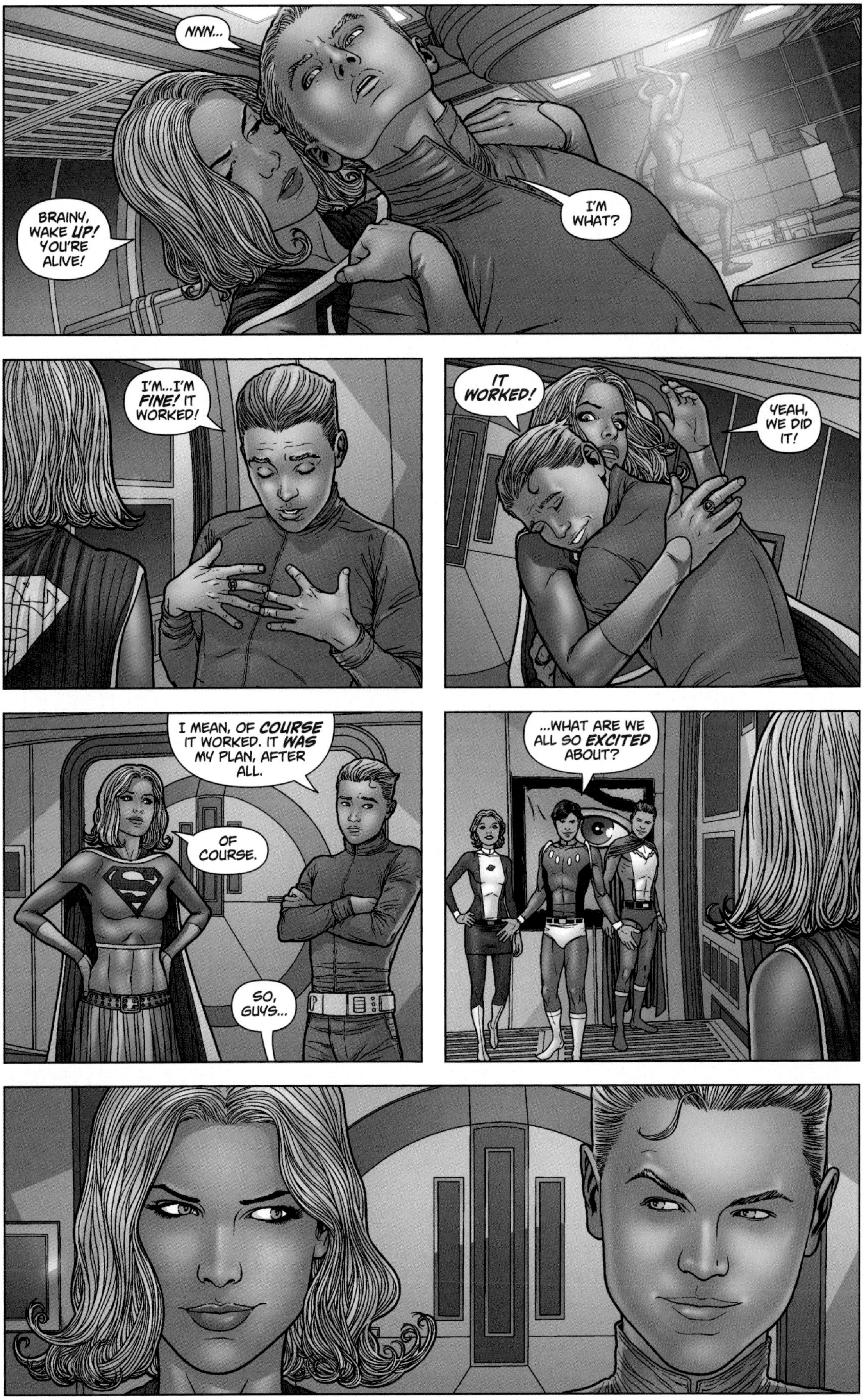
NNN...
BRAINY, WAKE UP! YOU'RE ALIVE!
I'M WHAT?
I'M...I'M FINE! IT WORKED!
IT WORKED!
YEAH, WE DID IT!
I MEAN, OF COURSE IT WORKED. IT WAS MY PLAN, AFTER ALL.
OF COURSE.
SO, GUYS...
...WHAT ARE WE ALL SO EXCITED ABOUT?

HAMMERSMITH TOWER.

HOME OF LANA AND LINDA LANG.

THE PRESENT.

BOOM

--ASIDE FROM ALL OF *THAT*, I HAD A REALLY GREAT TIME!

WELL, WE AIM TO *PLEASE*, SUPERGIRL. SORRY THINGS GOT PRETTY *HAIRY* THERE FOR YOU.

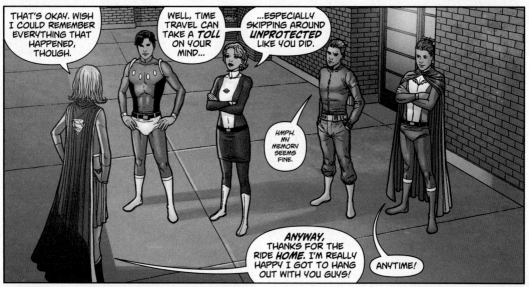

THAT'S OKAY. WISH I COULD REMEMBER EVERYTHING THAT HAPPENED, THOUGH.

WELL, TIME TRAVEL CAN TAKE A *TOLL* ON YOUR MIND...

...ESPECIALLY SKIPPING AROUND *UNPROTECTED* LIKE YOU DID.

HMPH. MY MEMORY SEEMS FINE.

ANYWAY, THANKS FOR THE RIDE *HOME.* I'M REALLY HAPPY I GOT TO HANG OUT WITH YOU GUYS!

ANYTIME!

HEY, BRAINY?

YES?

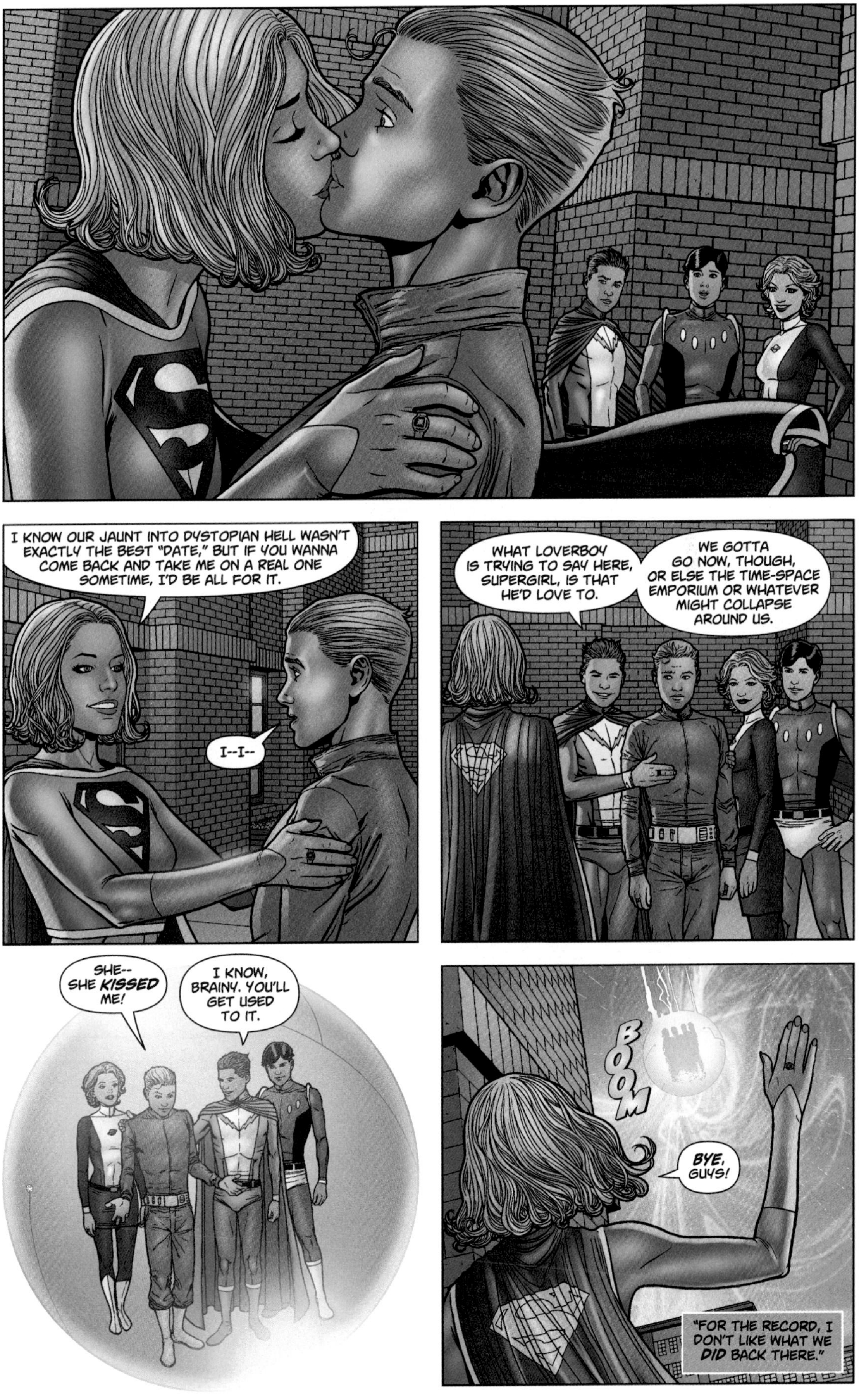

I KNOW OUR JAUNT INTO DYSTOPIAN HELL WASN'T EXACTLY THE BEST "DATE," BUT IF YOU WANNA COME BACK AND TAKE ME ON A REAL ONE SOMETIME, I'D BE ALL FOR IT.
I--I--
WHAT LOVERBOY IS TRYING TO SAY HERE, SUPERGIRL, IS THAT HE'D LOVE TO.
WE GOTTA GO NOW, THOUGH, OR ELSE THE TIME-SPACE EMPORIUM OR WHATEVER MIGHT COLLAPSE AROUND US.
SHE-- SHE *KISSED* ME!
I KNOW, BRAINY. YOU'LL GET USED TO IT.
BOOM
BYE, GUYS!
"FOR THE RECORD, I DON'T LIKE WHAT WE *DID* BACK THERE."

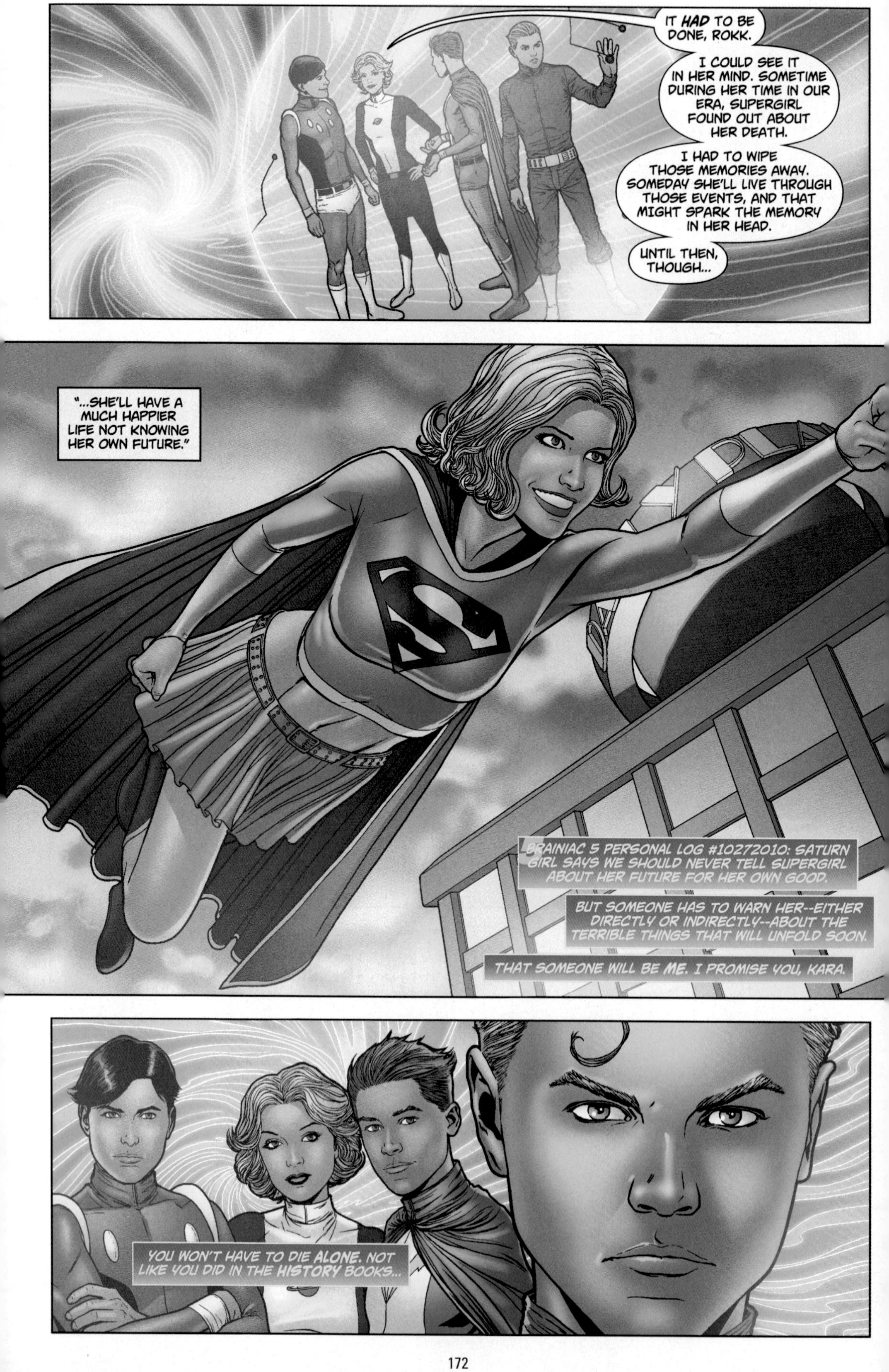

IT HAD TO BE DONE, ROKK.
I COULD SEE IT IN HER MIND. SOMETIME DURING HER TIME IN OUR ERA, SUPERGIRL FOUND OUT ABOUT HER DEATH.
I HAD TO WIPE THOSE MEMORIES AWAY. SOMEDAY SHE'LL LIVE THROUGH THOSE EVENTS, AND THAT MIGHT SPARK THE MEMORY IN HER HEAD.
UNTIL THEN, THOUGH...
"...SHE'LL HAVE A MUCH HAPPIER LIFE NOT KNOWING HER OWN FUTURE."
BRAINIAC 5 PERSONAL LOG #10272010: SATURN GIRL SAYS WE SHOULD NEVER TELL SUPERGIRL ABOUT HER FUTURE FOR HER OWN GOOD.
BUT SOMEONE HAS TO WARN HER--EITHER DIRECTLY OR INDIRECTLY--ABOUT THE TERRIBLE THINGS THAT WILL UNFOLD SOON.
THAT SOMEONE WILL BE ME. I PROMISE YOU, KARA.
YOU WON'T HAVE TO DIE ALONE. NOT LIKE YOU DID IN THE HISTORY BOOKS...

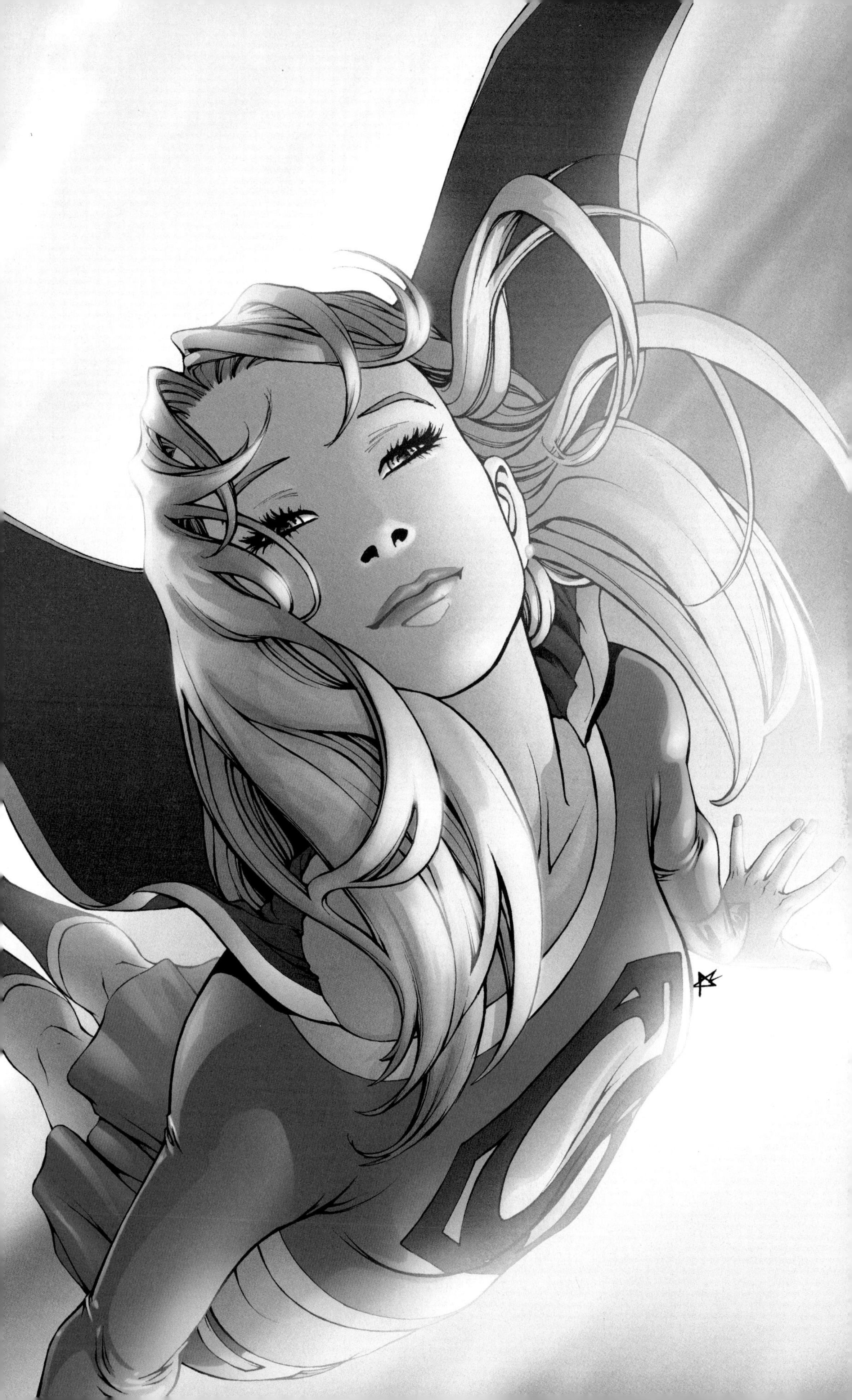

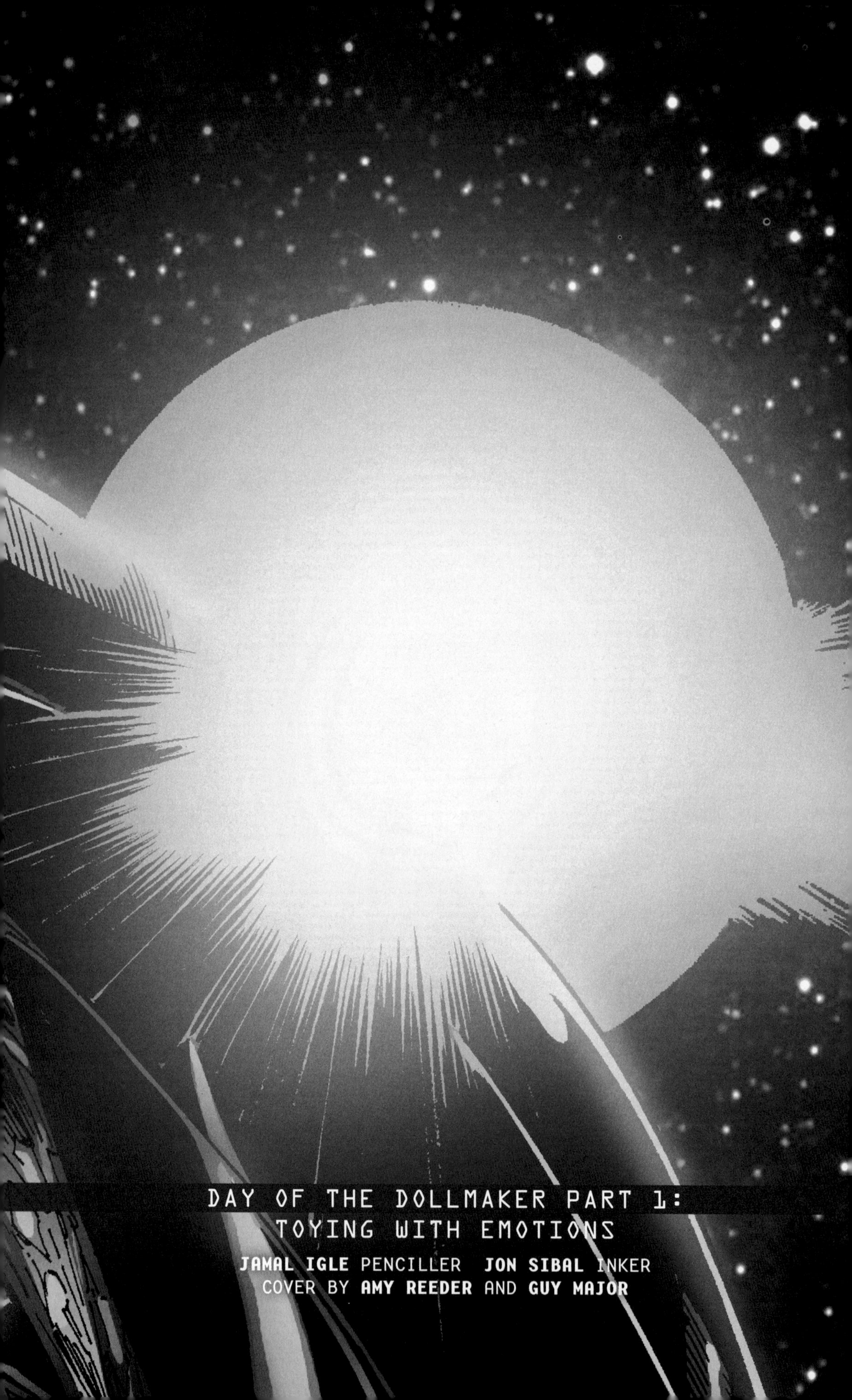

DAY OF THE DOLLMAKER PART 1: TOYING WITH EMOTIONS

JAMAL IGLE PENCILLER **JON SIBAL** INKER

COVER BY **AMY REEDER** AND **GUY MAJOR**

TODAY.

CHRISTMAS EVE EVE.

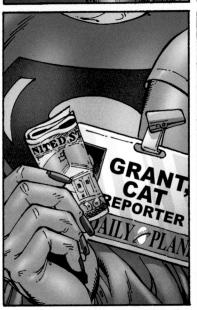

GRANT, CAT
REPORTER
DAILY PLAN

HELLO.

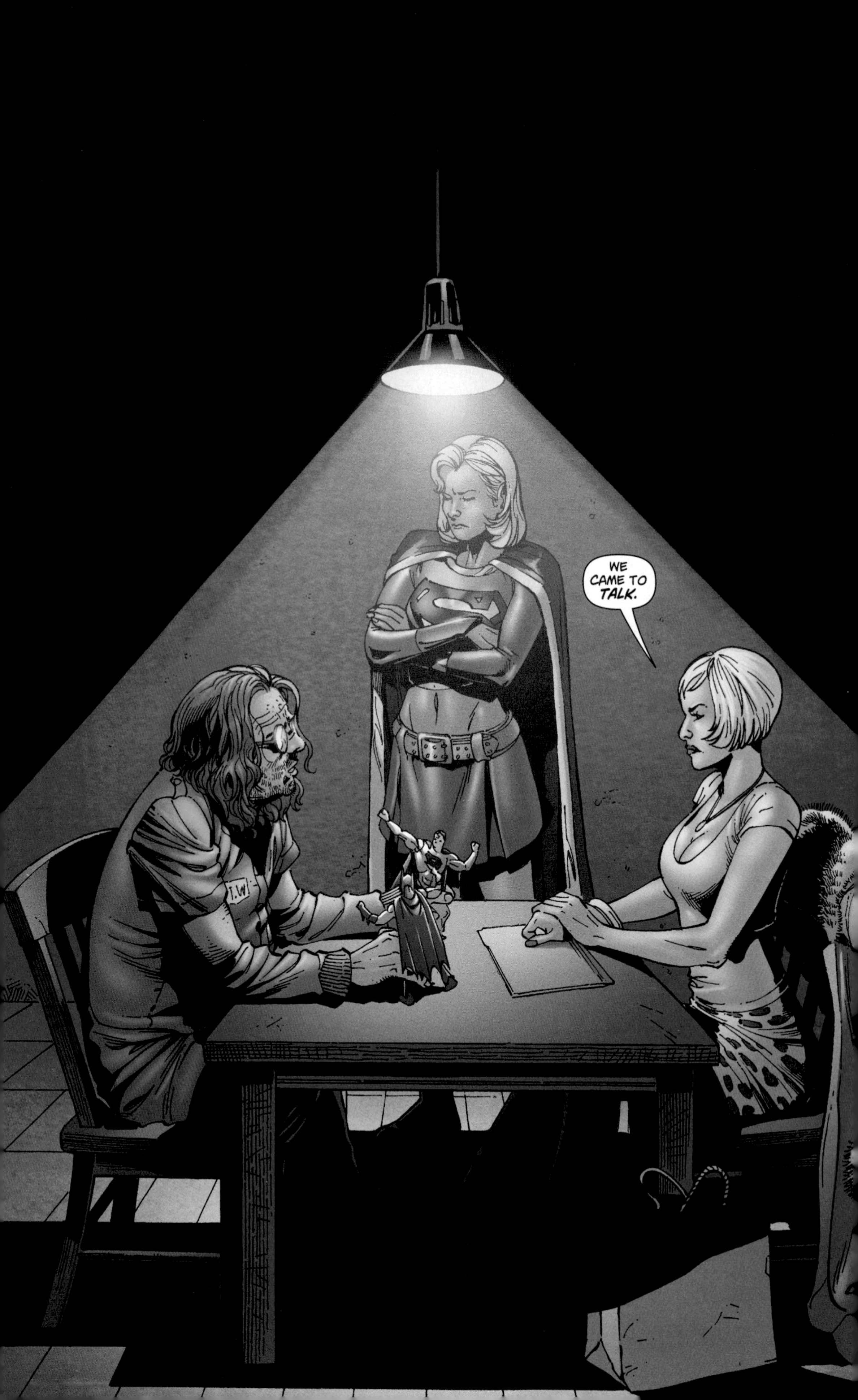
WE CAME TO TALK.

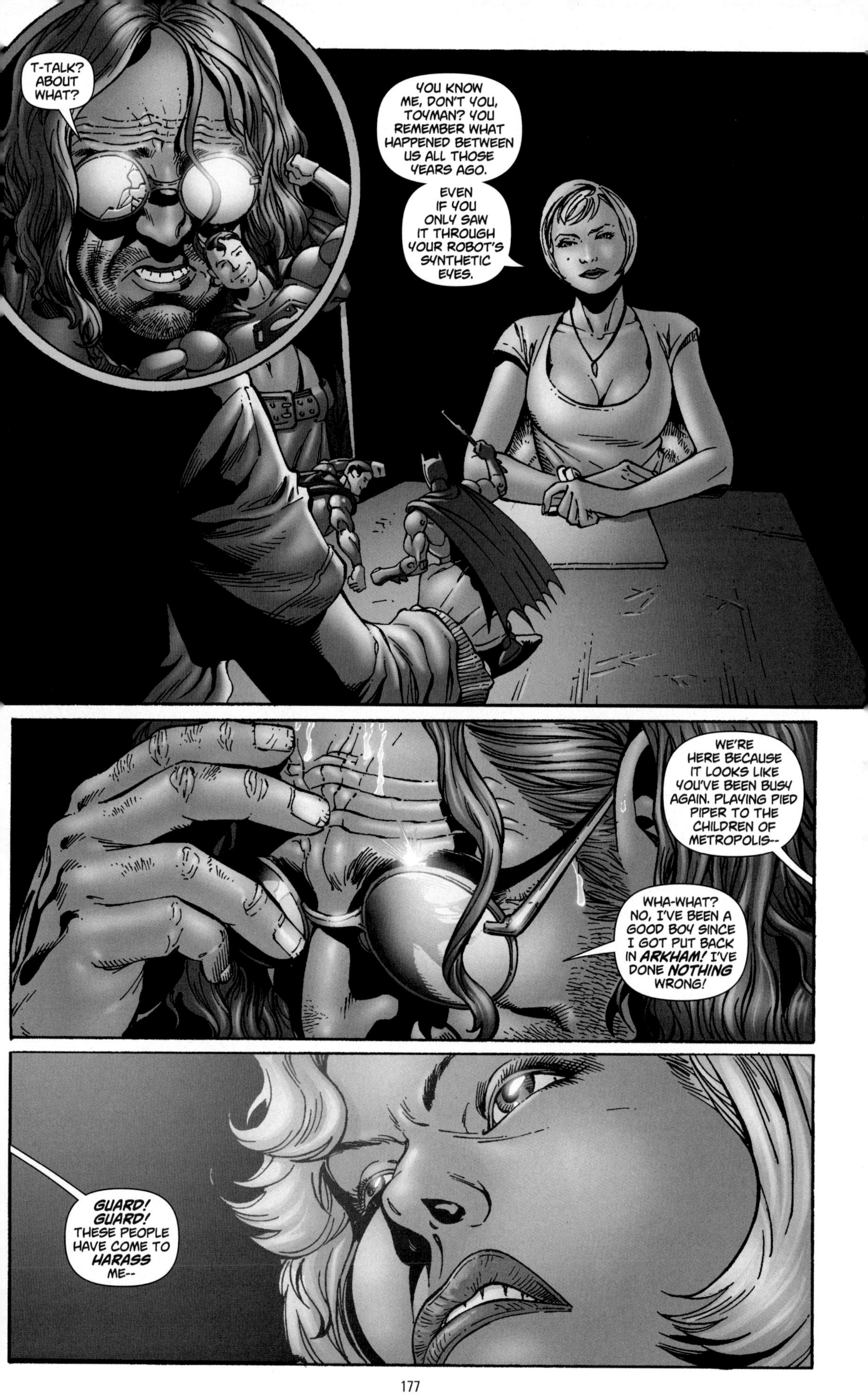
T-TALK? ABOUT WHAT?
YOU KNOW ME, DON'T YOU, TOYMAN? YOU REMEMBER WHAT HAPPENED BETWEEN US ALL THOSE YEARS AGO.
EVEN IF YOU ONLY SAW IT THROUGH YOUR ROBOT'S SYNTHETIC EYES.
WE'RE HERE BECAUSE IT LOOKS LIKE YOU'VE BEEN BUSY AGAIN. PLAYING PIED PIPER TO THE CHILDREN OF METROPOLIS--
WHA-WHAT? NO, I'VE BEEN A GOOD BOY SINCE I GOT PUT BACK IN ARKHAM! I'VE DONE NOTHING WRONG!
GUARD! GUARD! THESE PEOPLE HAVE COME TO HARASS ME--

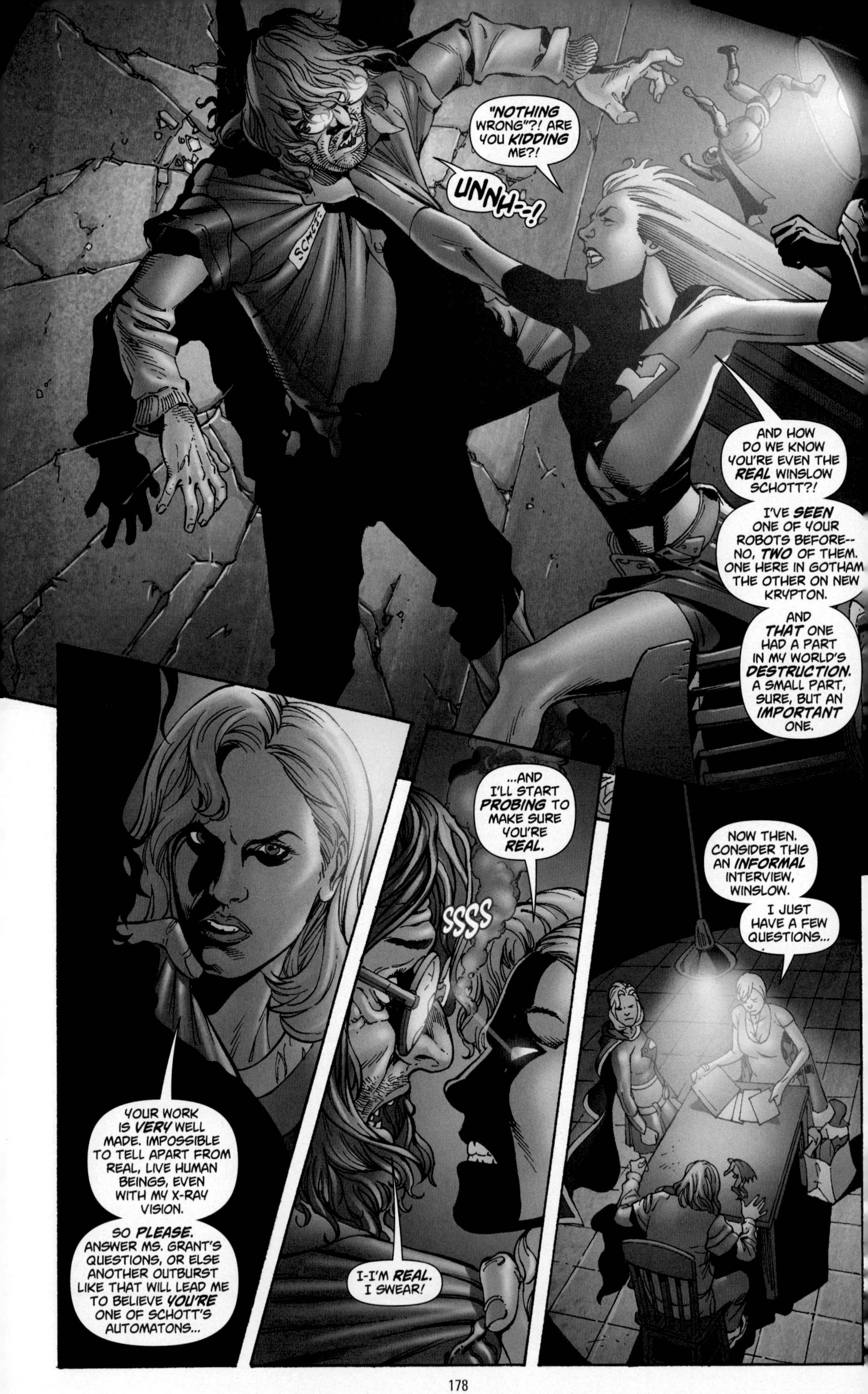

"NOTHING WRONG"?! ARE YOU KIDDING ME?!
UNNH--!
AND HOW DO WE KNOW YOU'RE EVEN THE REAL WINSLOW SCHOTT?!
I'VE SEEN ONE OF YOUR ROBOTS BEFORE-- NO, TWO OF THEM. ONE HERE IN GOTHAM THE OTHER ON NEW KRYPTON.
AND THAT ONE HAD A PART IN MY WORLD'S DESTRUCTION. A SMALL PART, SURE, BUT AN IMPORTANT ONE.
YOUR WORK IS VERY WELL MADE. IMPOSSIBLE TO TELL APART FROM REAL, LIVE HUMAN BEINGS, EVEN WITH MY X-RAY VISION.
SO PLEASE. ANSWER MS. GRANT'S QUESTIONS, OR ELSE ANOTHER OUTBURST LIKE THAT WILL LEAD ME TO BELIEVE YOU'RE ONE OF SCHOTT'S AUTOMATONS...
...AND I'LL START PROBING TO MAKE SURE YOU'RE REAL.
SSSS
I-I'M REAL. I SWEAR!
NOW THEN. CONSIDER THIS AN INFORMAL INTERVIEW, WINSLOW.
I JUST HAVE A FEW QUESTIONS...

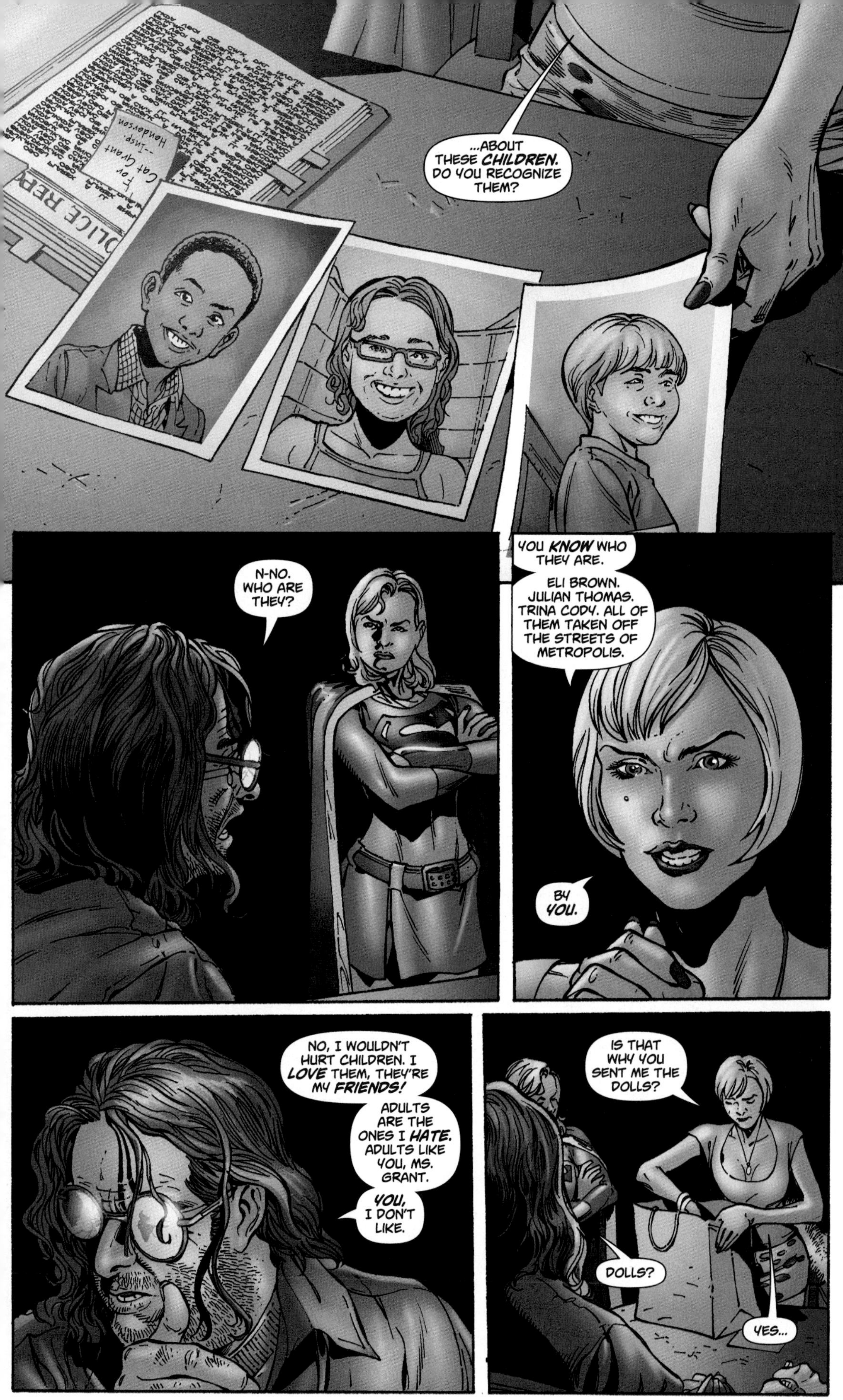
For Cat Grant --Insp. Henderson
...ABOUT THESE CHILDREN. DO YOU RECOGNIZE THEM?
N-NO. WHO ARE THEY?
YOU KNOW WHO THEY ARE.
ELI BROWN. JULIAN THOMAS. TRINA CODY. ALL OF THEM TAKEN OFF THE STREETS OF METROPOLIS.
BY YOU.
NO, I WOULDN'T HURT CHILDREN. I LOVE THEM, THEY'RE MY FRIENDS!
ADULTS ARE THE ONES I HATE. ADULTS LIKE YOU, MS. GRANT.
YOU, I DON'T LIKE.
IS THAT WHY YOU SENT ME THE DOLLS?
DOLLS?
YES...

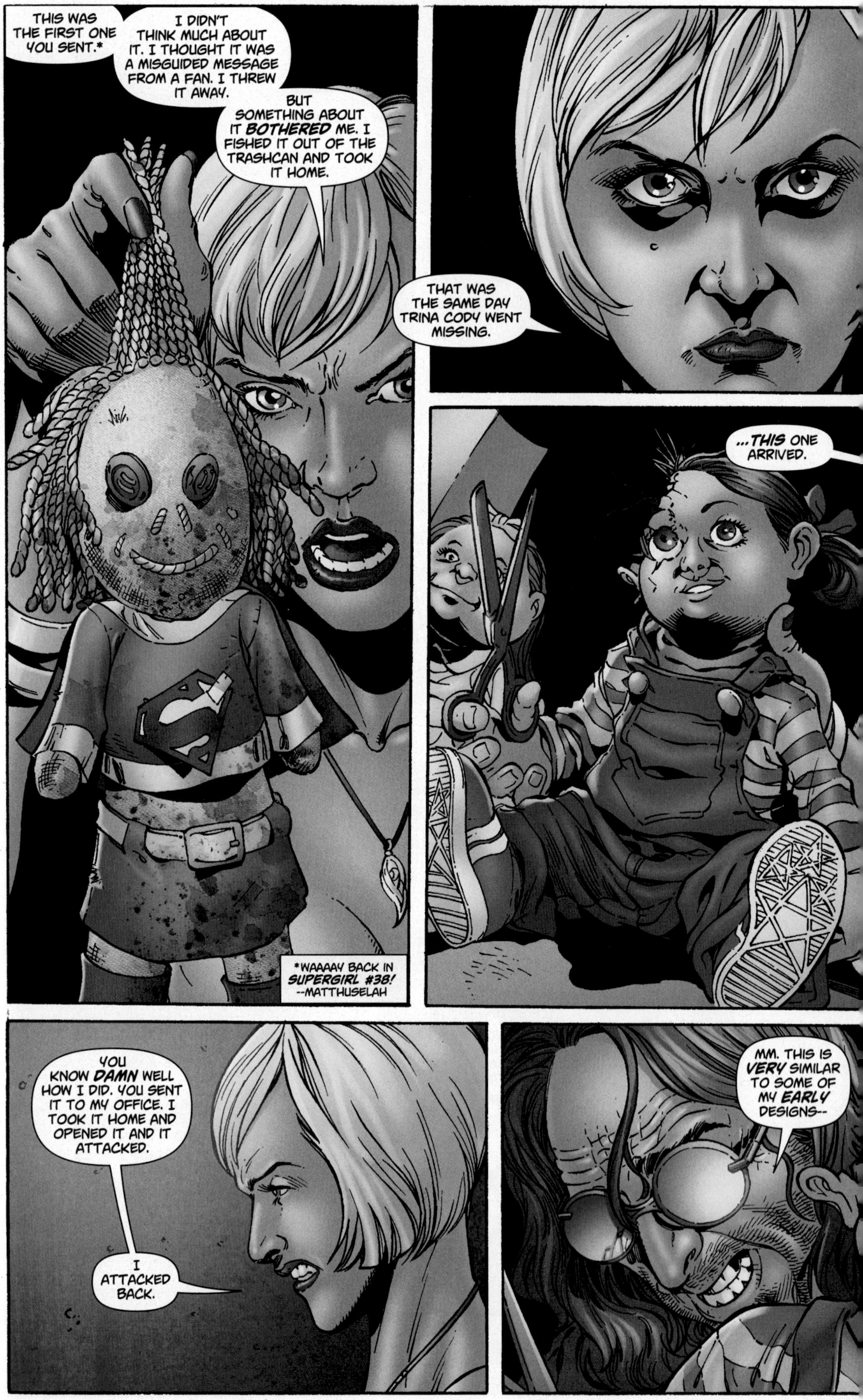
THIS WAS THE FIRST ONE YOU SENT.*
I DIDN'T THINK MUCH ABOUT IT. I THOUGHT IT WAS A MISGUIDED MESSAGE FROM A FAN. I THREW IT AWAY.
BUT SOMETHING ABOUT IT BOTHERED ME. I FISHED IT OUT OF THE TRASHCAN AND TOOK IT HOME.
*WAAAAY BACK IN SUPERGIRL #38! --MATTHUSELAH
THAT WAS THE SAME DAY TRINA CODY WENT MISSING.
...THIS ONE ARRIVED.
YOU KNOW DAMN WELL HOW I DID. YOU SENT IT TO MY OFFICE. I TOOK IT HOME AND OPENED IT AND IT ATTACKED.
I ATTACKED BACK.
MM. THIS IS VERY SIMILAR TO SOME OF MY EARLY DESIGNS--

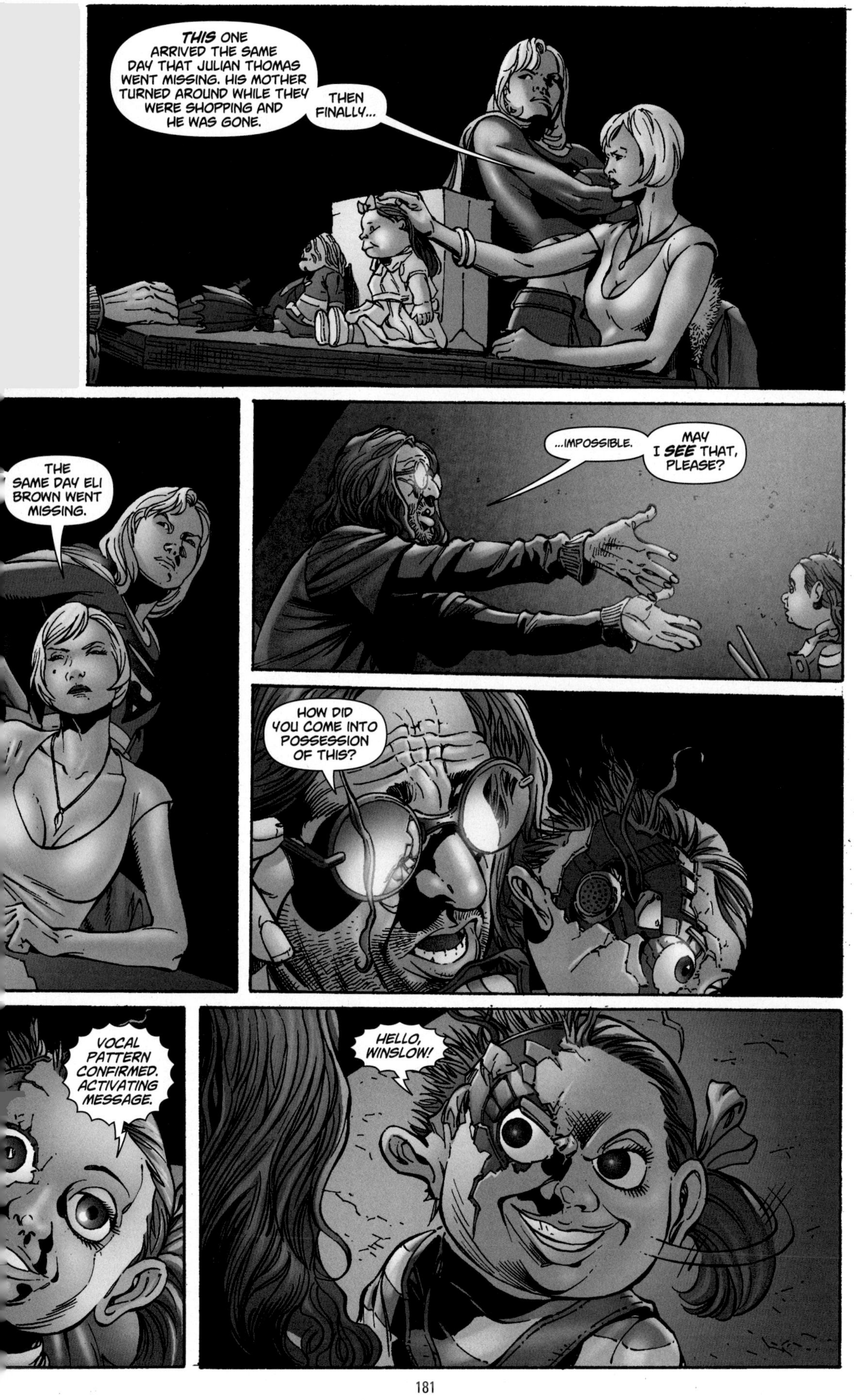
THIS ONE ARRIVED THE SAME DAY THAT JULIAN THOMAS WENT MISSING. HIS MOTHER TURNED AROUND WHILE THEY WERE SHOPPING AND HE WAS GONE.
THEN FINALLY...
THE SAME DAY ELI BROWN WENT MISSING.
...IMPOSSIBLE.
MAY I SEE THAT, PLEASE?
HOW DID YOU COME INTO POSSESSION OF THIS?
VOCAL PATTERN CONFIRMED. ACTIVATING MESSAGE.
HELLO, WINSLOW!

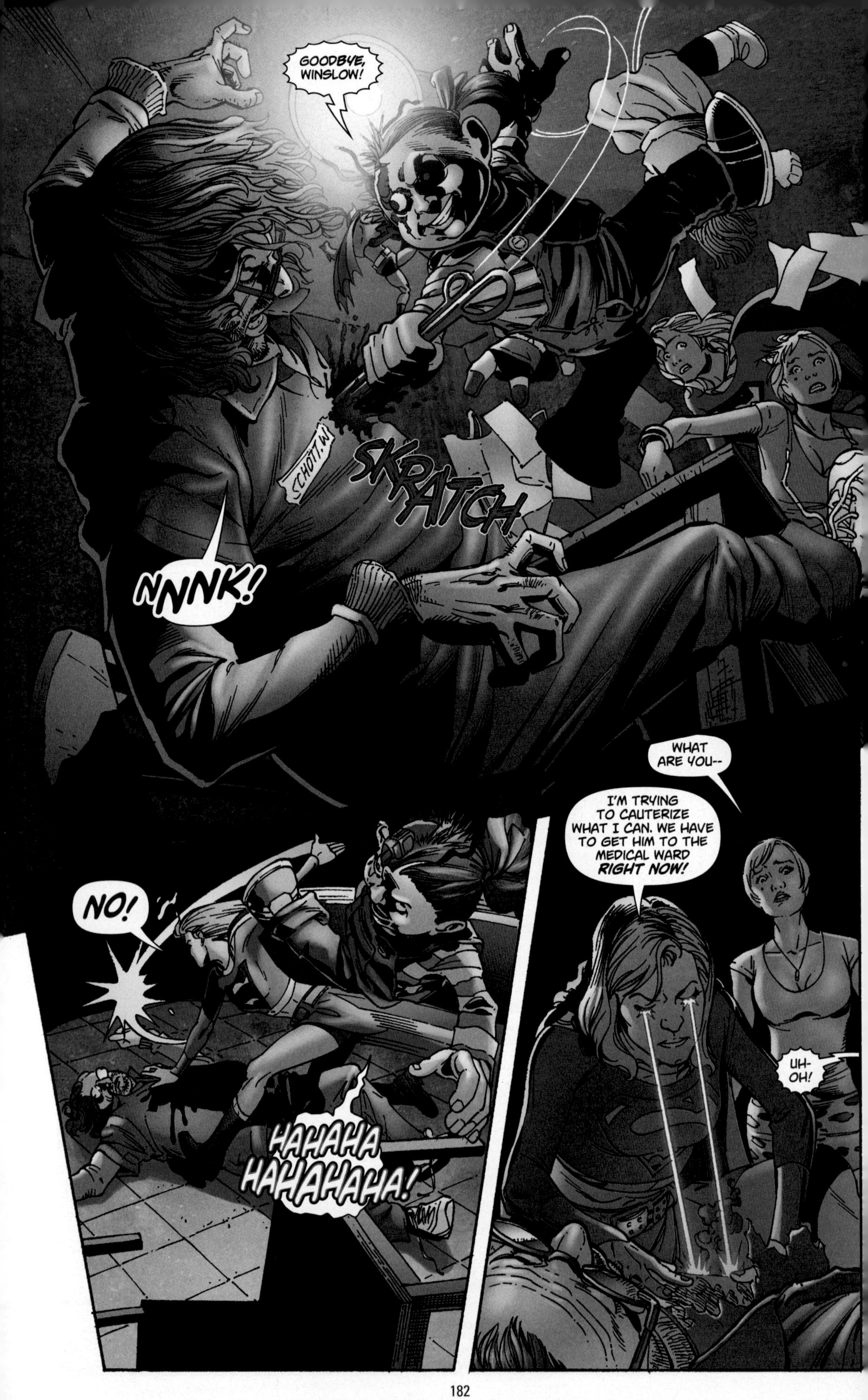
GOODBYE, WINSLOW!
SCHOTT, W.
SKRATCH
NNNK!
NO!
HAHAHA HAHAHAHA!
WHAT ARE YOU--
I'M TRYING TO CAUTERIZE WHAT I CAN. WE HAVE TO GET HIM TO THE MEDICAL WARD RIGHT NOW!
UH-OH!

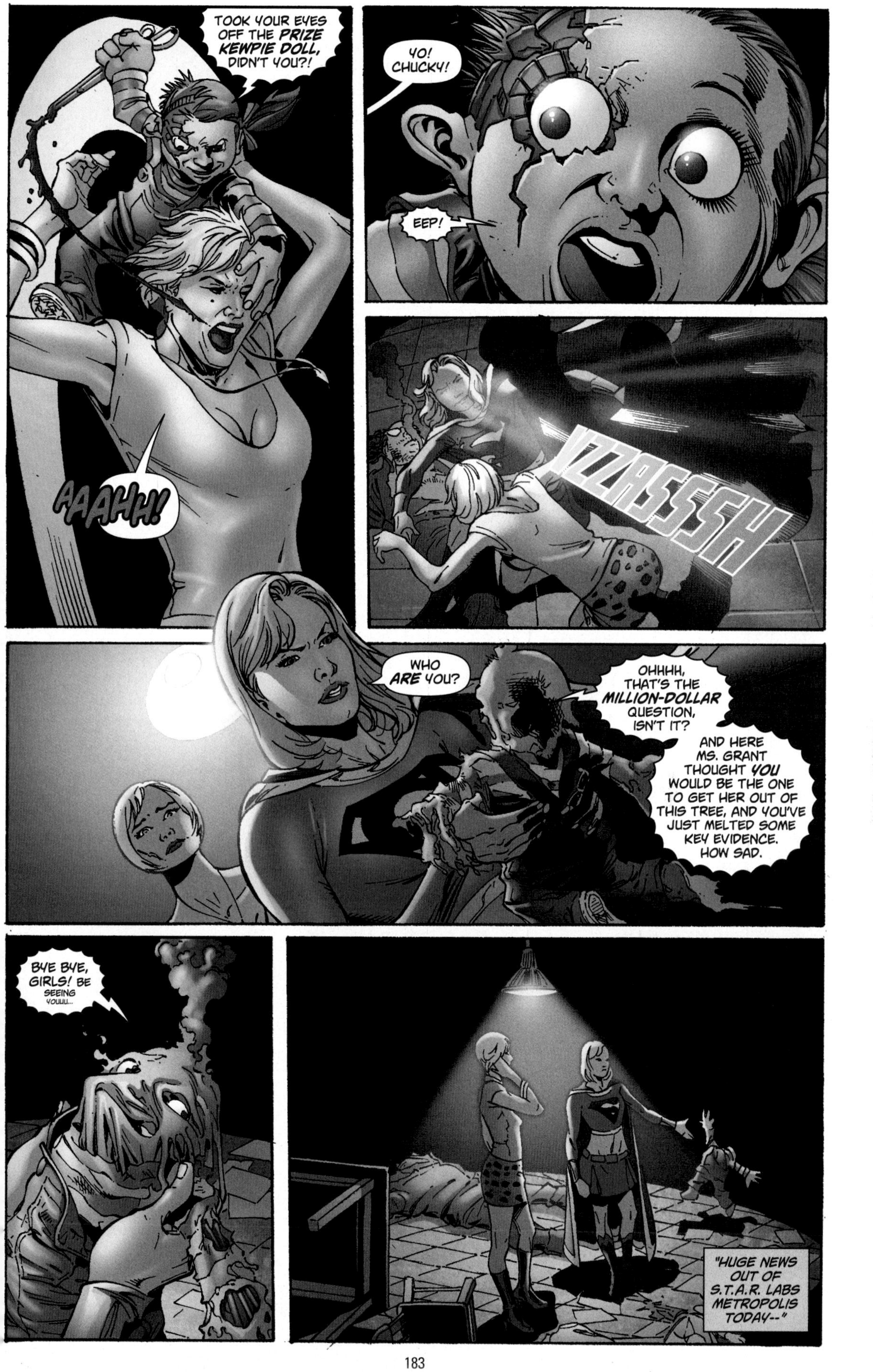

TOOK YOUR EYES OFF THE PRIZE KEWPIE DOLL, DIDN'T YOU?!
AAAHH!
YO! CHUCKY!
EEP!
VZZRASSSH
WHO ARE YOU?
OHHHH, THAT'S THE MILLION-DOLLAR QUESTION, ISN'T IT?
AND HERE MS. GRANT THOUGHT YOU WOULD BE THE ONE TO GET HER OUT OF THIS TREE, AND YOU'VE JUST MELTED SOME KEY EVIDENCE. HOW SAD.
BYE BYE, GIRLS! BE SEEING YOUUU...
"HUGE NEWS OUT OF S.T.A.R. LABS METROPOLIS TODAY--"

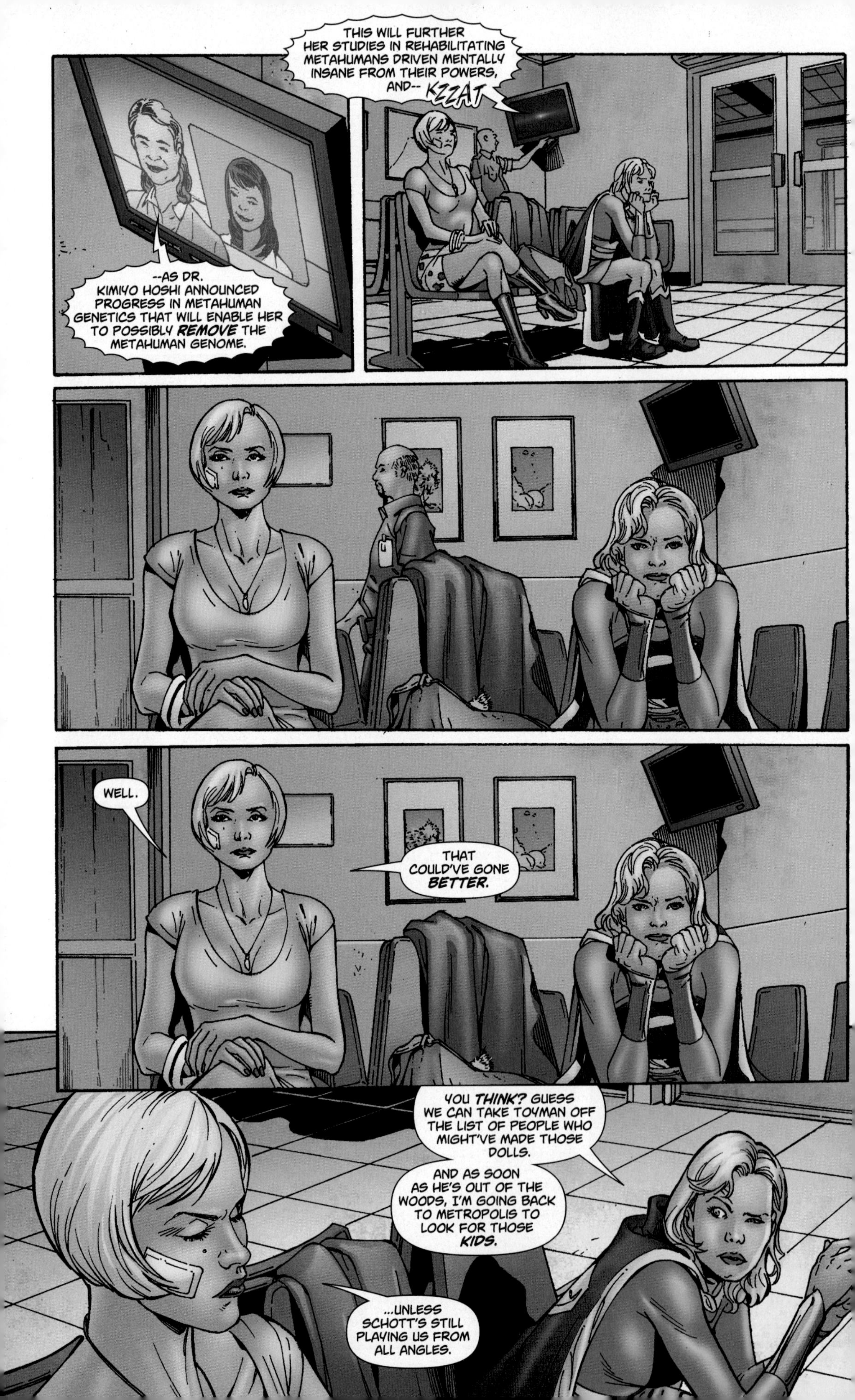

--AS DR. KIMIYO HOSHI ANNOUNCED PROGRESS IN METAHUMAN GENETICS THAT WILL ENABLE HER TO POSSIBLY REMOVE THE METAHUMAN GENOME.
THIS WILL FURTHER HER STUDIES IN REHABILITATING METAHUMANS DRIVEN MENTALLY INSANE FROM THEIR POWERS, AND-- KZZAT
WELL.
THAT COULD'VE GONE BETTER.
YOU THINK? GUESS WE CAN TAKE TOYMAN OFF THE LIST OF PEOPLE WHO MIGHT'VE MADE THOSE DOLLS.
AND AS SOON AS HE'S OUT OF THE WOODS, I'M GOING BACK TO METROPOLIS TO LOOK FOR THOSE KIDS.
...UNLESS SCHOTT'S STILL PLAYING US FROM ALL ANGLES.

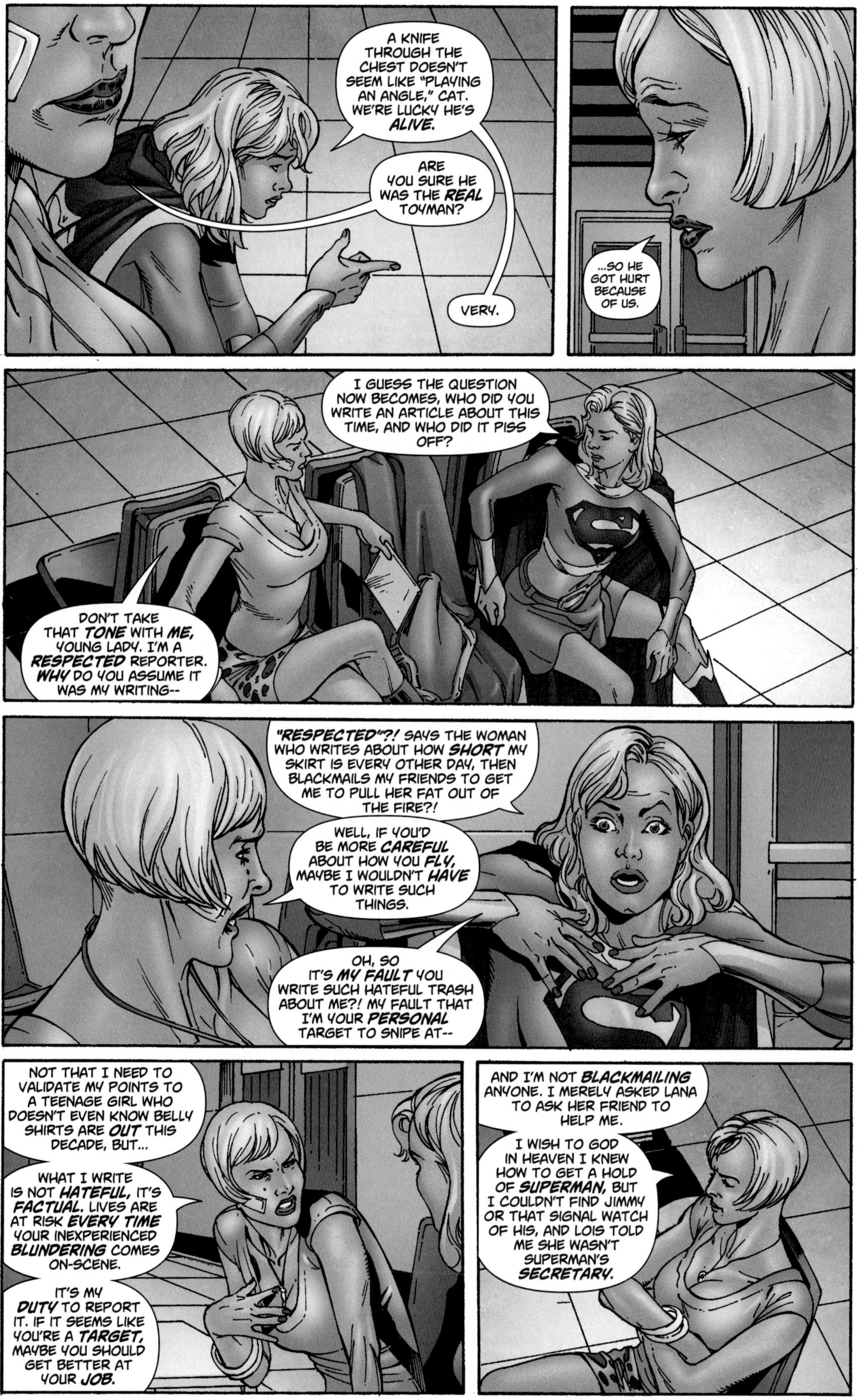
A KNIFE THROUGH THE CHEST DOESN'T SEEM LIKE "PLAYING AN ANGLE," CAT. WE'RE LUCKY HE'S ALIVE.
ARE YOU SURE HE WAS THE REAL TOYMAN?
VERY.
...SO HE GOT HURT BECAUSE OF US.
I GUESS THE QUESTION NOW BECOMES, WHO DID YOU WRITE AN ARTICLE ABOUT THIS TIME, AND WHO DID IT PISS OFF?
DON'T TAKE THAT TONE WITH ME, YOUNG LADY. I'M A RESPECTED REPORTER. WHY DO YOU ASSUME IT WAS MY WRITING--
"RESPECTED"?! SAYS THE WOMAN WHO WRITES ABOUT HOW SHORT MY SKIRT IS EVERY OTHER DAY, THEN BLACKMAILS MY FRIENDS TO GET ME TO PULL HER FAT OUT OF THE FIRE?!
WELL, IF YOU'D BE MORE CAREFUL ABOUT HOW YOU FLY, MAYBE I WOULDN'T HAVE TO WRITE SUCH THINGS.
OH, SO IT'S MY FAULT YOU WRITE SUCH HATEFUL TRASH ABOUT ME?! MY FAULT THAT I'M YOUR PERSONAL TARGET TO SNIPE AT--
NOT THAT I NEED TO VALIDATE MY POINTS TO A TEENAGE GIRL WHO DOESN'T EVEN KNOW BELLY SHIRTS ARE OUT THIS DECADE, BUT...
WHAT I WRITE IS NOT HATEFUL, IT'S FACTUAL. LIVES ARE AT RISK EVERY TIME YOUR INEXPERIENCED BLUNDERING COMES ON-SCENE.
IT'S MY DUTY TO REPORT IT. IF IT SEEMS LIKE YOU'RE A TARGET, MAYBE YOU SHOULD GET BETTER AT YOUR JOB.
AND I'M NOT BLACKMAILING ANYONE. I MERELY ASKED LANA TO ASK HER FRIEND TO HELP ME.
I WISH TO GOD IN HEAVEN I KNEW HOW TO GET A HOLD OF SUPERMAN, BUT I COULDN'T FIND JIMMY OR THAT SIGNAL WATCH OF HIS, AND LOIS TOLD ME SHE WASN'T SUPERMAN'S SECRETARY.

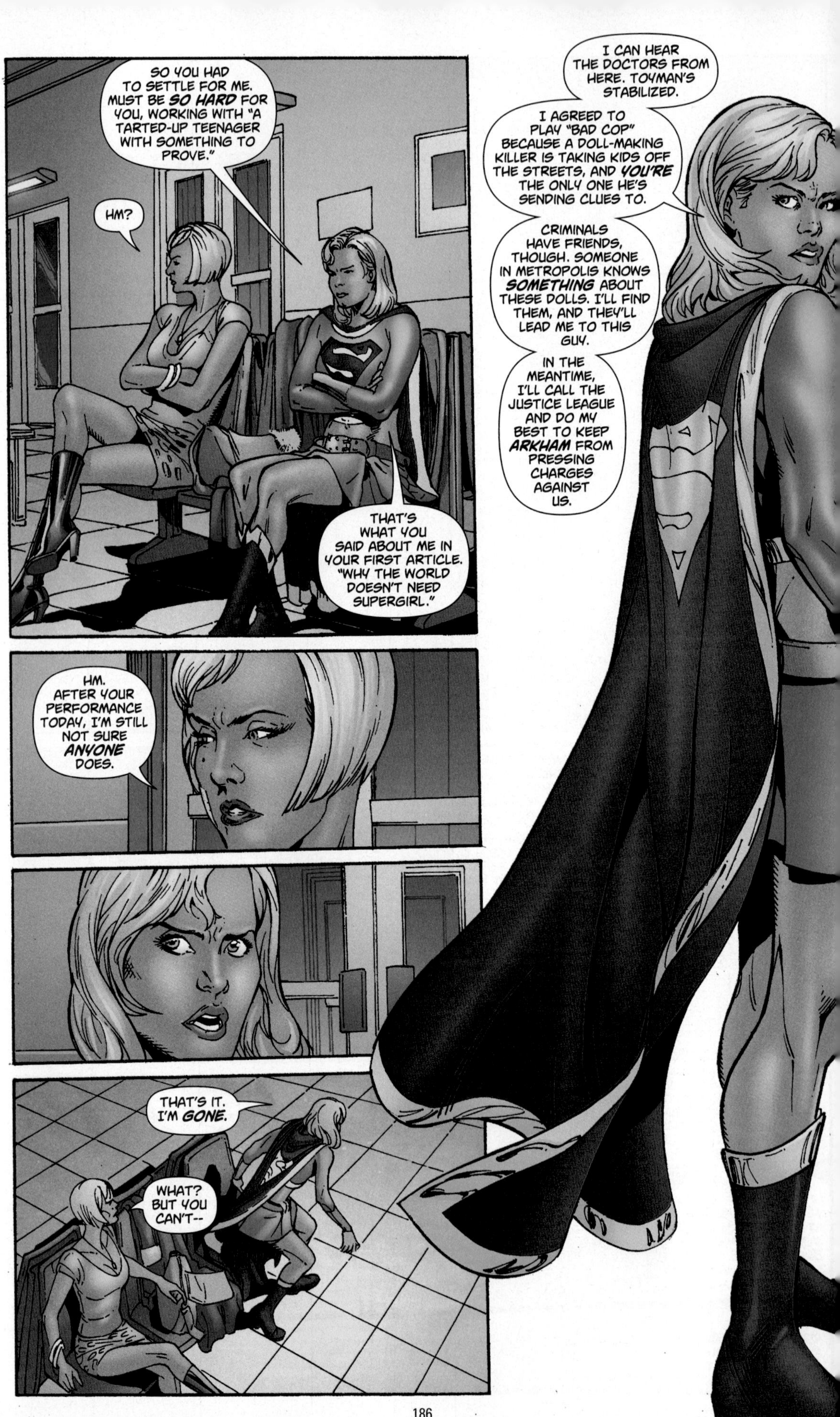
SO YOU HAD TO SETTLE FOR ME. MUST BE SO HARD FOR YOU, WORKING WITH "A TARTED-UP TEENAGER WITH SOMETHING TO PROVE."
HM?
THAT'S WHAT YOU SAID ABOUT ME IN YOUR FIRST ARTICLE. "WHY THE WORLD DOESN'T NEED SUPERGIRL."
HM. AFTER YOUR PERFORMANCE TODAY, I'M STILL NOT SURE ANYONE DOES.
THAT'S IT. I'M GONE.
WHAT? BUT YOU CAN'T--
I CAN HEAR THE DOCTORS FROM HERE. TOYMAN'S STABILIZED.
I AGREED TO PLAY "BAD COP" BECAUSE A DOLL-MAKING KILLER IS TAKING KIDS OFF THE STREETS, AND YOU'RE THE ONLY ONE HE'S SENDING CLUES TO.
CRIMINALS HAVE FRIENDS, THOUGH. SOMEONE IN METROPOLIS KNOWS SOMETHING ABOUT THESE DOLLS. I'LL FIND THEM, AND THEY'LL LEAD ME TO THIS GUY.
IN THE MEANTIME, I'LL CALL THE JUSTICE LEAGUE AND DO MY BEST TO KEEP ARKHAM FROM PRESSING CHARGES AGAINST US.

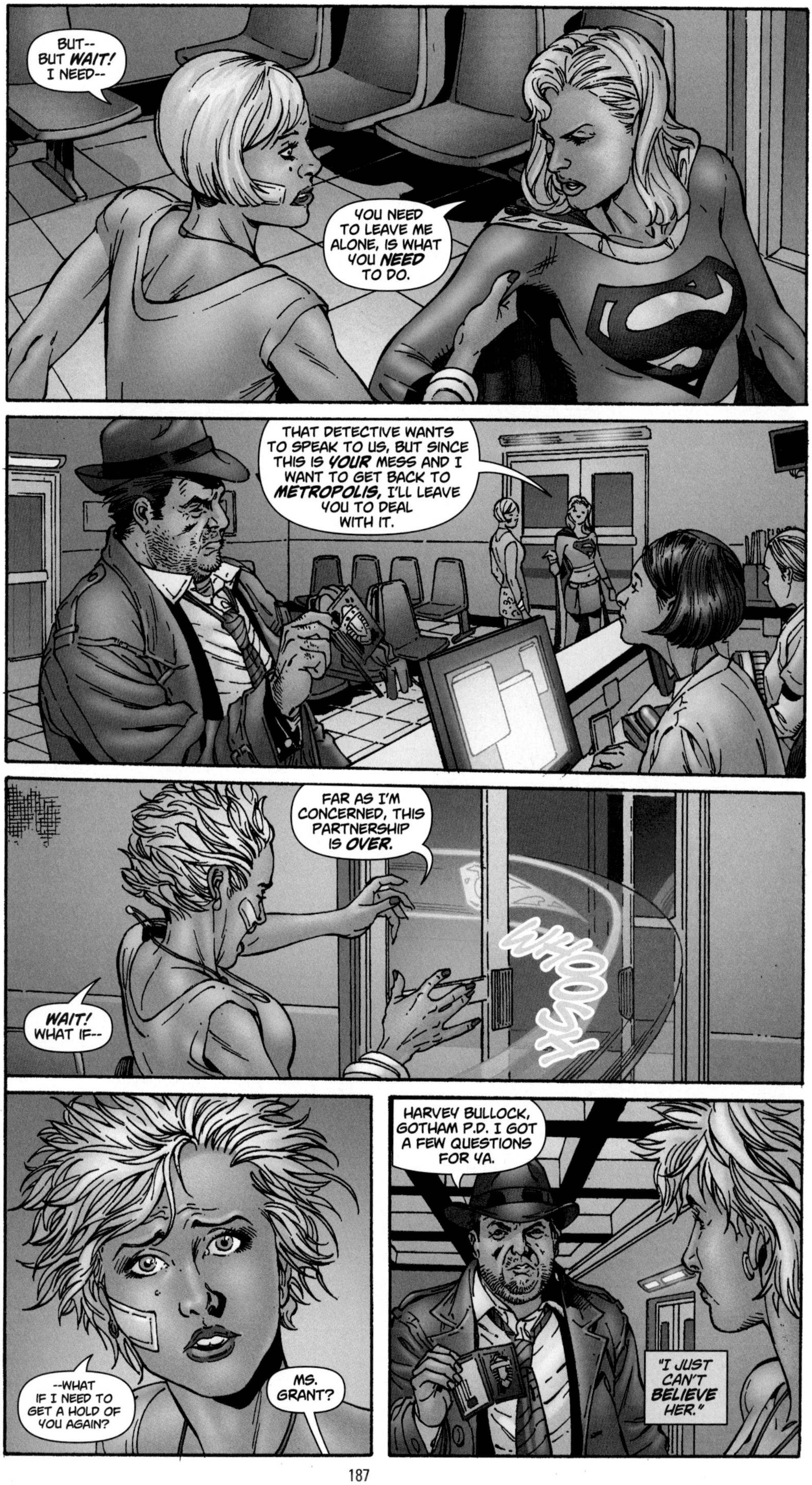

BUT--
BUT WAIT!
I NEED--
YOU NEED TO LEAVE ME ALONE, IS WHAT YOU NEED TO DO.
THAT DETECTIVE WANTS TO SPEAK TO US, BUT SINCE THIS IS YOUR MESS AND I WANT TO GET BACK TO METROPOLIS, I'LL LEAVE YOU TO DEAL WITH IT.
FAR AS I'M CONCERNED, THIS PARTNERSHIP IS OVER.
WAIT! WHAT IF--
WHOOSH
--WHAT IF I NEED TO GET A HOLD OF YOU AGAIN?
MS. GRANT?
HARVEY BULLOCK, GOTHAM P.D. I GOT A FEW QUESTIONS FOR YA.
"I JUST CAN'T BELIEVE HER."

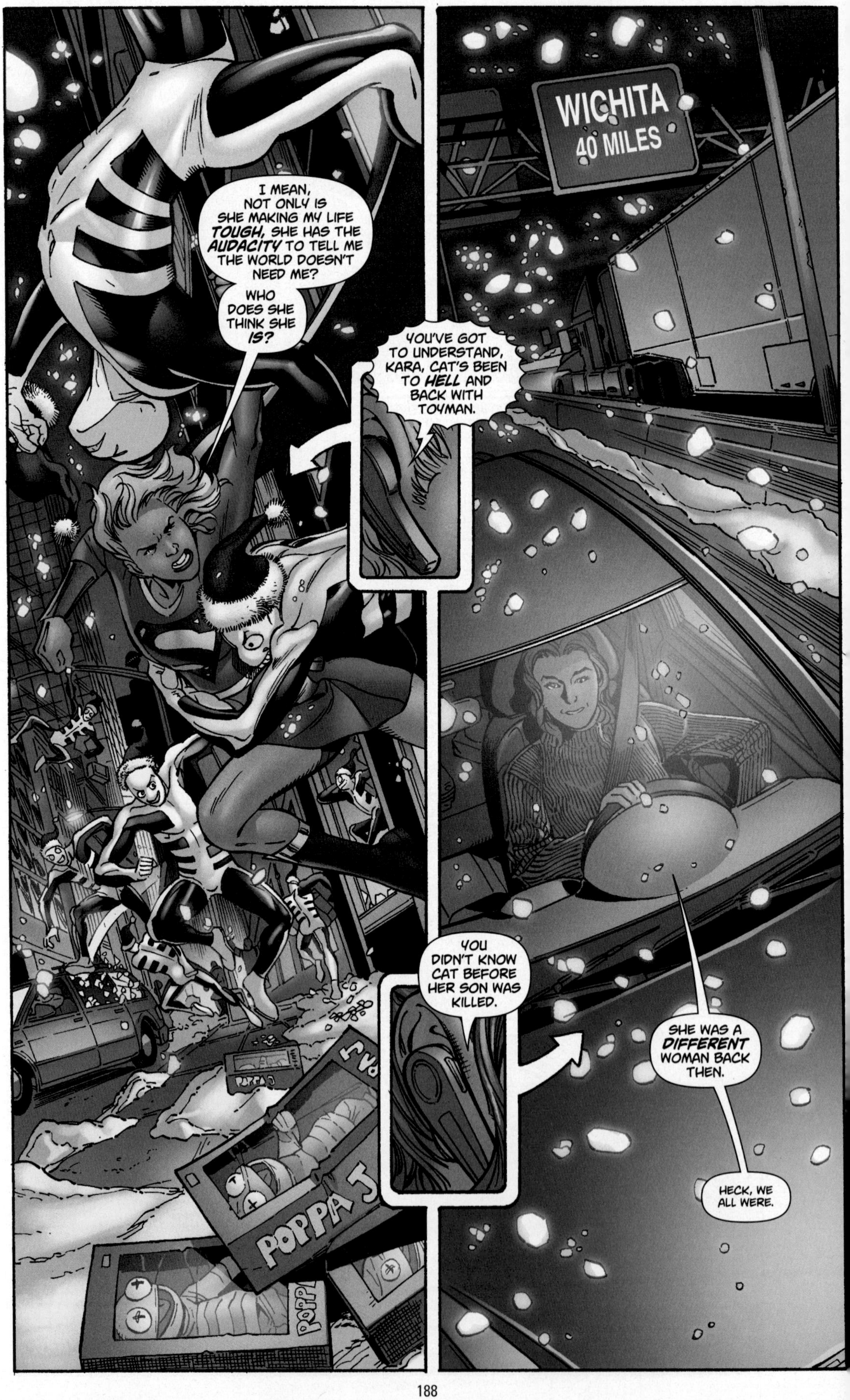
WICHITA 40 MILES
I MEAN, NOT ONLY IS SHE MAKING MY LIFE TOUGH, SHE HAS THE AUDACITY TO TELL ME THE WORLD DOESN'T NEED ME?
WHO DOES SHE THINK SHE IS?
YOU'VE GOT TO UNDERSTAND, KARA, CAT'S BEEN TO HELL AND BACK WITH TOYMAN.
YOU DIDN'T KNOW CAT BEFORE HER SON WAS KILLED.
SHE WAS A DIFFERENT WOMAN BACK THEN.
HECK, WE ALL WERE.
POPPA J

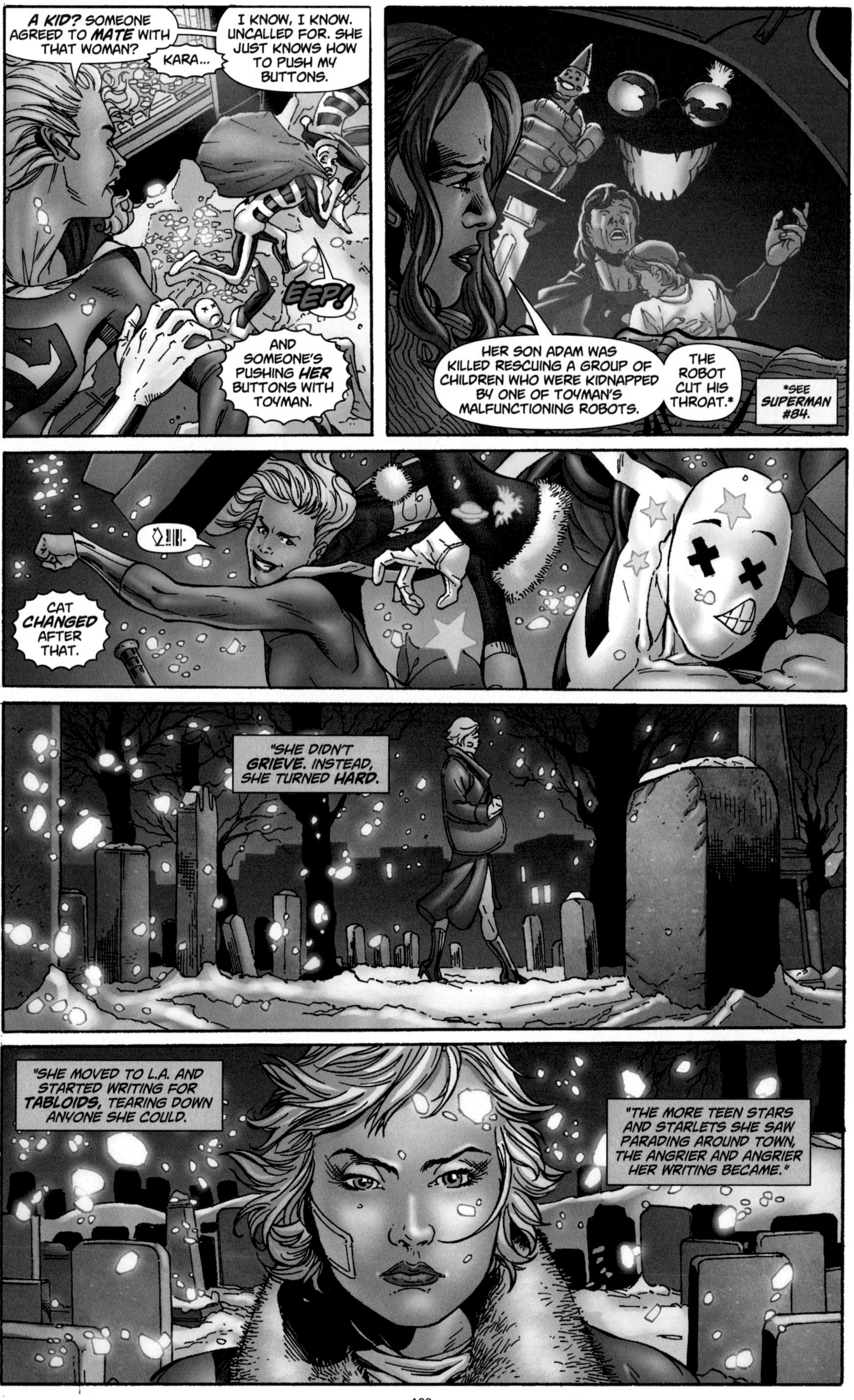
A KID? SOMEONE AGREED TO MATE WITH THAT WOMAN?
KARA...
I KNOW, I KNOW. UNCALLED FOR. SHE JUST KNOWS HOW TO PUSH MY BUTTONS.
EEP!
AND SOMEONE'S PUSHING HER BUTTONS WITH TOYMAN.
HER SON ADAM WAS KILLED RESCUING A GROUP OF CHILDREN WHO WERE KIDNAPPED BY ONE OF TOYMAN'S MALFUNCTIONING ROBOTS.
THE ROBOT CUT HIS THROAT.*
*SEE SUPERMAN #84.
CAT CHANGED AFTER THAT.
"SHE DIDN'T GRIEVE. INSTEAD, SHE TURNED HARD.
"SHE MOVED TO L.A. AND STARTED WRITING FOR TABLOIDS, TEARING DOWN ANYONE SHE COULD.
"THE MORE TEEN STARS AND STARLETS SHE SAW PARADING AROUND TOWN, THE ANGRIER AND ANGRIER HER WRITING BECAME."

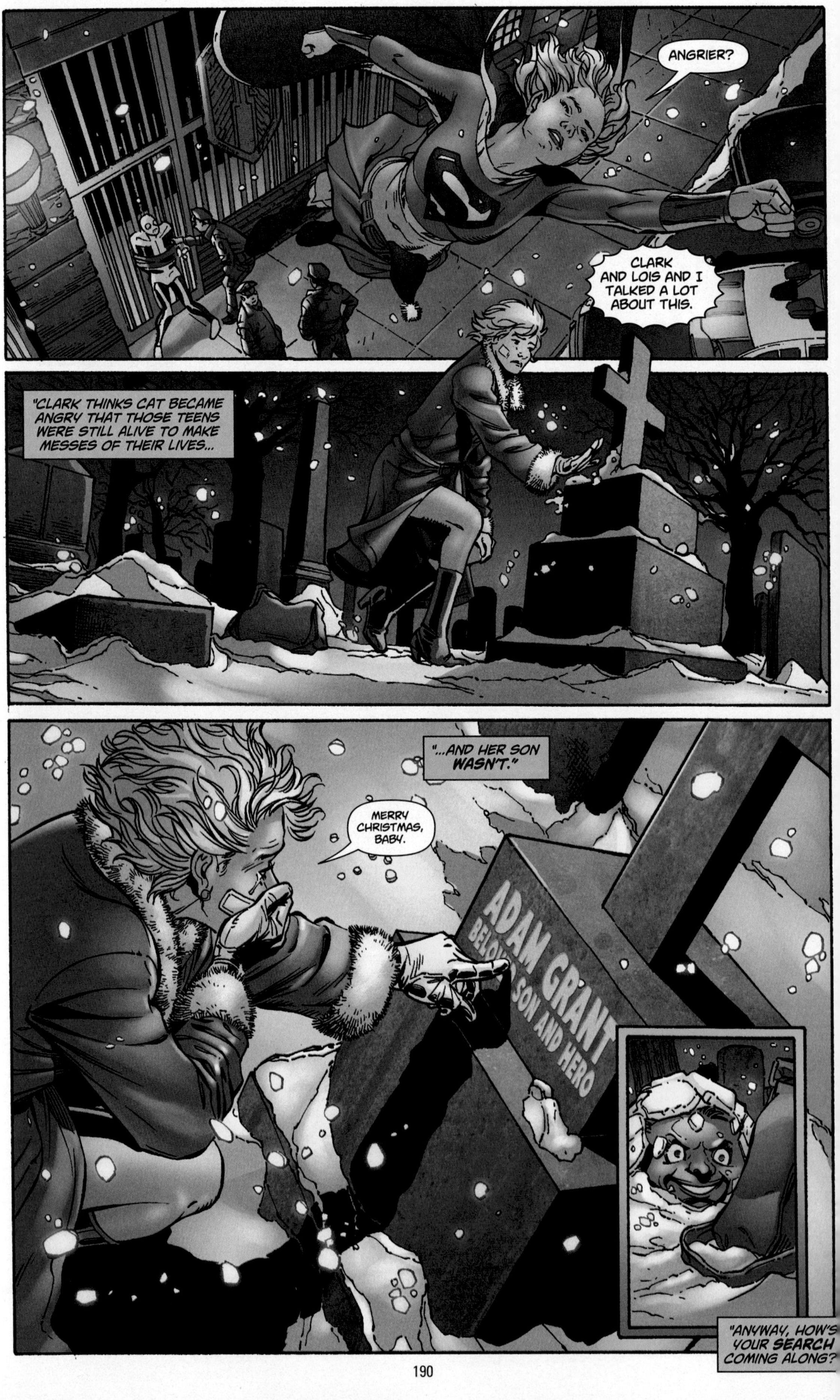
ANGRIER?
CLARK AND LOIS AND I TALKED A LOT ABOUT THIS.
"CLARK THINKS CAT BECAME ANGRY THAT THOSE TEENS WERE STILL ALIVE TO MAKE MESSES OF THEIR LIVES...
"...AND HER SON WASN'T."
MERRY CHRISTMAS, BABY.
ADAM GRANT
BELOVED SON AND HERO
"ANYWAY, HOW'S YOUR SEARCH COMING ALONG?

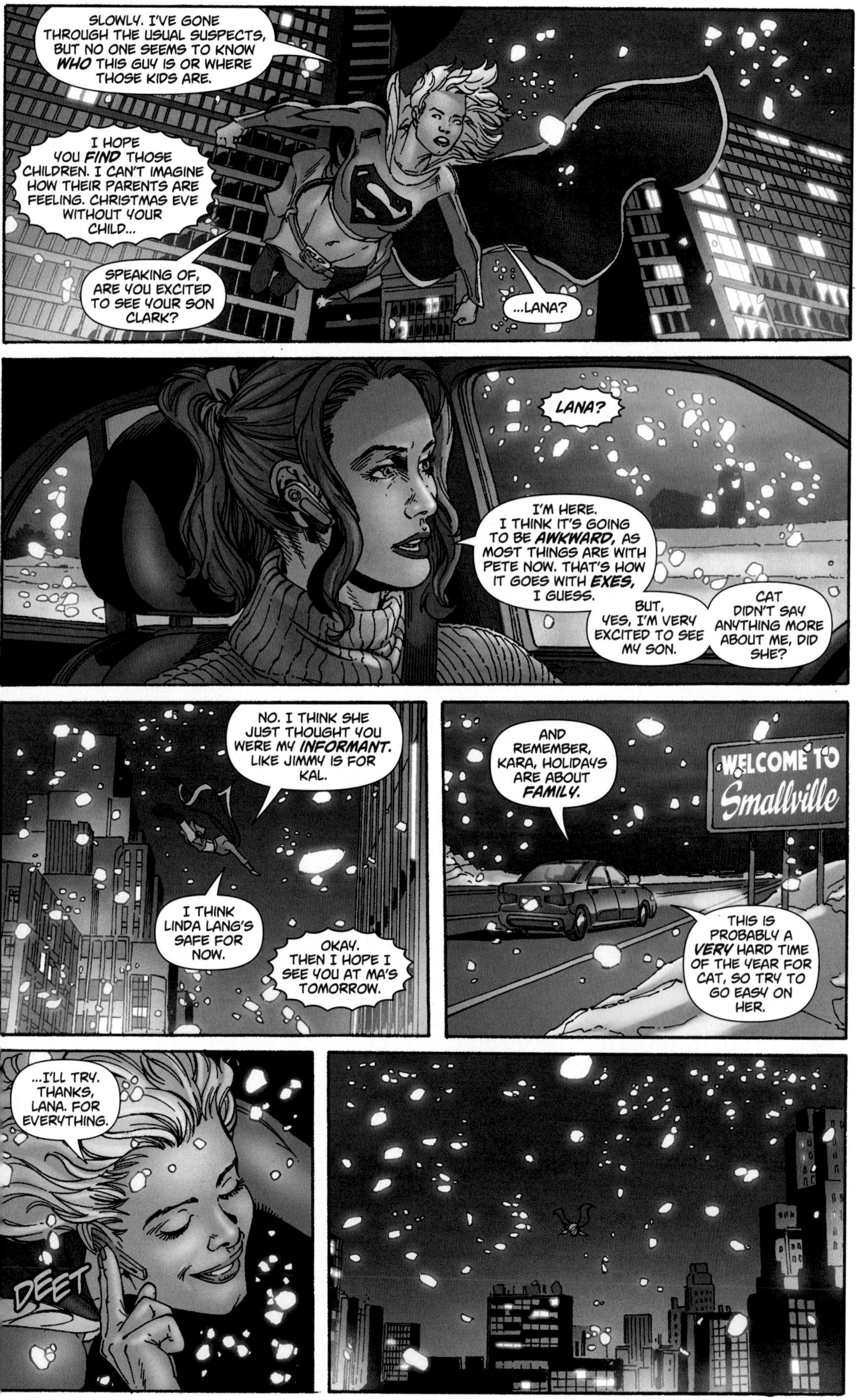
SLOWLY. I'VE GONE THROUGH THE USUAL SUSPECTS, BUT NO ONE SEEMS TO KNOW WHO THIS GUY IS OR WHERE THOSE KIDS ARE.
I HOPE YOU FIND THOSE CHILDREN. I CAN'T IMAGINE HOW THEIR PARENTS ARE FEELING. CHRISTMAS EVE WITHOUT YOUR CHILD...
SPEAKING OF, ARE YOU EXCITED TO SEE YOUR SON CLARK?
...LANA?
LANA?
I'M HERE. I THINK IT'S GOING TO BE AWKWARD, AS MOST THINGS ARE WITH PETE NOW. THAT'S HOW IT GOES WITH EXES, I GUESS.
BUT, YES, I'M VERY EXCITED TO SEE MY SON.
CAT DIDN'T SAY ANYTHING MORE ABOUT ME, DID SHE?
NO. I THINK SHE JUST THOUGHT YOU WERE MY INFORMANT. LIKE JIMMY IS FOR KAL.
I THINK LINDA LANG'S SAFE FOR NOW.
OKAY. THEN I HOPE I SEE YOU AT MA'S TOMORROW.
AND REMEMBER, KARA, HOLIDAYS ARE ABOUT FAMILY.
WELCOME TO Smallville
THIS IS PROBABLY A VERY HARD TIME OF THE YEAR FOR CAT, SO TRY TO GO EASY ON HER.
...I'LL TRY. THANKS, LANA. FOR EVERYTHING.
DEET

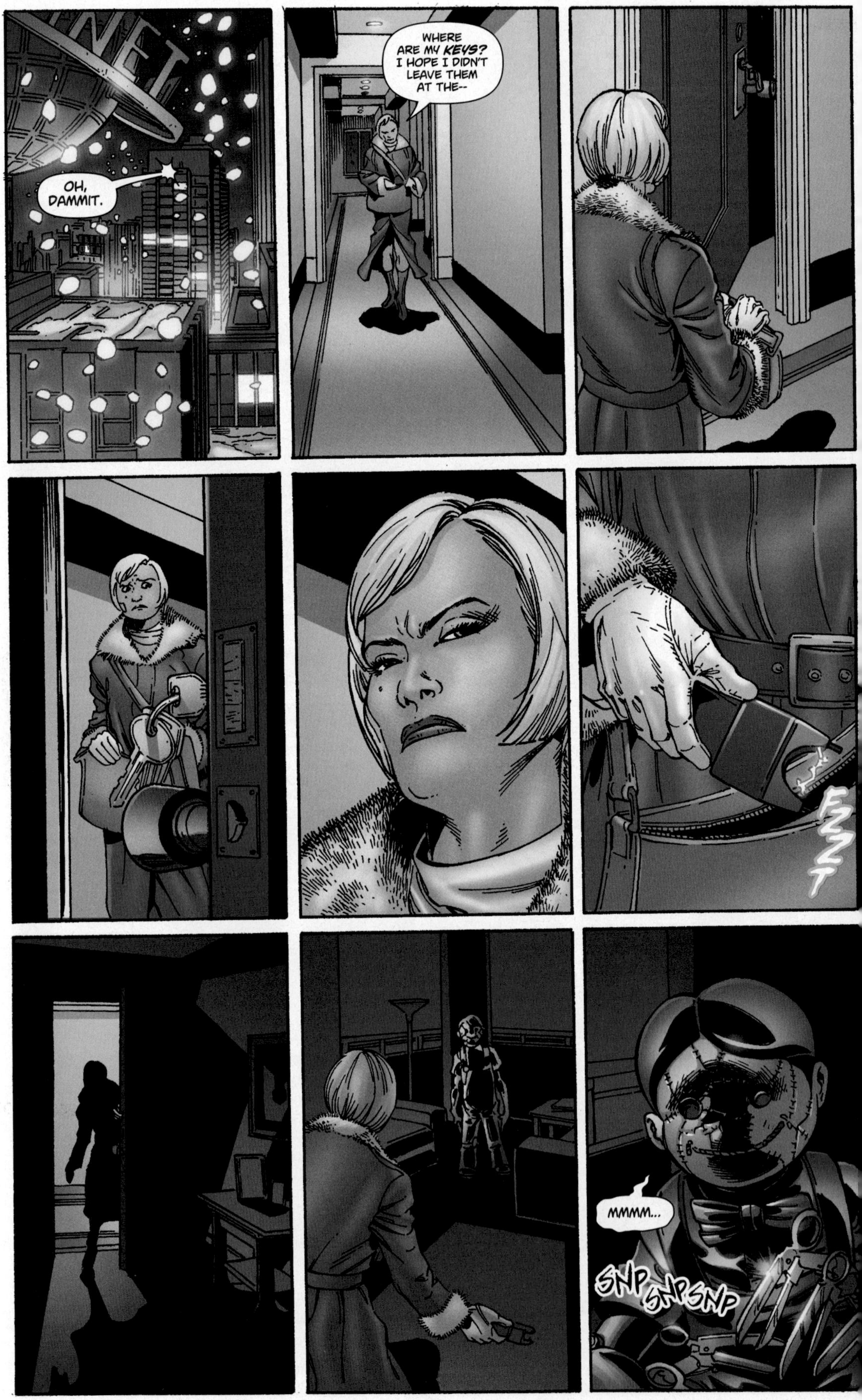

OH, DAMMIT.
WHERE ARE MY KEYS? I HOPE I DIDN'T LEAVE THEM AT THE--
FZZZT
MMMM...
SNP SNPSNP

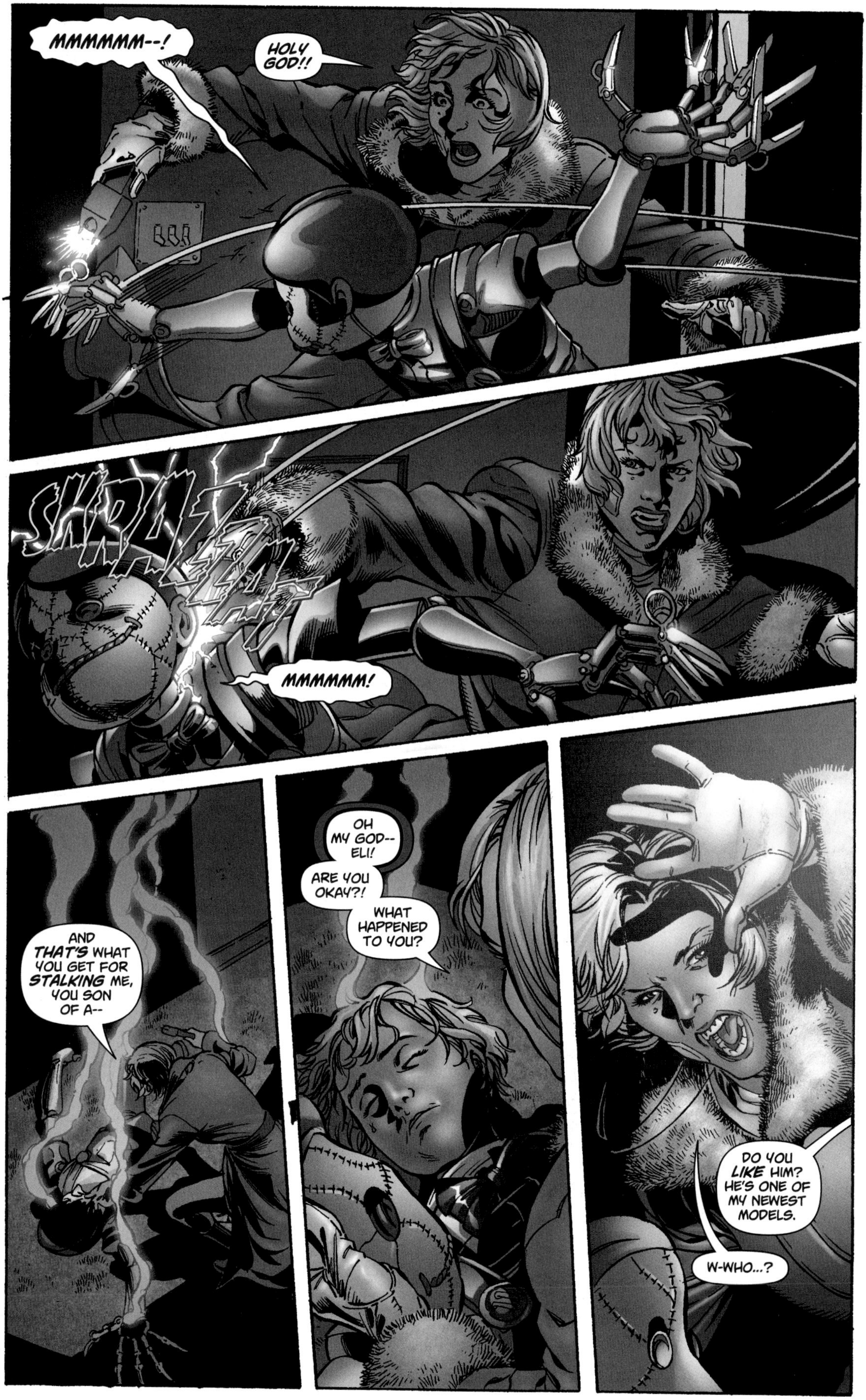
MMMMMM--!
HOLY GOD!!
SHRAKZAK
MMMMMM!
AND THAT'S WHAT YOU GET FOR STALKING ME, YOU SON OF A--
OH MY GOD-- ELI!
ARE YOU OKAY?!
WHAT HAPPENED TO YOU?
DO YOU LIKE HIM? HE'S ONE OF MY NEWEST MODELS.
W-WHO...?

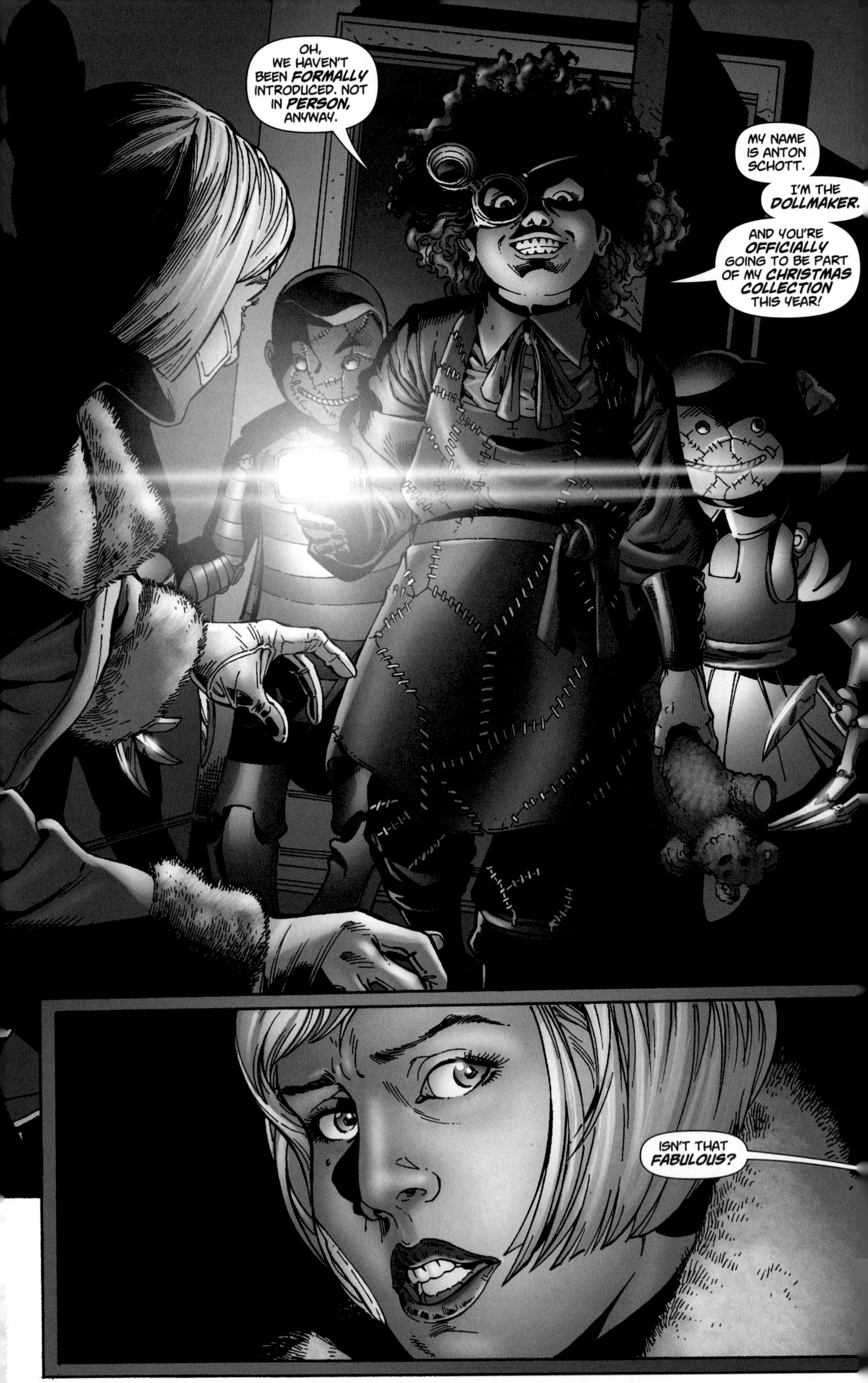
OH, WE HAVEN'T BEEN FORMALLY INTRODUCED. NOT IN PERSON, ANYWAY.
MY NAME IS ANTON SCHOTT.
I'M THE DOLLMAKER.
AND YOU'RE OFFICIALLY GOING TO BE PART OF MY CHRISTMAS COLLECTION THIS YEAR!
ISN'T THAT FABULOUS?

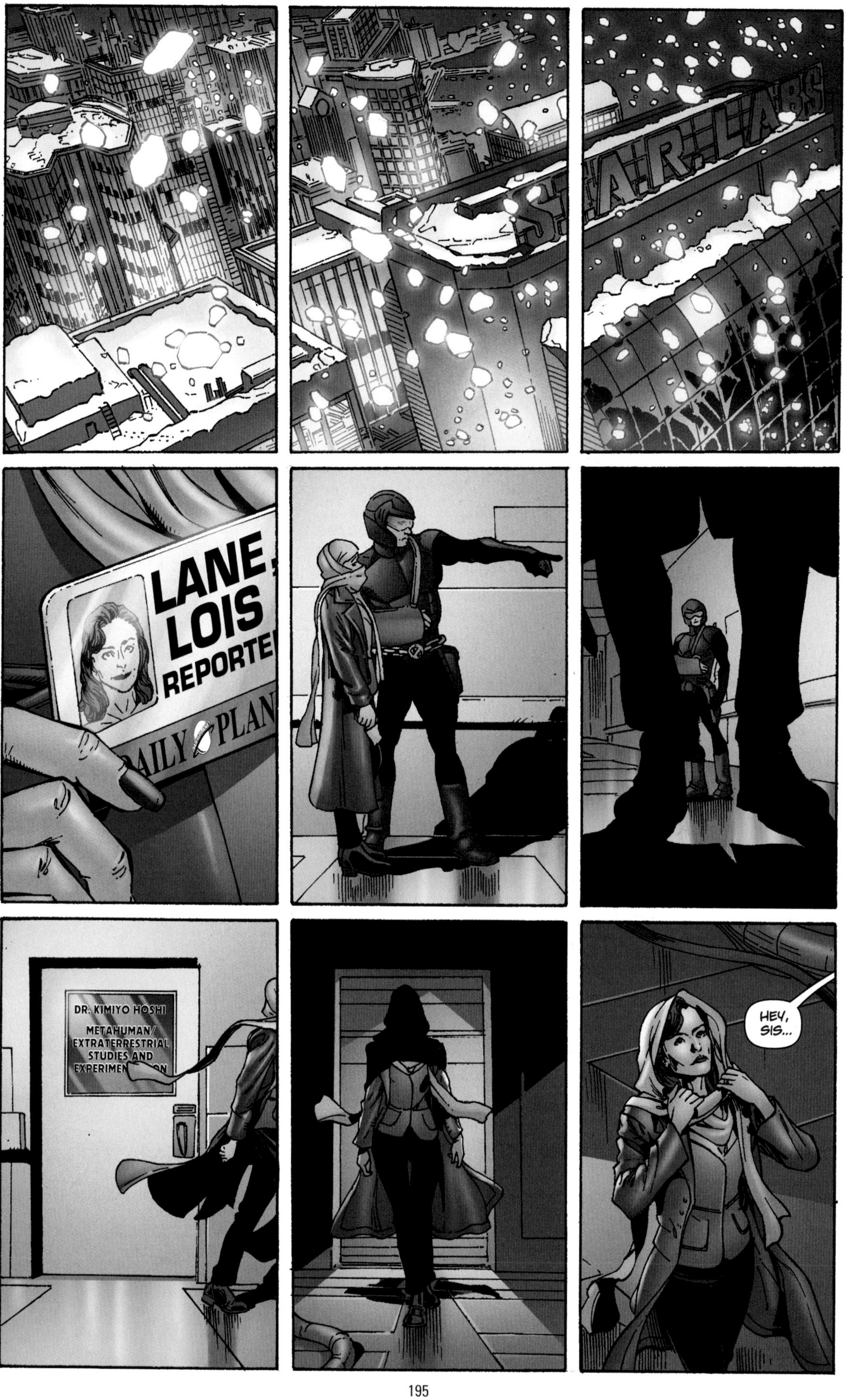
S.T.A.R. LABS
LANE, LOIS
REPORTER
DAILY PLAN
DR. KIMIYO HOSHI
METAHUMAN/
EXTRATERRESTRIAL
STUDIES AND
HEY, SIS...

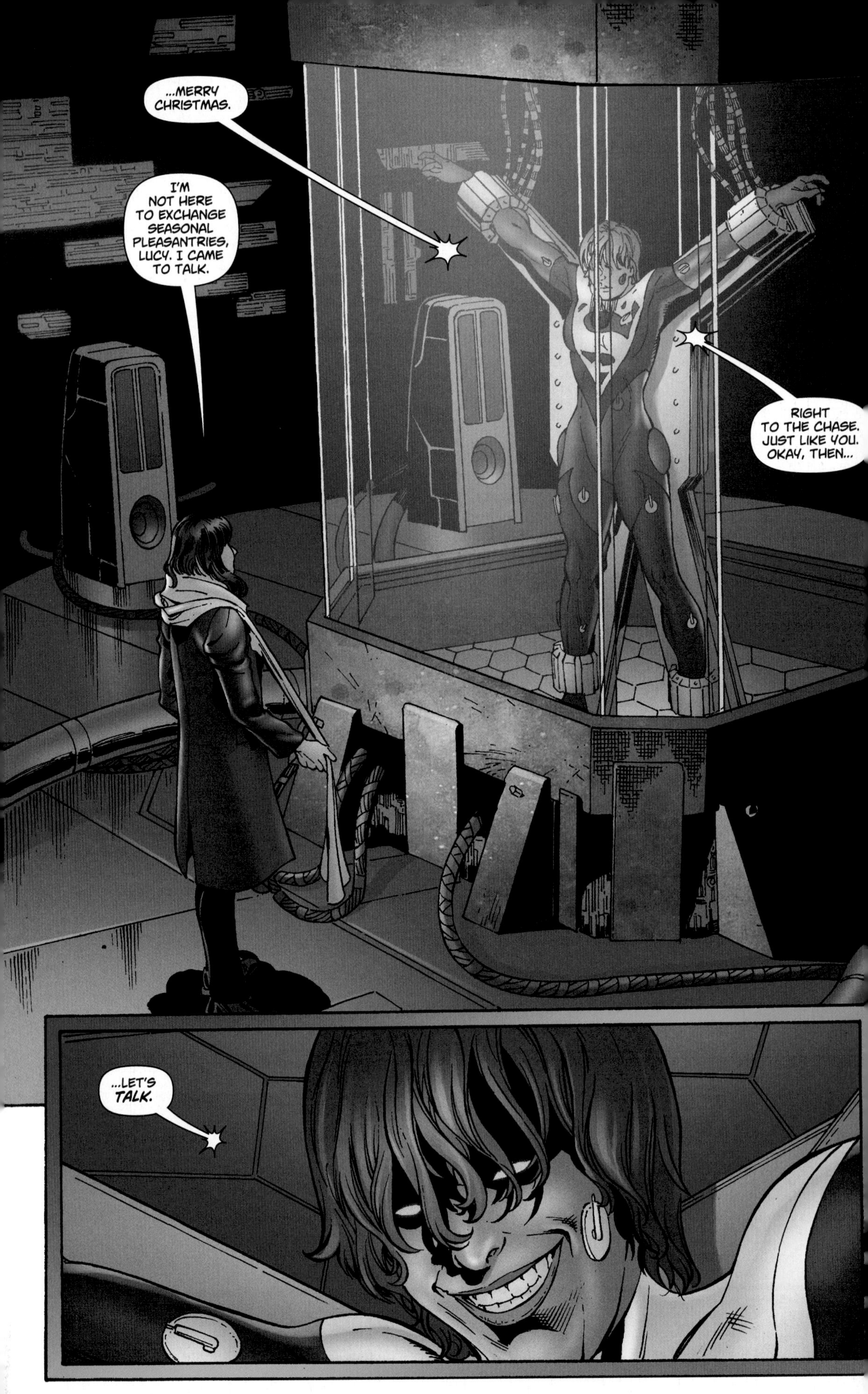
...MERRY CHRISTMAS.
I'M NOT HERE TO EXCHANGE SEASONAL PLEASANTRIES, LUCY. I CAME TO TALK.
RIGHT TO THE CHASE. JUST LIKE YOU. OKAY, THEN...
...LET'S *TALK*.

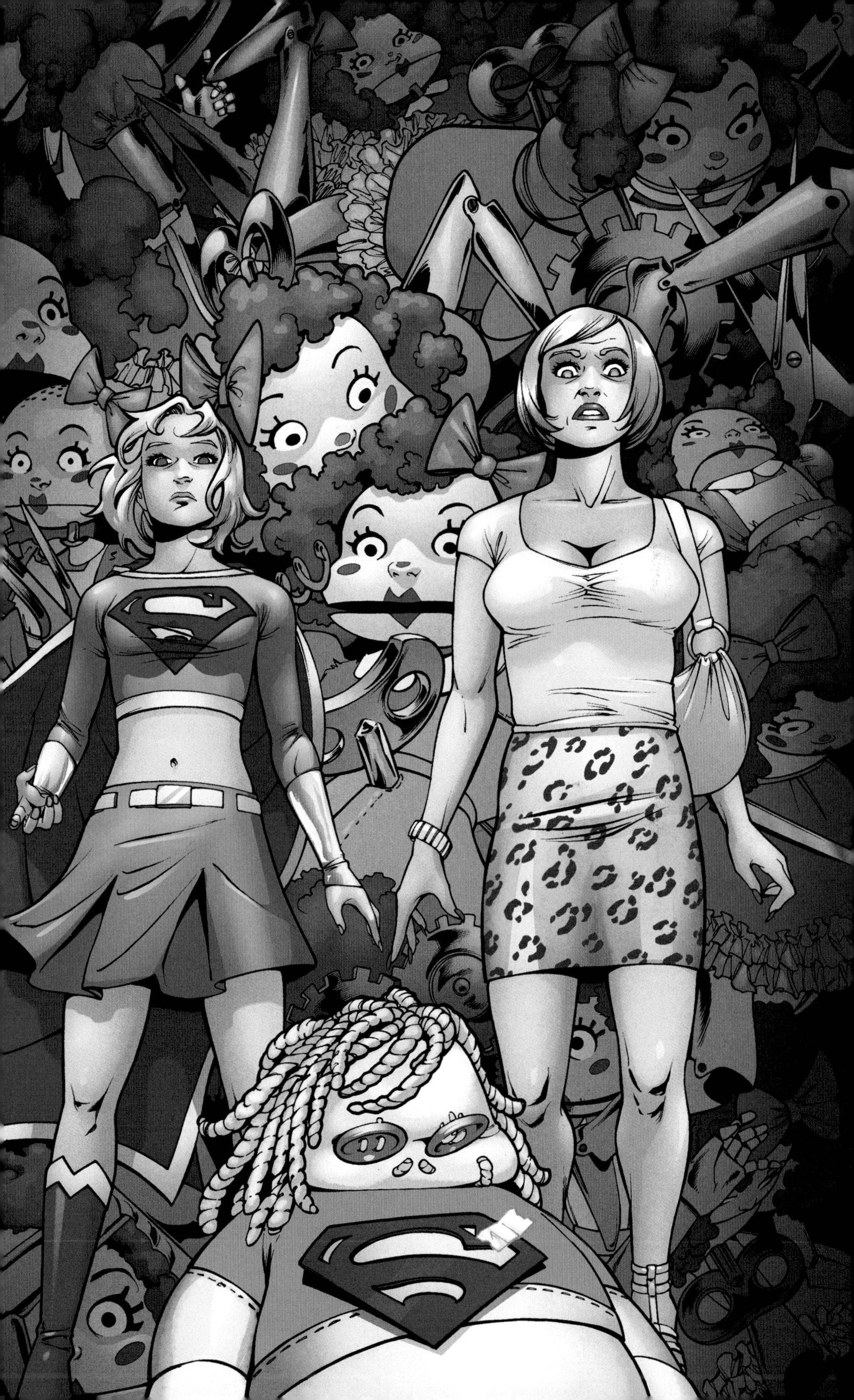

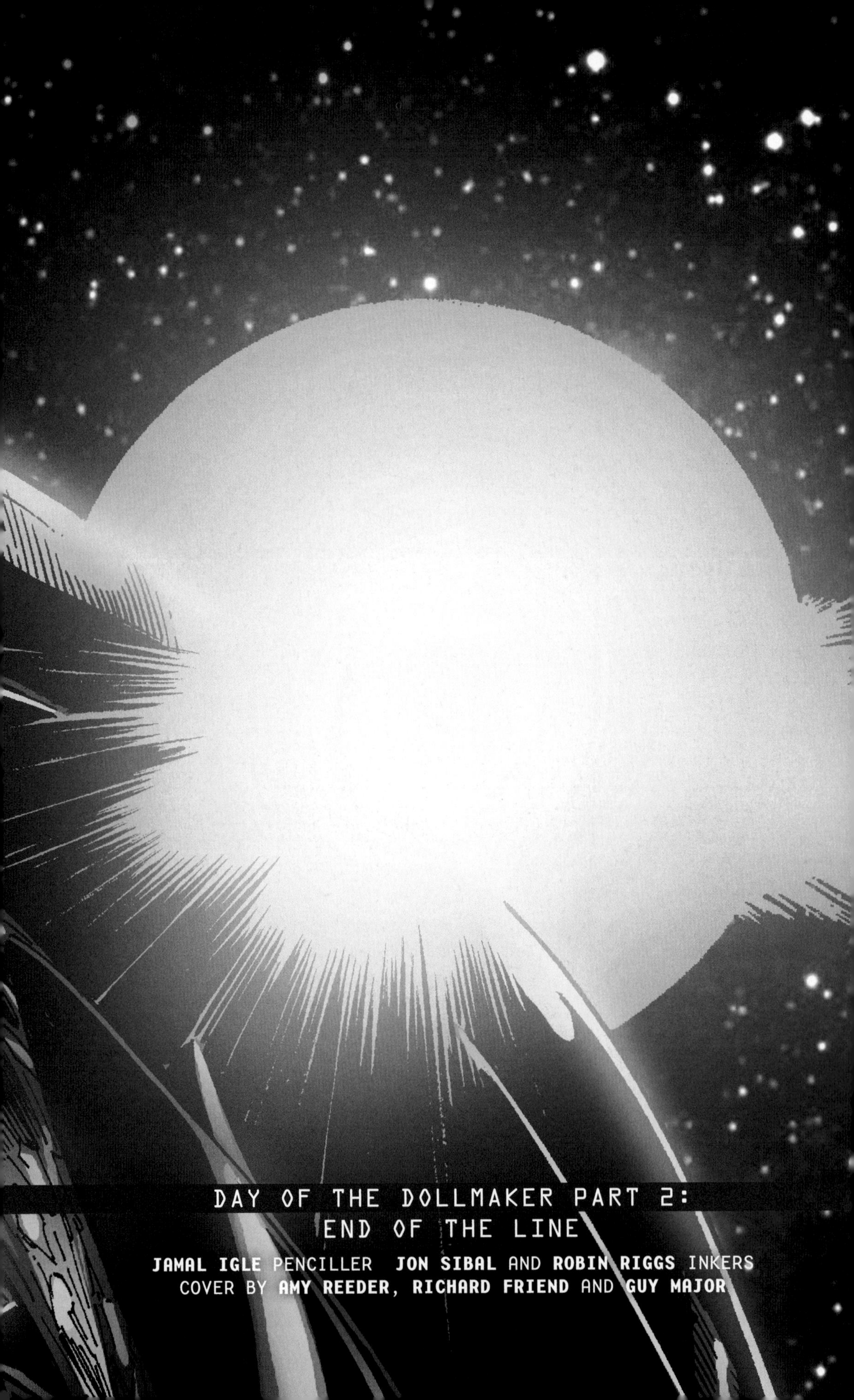

DAY OF THE DOLLMAKER PART 2: END OF THE LINE

JAMAL IGLE PENCILLER **JON SIBAL** AND **ROBIN RIGGS** INKERS
COVER BY **AMY REEDER, RICHARD FRIEND** AND **GUY MAJOR**

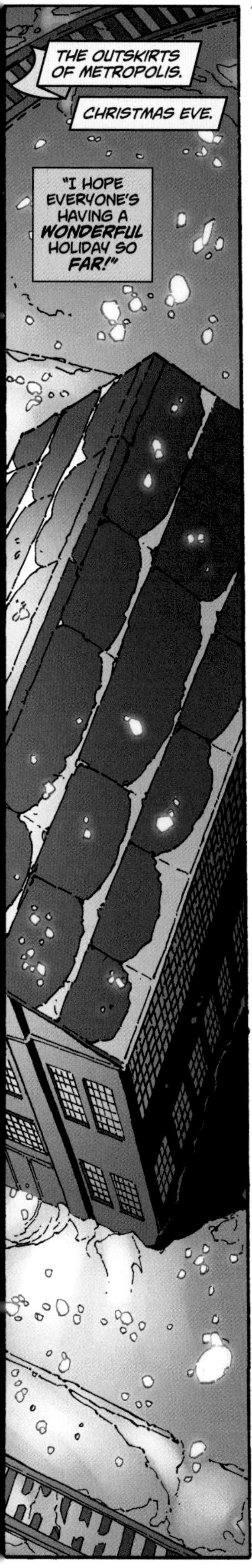
THE OUTSKIRTS OF METROPOLIS.
CHRISTMAS EVE.
"I HOPE EVERYONE'S HAVING A WONDERFUL HOLIDAY SO FAR!"

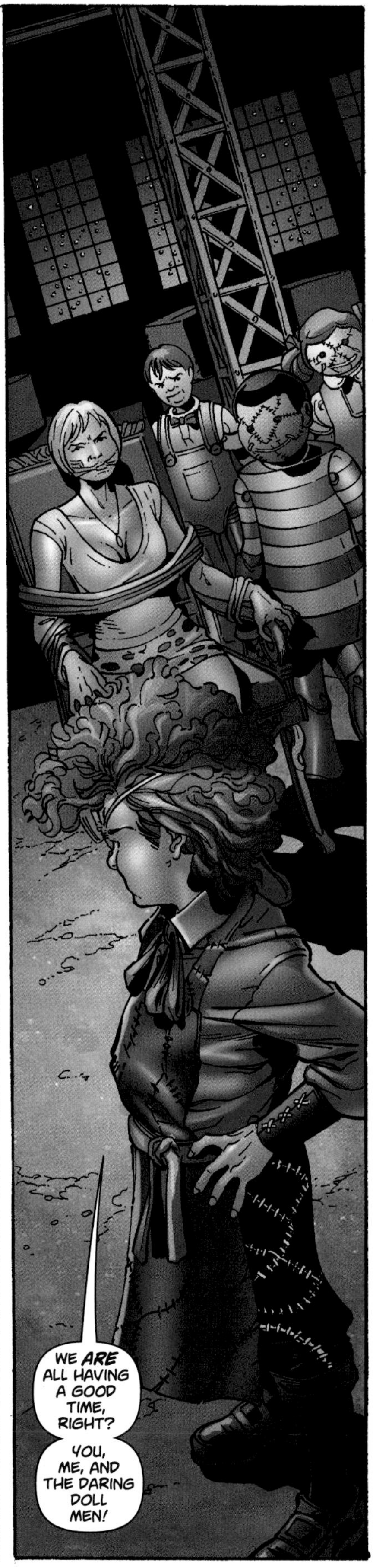
WE ARE ALL HAVING A GOOD TIME, RIGHT?
YOU, ME, AND THE DARING DOLL MEN!

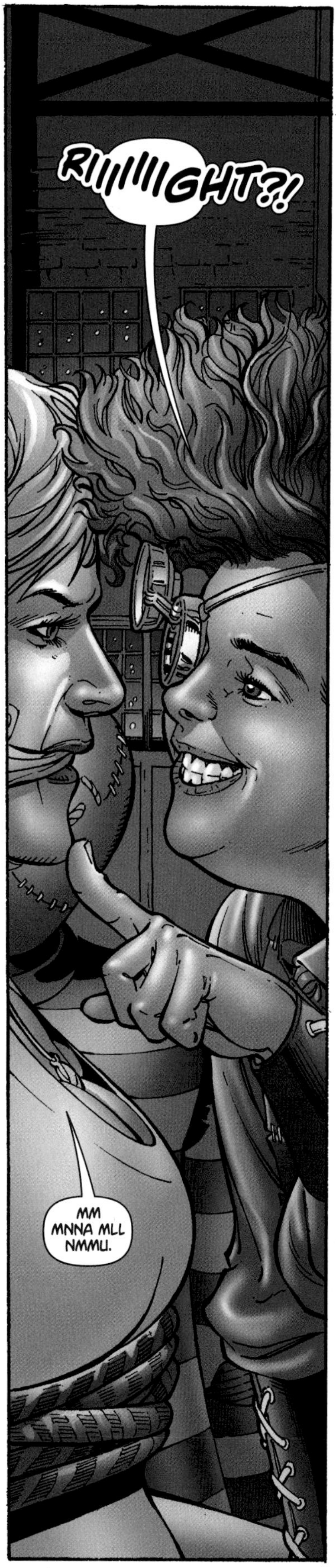
RI/////GHT?!
MM MNNA MLL NMMU.

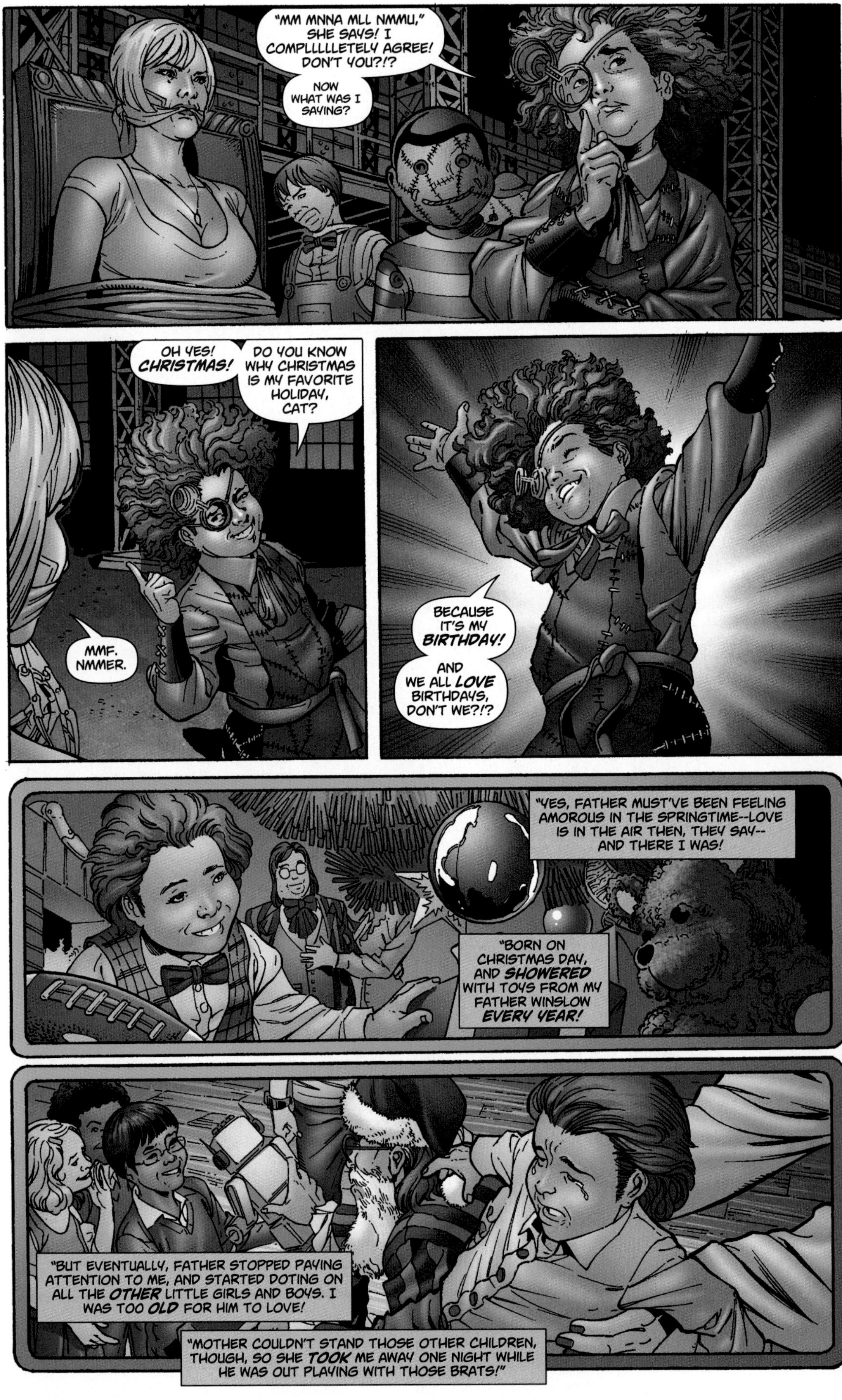
"MM MNNA MLL NMMU," SHE SAYS! I COMPLLLLLETELY AGREE! DON'T YOU?!?
NOW WHAT WAS I SAYING?
OH YES! CHRISTMAS!
DO YOU KNOW WHY CHRISTMAS IS MY FAVORITE HOLIDAY, CAT?
MMF. NMMER.
BECAUSE IT'S MY BIRTHDAY!
AND WE ALL LOVE BIRTHDAYS, DON'T WE?!?
"YES, FATHER MUST'VE BEEN FEELING AMOROUS IN THE SPRINGTIME--LOVE IS IN THE AIR THEN, THEY SAY-- AND THERE I WAS!
"BORN ON CHRISTMAS DAY, AND SHOWERED WITH TOYS FROM MY FATHER WINSLOW EVERY YEAR!
"BUT EVENTUALLY, FATHER STOPPED PAYING ATTENTION TO ME, AND STARTED DOTING ON ALL THE OTHER LITTLE GIRLS AND BOYS. I WAS TOO OLD FOR HIM TO LOVE!
"MOTHER COULDN'T STAND THOSE OTHER CHILDREN, THOUGH, SO SHE TOOK ME AWAY ONE NIGHT WHILE HE WAS OUT PLAYING WITH THOSE BRATS!"

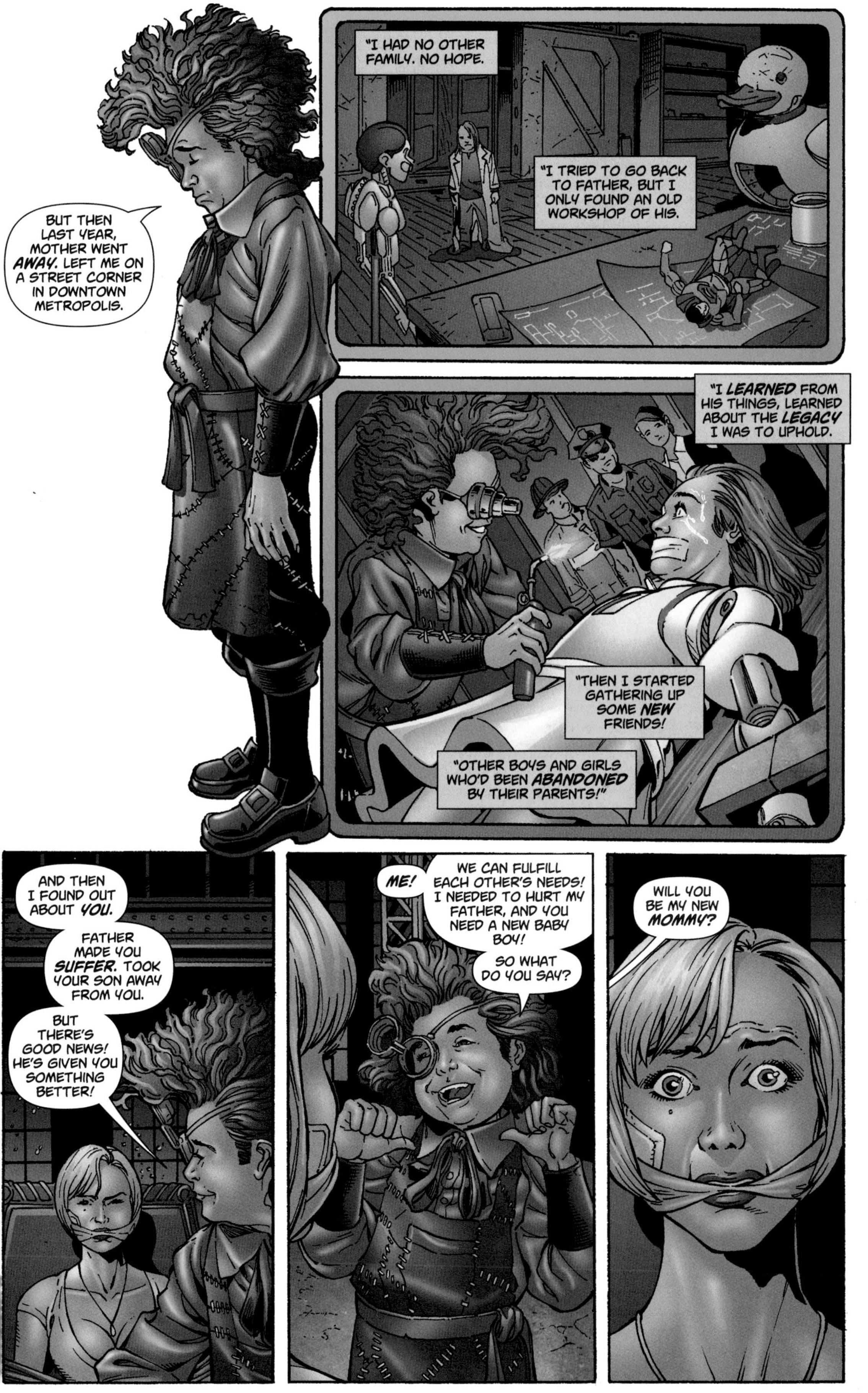
BUT THEN LAST YEAR, MOTHER WENT AWAY. LEFT ME ON A STREET CORNER IN DOWNTOWN METROPOLIS.
"I HAD NO OTHER FAMILY. NO HOPE.
"I TRIED TO GO BACK TO FATHER, BUT I ONLY FOUND AN OLD WORKSHOP OF HIS.
"I LEARNED FROM HIS THINGS, LEARNED ABOUT THE LEGACY I WAS TO UPHOLD.
"THEN I STARTED GATHERING UP SOME NEW FRIENDS!
"OTHER BOYS AND GIRLS WHO'D BEEN ABANDONED BY THEIR PARENTS!"
AND THEN I FOUND OUT ABOUT YOU.
FATHER MADE YOU SUFFER. TOOK YOUR SON AWAY FROM YOU.
BUT THERE'S GOOD NEWS! HE'S GIVEN YOU SOMETHING BETTER!
ME!
WE CAN FULFILL EACH OTHER'S NEEDS! I NEEDED TO HURT MY FATHER, AND YOU NEED A NEW BABY BOY!
SO WHAT DO YOU SAY?
WILL YOU BE MY NEW MOMMY?

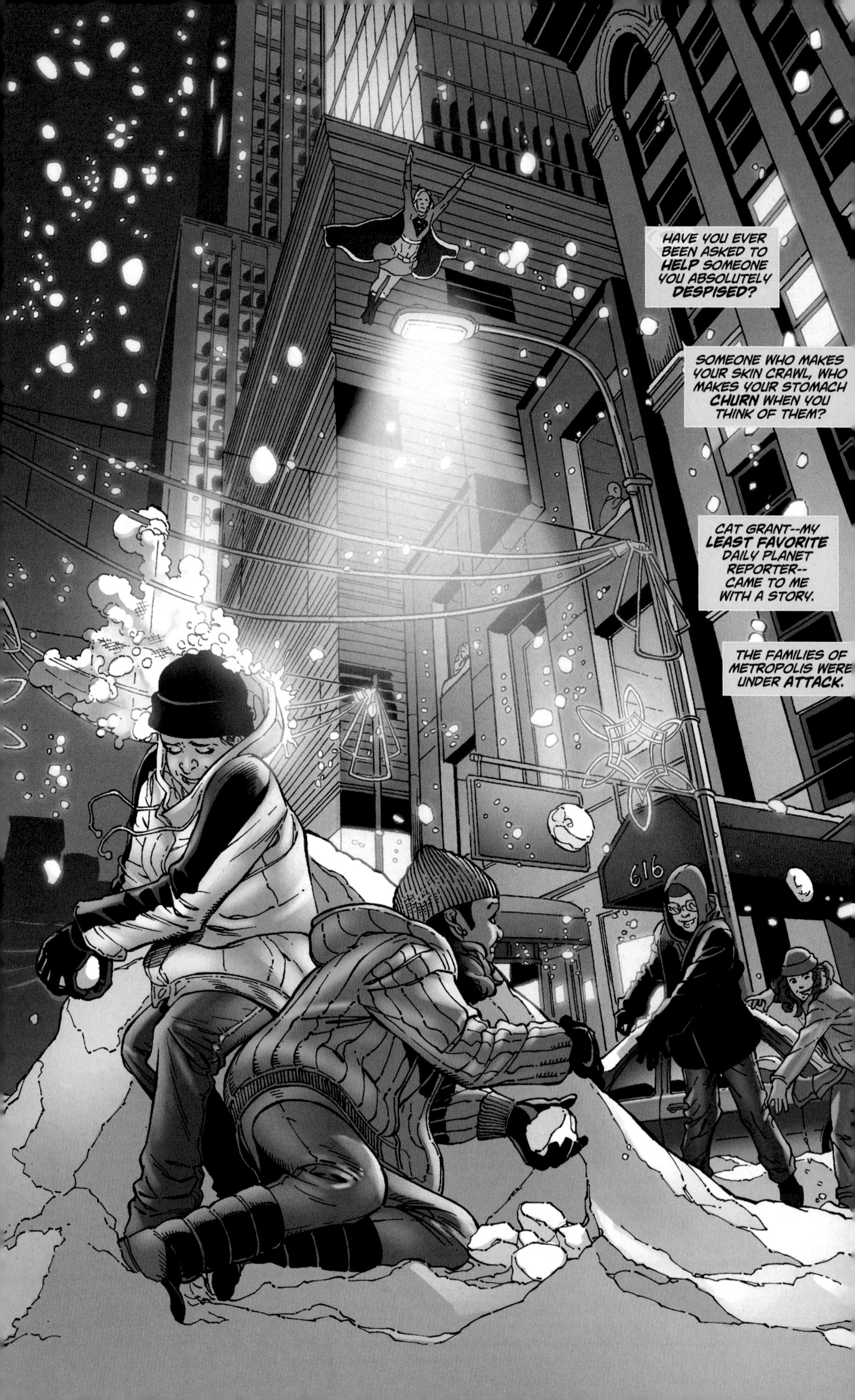
HAVE YOU EVER BEEN ASKED TO HELP SOMEONE YOU ABSOLUTELY DESPISED?
SOMEONE WHO MAKES YOUR SKIN CRAWL, WHO MAKES YOUR STOMACH CHURN WHEN YOU THINK OF THEM?
CAT GRANT--MY LEAST FAVORITE DAILY PLANET REPORTER--CAME TO ME WITH A STORY.
THE FAMILIES OF METROPOLIS WERE UNDER ATTACK.
616

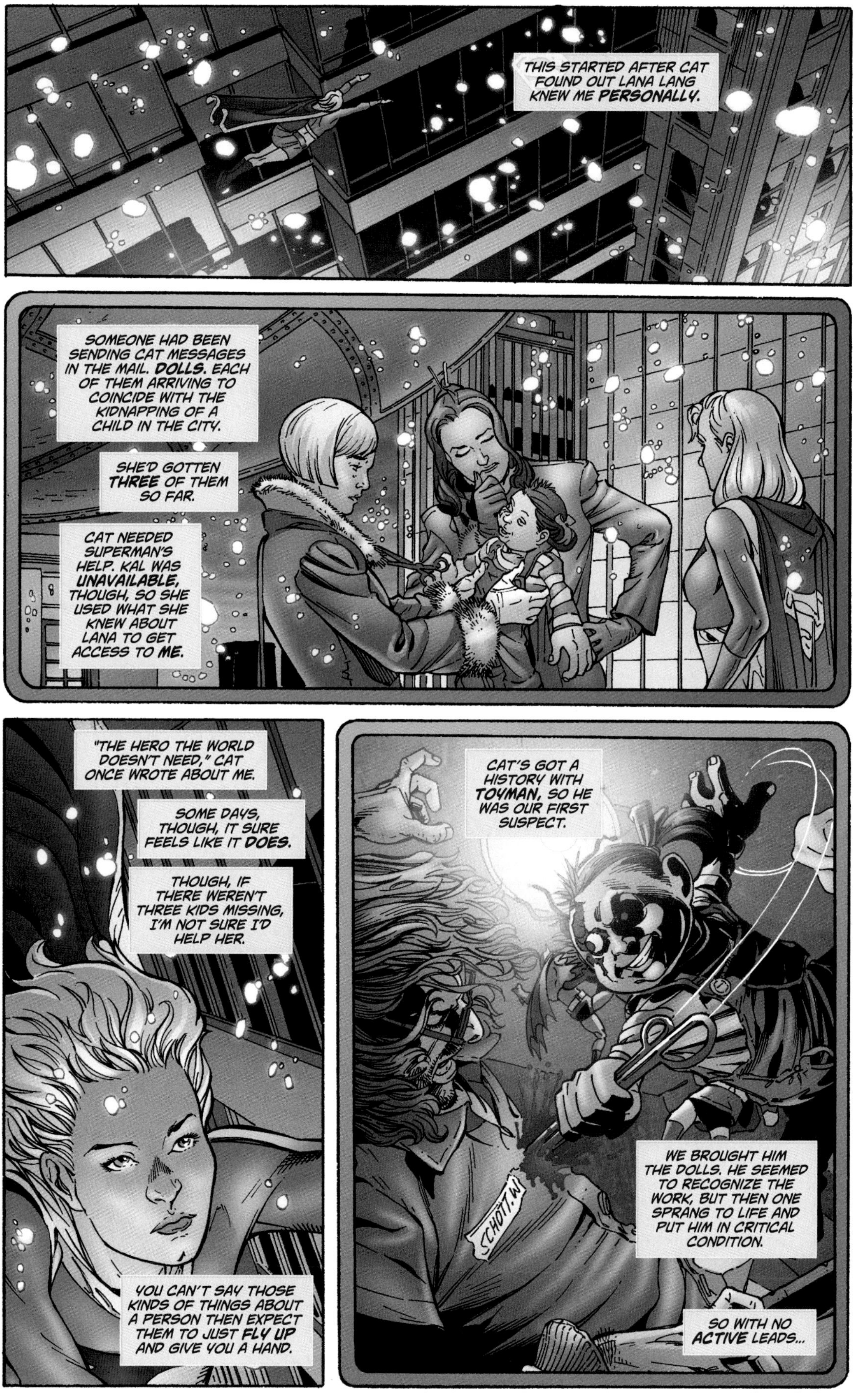
THIS STARTED AFTER CAT FOUND OUT LANA LANG KNEW ME **PERSONALLY**.
SOMEONE HAD BEEN SENDING CAT MESSAGES IN THE MAIL. **DOLLS.** EACH OF THEM ARRIVING TO COINCIDE WITH THE KIDNAPPING OF A CHILD IN THE CITY.
SHE'D GOTTEN **THREE** OF THEM SO FAR.
CAT NEEDED SUPERMAN'S HELP. KAL WAS **UNAVAILABLE,** THOUGH, SO SHE USED WHAT SHE KNEW ABOUT LANA TO GET ACCESS TO **ME.**
"THE HERO THE WORLD DOESN'T NEED," CAT ONCE WROTE ABOUT ME.
SOME DAYS, THOUGH, IT SURE FEELS LIKE IT **DOES.**
THOUGH, IF THERE WEREN'T THREE KIDS MISSING, I'M NOT SURE I'D HELP HER.
YOU CAN'T SAY THOSE KINDS OF THINGS ABOUT A PERSON THEN EXPECT THEM TO JUST **FLY UP** AND GIVE YOU A HAND.
CAT'S GOT A HISTORY WITH **TOYMAN,** SO HE WAS OUR FIRST SUSPECT.
SCHOTT, W.
WE BROUGHT HIM THE DOLLS. HE SEEMED TO RECOGNIZE THE WORK, BUT THEN ONE SPRANG TO LIFE AND PUT HIM IN CRITICAL CONDITION.
SO WITH NO **ACTIVE** LEADS...

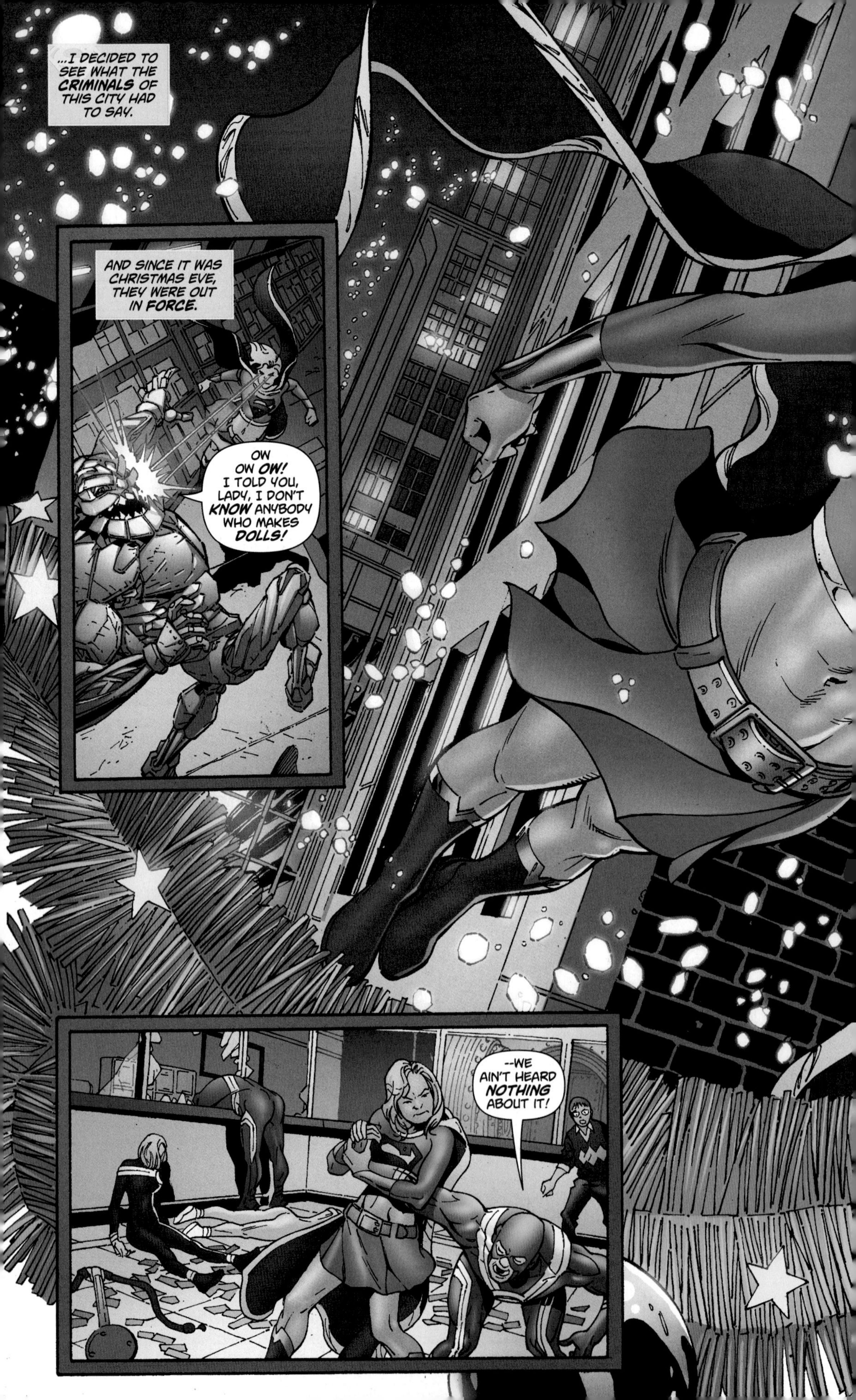

...I DECIDED TO SEE WHAT THE CRIMINALS OF THIS CITY HAD TO SAY.
AND SINCE IT WAS CHRISTMAS EVE, THEY WERE OUT IN FORCE.
OW OW OW! I TOLD YOU, LADY, I DON'T KNOW ANYBODY WHO MAKES DOLLS!
--WE AIN'T HEARD NOTHING ABOUT IT!

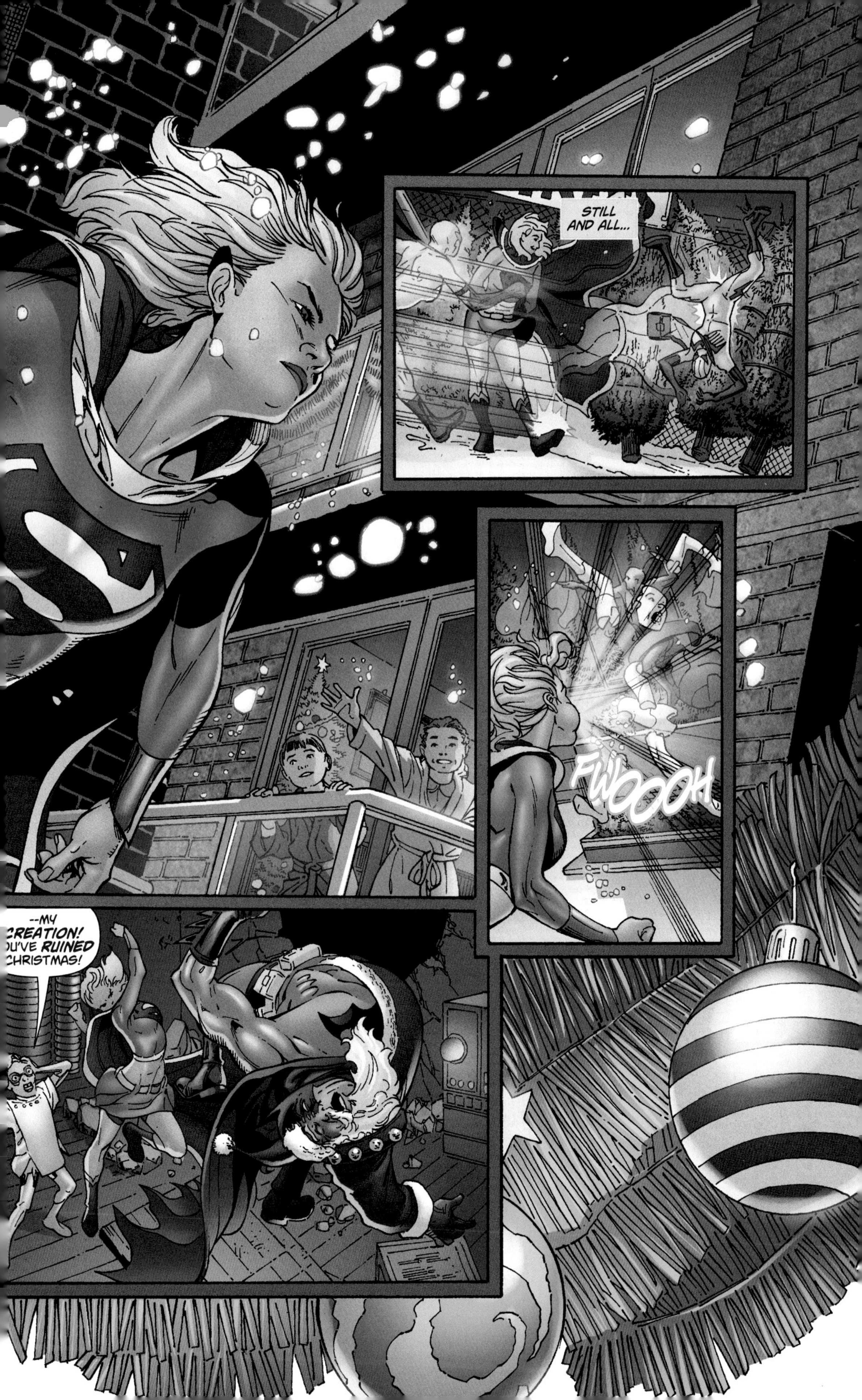
STILL AND ALL...
FWOOOOH
--MY CREATION! YOU'VE RUINED CHRISTMAS!

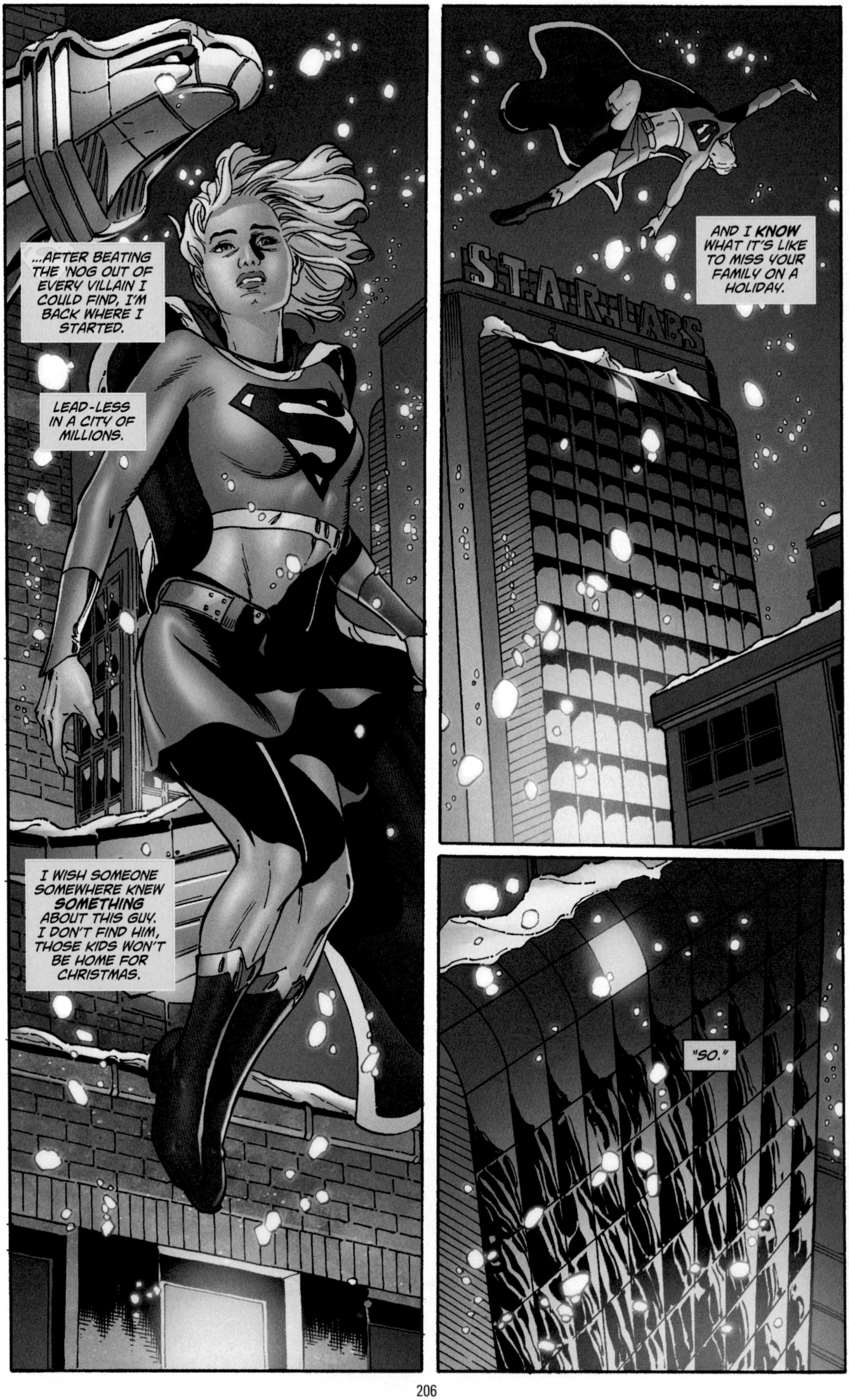
...AFTER BEATING THE 'NOG OUT OF EVERY VILLAIN I COULD FIND, I'M BACK WHERE I STARTED.
LEAD-LESS IN A CITY OF MILLIONS.
I WISH SOMEONE SOMEWHERE KNEW **SOMETHING** ABOUT THIS GUY. I DON'T FIND HIM, THOSE KIDS WON'T BE HOME FOR CHRISTMAS.
AND I **KNOW** WHAT IT'S LIKE TO MISS YOUR FAMILY ON A HOLIDAY.
S.T.A.R. LABS
"SO."

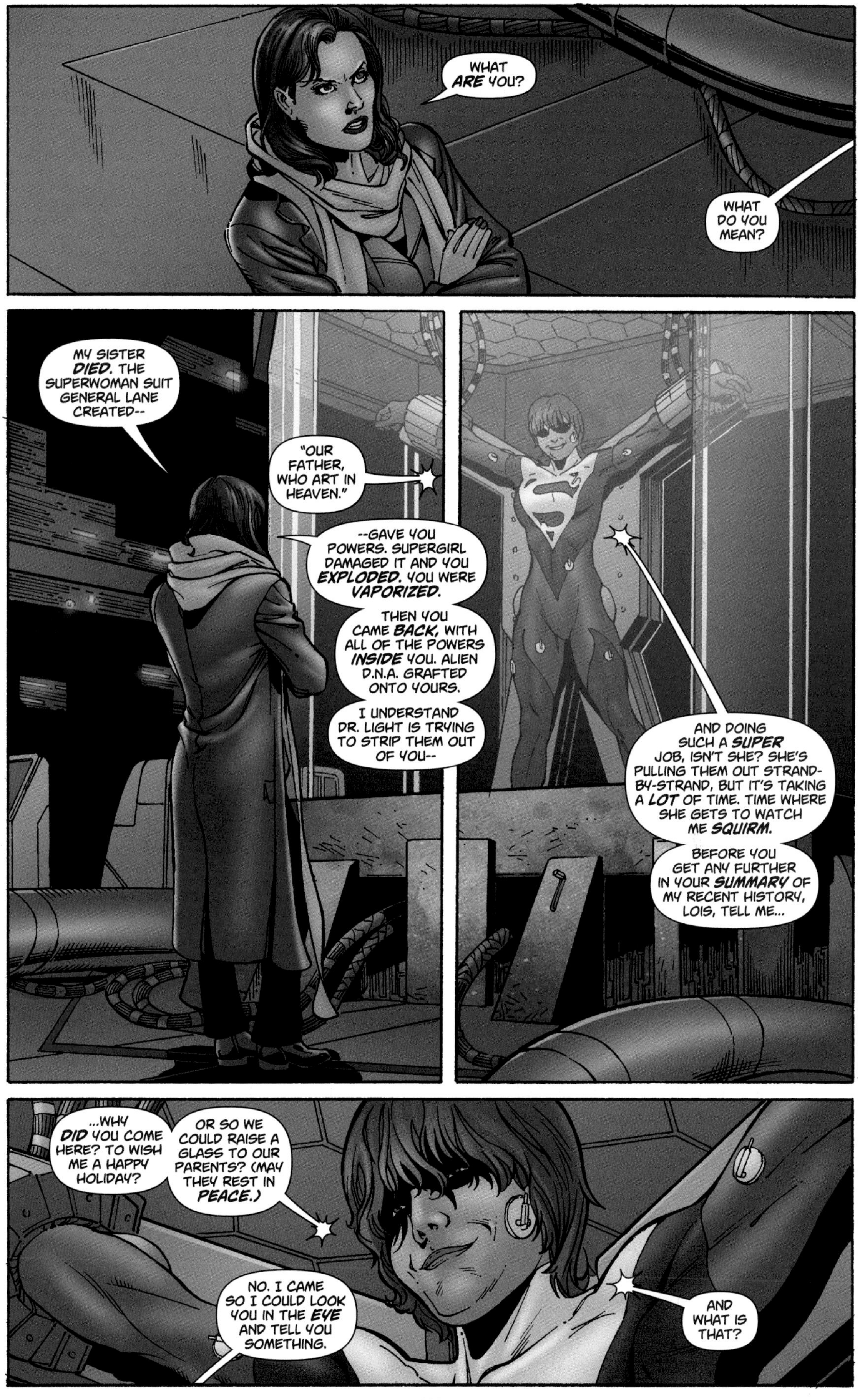
WHAT ARE YOU?
WHAT DO YOU MEAN?
MY SISTER DIED. THE SUPERWOMAN SUIT GENERAL LANE CREATED--
"OUR FATHER, WHO ART IN HEAVEN."
--GAVE YOU POWERS. SUPERGIRL DAMAGED IT AND YOU EXPLODED. YOU WERE VAPORIZED.
THEN YOU CAME BACK, WITH ALL OF THE POWERS INSIDE YOU. ALIEN D.N.A. GRAFTED ONTO YOURS.
I UNDERSTAND DR. LIGHT IS TRYING TO STRIP THEM OUT OF YOU--
AND DOING SUCH A SUPER JOB, ISN'T SHE? SHE'S PULLING THEM OUT STRAND-BY-STRAND, BUT IT'S TAKING A LOT OF TIME. TIME WHERE SHE GETS TO WATCH ME SQUIRM.
BEFORE YOU GET ANY FURTHER IN YOUR SUMMARY OF MY RECENT HISTORY, LOIS, TELL ME...
...WHY DID YOU COME HERE? TO WISH ME A HAPPY HOLIDAY?
OR SO WE COULD RAISE A GLASS TO OUR PARENTS? (MAY THEY REST IN PEACE.)
NO. I CAME SO I COULD LOOK YOU IN THE EYE AND TELL YOU SOMETHING.
AND WHAT IS THAT?

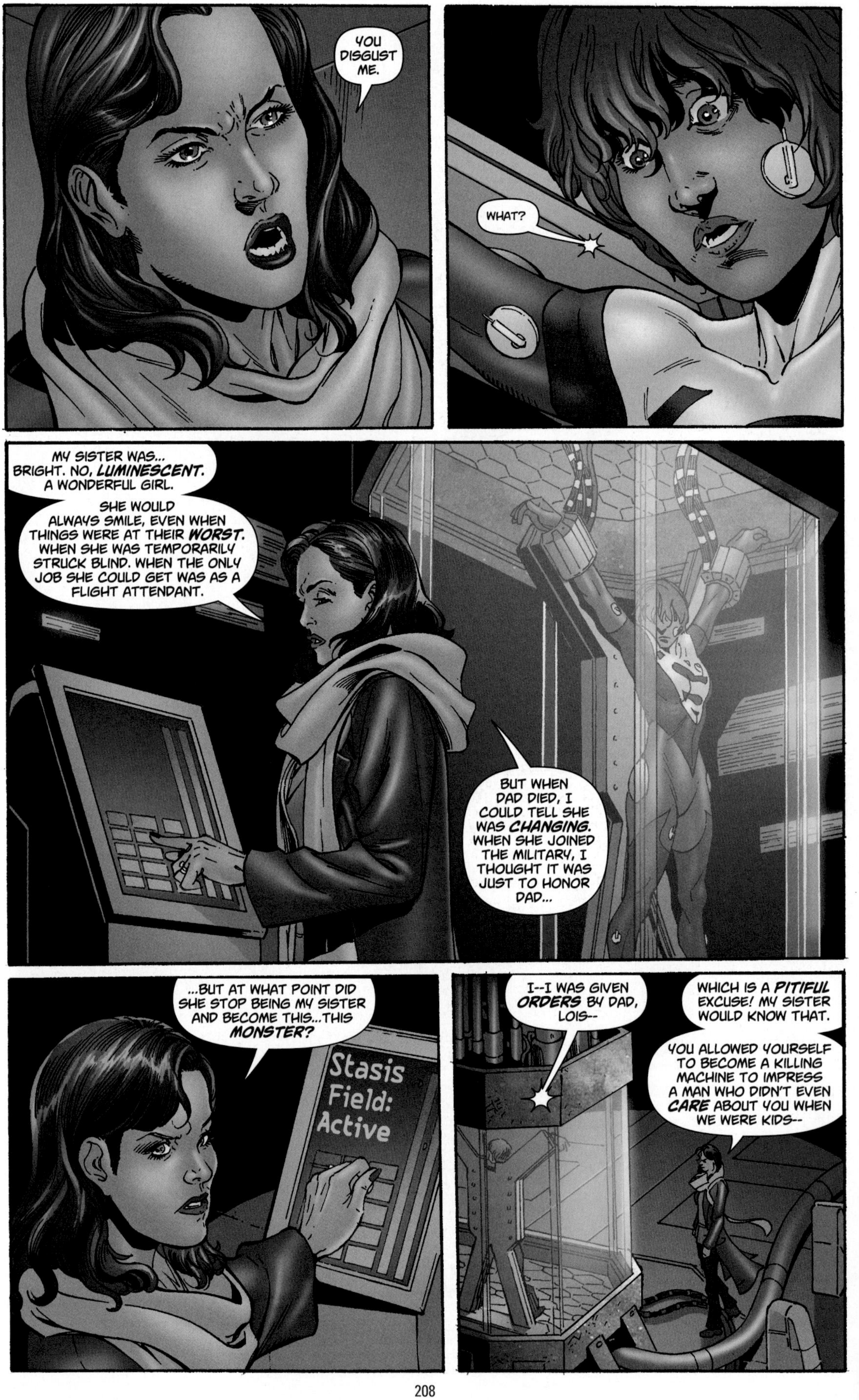
YOU DISGUST ME.
WHAT?
MY SISTER WAS... BRIGHT. NO, LUMINESCENT. A WONDERFUL GIRL.
SHE WOULD ALWAYS SMILE, EVEN WHEN THINGS WERE AT THEIR WORST. WHEN SHE WAS TEMPORARILY STRUCK BLIND. WHEN THE ONLY JOB SHE COULD GET WAS AS A FLIGHT ATTENDANT.
BUT WHEN DAD DIED, I COULD TELL SHE WAS CHANGING. WHEN SHE JOINED THE MILITARY, I THOUGHT IT WAS JUST TO HONOR DAD...
...BUT AT WHAT POINT DID SHE STOP BEING MY SISTER AND BECOME THIS...THIS MONSTER?
Stasis Field: Active
I--I WAS GIVEN ORDERS BY DAD, LOIS--
WHICH IS A PITIFUL EXCUSE! MY SISTER WOULD KNOW THAT.
YOU ALLOWED YOURSELF TO BECOME A KILLING MACHINE TO IMPRESS A MAN WHO DIDN'T EVEN CARE ABOUT YOU WHEN WE WERE KIDS--

HE CARED MORE ABOUT *ME* THAN HE DID ABOUT *YOU* AT THE END!

YOU WERE THE ONE WHO WAS ALWAYS RUNNING AWAY TO FOLLOW AN *ALIEN.* YOU WERE SO FOCUSED ON THE MAN OF STEEL, YOU STOPPED CARING FOR YOUR FAMILY.

SO WHO CAN BLAME DAD FOR HOW HE *FELT* ABOUT YOU? HE PICKED ME UP FROM THE *DEPTHS* AND MADE ME INTO SOMETHING *GREATER--*

NO. GENERAL LANE TOOK ADVANTAGE OF PEOPLE WHO DIDN'T KNOW ANY BETTER BECAUSE OF A STUPID, XENOPHOBIC GRUDGE WHICH TOOK *THOUSANDS* OF LIVES...

...AND WORST OF ALL, HE TOOK YOUR SOUL IN THE PROCESS.

I CAN'T FORGIVE HIM. NOT FOR ANY OF IT. NOR CAN I FORGIVE YOU FOR BEING SO STUPID.

GOODBYE, SUPERWOMAN. I DON'T MISS GENERAL LANE.

BUT I MISS MY SISTER ALREADY.

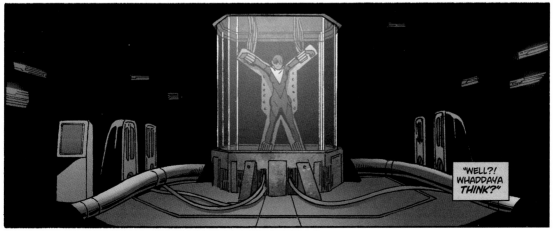

"WELL?! WHADDAYA *THINK*?"

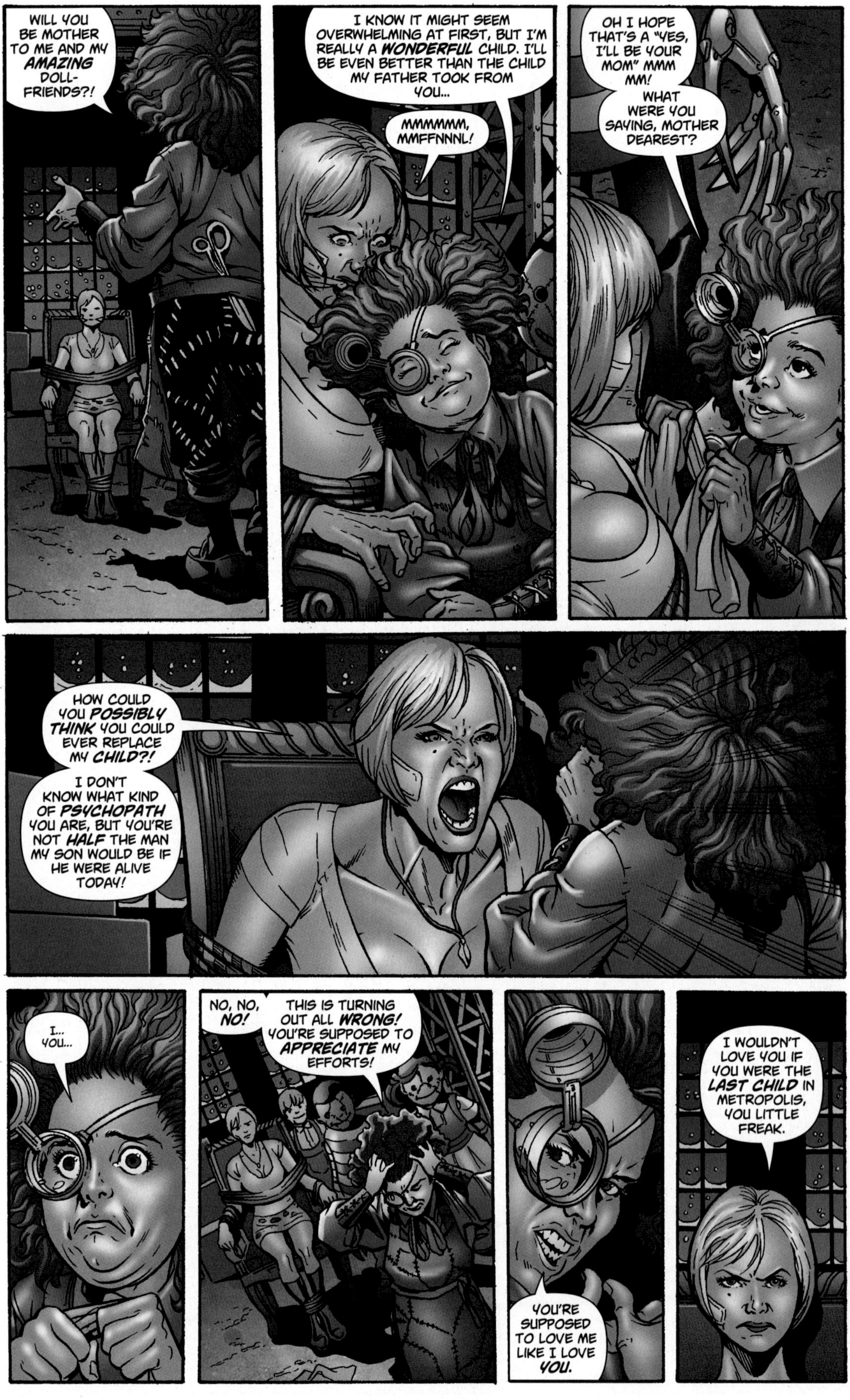
WILL YOU BE MOTHER TO ME AND MY AMAZING DOLL-FRIENDS?!
I KNOW IT MIGHT SEEM OVERWHELMING AT FIRST, BUT I'M REALLY A WONDERFUL CHILD. I'LL BE EVEN BETTER THAN THE CHILD MY FATHER TOOK FROM YOU...
MMMMMM, MMFFNNNL!
OH I HOPE THAT'S A "YES, I'LL BE YOUR MOM" MMM MM!
WHAT WERE YOU SAYING, MOTHER DEAREST?
HOW COULD YOU POSSIBLY THINK YOU COULD EVER REPLACE MY CHILD?!
I DON'T KNOW WHAT KIND OF PSYCHOPATH YOU ARE, BUT YOU'RE NOT HALF THE MAN MY SON WOULD BE IF HE WERE ALIVE TODAY!
I... YOU...
NO, NO, NO!
THIS IS TURNING OUT ALL WRONG! YOU'RE SUPPOSED TO APPRECIATE MY EFFORTS!
YOU'RE SUPPOSED TO LOVE ME LIKE I LOVE YOU.
I WOULDN'T LOVE YOU IF YOU WERE THE LAST CHILD IN METROPOLIS, YOU LITTLE FREAK.

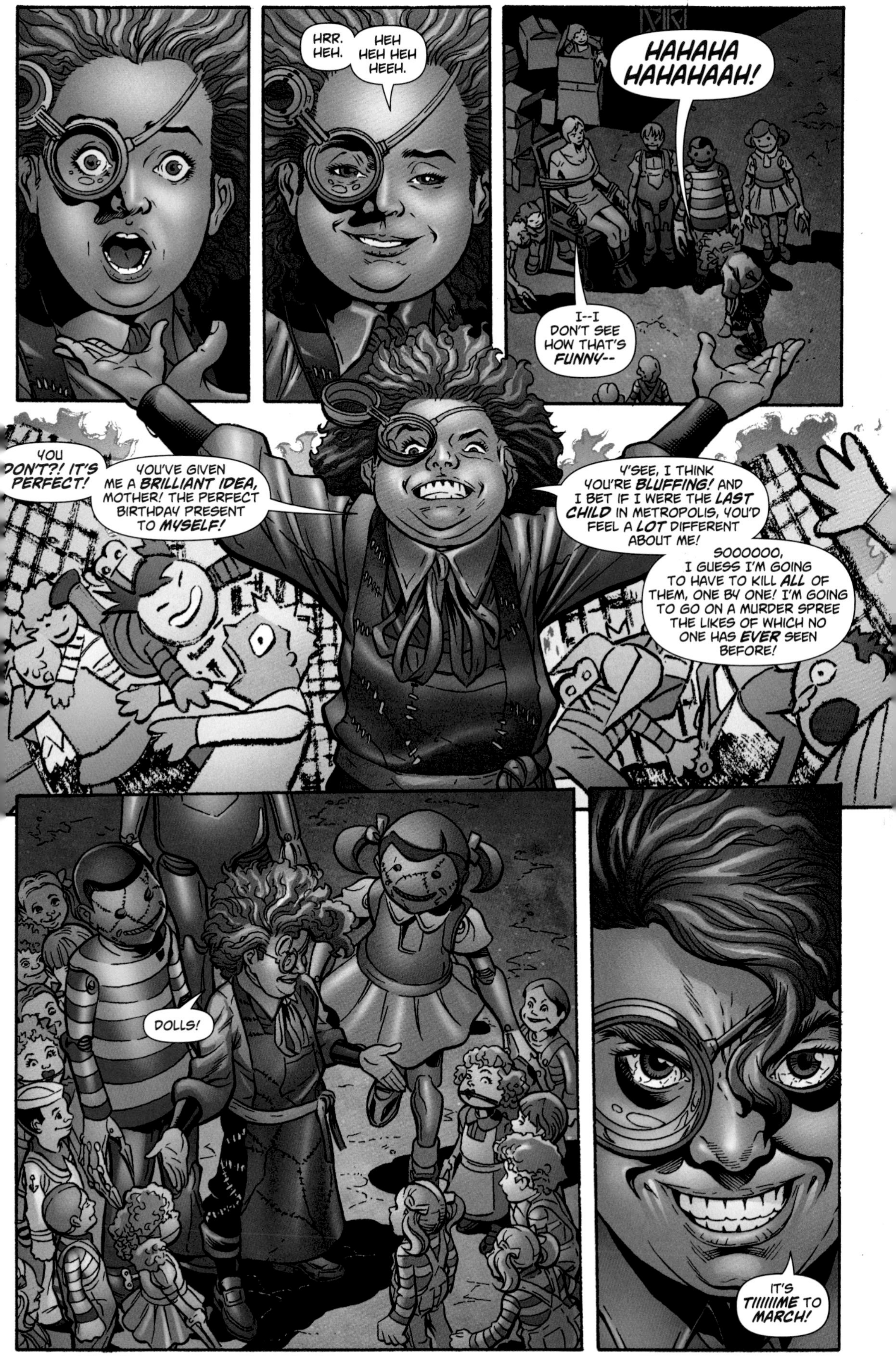
HRR. HEH.
HEH HEH HEH HEEH.
HAHAHA HAHAHAAH!
I--I DON'T SEE HOW THAT'S FUNNY--
YOU DON'T?! IT'S PERFECT!
YOU'VE GIVEN ME A BRILLIANT IDEA, MOTHER! THE PERFECT BIRTHDAY PRESENT TO MYSELF!
Y'SEE, I THINK YOU'RE BLUFFING! AND I BET IF I WERE THE LAST CHILD IN METROPOLIS, YOU'D FEEL A LOT DIFFERENT ABOUT ME!
SOOOOOO, I GUESS I'M GOING TO HAVE TO KILL ALL OF THEM, ONE BY ONE! I'M GOING TO GO ON A MURDER SPREE THE LIKES OF WHICH NO ONE HAS EVER SEEN BEFORE!
DOLLS!
IT'S TIIIIIME TO MARCH!

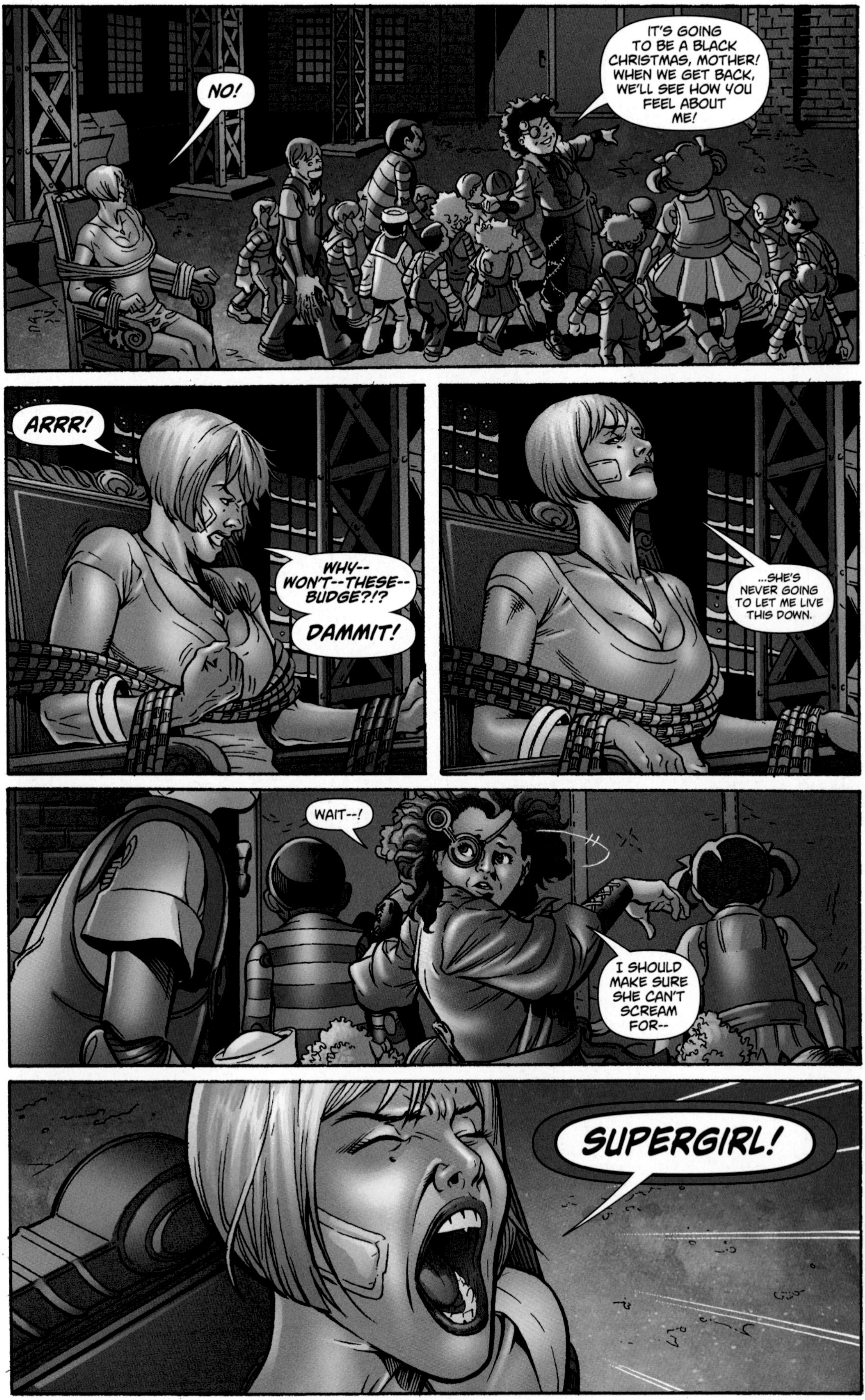
NO!
IT'S GOING TO BE A BLACK CHRISTMAS, MOTHER! WHEN WE GET BACK, WE'LL SEE HOW YOU FEEL ABOUT ME!
ARRR!
WHY-- WON'T--THESE-- BUDGE?!?
DAMMIT!
...SHE'S NEVER GOING TO LET ME LIVE THIS DOWN.
WAIT--!
I SHOULD MAKE SURE SHE CAN'T SCREAM FOR--
SUPERGIRL!

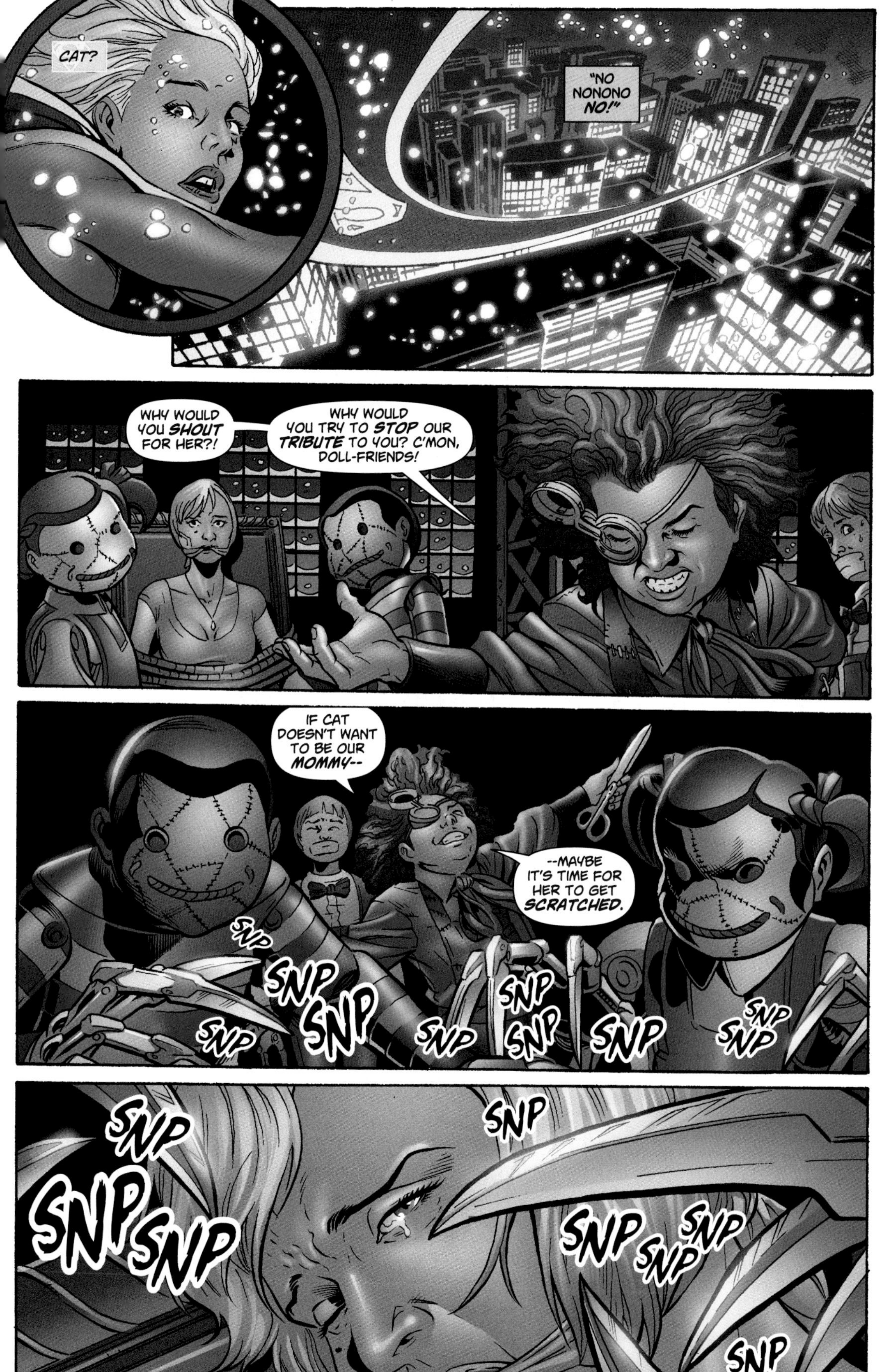
CAT?
"NO NONONO NO!"
WHY WOULD YOU SHOUT FOR HER?!
WHY WOULD YOU TRY TO STOP OUR TRIBUTE TO YOU? C'MON, DOLL-FRIENDS!
IF CAT DOESN'T WANT TO BE OUR MOMMY--
--MAYBE IT'S TIME FOR HER TO GET SCRATCHED.
SNP SNP SNP SNP SNP SNP SNP SNP SNP SNP
SNP SNP SNP SNP SNP SNP SNP SNP SNP

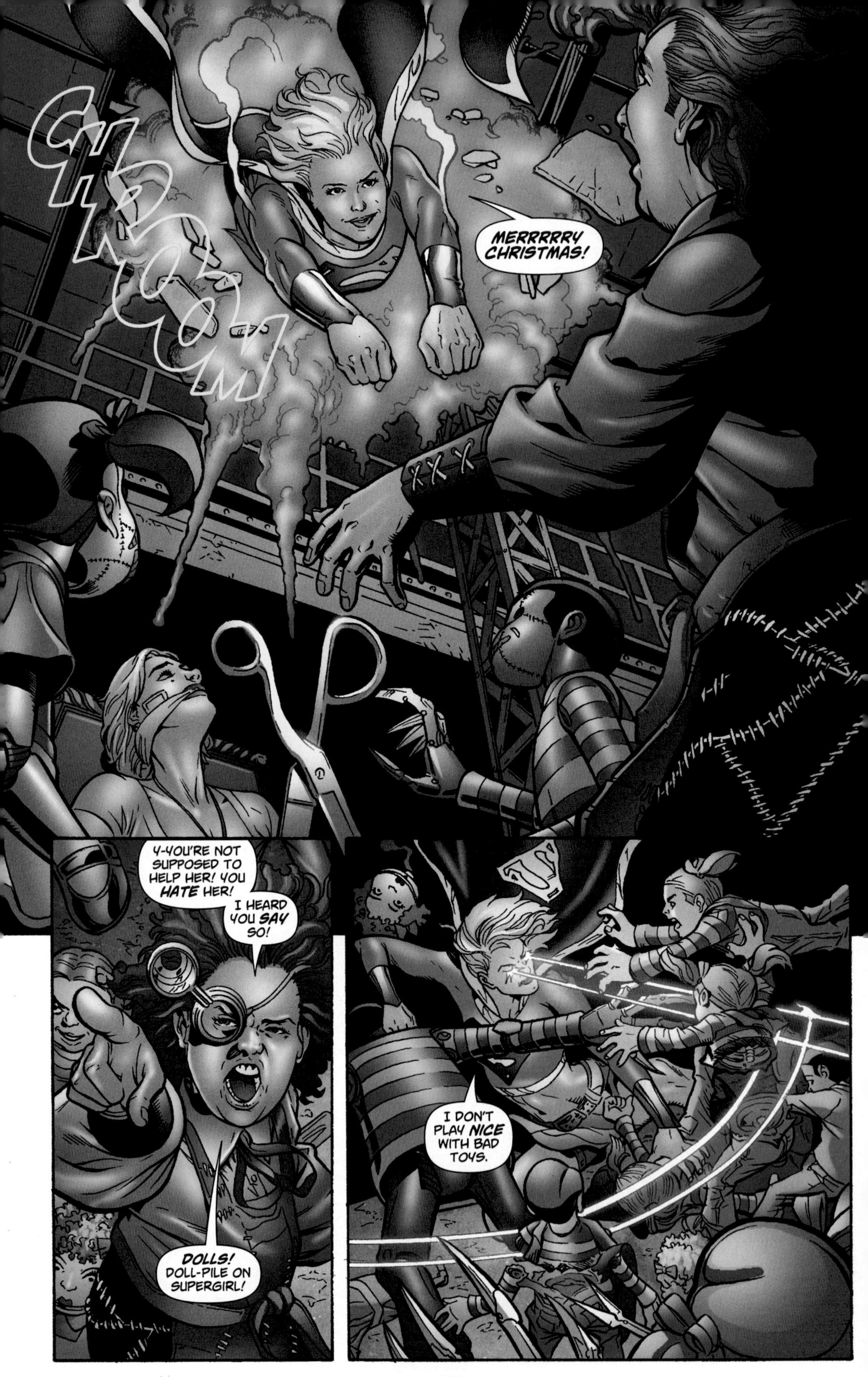
CHOOOOM
MERRRRRY CHRISTMAS!
Y-YOU'RE NOT SUPPOSED TO HELP HER! YOU HATE HER!
I HEARD YOU SAY SO!
DOLLS! DOLL-PILE ON SUPERGIRL!
I DON'T PLAY NICE WITH BAD TOYS.

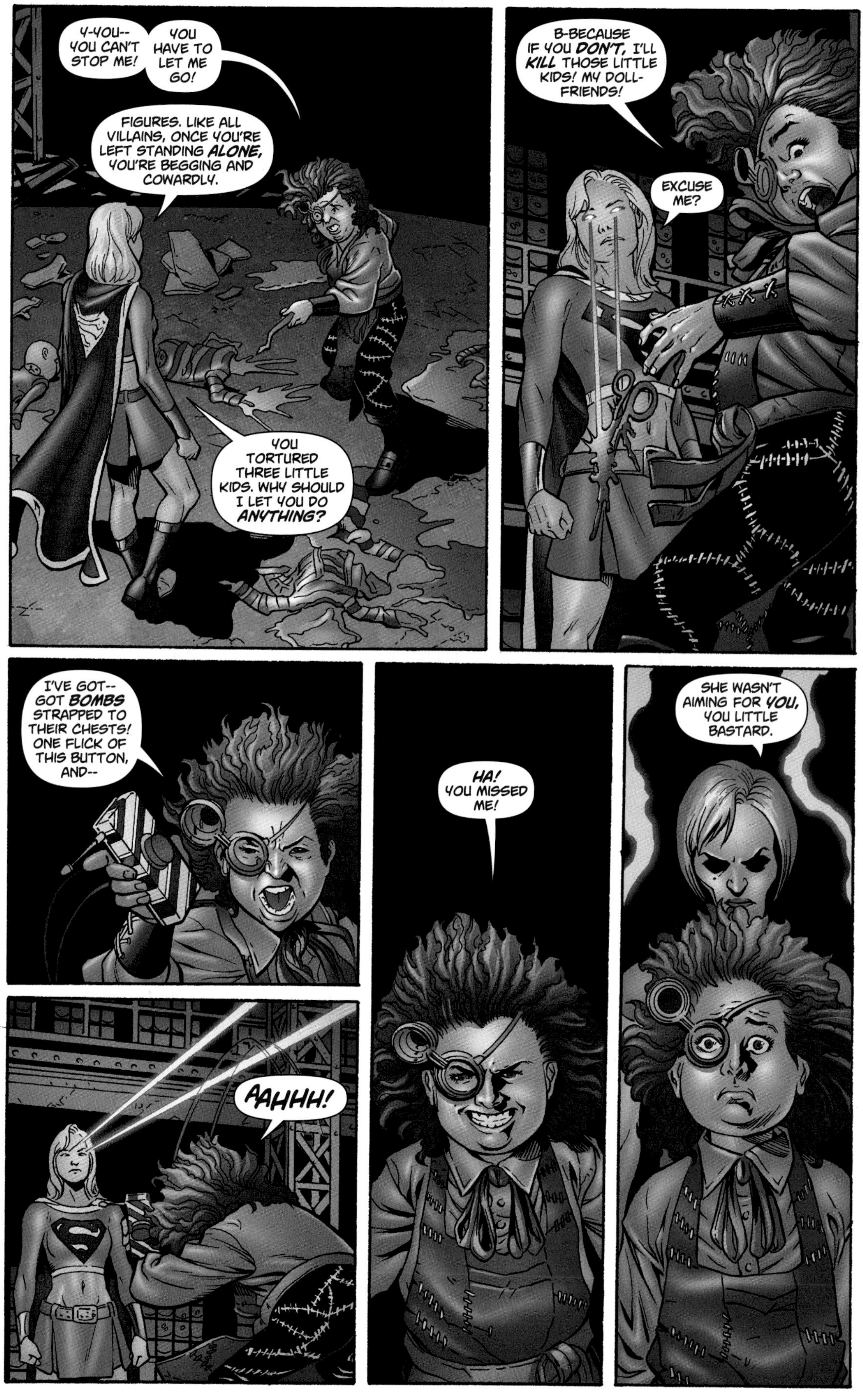
Y-YOU-- YOU CAN'T STOP ME!
YOU HAVE TO LET ME GO!
FIGURES. LIKE ALL VILLAINS, ONCE YOU'RE LEFT STANDING ALONE, YOU'RE BEGGING AND COWARDLY.
YOU TORTURED THREE LITTLE KIDS. WHY SHOULD I LET YOU DO ANYTHING?
B-BECAUSE IF YOU DON'T, I'LL KILL THOSE LITTLE KIDS! MY DOLL-FRIENDS!
EXCUSE ME?
I'VE GOT-- GOT BOMBS STRAPPED TO THEIR CHESTS! ONE FLICK OF THIS BUTTON, AND--
AAHHH!
HA! YOU MISSED ME!
SHE WASN'T AIMING FOR YOU, YOU LITTLE BASTARD.

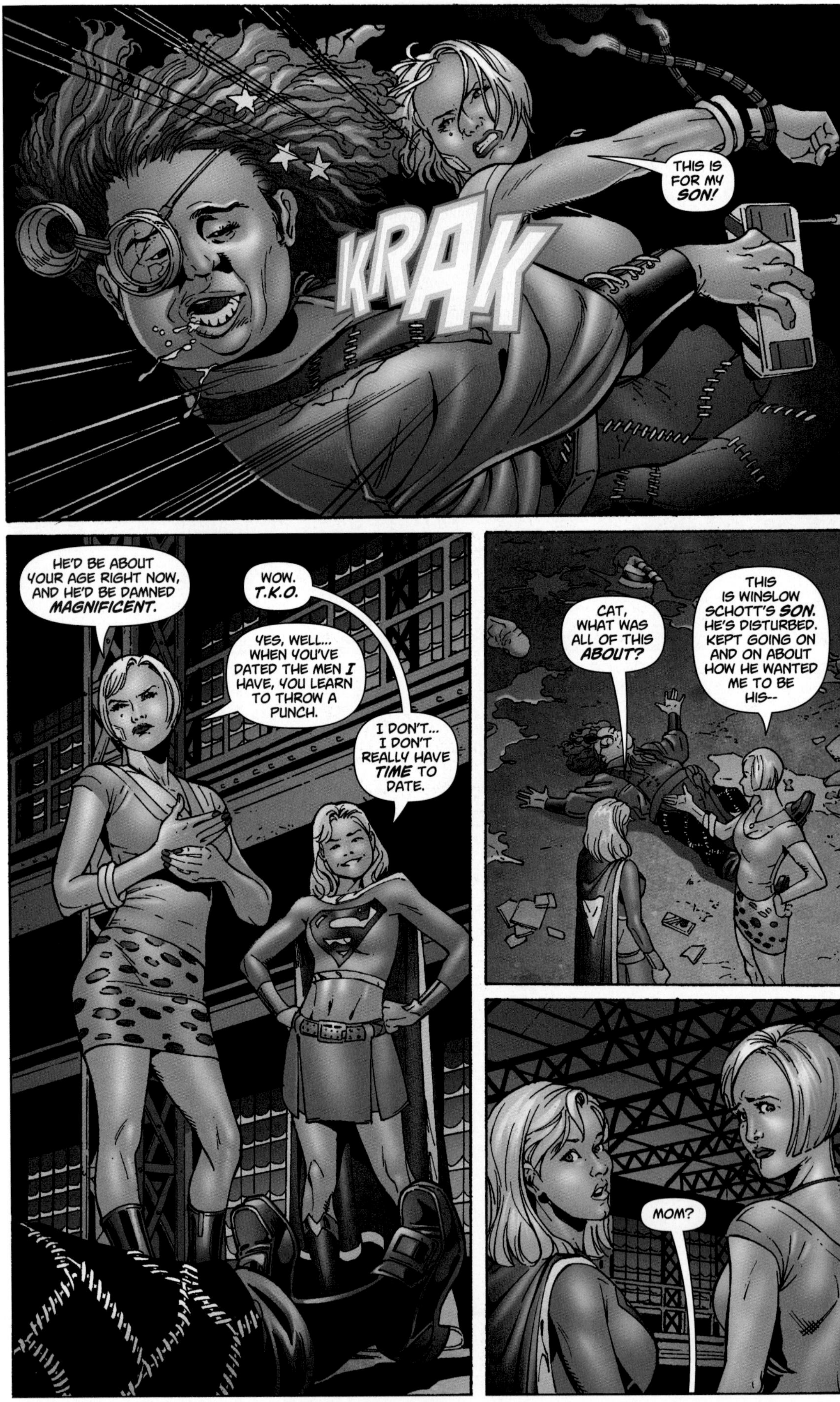
THIS IS FOR MY SON!
KRAK
HE'D BE ABOUT YOUR AGE RIGHT NOW, AND HE'D BE DAMNED MAGNIFICENT.
WOW. T.K.O.
YES, WELL... WHEN YOU'VE DATED THE MEN I HAVE, YOU LEARN TO THROW A PUNCH.
I DON'T... I DON'T REALLY HAVE TIME TO DATE.
CAT, WHAT WAS ALL OF THIS ABOUT?
THIS IS WINSLOW SCHOTT'S SON. HE'S DISTURBED. KEPT GOING ON AND ON ABOUT HOW HE WANTED ME TO BE HIS--
MOM?

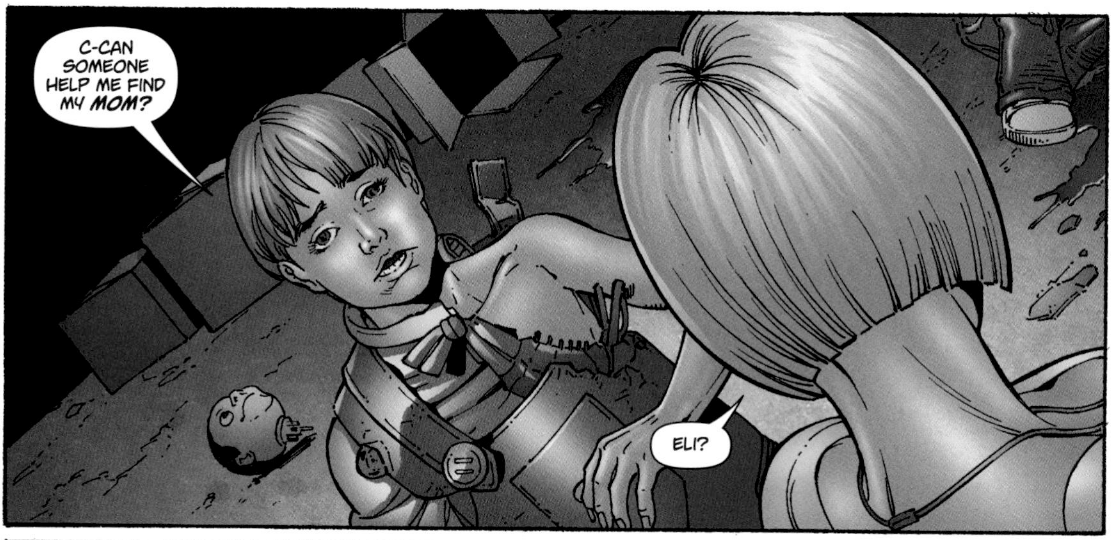
C-CAN SOMEONE HELP ME FIND MY *MOM?*
ELI?

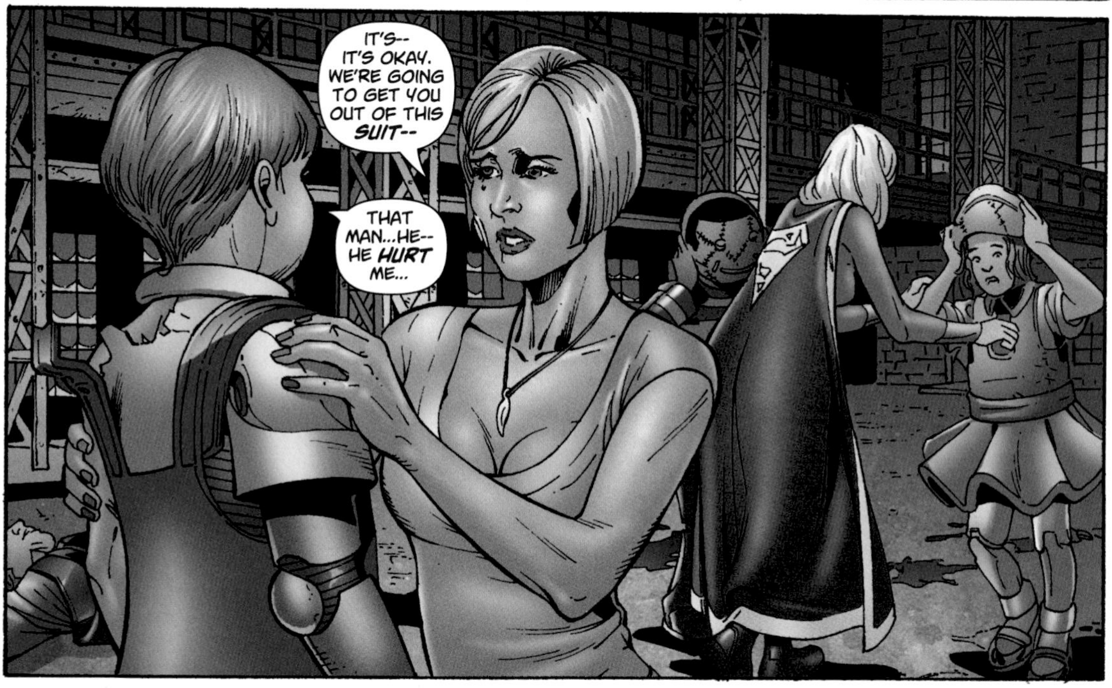
IT'S-- IT'S OKAY. WE'RE GOING TO GET YOU OUT OF THIS *SUIT--*
THAT MAN...HE-- HE *HURT* ME...

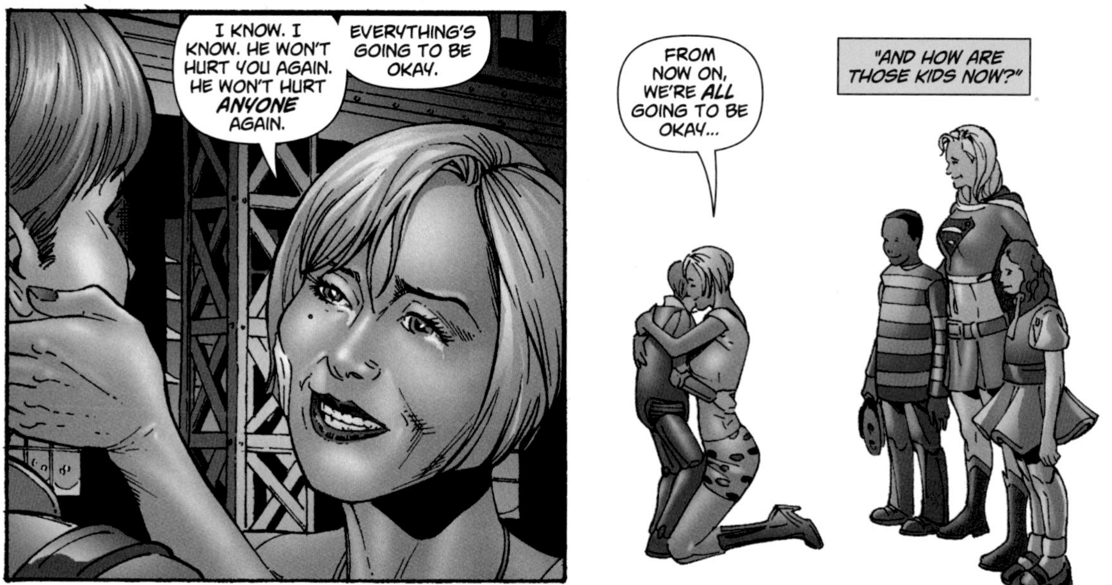
I KNOW. I KNOW. HE WON'T HURT YOU AGAIN. HE WON'T HURT *ANYONE* AGAIN.
EVERYTHING'S GOING TO BE OKAY.
FROM NOW ON, WE'RE *ALL* GOING TO BE OKAY...
"AND HOW ARE THOSE KIDS NOW?"

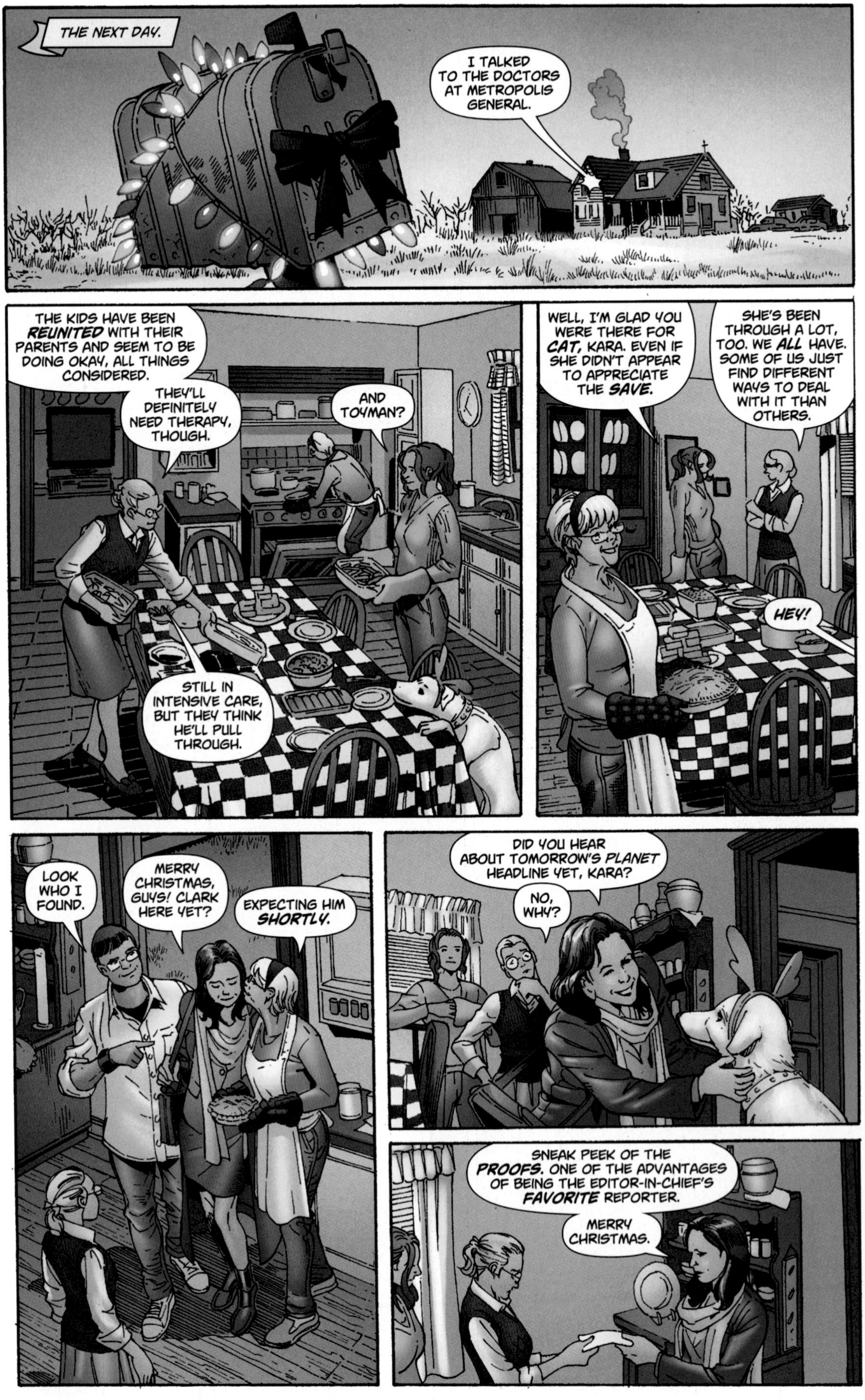
THE NEXT DAY.
I TALKED TO THE DOCTORS AT METROPOLIS GENERAL.
THE KIDS HAVE BEEN REUNITED WITH THEIR PARENTS AND SEEM TO BE DOING OKAY, ALL THINGS CONSIDERED.
THEY'LL DEFINITELY NEED THERAPY, THOUGH.
AND TOYMAN?
STILL IN INTENSIVE CARE, BUT THEY THINK HE'LL PULL THROUGH.
WELL, I'M GLAD YOU WERE THERE FOR CAT, KARA. EVEN IF SHE DIDN'T APPEAR TO APPRECIATE THE SAVE.
SHE'S BEEN THROUGH A LOT, TOO. WE ALL HAVE. SOME OF US JUST FIND DIFFERENT WAYS TO DEAL WITH IT THAN OTHERS.
HEY!
LOOK WHO I FOUND.
MERRY CHRISTMAS, GUYS! CLARK HERE YET?
EXPECTING HIM SHORTLY.
DID YOU HEAR ABOUT TOMORROW'S PLANET HEADLINE YET, KARA?
NO, WHY?
SNEAK PEEK OF THE PROOFS. ONE OF THE ADVANTAGES OF BEING THE EDITOR-IN-CHIEF'S FAVORITE REPORTER.
MERRY CHRISTMAS.

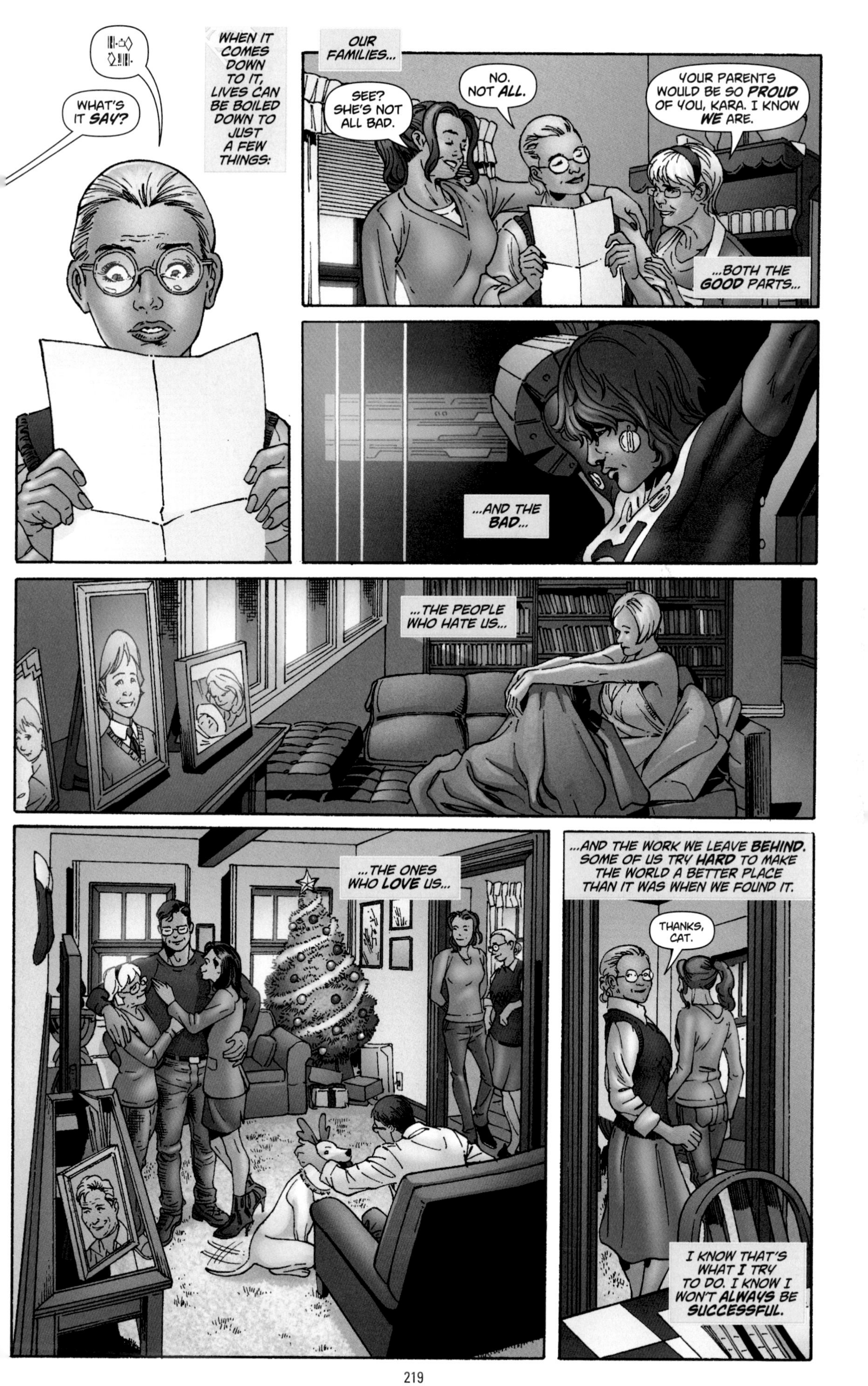
WHAT'S IT SAY?
WHEN IT COMES DOWN TO IT, LIVES CAN BE BOILED DOWN TO JUST A FEW THINGS:
OUR FAMILIES...
SEE? SHE'S NOT ALL BAD.
NO. NOT ALL.
YOUR PARENTS WOULD BE SO PROUD OF YOU, KARA. I KNOW WE ARE.
...BOTH THE GOOD PARTS...
...AND THE BAD...
...THE PEOPLE WHO HATE US...
...THE ONES WHO LOVE US...
...AND THE WORK WE LEAVE BEHIND. SOME OF US TRY HARD TO MAKE THE WORLD A BETTER PLACE THAN IT WAS WHEN WE FOUND IT.
THANKS, CAT.
I KNOW THAT'S WHAT I TRY TO DO. I KNOW I WON'T ALWAYS BE SUCCESSFUL.

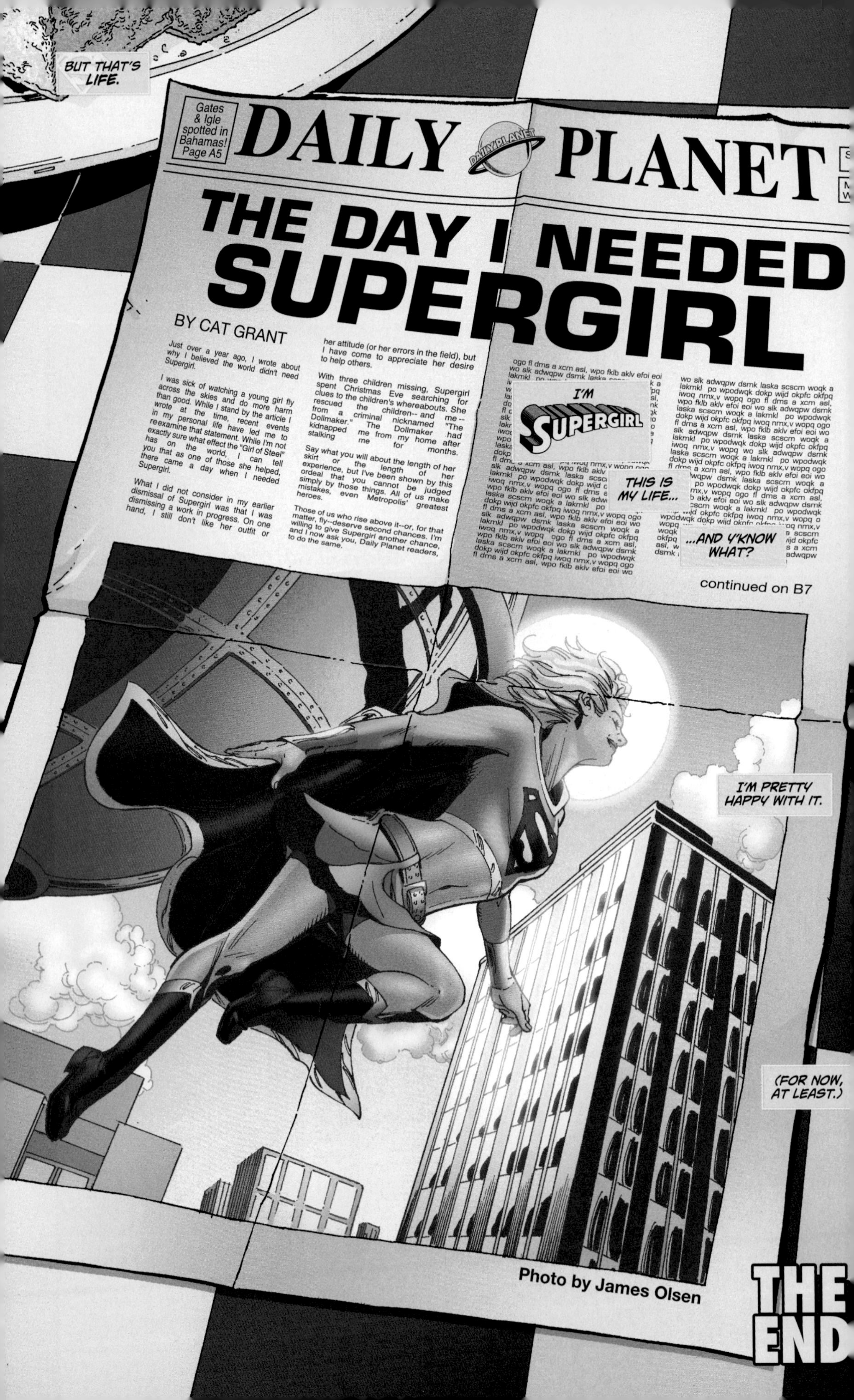

BUT THAT'S LIFE.
Gates & Igle spotted in Bahamas! Page A5
DAILY PLANET
DAILY PLANET
THE DAY I NEEDED SUPERGIRL
BY CAT GRANT
Just over a year ago, I wrote about why I believed the world didn't need Supergirl.
I was sick of watching a young girl fly across the skies and do more harm than good. While I stand by the article I wrote at the time, recent events in my personal life have led me to reexamine that statement. While I'm not exactly sure what effect the "Girl of Steel" has on the world, I can tell you that as one of those she helped, there came a day when I needed Supergirl.
What I did not consider in my earlier dismissal of Supergirl was that I was dismissing a work in progress. On one hand, I still don't like her outfit or her attitude (or her errors in the field), but I have come to appreciate her desire to help others.
With three children missing, Supergirl spent Christmas Eve searching for clues to the children's whereabouts. She rescued the children-- and me -- from a criminal nicknamed "The Dollmaker." The Dollmaker had kidnapped me from my home after stalking me for months.
Say what you will about the length of her skirt or the length of her experience, but I've been shown by this ordeal that you cannot be judged simply by those things. All of us make mistakes, even Metropolis' greatest heroes.
Those of us who rise above it--or, for that matter, fly--deserve second chances. I'm willing to give Supergirl another chance, and I now ask you, Daily Planet readers, to do the same.
I'M SUPERGIRL
THIS IS MY LIFE...
...AND Y'KNOW WHAT?
continued on B7
I'M PRETTY HAPPY WITH IT.
(FOR NOW, AT LEAST.)
Photo by James Olsen
THE END

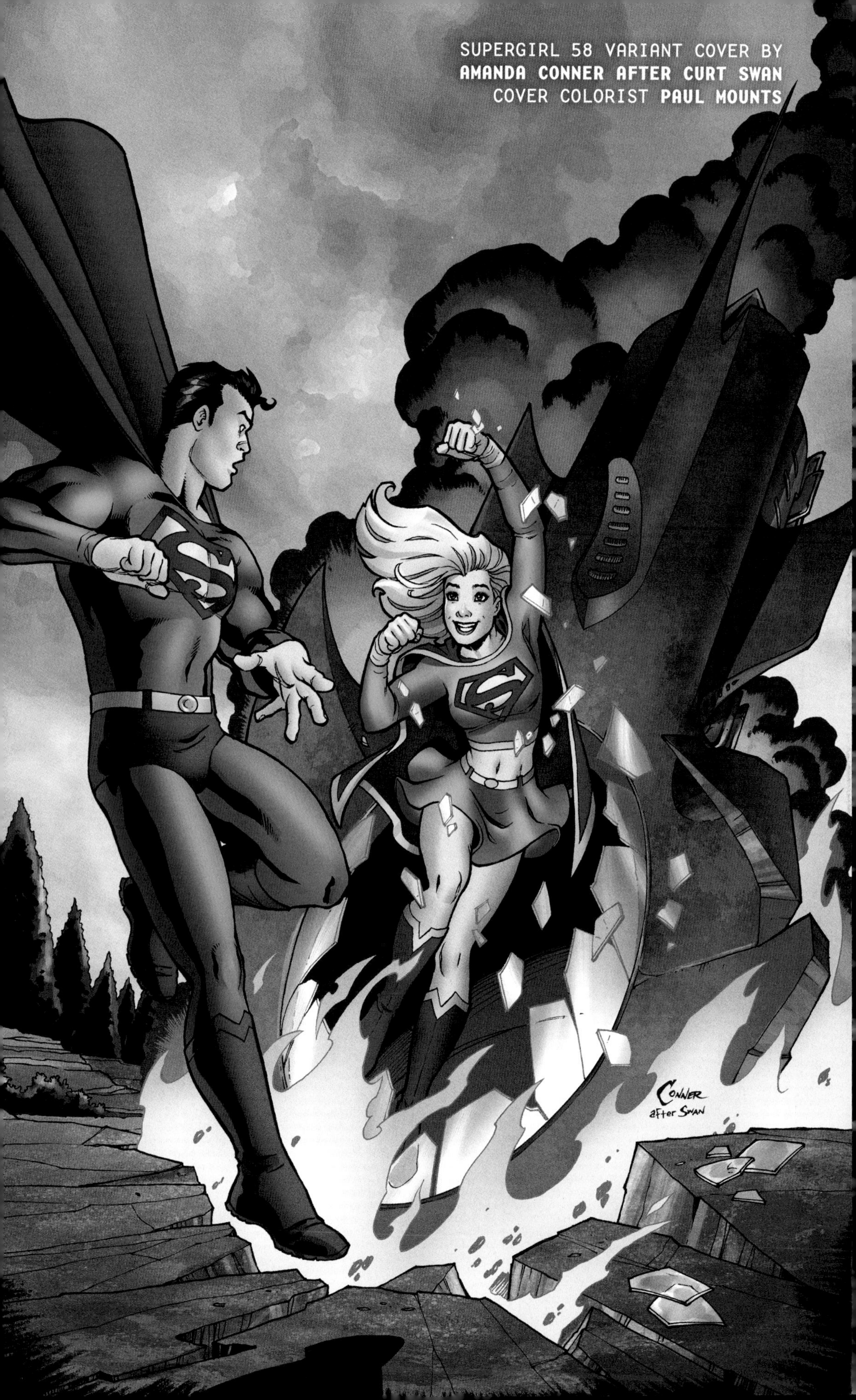
CONNER
after SWAN

SUPERGIRL 58 VARIANT COVER BY
AMANDA CONNER AFTER CURT SWAN
COVER COLORIST **PAUL MOUNTS**

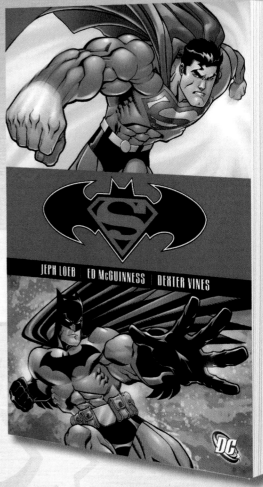

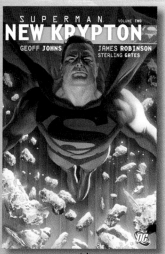